FEAR/LESS

FEAR/LESS

Library of Congress Control Number: 2024937371

ISBN (paperback): 978-1-963271-11-9
ISBN (ebook): 978-1-963271-12-6

ARMINLEAR

Armin Lear Press, Inc.
215 W Riverside Drive, #4362
Estes Park, CO 80517

FEAR/LESS

Why Your Lifelong Fears Are Probably Groundless

Edited by Wojciech Janicki

CONTENTS

"This is a world you'll never understand
and you always fear what you don't understand."

Carmine Falcone (Tom Wilkinson)
Batman Begins

INTRODUCTION

Wojciech Janicki

Evolution is a process in which all species adapt to changing environmental conditions. This adaptation process can be purely biological, with natural selection determining which specimens of a species will pass on their genes to future generations and which genealogical branches will die out. But this is not the only possibility. For *Homo sapiens*, cultural factors can strongly influence adapting to the circumstances surrounding us.

Culture consists of

- the values that define what is essential in life,
- norms, or the expected or desired behavior of humans and their communities in specific situations,
- institutions, or the social structures that uphold these norms; and finally
- artifacts, which are the products or aspects of our material culture.

Examples and behavior models are shaped by our social environment rather than our genes, much like the perception of the world that underlies the norms we follow. At the same time, our social environment operates based on imaginary orders to organize human life – a set of beliefs that do not stem from the worlds of physics or biology but from a collective, often informal social contract.[1]

These beliefs and convictions define what is proper and reasonable and what is wrong and undesirable, identify threats, and indicate how we should behave if those threats arise. Some threats (such as lightning strikes) can be objective, while others (such as solar eclipses) are subjective.

It is an objective truth that if we wish to increase our chances of survival, we probably should not climb the lone tree in the field during a thunderstorm. But it is not an objective truth that a solar eclipse manifests divine wrath, and the only way to appease the gods is to sacrifice a living being that a priest demands on behalf of supernatural beings. In the 21st century, we interpret both phenomena correctly – something impossible in, for instance, Ancient Egypt.

Natural phenomena are not humanity's only source of malaise, nor are they the only category of events or processes whose interpretation has proven challenging. Difficulties in understanding a specific facet of the world naturally lead to trouble in teasing out how society expects us to react. Should marijuana be freely and commonly available (as in coffee shops in the Netherlands or pharmacies in Canada), or should it be restricted (as in Germany and Australia)? Is the balance of costs and benefits from the extraction of shale gas trapped in formations from the Lower Paleozoic positive (as is believed by many in the United States) or negative (France)? Is cell phone usage safe for humans, or is it a lethal threat, especially with the advent of 5G?

Knowledge and acquiring knowledge provide us with the answers to all the questions above and many others. Knowledge constitutes (or should include) the only ground to resolve good, beneficial, harmful, and pernicious dilemmas. If we follow Plato in defining knowledge as a belief that is logically true and strongly supported by evidence, we arrive at the heart of the problem that the authors of this volume will tackle – namely, how humanity has, for centuries, defined and distinguished what is desirable, safe, and favorable from what is undesirable, dangerous, and threatening.

At first glance, the criterion identified above appears crystal clear, and the results of our evaluations should be unambiguous. However, questions about how to confirm the integrity of a given belief have remained unresolved since ancient times. Within the broad domain of philosophy, epistemology is the primary area that pursues such dilemmas, which proposes a wide spectrum of verification tools. However, the main problem persists: none of these tools have gained universal acceptance, and some philosophers even believe that, in most cases, such verification is impossible. Determining the necessary and sufficient conditions that must be satisfied for beliefs to be considered knowledge is sometimes impossible.[2]

The issue of whether our beliefs are true and when they are true – in other words, whether they can be regarded as objective knowledge – is a matter of debate in many different scientific disciplines as well. It has even spawned a separate branch of science called knowledge theory. To a psychologist, a person assimilates knowledge through the organs responsible for their senses. They encode in long-term memory, enabling them to talk about it or use the information and skills they possess to perform specific actions. An economist will treat knowledge as a data set with a particular market value, which can then be used to make rational economic decisions. In this view, knowledge can not only be acquired but also managed. In information science, the source of knowledge is information that appears in a specific context, acquired in a way conditioned by our experience. Cognitive science, conversely, clearly separates knowledge from data, treating the latter as the foundation for knowledge and explicitly stipulating that knowledge is always relative and always refers to a specific source of information or field of human activity.[3]

However we choose to define knowledge, the fact remains that the Platonic understanding of the concept envisions *Homo sapiens* enjoying access to an ever-expanding and evolving bank of cognitive acquisitions. For centuries, we have slowly and diligently narrowed the scope of our ignorance, eliminating the foundations of our understanding of the world based solely on faith and expanding those based on informed comprehension. Cognition, empirical observation, experience, analysis and synthesis, and simulations – these and other research methods have contributed to a gradual shift along the axis leading from pure faith to scientifically supported knowledge. Processes and phenomena whose causes or development humans previously could not fathom instilled fear in us. They were often attributed to supernatural forces – thunderbolts in Ancient Greece were cast by an angry Zeus, Poseidon's rage agitated the sea, and Hades triggered devastating earthquakes. Today, we look back at these beliefs with more than a grain of salt – so much so that, rather than calling them profoundly erroneous (even though they are profoundly wrong), we somewhat paternalistically brand them as myths and even teach them to children in schools.

The term myth is exceptionally broad, multifaceted, and, thus, highly ambiguous. Scholars from many scientific disciplines have spent years attempting to clarify its meaning, pursuing a slightly different direction with each iteration. All these efforts originate from ancient Greece, where the term was coined initially to describe a story about gods, demons, and other supernatural beings. Today, on this foundation, modern-day fields like literature, religious studies, ethnology, and structural anthropology build their respective canonical understandings of the myth. In this interpretation, the myth is a tale whose task is to enlighten humans about the meaning of their individual or collective experience or even the world. This tale is passed down from generation to generation so that the myth becomes part of the tradition of a given community. Myths may also be understood as a symbolic reflection of the vision of reality shared by a given society, as one of the main currents of contemporary sociology claims, or as a kind of heroic origin story of an ethnonational group, the latter being the favored lens of many political scientists. Other scientific disciplines, such as psychology and history, imbue the term with their unique interpretations.[4]

But let us return to the archetypal notion of the myth, as popularized by ancient Greece. In the eyes of Greek mythologists, myths and historical truth lay on opposite poles. The formation of myths was viewed as deriving from subjective perceptions and the effect of desperate attempts to explain the elements of reality that were considered wholly irrational and impossible to describe. This interpretation, attributed to Plato, can be viewed as a bridge to today's most common, popular understanding of myth. Modern society understands myths as superstitions or false and baseless assumptions about someone or something we give credence to without proof; in some cases, they are created by how we describe reality. After all, it is by telling the truth in each way that we understand and interpret it the way we do.[5] The myths we allow others to feed us – which we nourish with our stories and social behavior – become a part of our reality. Sometimes, they penetrate our consciousness so deeply that we cease to think about their integrity and take for granted supposed truths that are not truths at all.

Finding a rational explanation for specific events or phenomena is not always easy. Our efforts to understand and explain them continue only as long as we remain aware that we are dealing with a myth. Once we ascribe some supernatural origin to a phenomenon we do not understand or make value judgments about (good and evil, benefit and hazard) without first investigating its causes and dynamics, we mythologize it instead of admitting our ignorance. Everything we judge and evaluate becomes a myth – even if we do not understand it yet, cannot explain it, and fail to situate it in existing scientific frameworks. Why do we let this happen? Because knowledge is always more difficult to assimilate, it requires a concerted effort, a deliberate search for information, a focused analysis, and an understanding of specialized terms and concepts. On the other hand, myths are easily digestible; they explain the unexplained in accessible ways. They may be based on half-truths, understatements, and outright lies, but they have an advantage over knowledge by making simple explanations of complex matters easy to access.

Myths, as conceptualized and analyzed in this book, are therefore the product of ignorance, and broadening the scope of the knowledge available to us allows us to avoid mythologizing the unknown and explore it through the lens of empirical, experimental science – often physics, chemistry, and biology. Building on the established theory of spatial diffusion, this gradual process of pushing the frontiers of our knowledge – and especially disseminating the knowledge that has already been anchored and absorbed in one part of the world – can be called the diffusion of knowledge.[6] Before this can occur, fear often takes hold on either a local or universal level, driven by the prospect of facing the unknown.[7]

Myths give rise to fear. We fear supernatural forces, humbly bow our heads before the Absolute, and dutifully listen to priests, monks, and ministers who claim to be its emissaries. The Absolute may be religious, but it does not have to be. All it needs to represent is a natural phenomenon or a technical invention we do not understand so we can select the priests who will most effectively persuade us toward their interpretation of why the phenomenon occurs or how the design works. This is why people were so reluctant to use iron railroads for so long and feared using electric current – especially alternating current, which today provides electricity through every outlet on our walls. All it takes is for us to hear a convincing, if not necessarily accurate, diagnosis of the reasons for or future consequences of specific social or political phenomena so that, guided by the fears that its preachers create in us, we follow them without reflection, deeply convinced that we are guided by knowledge and logical thinking. The purveyors of fear ruthlessly exploit these anxieties, manipulating and managing us through them.[8]

With the passage of time and the march of progress, we attain higher levels of education and understanding. Still, the number of new inventions emerging every day is also increasing. As a result, although we no longer fear railroads or electricity, we continue to find new bogeymen. What we cannot verify experimentally, feel with our senses, or visualize and properly imagine may provoke anxiety and fear.

Fear is a state of intense emotional tension associated with an actual threat or the sensation that such a threat is present, which in animals triggers the fight-or-flight response. In humans, fear is one of the strongest emotions associated with biological changes in the body and behaviors that would not occur without it. This is why we can easily hit the lock on the door of a house or car with our keys when we walk up to it, but we fumble and drop them when we see a mugger running towards us wielding a knife.

The primal trigger for the emergence of emotions, including fear, remains mysterious. Is it the body's somatic reactions, as specific psychological theories propose? Is it human brain activity, as stipulated by contemporary neurology? Or is it mainly our thoughts, as cognitive scientists suggest? Charles Darwin argued that emotions play an adaptational role, allowing us to interpret the behavior of other individuals and react appropriately correctly. We intuitively decide to flee in danger because this will facilitate our survival. Many theories of emotion developed in psychology argue that the thoughts we harbor contribute significantly to how we experience emotions. An innocent knock on the door may trigger joy and cause our hearts to beat faster if we are expecting a visit from the one we love, or it may provoke fear or anger when the debt collector comes knocking. A barking dog may seem threatening, arouse fear, and increase our heart rate. Still, it does not have to – our assessment of whether the dog can jump over the fence that separates it from us affects the physiological reaction of our body and the occurrence of fear. In this sense, fear is not the result of any particular physiological reaction but rather our interpretation of that reaction. Our assessment of the fence's effectiveness as a barrier may be wrong, so fear is driven not by facts but by our consciousness.[9]

Across thousands of years of evolution, humankind has developed the capacity for abstract thinking, allowing us to gain awareness of the possible consequences of our actions or inactions. Thus, we fear what is happening here and now and what may happen in the distant future.[10] Because of this ability, myths give rise to such profound fear of the future, and the priests who purvey them enjoy such a large captive audience. These fears are not linked to bodily reactions in the same way that an aggressive dog attacking us or another situation of immediate danger is. Nevertheless, after being bred and regularly irrigated by those who frighten us with bleak visions of the future, these fears grow their roots deep inside us, become our constant companions, and, over time, evolve into part of our core beliefs, often unbeknownst to us. They merge with our knowledge of what we are sure will come.

Framed in this way, do our accumulated beliefs meet the criterion of objective knowledge? Are our fears of what the future will bring rational? Continuing the analogy of the barking dog, is the fence high enough to protect us? It isn't easy to find clear-cut answers to these questions. As long as our interpretations of reality are based on experience, we can be confident about how the future will unfold. When we drop an apple, it will fall to the ground, just like it did for Isaac Newton. The law of gravity remains in force today, just like it did yesterday and just like it will tomorrow. But when we want to project the course of social, economic, or political phenomena, the effects of using technological inventions, or natural events such as earthquakes, everything becomes uncertain: the time, the location, the intensity, and the details of the course of specific events. We only become wise in hindsight, and then we begin to explain to ourselves that how the events unfolded was evident in retrospect. It's a pity that almost no one could see how obvious it was sooner.[11]

What we think of as our knowledge about the future, if grown from the seed of fears planted in us by somebody else and carefully nurtured after that, may be a collection of fears and myths that have nothing to do with reality. Could they turn out to be true? Alas, there is no scale on which we can measure and weigh tomorrow to show how our fears about the future are justified. Any rational approach – because we all try to act like rational beings and generally consider ourselves as such – requires learning from the past. This does not mean simply extrapolating previously observed trends into the future. Instead, it means choosing such interpretations of reality that emerge as the most appropriate ones, given the knowledge available. In the absence of hard evidence, which we often lack concerning the future, we are guided in our choices by our cognitive intuition. It is not infallible.[12] This is precisely why it is essential to grasp that we have generally been wrong in the past – that life has addressed most of our past predictions through negative verification. When the future becomes the present, it usually turns out that it is not at all as we imagined it not so long ago. That we misinterpreted the events as they unfolded, that we were needlessly afraid of new inventions. Painting the future in the colors of doom and gloom usually means that the unhappiness is inside us, not that our future is bleak. In other words, it shows us that our fears were groundless. This is the central theme of this book and its contribution to the debate on myths.

All myths and fears can be divided into three groups. The first includes myths that have been completely dismantled and disproved because the associated phenomena that humans mythologized have been convincingly explained by science. This group encompasses lightning strikes, solar eclipses, the Flat Earth myth, alleged medieval witchcraft, and lesser known, more contemporary myths, such as the supposed dangers of building urban sewage systems for agriculture in the area. In a book with the notable title *The Sewer System of Warsaw as an Instrument of Judaism and Chicanery*,[13] published at the turn of the 20th century, the author argued with conviction and aplomb that the true purpose of building sanitation infrastructure in Warsaw was the insidious destruction of Polish agriculture and Polish society by Jews. Contemporary myths also include the widespread (since at least the 19th century) belief that shortening the number of hours worked will inevitably lead to loss of productivity and decreases in the volume of production,[14] the myth about tax revenues to the state treasury dropping as a result of tax cuts,[15] the tale about the need to ensure ethnic or national purity (as implemented to disgraceful proportions in the United States during the era of slavery and in Germany in the 1930s),[16] the myth about the usefulness of selecting members of the community in terms of their mental capacity and physical health (as implemented for several decades in Sweden and Australia),[17] the myth about HIV infections through handshakes, and countless others. The list of examples could continue, but the diffusion of knowledge on each topic above can be considered complete. At the same time, loose associations of conspiracy theorists, such as Flat Earth societies, are nothing more than local folklore.

The second group consists of myths we have only partially subdued. In some cases, the fragmented nature of efforts to disprove and conquer myths results from the fact that the cognitive processes that allow us to enhance our knowledge base and ultimately overturn a commonly held belief are still in progress. In other cases, this shift has already occurred in some parts of the world, while others are still in the process of overcoming baseless beliefs on the topic. This group includes the notion that we will be unable to feed the population of the world due to excessive population growth, the need to radically reduce the use of natural resources due to their rapid depletion, the idea that oil is the primary factor that fuels international rivalries over the Arctic, and the evergreen, recurring myth of the impending end of the world. Many will be outraged and appalled by the thought of combining these examples in a single sentence and view their author as an insurgent agitator. But, as Michał Heller has written, statements like these can and should be formulated to challenge the existing order:

> In every era, from the birth of modern experimental science to the present day, science has developed through two interlinked dynamics: in the center, we have the "hard core" defined by theses closely linked to empirical observation, and at the edges, we find a "belt" of bold (or extravagant, depending on one's point of view) hypotheses, not too far removed from what we usually classify as science fiction. As time goes by, some of these hypotheses move into the "core," acquiring a scientific status in the literal sense of the term. Other concepts – the vast majority are

> thrown outside the margins of "official science" and disappear. However, the "outer belt" plays an important role in defining directions of progress for our understanding of the physical world. Even hypotheses doomed to be sent into oblivion are of great heuristic significance – they inspire new research programs and directions.[18]

The myths outlined above are commonly reproduced nearly everywhere in the world, but the voices of those questioning them are becoming increasingly evident and resonant.

A second subcategory of myths that have only been partially vanquished are those still widespread in certain parts of the world, even if they have long been forgotten in others, which stigmatize behavior associated with them today. The examples here are just as comprehensive as in previous cases. Some of these myths are fading before our very eyes, such as the myth of the perils of women driving cars, which was embedded in the state policy of Saudi Arabia until 2018, or the notion that women should not travel alone, which is alive and well in the same country. Other myths are still widely accepted, though their decomposition has already begun. One example is the myth that homosexual tendencies and behavior are unnatural in humans – a myth overthrown in countries that have legalized same-sex unions. As Yuval Noah Harari points out,[19] the "unnatural" does not occur in nature.

In contrast, what does occur can be considered socially unacceptable according to the imagined order of things. Gravity is a natural phenomenon, and our choice of whether to accept it has zero bearing on its existence. Sexual attraction to people of the same sex is the same. The fact that some do not accept it stems from our propensity to filter facts through our values, convictions, and beliefs. Sometimes, we go so far in our interpretations and judgments of reality that, if facts provide ample challenge to our beliefs' correctness, then facts suffer. As Tom Phillips writes:

> Our brains hate finding out that they're wrong. Confirmation bias is our annoying habit of zeroing in like a laser-guided missile on any scrap of evidence that supports what we already believe and blithely ignoring the possibly much, much larger piles of evidence that suggest we might have been completely misguided. [20]

This is probably why myths, and their derivatives, are so entrenched in our minds and societies – and so difficult to root out. It is particularly challenging to alter those beliefs that cannot be empirically verified with one's own experience or someone else's. No one questions that a hunting dog runs faster than a human being; we can confirm this is true from everyday empirical observation. Those who wish to understand the reasons for this and explain why it happens can do so by drawing on the biological sciences. An airplane can fly despite weighing tens of thousands of pounds, significantly exceeding the weight of the air surrounding it; a human possesses no such ability despite weighing much less than even the most miniature aluminum aircraft. We find this more challenging to comprehend because to do so, we would have to possess at least an elementary understanding of physics, yet we all accept the fact that planes can fly.

It is much more challenging to accept social or economic phenomena as fact, as they do not undergo the same kind of direct verification as physical, biological, or chemical processes. As a society, we are not willing to accept that no government has its own money, that all of them redistribute cash that belongs to the taxpayers, and that if they promise something to one group, they will first have to take it away from another – or the same one. We can quote Margaret Thatcher's 1983 speech to the Conservative Party Conference – in which she underscored this exact point – a thousand times over to no avail. People worldwide want to believe that the government that gives them something is the government that does the right thing. The myth of the government that manages its coffers is alive and well in many parts of the world.

For this reason (among others), the Law and Justice party in Poland has continued to enjoy an overwhelming advantage over opposition groups and has ruled the country independently for two terms in a row. One of the party's flagship projects is *Family 500+*, under which the party generously fills citizens' pockets with cash transfers using money siphoned off from those pockets. The program was marketed to encourage higher birth rates, assuming that families would be more likely to have children because the government will provide monthly payments of 500 PLN (about 125 USD; since 2024 it is 800 PLN, or 200 USD) per underage child. The funds were disbursed to all parents, regardless of their level of income, and the program's proponents framed this feature of its design as an argument against the notion that it was purely a social welfare scheme. And yet, Polish citizens have accepted the stated purpose and the cash flow that it brought them with no objections, no concerns about the experiences of other European countries that had fruitlessly pursued similar policies, and no recognition of the abundant scientific studies explaining demographic fluctuations (including fertility rates)[21] or even the fact that the program itself has had almost no demographic effects whatsoever.[22] As individuals and social collectives, we strive to remain firmly convinced of the validity of our own beliefs, regardless of the facts. As a result, the diffusion of knowledge is still ongoing concerning myths that have only been partially conquered.

The third group is made up of myths that – despite the lack of reliable knowledge based on empirical experience on the subject and solid scientific foundations – are still experiencing their heyday. While attempting to identify specific myths from the second group carries a significant risk because it exposes those questioning them to attacks and accusations from those who embrace them, merely raising an example from the third group would antagonize almost everyone. Because of their highly controversial nature, these myths will only be tackled in the final part of this book. Perhaps then, once our readers have processed the trajectories of tales that have been entirely or partially put to rest, they will grasp just how convinced humankind was of the validity of its "truths" in previous eras – until they ceased to be truths, which implies that they were never true, to begin with. This will enable us to critically engage with the final challenge and ask ourselves to what extent specific ubiquitous fears of the modern age are fully anchored in reality. Only the future will show how much of this fear is either rational or not, as explanations for phenomena that are not fully understood today will emerge sooner or later.

The state has played or continues to play a role in some of the abovementioned myths. As a political entity embedded in a specific space and equipped with mechanisms of power and oppression, the state should act on behalf of its citizens – at least in democratic societies, where those powers are granted to the government as part of a social contract that involves surrendering part of their own, individual sovereignty. It is impossible to simultaneously work for the benefit of every citizen, given multiple opposing interests among groups and individuals; after all, the security blanket of state subsidies is always too short on one end, and a wage increase for miners means no equivalent increase for nurses. However, there are situations where the state can and should maintain maximum objectivity and make honest, fact-based assessments. Much like the board members of a listed company strive to carry out their duties in the interest of the shareholders who appointed them through a supervisory board, government officials should act in the citizens' best interest. This rule should be apparent in democratic states.

Unfortunately, in both cases, these ideal assumptions collide with a harsher reality – one in which the company's board of directors is guided by the desire to maximize its revenues rather than the benefits of the company and one in which the government does not act in the interest of its citizens but seeks to stay in power at all costs. If the objective truth must be offered as a sacrificial lamb at the altar of success, neither entity will hesitate to condemn it to death. The list of examples confirming this statement is extended in every modern state. One needs to look at certain decisions that ultimately chart a course for the transformation of the structure of energy production under a specific resource regime. Whether a given location becomes the home of a brand-new coal-fired power station, an atomic power plant, a gas-fired plant, or a wind farm is not determined by a careful economic analysis that considers all the necessary social and environmental factors but by political decisions made by political actors. These decisions can result in an increase or a decrease in the level of public support for a given policy option and political formation. To boost this support, politicians argue that they are defending the interests of their constituents – all the while ruthlessly capitalizing on their power to mold their citizens' fears while governing *through* fear, as Frank Furedi has noted.[23] Depending on the results of their political calculus, they can weaponize everything from particulate matter and carbon dioxide to the fear of an atomic apocalypse, from the noise pollution of wind farms to the environmental fallout of natural gas extraction. There is no doubt whatsoever that humanity needs electricity. But how and where it should be obtained to make it accessible, inexpensive, and clean is a question dominated by political tugs of war. These dynamics escalate fear and reaffirm the masses' deeply entrenched beliefs, which they see as their own. Leszek Kołakowski described this brusquely in the context of atomic power plants:

> . . . protests against nuclear power plants continue unabated. The ignorant masses in the streets say what amounts to this: "You, those in power, are to give us as much electricity as we desire, but without nuclear reactors, without harming the environment, and without spoiling our beautiful landscape. You have to come up with something – and what that something will be is your problem.[24]

In the next part of this book, we will draw myths from the first two groups and analyze them in detail. The myths from the first group, that is, that have already been successfully disproved will be presented primarily to show how deadly serious the entire world (including the world of science) was about placing its faith in something that is not worth a dime today. The myths from the second group will illustrate how certain phenomena or processes that have until recently been presented as unequivocally negative are transforming and moving further along the faith-to-knowledge axis. Based on this, we should conclude that because the world is constantly evolving and scientific progress is achieving ever greater heights, specific processes and events exist in the world today that are almost universally feared – and that they should instead be placed into the third group of myths, that is, those that will one day be dismantled.

This book's main objective and purpose is to show that we should not submit to excessive fears. All we need to do is wait for the moment when the causes and effects of the phenomena and processes we fear and mythologize today will be effectively explained. Our experience to date shows that this evolutionary path will hold in most cases – ultimately, many of our past fears turned out to be overblown, a product of our penchant for misinterpreting reality and falling prey to a doom-and-gloom mindset.

There are countless events, phenomena, and processes that people have unnecessarily feared in centuries past. We selected those that ultimately formed the chapters of this book using several criteria: their universal occurrence, their spatial scope, and the scale of their impact on human consciousness. At the same time, we tried to illuminate fears linked to various dimensions of everyday human life: technology, space, energy, religion, the environment, or consciousness. We selected myths from both the first and second groups described above to undergird the thesis that there is no rational need to fear the myths from the third group. Thus, in the following chapters, we talk about how, until very recently, the fear of railroads and electricity was ubiquitous and powerful across societies, even though today, we all know how irrational it is. We then discuss how many of us, to this day, harbor severe fears of the imminent end of the world and try to prepare for its arrival, then tackle the fear of nuclear power, overpopulation, and the rapidly approaching depletion of essential mineral resources on Earth. In Chapter 7, we look for a common denominator for all our fears and an explanation for why they exist, anchoring the narrative in the widespread fear of an uncertain future. In the concluding chapter, we draw on all the preceding threads to showcase phenomena that belong in the third group – those whose myth-generating power has yet to be defused.

Although this book is the work of seven authors, to maintain internal consistency, we establish a common analytical structure that applies across all the myths and the fears accompanying them. We begin by identifying the historical circumstances and location in which the legend was born. Secondly, we describe the phenomenon or process in question, complete with the arguments used by those who claim it is dangerous to human life, health, or the well-being of current or future generations. Next, we present illustrations of the "propaganda of fear" that has stoked that fear in the populace's minds; this includes posters, excerpts from scientific works, popular science publications, newspaper articles, radio and television shows, and school textbooks. In pertinent cases, we also explore the state's role in fomenting the fear in question and the tools it uses to bring its goals to fruition. In the final part of each chapter, we present the process of conquering the myth in question and arriving at truths that liberated humanity from fear, as well as how this fear was conquered. We visualize this process across time and space to show precisely how the diffusion of knowledge unfolded – or, for the myths in the second group, continues to unfold today.

ONE
OFF THE RAILS: THE PERILS OF THE RAILROAD

Karol Kowalczyk

It may seem complicated to believe today, but the railroad, invented less than 200 years ago, generated fear for almost the entire first century of its existence. Those who propagated the fear of steam trains included the usual suspects, that is, the owners of then common means of transportation threatened by the competition that the railroads presented, such as stagecoaches or inland waterway vessels, and representatives of conservative religious movements. But the opposition also included some of the most educated and enlightened people in society: writers, philosophers, and doctors. Railroad rejectionists sometimes dismantled newly constructed railroad tracks, driven by their opposition to and fear of the iron monsters that rode them. They ascribed diabolical origins to the new form of transportation. They saw it as amoral – or even, in some cases, as an instrument of future depopulation, with serious, respectable scientific journals advancing dramatic evidence of their harmful effects on human health. Although there have been many attempts to halt the development of railroads, and every accident has been treated as evidence in the case against their further development, today, we enjoy fast and comfortable trains, and we look back on 19th-century views on the matter with bemusement.

THE BIRTH OF A GREAT AND TERRIBLE INVENTION

Milestones in the development of world civilization have always met with a plethora of opinions and attitudes. The initiators, disseminators, and enthusiastic groups who spearheaded the acceptance of the newest invention always came in tandem with skeptics – "brakemen" whose collective size and influence can vary depending on the extent to which the innovation interferes with the status quo. These groups identify with the old order; they see it as the optimal state of affairs, one that does not require change. In extreme situations, the clash of old and new can trigger defense mechanisms and responses that delay the diffusion of knowledge about an invention or innovation, especially in places where large groups of opponents can circulate numerous myths about it. Yet even there, in time, such groups eventually conquer their fears and apprehensions, and the innovation that they feared becomes a component of everyday life.

The railroad is the archetype of a milestone that was both enthusiastically received and met with trepidation and hostility, especially in the first decades of its existence. But fear did not halt its progress. Railroads have gone through a technological evolution from horse-drawn wagons to steam engines and electric, diesel, and magnetic levitation trains. Today, none of us fears traveling by train at speeds above 200 kph (124 mph). On the contrary, fast travel makes a given mode of transport more attractive, and constantly improving safety standards minimizes the risk of accidents.

However, the landscape was very different when railroads were in their infancy in Europe and North America and when they first reached other continents. For people accustomed to horse-drawn carriages that reached speeds of several to little more than a dozen kilometers per hour, changing to trains was an experience unlike any other. Railroads elicited admiration but also trepidation, which was accompanied by myths, some of which were stoked by authorities in the fields of science, art, and religion.

How old is the railroad?

Pinpointing the exact date when the railroad was born is not a simple task. Many publications cite September 27, 1825. On that day, the first public service railroad opened between Stockton and Darlington in the northeast of England, using a combination of steam and horse traction. September 15, 1830, is cited just as often as it was the launch date of the Liverpool & Manchester Railway, the first ever inter-city passenger service to be operated using solely steam locomotives. This line was also the origin of the standard gauge – 4 feet 8.5 inches (1435 mm) wide – which is used in many countries today.[25]

Yet the actual genesis of the railroad can be traced much farther back. Distinct methods of transportation that resembled the railroad may have existed in antiquity. Still, the direct roots of the invention lie at the beginning of the 16th century and in mining operations in what is now Germany and Austria. The technical solutions developed then were successfully adapted and improved by the British industry in the following century. The growing weight of the rock extracted from quarries and mines generated a need to improve the means of transportation that took them from their points of extraction to reloading depots, which were located on dirt and gravel roads, canals, and navigable rivers. Notable transportation routes were created for primitive horse-driven freight cars (chaldron wagons) and variously called *waggonways*, *plateways*, *tramways*, *tramroads*, *dramways*, *gangways*, *gangroads*, *railways*, and *railroads*. Most of these words have fallen out of use, displaced by the latter two terms, which were initially used interchangeably. Over time, the *railway* became the dominant form used in British English, while the *railroad* became widely adopted in American English.[26]

The high demand for ways to efficiently transport excavated material catalyzed the evolution of rails – the essential element distinguishing the new method of transportation from conventional vehicles that moved freely on the road. The first rails were made entirely of wood; their successors were covered with strips of cast iron and finally made exclusively of cast iron or wrought iron. Their susceptibility to fracture from the vibrations of passing trains led to the replacement of iron with steel as early as the 1850s. Rails were first used in regular passenger traffic in 1807 in southern Wales, with the Swansea & Oystermouth horsecar railway service, which was operated by specially designed stagecoaches. In the years that followed, similar railways were established in several other locations on the European continent and on the East Coast of North America.[27] However, it was not the expansion of horsecar railways that produced the first tremors of fear. Fear only became a factor after the birth of the second "child" of the Industrial Revolution – the steam-powered locomotion (Fig. 1). The unprecedented speed it enabled provoked terror, as did the power of steam itself, which combined two elements: fire and water.

Fig. 1. A "child" of the Industrial Revolution, as depicted in 1885 by Polish painter Jan Matejko in a drawing from the collection of the National Museum in Krakow titled *Wynalazek kolei żelaznej* [*The Invention of the Railway*] (part of the series *Dzieje Cywilizacji Ludzkości* [*History of Human Civilization*]). The artist used symbolic ambiguity: the word *para* in Polish means both *couple* and *steam*, the latter of which gave birth to the railway.[28]

TOWARDS THE STEAM LOCOMOTIVE

English blacksmith Thomas Newcomen's construction of a low-pressure steam engine in a coal mine in Devon County around 1712 is often considered the symbolic starting point of the Industrial Revolution. The design was later refined and popularized by Scottish inventor James Watt in the 1760s. The use of steam in vehicles was possible only after increasing its pressure, which from the very beginning created the risk of exploding boilers. Before the first self-propelled rail vehicle was developed, trials were conducted using road vehicles. French designer Nicolas-Joseph Cugnot was a pioneer in this area. His three-wheeled steam vehicle, the famous *Fardier à vapeur* built in 1770, made history when it crashed into a wall, interrupting further development. Similar experiments were conducted in Cornwall by Richard Trevithick, the future "father" of locomotives. Trevithick was still making miniature steam-powered models as late as the end of the 18th century and built a full-sized vehicle in 1801. This was a self-propelled road locomotive called the *Puffing Devil*, which got its name from a fire caused by the inattention of the builder himself. The *Puffing Devil* had been stashed in a shed due to a technical fault; however, the firebox had not been extinguished, causing water to evaporate from the boiler and the machine to ignite.[29]

Trevithick organized the first demonstration of his steam locomotive on cast-iron rails in 1804 in South Wales, on a 9.75 miles (15.7 km) stretch between the Penydarren Ironworks (near Merthyr Tydfil) and the village of Navigation (now Abercynon). The success of the attempt was the subject of a wager between the owner of the ironworks in question and one of his competitors, who did not believe in the capabilities of the steam locomotive. The wager was for a sum that was gigantic at the time – 500 guineas. The train, carrying 70 passengers and 10 tons of iron, completed its route in 4 hours and 5 minutes, with a maximum speed of 5 mph (8 kph). Four years later, Trevithick presented his steam locomotive to the citizens of London. It ran on an elliptical track, once again carrying passengers. However, this one was a new machine named *Catch me who can*, which could already reach a top speed of 15 mph (24 kph). Nevertheless, the innovation did not garner sufficient public interest, and the creator himself prematurely abandoned further work with no inkling of how events would unfold.[30]

Demand for the previously unappreciated invention was revived with the onset of the economic crisis caused by Britain's wars with France between 1803 and 1815. The country's large reserves of coal proved to be a salvation in light of rising horse feed prices. Bit by bit, inventors began to design and build coal-fired steam locomotives. Chief among numerous British engineers was George Stephenson, initially a specialist in operating stationary steam engines working in the mines near Newcastle. Stephenson built his first locomotive in 1814, ten years after Trevithick's Welsh success. However, he achieved his greatest fame through two later machines: *Locomotion No. 1* (also known as *Active*) and *Rocket*, which he designed together with his son Robert. The former was built in 1825 for the Stockton & Darlington Railway. The latter, dating from 1829 (Fig. 2), won a contest to operate the Liverpool & Manchester Railway, with a top speed of 30 mph (48 kph).[31]

Fig. 2. The steam locomotive *Rocket* in an engraving published in 1874 by *Harper's New Monthly Magazine* in New York.[32]

THE BEGINNINGS OF GLOBAL DIFFUSION

These achievements were closely observed by envoys from other parts of Europe and the world, who became the first carriers of information about them. Among these envoys were both supporters and opponents of the invention, which resulted in the simultaneous spread of facts and myths about it. The diffusion of knowledge at the initial stage of railroad development was limited to narrow groups of organizers and had a minor impact radius. The farther away from the area served by a particular railroad, the more scant and rudimentary the information that other social groups received. This encouraged the spread of myths. Knowledge only started to gain the upper hand after some time, thanks to ever denser and more extensive railroad networks in individual areas (Fig. 3 and 4).

In 1830, the first steam railroad in the United States – the Baltimore & Ohio Railroad – was opened to the public.[33] By the late 1830s, railroads existed in Canada and several countries in continental Europe: Belgium, Germany (Bavaria), France, Austria, Russia, Italy (Kingdom of the Two Sicilies), and the Netherlands. They ran steam locomotives imported from Great Britain before domestic industry learned to produce them.

The following decades were characterized by an increase in train speeds and the rapid development of rail networks on all the inhabited continents (Fig. 3), bolstered by colonialism and its policies. In the 1850s, the invention appeared in Latin America, Australia, and the Indian Peninsula. It first arrived in South Africa (in the Cape Colony) in 1860 and reached East Asia in the 1870s. The railroad had a particularly rocky start in China, which today is the world leader in the construction of high-speed lines.[34]

In operation since:	Country:	Length of rail network (km) in:							
		1830	1840	1850	1860	1870	1880	1890	1900
1825	Great Britain and Ireland	279	2,053	10,660	16,797	24,383	28,854	32,726	35,296
1830	United States	65	4,509	14,515	49,277	85,151	150,113	263,228	311,287
1835	Belgium	-	331	861	1,729	2,897	4,112	5,207	6,345
1835	Germany	-	466	6,053	11,724	19,719	33,888	42,869	51,391
1836	Canada	-	25	106	3,323	4,211	11,035	21,160	28,410
1837	France	-	493	3,010	9,439	17,733	25,925	36,672	42,826
1837	Austria	-	143	1,579	4,543	9,589	18,512	26,553	36,883
1837	Russia	-	27	500	1,591	11,236	23,524	30,940	48,107
1839	Italy	-	7	426	1,800	6,208	8,713	12,907	15,787
1839	Netherlands	-	18	176	335	1,419	1,841	2,610	2,743
1844	Switzerland	-	-	25	1,058	1,442	2,470	3,198	3,783
1847	Denmark	-	-	211	485	764	1,592	1,986	3,001

In operation since:	Country:	Length of rail network (km) in:							
		1830	1840	1850	1860	1870	1880	1890	1900
1848	Spain	-	-	28	1,918	5,475	7,480	9,878	17,357
1850	Mexico	-	-	11	32	349	1,120	9,713	15,454
1853	British India	-	-	-	841	4,840	14,729	26,299	39,634
1854	Brazil	-	-	-	295	786	3,500	9,800	14,798
1854	Australia	-	-	-	363	1,807	7,823	18,732	25,151
1855	Sweden	-	-	-	531	1,734	5,761	8,018	11,320
1857	Argentina	-	-	-	39	732	2,313	9,255	17,047
1860	Ottoman Empire	-	-	-	66	291	1,394	1,719	3,142
1860	Cape Colony (South Africa)	-	-	-	5	167	1,616	3,262	4,931
1872	Japan	-	-	-	-	-	122	2,333	5,858
1876	China	-	-	-	-	-	0 (15)	145	1,070
Legend (square area proportional to the network length):		1,000	5,000	10,000	25,000	50,000	100,000	200,000	350,000

Fig. 3. Development of steam railroads for public use in selected countries until 1900.[35]

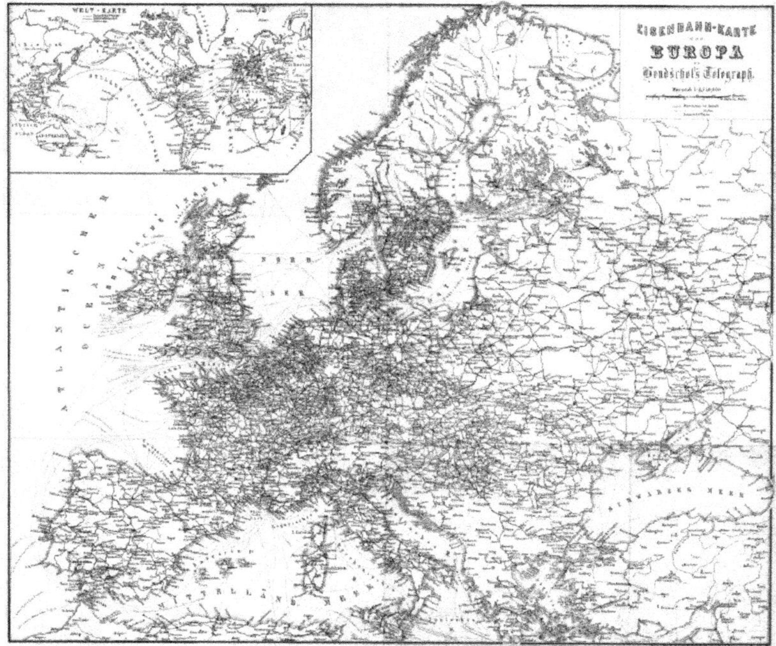

Fig. 4. The European rail network and the world's major transportation routes in the late 19th century. The spider web of rail lines demonstrates the successful conquest of fear. The map served as an appendix to a German timetable titled *Hendschel's Telegraph: Übersicht der Eisenbahn-, Post, Dampfschiff- und Telegraphen-Verbindungen*.[36]

Hell on wheels: The oldest railroad myths

The black puffing monster

Suppose we wish to follow the trail of railroad myths. In that case, we should begin with the original notion of the steam locomotive as an invention from hell, the embodiment of evil, a source of moral depravity, and a vehicle whose existence flew in the face of nature. This image, while stemming from the propulsive power of the machine itself, encompassed all aspects of the new branch of transportation in practice. Myths began to spread in specific locations during the initial phase of the development of the railroad network, sometimes as early as the planning stage of the route of the first line when disturbing accounts of outside witnesses observing the implementation of the invention in other places circulated vigorously.

One category of human communities was particularly vulnerable to the spread of fear: communities that remained firmly attached to their religious beliefs, shaped in the realities of the centuries-old "Age of the Horse," whose origins can be dated to the third millennium BC.[37] Contrary to appearances, myths were not the exclusive domain of poorly educated social groups, who were sometimes treated as objects of ridicule by the bourgeois elite (Fig. 5). At the same time, various authorities and opinion shapers of that era espoused equally controversial visions, acting them out on a local, regional, or even global scale.

Fig. 5. The idea of a steam locomotive in the eyes of German peasants, caricatured in 1854 in the Munich satirical weekly *Fliegende Blätter*.[38]

The first sparks of fear of the railroad emerged in various strands of Protestantism as a result of the distinctive sequence of spatial development of railroads around the world. Let us move then to a hinterland of the United States. In 1828, when construction on the Baltimore & Ohio Line began, the town of Lancaster (Ohio) planned to hold a debate on the latest technological advances on its school grounds. The school board, however, refused to make the premises available, responding with a letter that conveyed the following reasoning:

> . . . such things as railroads and telegraph are impossibilities, and rank infidelity. There is nothing in the Word of God about them. If God had designed that His intelligent creatures should travel at the frightful speed of fifteen miles an hour by steam, He would have clearly foretold it through His holy prophets.[39]

At times, specific business interests were behind objections that were based on an overly literal interpretation of religious texts. Before steam locomotives took hold in Britain and the United States, a network of navigable inland canals had flourished there and were of great interest to investors. The new mode of transportation posed severe competition. One of the ways in which the old system resisted the coming changes was by spreading the myth of the infernal origin of the railroad. This is perfectly illustrated by this anonymous statement from a concerned American, recorded in the 1840s:

> Canals, sir, are God's own highway, operating on the soft bosom of the fluid that comes straight from Heaven. The railroad stems direct from Hell. It is the Devil's own invention, ..., spreading its infernal poison throughout the fair countryside. It will set fire to houses along its slimy tracks. . . . It will leave the land despoiled, ruined, a desert where only sable buzzards shall wing their loathsome way to feed

> upon the carrion accomplished by the iron monster of the locomotive engine.[40]

Occasionally, and in some circles, the belief in such myths did not cease even after the railroad had successfully taken root. One example was Sabbatarianism, a doctrine in Scottish denominations of Reformed Protestantism that forbade all entertainment on Sunday, as it was considered the Lord's Day. Rail travel was one of the pleasures from which followers were instructed to abstain.[41] Meanwhile, in Great Britain in the 1840s, Sunday excursions were gaining popularity, with the rapidly expanding railway companies offering tickets at attractive prices. But such pastimes were in apparent contradiction to the principles of Sabbatarianism, and this sometimes provoked peculiar reactions. In response to a public announcement regarding an excursion that was to leave Newcastle on August 29, 1841, a visiting pastor, William Chalmers Burns, plastered the city with warnings that read: "A Reward for Sabbath Breaking. People taken safely and swiftly to Hell! Next Lord's Day, by the Carlisle Railway, for 7s. 6d. It is a pleasure trip!"[42]

The pastor's protest ultimately had the opposite effect – it acted as an eye-catching advertisement for the travel agency. Nevertheless, defenders of the Christian Sabbath persisted in their beliefs for decades to come, exerting pressure on companies, sometimes resulting in significant reductions in train service on Sundays. In 1865, the Scottish weekly *Stirling Observer* reported on a public deliberation involving representatives of several religious associations under the title "Railway Sabbath Traffic." Of particular note was a statement made by one of the pastors:

> [R]ailway companies may make money by running their trains on the Sabbath day, but there can be no blessing in the money they make. There is a mark

> on every shilling they put into their till. There is a mark of God's disapprobation . . . that money is not lawfully got, it belongs not to you . . . for that money you have a fearful account to give.[43]

THE RAILROADS OF CATHOLIC EUROPE

As the railway spread throughout continental Europe, it reached areas with a strong Catholic influence. At first glance, it would seem that this "terrible invention" should be met with immediate and forceful resistance from rulers and heads of state who vocally declared their affiliation with the Catholic Church. As it turned out, the vast majority, upon hearing about the economic benefits of the railway in Great Britain and the United States, accepted it with great openness, with the exception of one European monarch – Pope Gregory XVI. When he became head of the Papal States in 1831, the territories directly administered by him occupied the entire central part of the Italian Peninsula. Despite numerous requests from influential subjects, Gregory XVI did not build a single kilometer of railways during his 15-year pontificate.[44] At the same time, several neighboring countries had already opened their first sections – the Kingdom of the Two Sicilies (1839), the Kingdom of Lombardy-Veneto (1840), and the Grand Duchy of Tuscany (1844) – and construction was beginning in the Kingdom of Sardinia. The lack of approval from the authorities of the Papal States meant that the future railway connection of the southern part of the peninsula with the rest of Europe was delayed, and the State itself remained isolated in relation to its neighbors. The railway did not reach Rome until 1856 in the form of a 24-kilometer section leading to Frascati.[45] But it was done under the rule of Pius IX, Gregory XVI's successor. The spatial situation can be observed on a German map from that year: *Post- und Eisenbahn- Reisekarte*, which is now available in the digital collections of the Library of Congress.[46]

Gregory XVI's motives were not known to the public at the time. There was no official document justifying the direction of his policy, and all proposals for the construction of railways in the Papal States made before 1846 were met with a wall of silence in the Vatican.[47] This gave rise to all sorts of conjectures which, on the one hand, perpetuated the negative image of this pope among supporters of progress and, on the other, fueled belief in the myth of the infernal origin of the railway among those who clung to the old order. It was not difficult for the latter to conclude that, since the pope himself opposed its construction, the invention must be the work of Satan. Among other things, it was claimed that Gregory XVI, in expressing his opposition, used a French play on words: *chemin de fer, chemin d'enfer* – that is, *the iron road, the road to hell*.[48]

News of the pope who railed against the railway reached places where the invention was developing dynamically and no longer aroused fear among some religious groups. The sluggish pace of construction was sometimes attributed to the pope's desire to protect the Eternal City from the influx of new currents of thought.[49] However, according to one of the texts included in the 103-volume dictionary of ecclesiastical knowledge *Dizionario di erudizione storico-ecclesiastica* (authored by Gaetano Moroni, a close associate of Popes Gregory XVI and Pius IX), the actual motives for this hostility were not religious. The problem lay not in the "infernal" propulsive power of the vehicle (the pope had supported steam navigation on the Tiber) but in fears of the adverse effects of railroads, including accidents and their lack of profitability.[50]

Radical changes came only with the pontificate of the next pope, Pius IX, who already in 1846 initiated the construction of railroads in the Papal States, and in 1849, became the first pope to travel by train in the vicinity of Naples, at the invitation of the

Neapolitan monarch. This is a storyline we will return to again in the section "Church on Wheels."

Now, let us leave the Italian Peninsula and move to Central and Eastern Europe, where the railway arrived more or less contemporaneously. The implementation of the invention was preceded by stories of people who had already experienced riding the new means of transport during their stays abroad. Some expressed delight; others were terrified. In 1847, not long before the opening of the first line to Kraków, the Polish geographer, and poet Wincenty Pol, otherwise a staunch proponent of the development of rail transport, included a colorful description inspired by Central European mythology in a written account of his trip to Silesia. Even for him – a man who was curious about the world and appreciated the advantages of innovative technology – the steam train inspired awe:

> Like a dragon's eyes the two bloody lanterns at the front of the steam wagon pierce the darkness . . . it seems as if the entire rolling stock is barreling straight into hell's throat, and when the shrill whistle of the steam pipe mixes with the sulfurous odor that emanates from time to one is reminded, if not of the devil of the old Polish tradition, then at least of Goethe's Mephistopheles.[51]

However, in Pol's case, knowledge quickly overcame fear: "Reliably something good must grow out of these iron railroads for the people . . . the thought of this easy passage through the world makes such a vivid, such a warming impression on everyone's mind!"[52]

In the Land of Broad-Gauge Tracks

Since we are already in Europe at this point in the story, let us travel to its eastern fringes. In the Russian Empire, as in the United States, railways proved to be an effective tool for colonizing the interior. However, at the outset, there was no shortage of dissenting voices, including those motivated by religion. Some Orthodox clergymen expressed concern about the transformation in how people traveled. Among them was Metropolitan Philaret (Drozdov) of Moscow, who, in his correspondence with the abbot of the Trinity Lavra of St. Sergius, vividly compared the old order with the new, the arrival of which was purportedly associated with a deadly threat:

> Would it not have been better to hold on to the simple mechanism, which threatened no one with death? In days past, one drove on ordinary roads quietly and bumpily, but was unharmed; now, on the railroad, one flies – with the danger of losing one's head every minute.[53]

The excerpt above is from 1839 when only a 27-kilometer stretch of railway (the Tsarskoye Selo Railway near St. Petersburg) existed in Russia, and most of the population had not yet had time to experience train travel. Metropolitan Philaret himself was among them. This did not prevent him from casting doubt on the economic viability of the railway and from prognosticating its negative impact on believers' morality. Two decades later, he continued to adhere to his position. In 1859, in connection with plans to build a railroad between Moscow and Sergeyev Posad, he purportedly argued that "[p]ilgrims would come to the monastery in railroad cars, on which all sorts of tales can be heard and often dirty stories, whereas now they come on foot and each step is a feat pleasing to God."[54]

When the line was opened three years later, the 80-year-old Philaret took part in the inaugural ride on a special train, which he had sprinkled with holy water.[55] After getting off the train, he had a sudden change of heart and relayed his positive impressions in an enthusiastic speech, stating: "I recommend the railroad. How much art, effort, and money it takes to drive an hour and a half instead of five."[56]

At the same time, the secular moral authority of Tsarist Russia, the world-famous novelist Leo Tolstoy, remained implacable in his disdain for the railway. During his travels around Western Europe in 1857, he was sometimes forced to travel by train, which, unlike stagecoaches, he abhorred without disguising it. Disgusted with the social life of Paris, he moved to Geneva, from where he wrote a letter addressed to another luminary of Russian literature, Ivan Turgenev. He described his attitude toward rail travel in trenchant terms:

> I did very well to get away from that Sodom. For goodness sake get away somewhere yourself too, only not by railway. The railway is to travelling what the brothel is to love – just as convenient, but just as inhumanly mechanical and deadly monotonous.[57]

Tolstoy maintained his aversion throughout his life, which left its mark on his literary work. It surfaces in the pages of his famous *Anna Karenina* but also less popular works. In 1889, when Russia had already built approximately 30,000 kilometers of railway lines, Tolstoy imbued the main character of his novella *Kreutzer Sonata* with the same distaste for the rails: "Oh, I am afraid, I am afraid of railway carriages. Fear seizes me."[58] Ironically, Tolstoy's life ended at a small train station located between Moscow and Voronezh after he fell ill with pneumonia on the train when he secretly left his family estate in search of a new place to live. The carrier, incidentally, was not to blame for the fate of the celebrated writer. It was its passenger's failing health and advanced age that were to blame.[59]

AT THE ANTIPODES

Fear did not recognize political borders or natural barriers in the form of seas and oceans. The indigenous people of Panama, where Catholic missionaries had been active since the 16th century, experienced their first encounter with a steam locomotive. In 1855, the Panama Railroad Company opened a line that connected the coast of the Caribbean Sea and the Pacific Ocean, thus improving what was then the fastest transport route from the East Coast of the United States to the West Coast.[60] Traveler Thomas Knox recalled this event in one of the adventure books that form part of his *The Boy Travelers* series.

> There was great excitement, which reached the pitch of terror when the creature came into the midst of the crowd, and the whistle was blown. The whole crowd fled to the river, and many of them jumped in, expecting they would be pursued, and possibly devoured. . . . They sent forward their priest to examine the animal; he surveyed it carefully, and then informed his followers that it was not an animal, but a machine, in which there was a veritable demon chained, and compelled to work the crank which propelled it. The explanation was sufficient; the good priest knew it was hopeless to attempt to enlighten them on the uses of steam . . . .[61]

The railroad in Australia was inaugurated the previous year. But fear was still evident there as late as the 1880s. Some among the pedestrians traversing the crowded streets of Sydney were terrified of the steam-powered streetcars that increased in the city. This innovation was acquired in 1879 from the United States for the Sydney International Exhibition. Shortly after that, the tramway network expanded its spatial reach. The noisy, smoky invention frightened horses, and its long braking distance resulted in a number of accidents involving pedestrians, many of which were fatal.[62] Steeped in this foreboding atmosphere, street traffic in the city evoked infernal associations among its residents, which the satirical magazine *Sydney Punch* skillfully illustrated. The magazine's 1881 issue included a cartoon titled "The Steam Fiend," depicting a streetcar in the shape of a skull, speeding along the rails and driven by the Devil. The scene is accompanied by a quote from Shakespeare's play, *King John*: "The jaws of danger and of death." Trove digital library managed by the National Library of Australia provides us an opportunity to look at this cartoon.[63]

Leaving aside extreme attitudes, the initial prejudice against the new means of transport was not entirely irrational. The overwhelming blackness of the smoke and soot, the loud noise, and the foul smell were far removed from the sensations to which humankind had become accustomed in earlier centuries when we moved at speeds that never exceeded those of a draft horse. Even the fastest stagecoaches, introduced in the 18th century, were considered embraced as a regular part of reality. Everyone understood animal power, unlike the mysterious power of the steam engine.[64] A large percentage of the population at the time was illiterate, and the average level of education did not allow for the knowledge contained in the writings of the pioneers of the railroad to be disseminated widely.

Furious delirium: Pathogenic effects of train travel

Early medical prognosis and diagnosis

However, some feared the railroad for hardly religious reasons; instead, what they saw in riding the rails was a real danger to human health. In 1835, members of the Academy of Lyon reacted to a series of trials in which people were transported on the Saint-Étienne–Lyon industrial railroad in coal cars – wagons that were profoundly unsuitable for human transport.[65] Concerned for the health of their fellow citizens, they presented a list of various diseases that they believed would arise with the spread of the invention throughout France:

> The overly hasty transition from one climate to another will produce lethal effects in the respiratory tract . . . . The swaying and shaking will give rise to nervous illnesses . . . while the rapid succession of views will lead to inflammation of the retina. The dust and smoke will cause bronchitis and pleural adhesions. Finally, the anxiety of constant exposure to danger will keep travelers in a state of perpetual alertness and presage cerebral affections. For pregnant women, any railway trip will unfailingly lead to a miscarriage, with all its consequences.[66]

Some went even further, viewing the new mode of transportation as a tool for future depopulation: "those who were not yet in a state of declared pregnancy would have to give up all hope of motherhood if they boarded the wagon so that this invention would have a very pronounced Malthusian character."[67]

Fear-inducing medical speculation was, of course, not exclusively a French specialty. Similar reactions followed shortly after the first rail line was opened in what is now Germany, between Nuremberg and Fürth (Bavarian Ludwig Railway). Let us take a look at a recommendation dating from around 1835, issued by the Königlich Bayrisches Obermedizinalkollegium (Royal Bavarian College of Senior Physicians):

> Travel in cars drawn by a locomotive ought to be forbidden, in the interest of public health. The rapid movement cannot fail to produce among the passengers the mental affection known as "delirium furiosum." Even if travelers are willing to incur this risk, the government should at least protect the public. A single glance at a locomotive passing rapidly is sufficient to cause the same cerebral derangement; consequently it is absolutely necessary to build a fence 10 ft. in height, on each side of the railway.[68]

In a slight twist of irony, the postulate of building barriers to protect the public was fulfilled in the 21st century when acoustic screens were installed along certain sections of railroad lines. The effect is essentially the same, although with a minor difference. Instead of hiding the train from the eyes of terrified passers-by, the screens obscure the landscape outside the window. This makes the journey uncomfortable for the passengers, but in the end, everyone makes it out unscathed despite traveling at 200 or 300 kph (124 or 186 mph). In comparison, the steam locomotive *Adler* (German word for "eagle"), which was the suspected culprit of the above afflictions among the people of Bavaria, could reach a top speed of about 65 kph (40 mph), while in regular operation it chugged along at only 35 kph (21 mph). The vehicle was bought in Britain and manufactured at George and Robert Stephenson's works in Newcastle.[69] Ceremonial opening of the Bavarian Ludwig Railway took place on December 7, 1835. A colored copper-plate engraving of that time by Conrad Wiessner highlights a huge public interest in the ceremony. One of the copies belongs to the Science Museum (London) and can be viewed on Google Arts & Culture.[70]

The adverse health effects of trains were also the subject of fears among British doctors. Tunnel crossings were one source of their concern. In 1836, amid plans to run a railway between London and Brighton, a discussion arose among the medical community, which advocated a route that would eliminate the need for tunnels along the way. According to Sir Anthony Carlisle, Vice-President of the Royal College of Surgeons and a physician with more than 40 years of experience:

> [T]he variations in temperature . . . will be sufficient to put persons even in health in danger of cold . . . a person is subjected to all the modifications of disorder of the lungs . . . and also erysipelas, a very dangerous disease, is known very frequently to happen from sudden transitions from heat to cold . . . . I would not permit one of my patients to go to Brighton by a railway that had a tunnel in it; I should endeavour to dissuade . . . from subjecting himself to such perils. . . . apprehend it would be impossible to change the atmosphere of a tunnel 600 yards long.[71]

The concerns raised were ultimately left unaddressed. The line was opened in 1841, complete with five tunnels that are still in use today. The longest of them – Clayton Tunnel – is 1 mile 499 yards (2066 m) long.[72]

"The Lancet": A source of myths?

Scientific journals also contributed to railway paranoia by pointing out the potential harms of riding the rails. Such was the case of the scientific journal *The Lancet*, widely recognized as prestigious even then. In 1862, it published a special pamphlet containing a collection of articles with the standard title, "The Influence of Railway Travelling on Public Health," all of which had previously appeared in separate issues of *The Lancet*.[73] The timing of its publication – nearly four decades after the debut of the first passenger trains – made some of the ideas presented there seem quite reasonable from today's point of view. However, there are a few that we can confidently categorize as myths. One shocking example is the theory about the harms of gazing out the window while riding the train:

> The rapidity and variety of the impressions necessarily fatigue both the eye and the brain. The constantly varying distance at which the objects are placed involves an incessant shifting of the adaptive apparatus by which they are focused upon the retina; and the mental effort by which the brain takes cognizance of them is scarcely less productive of cerebral wear because it is unconscious; . . . that excessive functional activity always implies destruction of material and organic change of substance.[74]

Looking through the brochure, we can come across another nevertheless controversial assertion. It turns out that even the use of season tickets was thought to be harmful. Daily travel was said to accelerate aging, as one doctor established while traveling on commuter trains on the above-mentioned London–Brighton line. He claimed that "a [daily] railway journey of an hour, at the rate of fifty miles an hour, is almost as fatiguing as half a day's journey on the road."[75]

To lend credence to these reports, the journal editors supplemented the quoted statement with statistics showing that the number of people using season tickets in England and Wales between 1859 and 1860 had declined by nearly 5,000.[76]

Diseases of the late 19th century

More than half a century of operation and continuous expansion did not deter further discussion on the health effects of traveling by rail at the end of the 19th century. Despite numerous improvements in passenger comfort and safety, British neurologist John Russell Reynolds returned to the subject in 1883, publishing an article titled "Travelling: Its Influence on Health." He wrote with conviction about the stresses that the human body can experience as a result of moving long distances by train in a relatively short period, pitting railways against other modes of transportation.[77]

Reading on the move was a standard method of curing alleged ailments, and railway stations jumped at the opportunity by providing increasingly well-stocked kiosks featuring abundant reading material. However, this behavior was also criticized by the author of the article, who regarded reading while traveling by train as another strain and an additional cause of fatigue. According to Reynolds, the use of suburban trains was even more harmful to human health, harkening back to the ideas published twenty years earlier in *The Lancet*:

> [A] journey in a 'stopping train,' with all the modern appliances of starting quickly and pulling up abruptly . . . [involves] an amount of muscular annoyance and moral vexation that is proportionate to the number of stoppages.[78]

Reynolds further attempted to prove that the time saved in travel is then wasted in the process of compensating for fatigue or treating disease, so it would be healthier and better to walk a few miles rather than take the train.

Before the railroad fully liberated itself from its hellish, morbid image, there was an innovation that revolutionized the mass transportation of people in London while instilling fear among some of its users. In 1863, London was the venue for the opening of the world's first underground railroad – the Metropolitan Railway. Initially, 3.75-mile (6 km) section (which still exists today) was built between Paddington and Farringdon stations, and the railway network was subsequently extended over the years. Its original design, however, differed from what we are used to from the various urban rail transport systems. Instead of electric power, which was introduced at the turn of the 20th century, the trains were powered by steam locomotives. Inefficient ventilation made the air in the tunnels oppressive and uncomfortable for passengers. In 1887, American journalist Ralph David Blumenfeld traveled on the London Underground while serving as a correspondent in Great Britain. This iteration of the invention was not yet known overseas, and the journalist's account was brimming with disapproval. His description of his impressions after stepping off the trains combines two significant fears: hell and loss of health.

> I had my first experience of Hades to-day, and if the real thing is to be like that I shall never again do anything wrong. I got into the Underground railway .... The atmosphere was a mixture of sulphur, coal dust and foul fumes from the oil lamp above; so that by the time we reached Moorgate Street I was near dead of asphyxiation and heat.[79]

Ridiculous Advocates

In reality, not all 19th-century physicians were skeptics, but myths sometimes sprang up even among advocates of the railroad. James Johnson was the editor of *The Medico-chirurgical Review and Journal of Practical Medicine*, a journal whose considerable reach derived from its being published on both sides of the Atlantic. In 1837, he wrote about the therapeutic properties of regular rail travel:

> The vibratory, or rather oscillatory motion communicated to the human frame, is very different from the swinging and jolting motions of the stage coach, and is productive of more salutary effects. It equalizes the circulation, promotes digestion, tranquillizes the nerves (after the open country is gained), and often causes sound sleep during the succeeding night .... The railroad bids fair to be a powerful remedial agent in many ailments to which the metropolitan and civic inhabitants are subject civic inhabitants are subject .... I have no doubt that to thousands and tens of thousands of valetudinarians in this overgrown Babylon, the run to Boxmoor or Tring and back, twice or thrice a week, will prove a means of preserving health and prolonging life, more powerful than all the drugs ....[80]

Just as fears of railroad-induced diseases sound like nonsense from today's vantage point, some overly optimistic opinions also come off as detached from reality. Thus, not only the fearful but also the uncritical enthusiasts of the rails were known to say far-fetched, implausible things.

Between myth and reality: Rail accidents and the propaganda of fear in the 19th century

The death train

Soon after the railroad was put into service, more and more accidents began to occur, a number of which had fatal repercussions. For some, this clearly validated their prejudices. Others were only beginning to experience fear as a result of press reports or their own observation. The fear of taking a ride into the bowels of Hell was gradually replaced by the fear of losing one's life or health during the journey. This comes through in illustrations from the era that were intended to evoke a feeling of terror in their audience. In short, the Devil chose to descend from the steam locomotive to make room for Death. An expressive example is the engraving titled "The Horrors of Travel" from the New York magazine *Harper's Weekly*, which we can access today through HathiTrust Digital Library.[81] The image, first published in 1865 (four months after the end of the American Civil War), was accompanied by disturbing description:

> During the present year Death appears to have set his mark upon the traveler .... There has come to be a general feeling of insecurity and distrust, and every man or woman who steps out of a railway car or steamboat at the termination of their journey unhurt does so with feeling of sensible relief. It is a fact that more lives have been lost by accident this year than in some of the severest battles of the war.[82]

Death could come from a range of directions: derailments and collisions, construction disasters and fires. Not all of these could be attributed to mistakes made by the crew or the railroad itself, through design flaws in the train's mechanical components or the infrastructure that maintained it. Some accidents were prompted by natural factors as well as by the absent-mindedness or deliberate actions of bystanders.[83] Regardless of the objective reasons, some observers launched attempts to find an overarching cause for all the incidents. For instance, the collection mentioned above of articles from *The Lancet* put forward some unique biological conjecture:

> In animal bodies the means of motion are muscle and tendon. Tigers or cats can leap from many times their own height without damage. A railway engine or carriage would be destroyed by a very small fall. Removed from the rail to a paved road, either it or the road, or both, would be rapidly destroyed. The reason is that there is great deficiency in the mechanical appliances which should represent muscle.[84]

But let us go back for a moment to the first public railway line from Stockton to Darlington and the investments that were planned in its wake. At that point in time, most of the English public had not yet experienced train travel personally. Thus, they based their perceptions on hearsay, much of which was disjointed. They tried to contrast the accounts they received with their previous experience of travel by horse-drawn carriages or vessels, including steamships. The new rail vehicles purportedly moved at a ferocious speed, arousing considerable fear. The prospect of accelerating to high speeds was hard to fathom and instantly created visions of inevitable, fatal accidents. The supposed dangers of rail travel at the frenetic speed of four hundred miles a day were contrasted with idyllic descriptions of steamship travel. Granted, one could drown, get killed by an exploding boiler, or suffer severe seasickness – but this was nothing compared to the risk of dying due to "high-speed" rail travel.[85]

ACCIDENTAL PANIC

Since the 1830s, the spread of fear has also been fed by actual accidents, not their projections. The ceremonial opening of the Liverpool & Manchester line, attended by the elite of the political and business community at the time, also had a dark side. On September 15, 1830, William Huskisson, a minister in several governments and a Tory member of the House of Commons, fell under the wheels of the famous *Rocket* steam engine. The locomotive sheared his leg off, and the blood loss was so severe that he died the same evening despite receiving prompt assistance. Huskisson became the first railroad accident victim known to the general public. The press eagerly seized the opportunity to increase reader interest. It covered the accident vividly, emotionally, and in great detail, thus helping to reignite the spiral of fear of the railroad.[86]

Subsequent accidents and the way they were reported in the media brought this fear to people who were not participants or even witnesses of the original events. The French economist and physician Louis René Villermé was shocked upon hearing of a train crash on May 8, 1842 – the feast day of King Louis Philippe. The accident occurred at Meudon, near Paris, on the Versailles–Paris line, which had been in operation for over two years. He recorded his feelings in letters to the Belgian scholar Lambert Adolphe Quételet. Interestingly, he believed that such bad experiences would be superseded in the long run and would not discourage people from using the railway:

> Although I stayed in Paris on the 8th, I felt for four days in a row a tightening of the chest, an oppression similar to what an enormous weight would produce. I witnessed 20 battles and skirmishes, and I believe the thousands of dead or wounded I saw never affected me so painfully. But one becomes accustomed to

> everything and the general pain that was caused here by the horrible disaster is already significantly weakened. We are in a time when impressions follow one another quickly and are no less quickly forgotten. This will not, moreover, prevent a single reasonable person from boarding a train.[87]

The disaster at Meudon was documented in numerous engravings and paintings that stimulated the public's imagination. Some of them are displayed in the Gallica – a digital collection of the National Library of France.[88] It was the first accident in the history of the world's railroads with such a high number of casualties. Out of 770 passengers and crew, 55 were killed and more than 100 injured. The tragic tally was the result of a fire that broke out after part of the train, which was pulled by two steam locomotives, derailed. The disaster occurred when an axle broke in one of the locomotives. Both fell off the rails, and fiery embers of coal spilled out of their fireboxes and onto the twisted metal of the cars crushed against the wreckage. The evacuation of the passengers was complicated by the fact that the compartment doors were locked from the outside for the duration of the ride – ironically, for safety reasons.[89]

All railroad companies operating in Europe, having learned from experience, abandoned this inherently dangerous practice. However, they retained the stagecoach-like construction of their passenger carriages, including unconnected compartments with separate entrances. Soon, this, too, proved to be an ineffective solution, as it began to encourage crime. The United States took a different approach: from the very beginning, American trains opted for open-space railroad cars without compartments, thus giving passengers a greater sense of security.[90]

Returning to the subject of rail accidents, the fatal events described above and others like them occurring on the railroad made a great impression on the public due to the high number of casualties. Even the very numerous but scattered deaths under the wheels of horse-drawn vehicles did not evoke such emotions. But the fear of dying in a train crash, even during the period of heightened risk that flowed from the vehicles' technical inadequacies, was sometimes overblown. According to *The Lancet*, in the United Kingdom, between 1857 and 1860, 242 train accidents resulted in 111 deaths and 2,025 injuries, while in London alone, in 1859, 70 people died in road accidents and 910 were injured. The average number of deaths in the coal mines – 1,000 per year – was also cited for comparison.[91]

The same publication includes a comparison of the risk of suffering a fatal railroad accident for several countries in the world, calculated as the ratio of the number of deaths to the total number of journeys passengers make in a given year. For France, a value for accidents involving stagecoaches is additionally provided, which gives an idea of the real difference in levels of safety between the two modes of transport. The probability of losing one's life during a journey by stagecoach was almost 21 times higher than by train – 1:335,000 versus 1:7,000,000.[92]

Now, let us abandon the world of numbers and move on to the world of literary fiction. Charles Dickens, though more widely known as the author of *A Christmas Carol*, also made his mark in railroad fear propaganda. Inspired by two accidents – a train collision at Clayton Tunnel that was reported in the press (August 25, 1861) and his own experience of being a passenger in a derailment that occurred at Staplehurst (June 9, 1865) – he wrote a story titled *The Signal-Man*. It was published in a special Christmas issue of the weekly literary magazine *All the Year Round*, whose increased circulation for the issue enhanced the social impact of the periodical. The paranormal phenomena described in the story activated readers' imagination, arousing fear among those who used rail services daily.[93]

The wizards of the 19th-century advertising world were perfectly capable of exploiting the readers' freshly created impressions. The back cover of the original copy of *Mugby Junction* – the same set of short stories in which *The Signal-Man* was published – displays an advertisement for insurance against railroad accidents that begins with the words: "Accidents will happen! Everyone should, therefore, provide against them! £1000 in case of death, or £6 per Week while laid-up by injury . . . ." Unlike the weekly magazine, which sold for four pence each, there was much more money to be made on insurance policies purchased under the duress of fear. The lowest annual premium was £3. By comparison, the weekly wages of Manchester boiler factory workers at that time were about £1-2. Today, the cheapest life insurance in the UK costs around £170 a year, while median income stands at approximately £25,000.[94]

The Tay Bridge disaster, which occurred on a bridge over the Firth of Tay near Dundee in Scotland on December 28, 1879, aroused great emotions on both sides of the Atlantic thanks to relentless media coverage. The open-lattice structure, which had been in operation for less than two years, aroused both admiration and fear even before the tragedy. It had a length of about 2 miles – a world record at the time. A few months before the incident, Queen Victoria herself had crossed the bridge on her way back from her summer residence at Balmoral. The monarch thus personally vouched for the structure's safety, as reported in the *Illustrated London News*. However, favorable press proved inferior to the laws of physics. The spans and piers of the bridge were not sufficiently resistant to wind. During a severe storm, some of them collapsed under the additional pressure of a moving train, and 75 people plunged to their deaths in the turbulent waters of the bay. The only survivor was the locomotive, which later received the nickname "The Diver." After undergoing repairs, it returned to service. On the 29th anniversary of the disaster, she managed to run one more time over the Tay Bridge, which was rebuilt in 1887. The engine remained in operation until 1919.[95]

The bridge disaster occurred on a Sunday, reawakening fears rooted in the teachings of Sabbatarianism, which we have already explored. An early-January 1880 issue of the weekly *Christian Herald and Signs of Our Times*, published in London and New York, featured on its cover page a frightening engraving of a sinking train amidst rough waves and damaged spans. Two different digital copies of this page can be found on the Leisure & Culture Dundee website and in the Internet Archive.[96] The magazine described the tragedy and its aftermath as divine retribution. The British edition included the following statement: "This catastrophe at Dundee may be regarded as a Judgement of the Almighty upon those who, in a land of Sabbath observance like Scotland, commit the outrage of violating the sanctity of the Lord's Day by unnecessary railway travelling."[97] Another London-based periodical *Truth* offered a witty retort: "Were there only railroad accidents in Scotland on Sundays this theory might be tenable, but it seems to me upset by the fact that persons in Scotland who travel on other days of the week are also occasionally maimed or killed, whereas had they deferred their journeys until the next Sunday, they would have reached their destination in perfect safety."[98]

That wasn't the first and only railroad bridge disaster caused by design errors. More than three decades earlier, another tragic incident took place and rocked the career of Robert Stephenson, the son of George Stephenson. In addition to constructing locomotives, he was involved in bridge engineering. On May 24, 1847, about six months after being put into service, his creation, the Dee Bridge near Chester in England, collapsed as a local passenger train passed over it. Five people were killed and many injured when almost the entire rolling stock, excluding the locomotive, fell into the river. It was one of the bridges built on the line connecting London and Holyhead in Wales. Stephenson proposed a lightweight structure using cast iron girders reinforced with wrought iron trusses and resting on two pillars. This kind of river passage was advocated by waterway companies. A masonry arch bridge with several pillars was considered an obstacle to navigation. It was also worried that the foundations of such a heavy structure would be unstable with frequent changes in water levels induced by tides. Applying iron castings, however, proved to be fatal. The disaster occurred due to deformations and fractures within too long girders which appeared because of repeated loading cycles leading to metal fatigue. To make matters worse, shortly before the accident, under Stephenson's orders, the bridge was topped with an extra layer of ballast to reduce the risk of fire to the wooden crossties supporting the tracks. This further deteriorated the strength of the structure.

Although the record of casualties wasn't as high as that of the Tay Bridge, the incident shocked the public and became a sensation in the press. Robert Stephenson came close to being charged with manslaughter. But he was cleared following an investigation.[99] The jury found no one to blame, while sowing fear of any cast iron bridges by the final report:

> [N]o girder bridge of so brittle and treacherous a metal as cast iron alone, even though trussed with wrought iron rods, is safe for quick or passenger trains. And . . . there are upwards of one hundred bridges similar, in principle and form, to the late one over the river Dee, either in use, or in course of being constructed, on various lines of railway. We consider all these unsafe, more or less so, in proportion to the span; still all unsafe.[100]

Conclusions of the report were reprinted in many newspapers. This was another cause of anxiety among passengers, who were wondering if any of the suspicious bridges might be on their route. Nevertheless, Stephenson continued to argue that cast iron girders could be safe and useful. He decided to strengthen his bridges by stacking more girders on top of the existing ones.[101]

FOR THOSE WHO SURVIVED THE DISASTER

Our exploration of railway disasters is an excellent opportunity to get off and stretch our legs by returning to a familiar topic: medical afflictions. Notably, a supposed disease known as the *railway spine* sits firmly at the intersection of myth and reality. It was thought to affect victims of accidents who had suffered no physical injuries or only minor ones. It would only manifest itself after some time through the deterioration of the patient's psychological and physical condition, ultimately leading to disability. Individual fatalities were also reported. The medical community posited that the cause of these symptoms lay in microscopic spinal cord injuries caused by mechanical shock during the accident. Thus, passengers who were familiar with the views circulating in the medical community probably feared not only losing their lives but also the aftermath of lucky escapes. It was only with time, thanks to clinical observations, that doctors began to explain the causes of the syndrome in different terms. Instead of looking for mechanically induced pathological changes, they explored the psychological dimensions of the problem. Thus, the traumatic experience and emotional shock of an accident were deemed to determine the symptoms of the disease, and the state of the victim's psyche was determined by disorders within the parts of the brain that control the senses and motor coordination.[102]

In the context of train accidents, it is impossible not to mention the British satirical weekly *Punch, or The London Charivari*, published since 1841. The magazine was famous for its blunt language and original cartoons. *Punch* was critical of the railway magnates, whom it accused of putting economic interests before the safety of passengers, among others.[103] Accidents were a relatively common subject of its satire; when combined with the profile of the magazine, this took the form of black humor, as in this brief commentary, titled "The Steam Annihilator": "It is said that 'Steam annihilates both Time and Space.' It is a thousand pities, for our comfort in railway travelling, that its annihilating powers will sometimes extend, also, to – human beings."[104] One of many illustrations mocking the safety of rail travel, published in 1850, is available for viewing in the Digital Library of Heidelberg University, which archives all issues of *Punch.*[105]

For many readers, this may have been a way to take the danger with a grain of salt and overcome their fear. Presumably, there were also those for whom reading the weekly did not help or even intensified their fears. The inspiration to write and sketch did not come out of thin air; it often echoed real-life events.

Railroad crime

The press was engaged in fearmongering by amplifying reports of murders, rapes, and assaults on trains. In Britain, the problem of railway crime was particularly well-publicized in the second half of the 19th century, when the new mode of transport became increasingly accessible to the public. This encouraged criminals to move their sordid activities to a new physical space. It is commonly thought that the first crime committed on the English railways was the murder of banker Thomas Briggs in 1864. He was beaten with his own walking stick and thrown from a running train.[106] Under these circumstances, *The Times* reported:

> A railway carriage is a place where we are cut off for a time from all chance of assistance, and this feeling of helplessness in case of emergency has been a bugbear to many travellers, male as well as female. Without the means of communications with the guard we are almost at the mercy of fire, collisions and fellow passengers. This last danger is to most minds by far the most intolerable of the three. The idea of being shut up with a madman has frightened sane persons into posting, and that of being shut up with a murderer is still more intolerable.[107]

The design of passenger carriages on European trains – which were divided into compartments – meant that perpetrators were able to commit their crimes discreetly and sometimes escape from the scene unscathed. Passengers felt paralyzed by the awareness – which was fueled by the newspapers – that an unknown criminal or lunatic was at large and might attack again. Because of this, wealthy people preferred to travel in the more crowded second or third class instead of in first class. Panic also increased among women who feared sexual violence while traveling alone. Subsequent modifications to the design of the railway carriages to add a passageway between compartments proved to be a reasonable way of reducing danger. In the United States, however, robberies abounded. The masterminds of railroad heists had to take into account the presence of a more significant number of witnesses riding in the open cars, so attacks were carried out in gangs of several people equipped with firearms. This gave the passengers a better chance of escaping with their lives, as the criminals were mainly interested in getting their hands on valuable loot.[108]

HORSE VS. HORSEPOWER: THE FEAR OF COMPETITION

ECONOMIC DISASTER

Even at the very dawn of steam-powered railroads, there was growing opposition from many interest groups who feared losing their existing market positions or experiencing a decline in the value of their accumulated assets with the advent of competition. These included, in particular, horse breeders, producers of fodder and various types of horse-drawn vehicles, enterprises that managed navigable rivers, canals, and turnpikes, companies that offered stagecoach passenger services, owners of inns and taverns located along existing routes, and landowners. Each of these groups found it beneficial to constrain the role of this innovative branch of transport that could take over a significant portion of the industry, resulting in the marginalization or bankruptcy of businesses engaged in traditional transportation. As a further consequence, some sectors of the economy that manufactured products or provided services to these companies would be rendered unnecessary. The prospect of the end of the old order thus provoked a variety of defensive reactions.

In the mid-1820s, the established players still felt powerfully entrenched. They did not give credence to scenarios that involved the expansion of the railroad, which they regarded as one of many experiments without much of a future. They expressed profound skepticism towards the lines that were being planned and built at the time, even questioning the core assumptions of the projects. They argued that the economic viability of the railroads was nil and that ticket sales would not be sufficient even to cover the cost of the coal needed to power the locomotive's engine.[109] They also predicted that an economic disaster was coming, and it would begin with society abandoning the use of horses as a means of providing propulsive power. The resulting domino effect would imperil horse breeders, force farmers to stop cultivating oats and lead them to bankruptcy while depriving coach drivers of their jobs. Some claimed that horse breeding could easily be replaced by sheep and cattle breeding and that barley and wheat could be grown instead of oats, which would make meat and bread cheaper. However, they were dismissed with the paternalistic argument that this all flowed from "that ridiculous spirit of innovation" – a characteristic line among all kinds of opponents of development and progress, regardless of where they are in the world and the type of innovation they do not believe in.[110]

CAN A HORSE BE FASTER THAN A STEAM ENGINE?

The proponents of horse-drawn propulsion were bolstered in the competitive struggle by one of the participants of a contest organized by the emerging Liverpool & Manchester Railway for the best locomotive. The event called the Rainhill Trials, took place in October 1829 near Rainhill in Lancashire (now Merseyside). The competition was open and public. In addition to the Stephensons' *Rocket*, other machines entered the trial. Among them was the *Cycloped*, built by Thomas Brandreth. Unlike its competitors, the vehicle was not powered by steam. It moved on rails thanks to a horse positioned on the surface of the railway platform, which used its gait to move a treadmill that was connected to the wagon wheels by a gear. This middle-ground solution was primarily an attempt to maintain the old status quo of the horse industry, but it did not bring satisfactory results. When pitted against steam locomotives, the *Cycloped* fared the worst, reaching a top speed of only 10 mph (16 kph) – three times slower than the *Rocket*, which won the contest.[111] In turn, American engineer Christian E. Detmold constructed a similar vehicle named *Flying Dutchman*, which was additionally equipped with passenger seats. It was tested at the same time by the South Carolina Canal and Railroad Company. An image of this horse-powered locomotive appears in an 1874 book *The*

History of the First Locomotives in America, which is provided by Cornell University Library via HathiTrust.[112]

The anti-railroad lobby received a boost through the outcome of another famous race between a horse and a steam engine; this time, it was the horse that emerged victorious. The race took place on August 28, 1830, on the emerging Baltimore & Ohio line. The industrialist Peter Cooper – creator of the steam locomotive *Tom Thumb* – organized a demonstration race between his locomotive and a horse in an effort to convince investors to purchase the machine. The vehicle was able to reach a speed of 18 mph (about 29 kph), which impressed the public. However, it had weaker acceleration, and the horse got the upper hand near the start of the race. The steam locomotive eventually caught up with and overtook the galloping steed but soon developed a technical fault that turned off the machine. Still, the unlucky finale of the race ultimately failed to dissuade investors from choosing Cooper's product.[113] This unusual event was also illustrated in the above-mentioned book.[114]

The transition from horse to steam traction frightened entrepreneurs not only in Great Britain and the United States, though their resistance in those two countries was particularly vigorous, owing to robust investment in a functioning system of roads and canals, among other factors. On July 3, 1833, five years before the opening of the first railway line in Prussia (Berlin–Potsdam),[115] the daily *Magdeburgische Zeitung* printed an opinion piece on the anticipated effects of the coming changes on feed producers and the entire local economy:

> The farmer will have to pay higher interest rates; he will no longer be able to grow oats when the horses go off course because we are running on steam, and he will suffer a substantial loss of oats as well as straw and hay, while for coal, which we do not have,

> at least not in Prussia, the money still goes out of the country![116]

Unfair competition

When various interest groups realized that they would not be able to win against the railroads in a fair fight, they began to pressure government agencies to ensure that the acts that set the conditions for the construction and operation of individual railroads included provisions to guarantee that they would receive satisfactory compensation for lost property or profits. In practice, this involved artificially raising the operating costs of the railroad companies. Sometimes canal managers, when a railroad crossed their land or ran close by, were able to charge a toll every time a train passed through. For example, until 1851, there was a regulation enacted by the government of the State of New York, under which any railroad company whose line was within 30 miles of the Erie Canal was required to pay the equivalent of the tolls incurred by vessels on the canal.

As always, the financial consequences ultimately fell on the passengers, who ended up paying inflated ticket prices. However, financial and bureaucratic obstacles failed to stop the further expansion of the railroads. Over time, to retain customers, competing companies began to reduce rates for the use of infrastructure (canals, roads) or transport services (stagecoaches), leading to bankruptcies and the partial disappearance of industries originating from the horse era.[117]

Railbenders: Verbal and physical resistance to railroad construction

The fear of change that would destabilize the long-established order stimulated actions that went beyond pure economics. Efforts to preserve the status quo sometimes took the soft form of verbal resistance, which was especially common among specific interest groups or influential figures seeking to thwart plans to run the railroad through a particular location. And where the contrast between the old and the new was particularly stark, objectors resorted to extreme solutions by disrupting ongoing construction or even physically dismantling already established rail infrastructure.

THE WARS OF THE WORDS

An 1839 information campaign inspired by the anti-railroad lobby in the state of Pennsylvania became a permanent part of the history of verbal resistance. The campaign used posters addressed to the citizens of Philadelphia that were meant to evoke public opposition to the inclusion of the city's center in the Camden & Amboy Railroad network, one of several lines that had already reached the city's outskirts.[118] A number of slogans were used to play on the emotions of different groups of recipients. The need to stop the railroad was motivated by concern for the welfare of children and the desire to protect local businesses. The activist organizers even played on the Philadelphians' ambitions and fears by scaring them about the inevitable marginalization of the city once it is absorbed into the New York metropolitan area. The poster used by the campaign consisted of a steam train belting out smoke and spreading fear among people, ramming the horse-drawn vehicles it encountered on its way. A dire warning on the poster read:

> Mothers, look out for your children! Artisans, mechanics, citizens! When you leave your family in health must you be hurried home to mourn a dreadful casualty! . . . a Locomotive Rail Road! Through your most Beautiful Streets, to the ruin of your trade, annihilation of your rights and regardless of your prosperity and comfort. Will you permit

> this? Or do you consent to be a Suburb of New York!! . . . Outrage![119]

It is hard to say if the poster had much to do with it, but for the next four decades, passenger stations serving Philadelphia were located outside of the downtown area. A large station terminal near Broad Street and City Hall did not open until 1881.[120]

Certain prominent figures who were hostile to the rapid expansion of the railroads believed that they contributed to excessive mobility among the working-class and peasant communities. However, their verbal battles proved unsuccessful. These individuals advocated the elitist use of the new mode of transportation and wished to keep certain benefits and affordances for themselves. King Ernest Augustus of Hanover, an uncle of Great Britain's Queen Victoria, is reported to have said, "I don't want a railroad in the country! I don't want every cobbler and tailor to be able to travel as fast as I do!"[121] The first rail line in the Kingdom (Hanover–Lehrte) opened in 1843, six years after Ernest Augustus took the throne.[122]

The famous English poet William Wordsworth, considered a luminary of Romantic literature, embraced a distinctive approach to the railways. Fascinated by the beauty of nature, in 1813, he took up residence in the charming Lake District in Cumbria (northwestern England). There, he produced a guidebook for travelers titled *Guide to the Lakes*, which, in the mid-1830s, became very popular among residents of large cities who wished to relax in nature. According to Wordsworth, tourism then was something utterly different from our understanding of it today, according to which it is essentially an industry. Through his guidebook, the poet wanted to promote elite tourism for travelers with refined aesthetic taste while excluding all aspects that would popularize it for the masses. He did not anticipate, however, that his message about the attractions of the Lake District would reach a large audience wishing to visit this extraordinary corner of the country, including many in the lower social strata. Meanwhile, the railways began to cater to the proletariat by offering them low fares for 3rd-class travel. In August 1844, plans emerged to build the Kendal & Windermere Railway, improving the Lake District's transport accessibility. Upon hearing of this, William Wordsworth became an ambassador for the opponents of the project, speaking on behalf of himself and the local population. Aware of his position, he hoped to gain more comprehensive support for his proposals. In some ways, he was an influencer of his time.[123]

The first manifestation of Wordsworth's verbal resistance was a sonnet dated October 12, 1844. It begins with the famous words: "Is then no nook of English ground secure / From rash assault?"[124] This work was reprinted in more than 60 newspapers throughout the United Kingdom, which shows the power of the author's influence.[125] The poet was not an absolute opponent of the new means of transport. Still, he believed that its spatial development must not be thoughtless and infringe on areas with valuable natural assets. As he wrote in one of his letters to the London daily *The Morning Post*: " . . . the very word [summer tourists] precludes the notion of a railway."[126] Wordsworth feared that, by allowing a mass influx of simple working-class people, the railway would contribute to the devastation of the region's natural beauty. Nowadays, the arguments he used are sometimes seen as shocking; in fact, they are the opposite of the doctrine of social inclusion and the struggle against exclusion from transport services that prevails today.

Wordsworth's attempts to show the discrepancies in how sensitive different social classes were to beauty are also highly controversial. The poet tried to argue that the working-class and peasant population, as well as the petty bourgeoisie, would not be able to fully appreciate the qualities of the Lake District so they could do without the railways. They would derive greater benefit from simply refraining from travel and taking advantage of cheap and easy forms of entertainment. Seasoned travelers would also be satisfied with this approach. On their expeditions, they would not have to mingle with poor people who could not pay for the stagecoach fare: "[T]he imperfectly educated classes are not likely to draw much good from rare visits to the Lakes performed in this way, and surely on their own account it is not desirable that the visits should be frequent."[127] On top of this, there were fears of moral corruption emanating from the industrial cities and the violation of the sanctity of the Sabbath, which, for Wordsworth, was an obvious consequence of the descent of throngs of proletarians on the virgin areas of the Lake District. He was particularly critical of the employer-organized leisure trips that were made possible by the development of rail networks: "The rich man cannot benefit the poor, nor the superior the inferior, by anything that degrades him. Packing off men after this fashion, for holiday entertainment, is, in fact, treating them like children."[128] Finally, he expressed concern for the state of the environment: "Alas, alas, if the lakes are to pay this penalty for their own attractions! . . . Sacred as that relic of the devotion of our ancestors deserves to be kept, there are temples of Nature, temples built by the Almighty, which have a still higher claim to be left unviolated."[129]

Against the background of all these statements, Wordsworth's assertion about the railway as such is rather intriguing: "Once for all let me declare that it is not against Railways but against the abuse of them that I am contending."[130]

Neither Wordsworth's position nor his arguments halted the construction of the railway, which was fully opened to passenger traffic on April 20, 1847. The line was a branch of the Lancaster & Carlisle Railway. It ran from Oxenholme junction station to an area surrounding Windermere, England's largest lake. The village of Rydal, where Wordsworth's estate, Rydal Mount, was located, distanced about 6.3 miles (10.1 km) from Windermere station. A course of the line is seen on J. Otley's 1849 map, which serves as an appendix to *A Descriptive Guide to the English Lakes and Adjacent Mountains*. A copy of this guide was digitized by Cornell University Library and posted on HathiTrust.[131]

Yet it was not the only railway line to reach the Lake District. Other sections were built after the poet's death, to the delight of the growing crowds of tourists.[132] His vision of exclusivity did not stand the test of time. In the 1930s, one of the four railway companies in operation – the London, Midland and Scottish Railway (LMS) – included the following slogans on its advertising posters: "The Lake District for Holidays; The Lake District: Cheap Fares by Rail; Ullswater – English Lake-Land: It's Quicker by Rail."[133] Today, however, rows of bungalows dot the shores of Windermere. Could it be that the nightmare of a former influencer has come true?

LET'S BREAK THIS TRACK

The development of railroads in North America, originally from the East Coast to the West, was an essential factor in the colonization of new territories. Along the iron roads, settlements and then cities sprang up, populated by a white immigrant population consisting of railroad workers, among many others. The infrastructure they built threatened the hunting grounds of indigenous peoples, who had been divided into numerous tribes for centuries. The indigenous population, hostile to the newcomers, rightly feared for their continued existence, which came into question with the mass importation of inventions from a foreign civilization. In the face of this perceived threat, physical resistance to the colonizers and the lasting traces of their activities, including railroads, emerged.

Attacks by indigenous warriors intensified during the construction of the First Transcontinental Railroad. Two independent companies carried out the undertaking. The Central Pacific Railroad began construction first, traveling eastward from Sacramento (California) starting in January 1863. The Union Pacific Railroad headed west in December, departing from Omaha (Nebraska). Most of the clashes with Native tribes occurred on the Great Plains, which the Union Pacific route crossed. Attacks on poorly armed survey and construction crews often decimated them, temporarily halting further work. Whenever they did manage to open a section, indigenous groups opposed to their furtherance sabotaged the tracks and derailed the trains that rode them. Only government support, which resulted in the placement of military posts along the line, improved safety on the railroad at the expense of increased Indian casualties.[134]

The Transcontinental Railroad was completed on May 10, 1869, against all odds, after approximately 1,750 miles (2,816 km) of track had been laid. That day, the Union Pacific and Central Pacific construction teams met in Promontory, Utah, and the final golden spike was driven into a wood cross tie. A third company, Western Pacific, soon opened a branch from Sacramento to San Francisco. As a result, by 1870, the entire route from San Francisco to New York could be traveled by train. According to a poster advertising the service, the trip would take six days and 20 hours instead of the several weeks that it took for a stagecoach to traverse the same distance.[135] However, the excellent engineering triumph came at the cost of countless casualties on both sides of the conflict, contributing indirectly to the physical displacement of the native population and the gradual disappearance of their culture.

Another interesting instance of physical opposition, this

time resulting in the rapid dismantling of the tracks, unfolded on the first railroad in the Chinese Empire under the Qing Dynasty. The Woosung Road was a narrow-gauge line and was only 14.9 km (9.25 miles) long. Between 1876 and 1877, it connected Shanghai with the port town of Woosung. It was built at the behest of foreigners who had settled there and engaged in trade with China – mainly Englishmen and Americans who established a company to execute the project. This was not the first attempt to introduce the invention in China, but it was the first to lay tracks and initiate operations successfully. Local authorities gave their preliminary approval for construction, unaware of the investors' ulterior motives. However, when they learned that the tracks were meant for a steam-powered vehicle, they alerted the imperial authorities in Beijing. They received instructions that prompted a complete reversal of their position.[136]

The lack of approval did not deter the investors. They decided to continue construction and present the Chinese authorities with a *fait accompli*. They also made significant investments in rolling stock, importing four locomotives and a set of wagons from Great Britain. They hoped that, once the railroad opened, the authorities would appreciate its advantages and allow it to continue. Unfortunately, they were wrong. When the line was transferred to Chinese management under a separate agreement, trains were banned. A prominent government official, Shen Baozhen, Viceroy of the Liangjiang region, made the final decision to liquidate the railroad. Dismantled in late 1877 – less than two years after construction began – the tracks and equipment were transported along with the rolling stock to a port in Taiwan and stored there. The plan was to run the railroad there for industrial purposes. However, this was not brought to fruition, and the rolling stock, with almost no mileage on it, was progressively consumed by rust and termites due to poor storage conditions. Interestingly, the first railroad that received full acceptance on the part of the Chinese authorities was built just four years later, in 1881.[137]

This peculiar "clash of civilizations" was predicted by *Punch* 23 years before the opening of Woosung Road. This satirical weekly observed the tensions between the Chinese government and Western trade representatives. In an 1853 issue, *Punch* included a fold-out cartoon depicting Chinese resistance to the destructive progress arriving from Europe, represented by the steam engine (Fig. 6). The existential threat to the Empire was manifested, among other things, in the devastation of local culture. In the background, near the front of the locomotive, one can see a barber's scissors cutting off a male braid, the so-called *queue*, which was a popular hairstyle during the Qing dynasty.

THE GREAT BARBARIAN DRAGON THAT WILL
T UP "THE BROTHER OF THE MOON," &c. &c. &c.

Fig. 6. The invasion of progress and Chinese opposition in a distorted version of reality presented in the weekly magazine *Punch*. The caption reads, "The Great Barbarian Dragon that will eat up the Brother of the Moon." "Brother of the Moon" refers to the Emperor of China, who was titled in various ways.[138]

Come along and ride this train! The conquest of fear and its evolution

Next station: Knowledge

The passage of time and the knowledge that spread with it were crucial in overcoming the fears and myths described above. Initially, the dissemination of intangible knowledge was preceded by the dissemination of tangible technical solutions, which were sometimes imposed from outside against a distinctive interpretation of local interests. It was only the gradually increasing social acceptance of invention, which stemmed from the diffusion of information beyond a narrow circle of insiders, that caused knowledge to stimulate the further diffusion of technical innovations. As a result, the second half of the 19th century saw the rapid development of rail networks around the world (see Figs. 3 and 4).

The process of knowledge diffusion took place in various ways, depending on the specific circumstances of the community in question. Over time, passengers became convinced that trains were not possessed, that their brains would not stop working, and that the probability of an accident was lower than media messaging suggested. Doctors discovered that their patients had gradually stopped associating their ailments with the "railroad epidemic." Railroad designers and workers learned from past failures, constantly improving track design, rolling stock, and train traffic management systems to be more resilient to extraordinary situations. In contrast, interest groups for whom railroads had become competitors had to come to terms with the irreversible loss of their previous market position. This led some entrepreneurs to change careers and invest in railroad stocks. This was not always successful, as in the case of the famous speculative bubble known as the Railway Mania of the 1840s.[139] At best, they had to grit their teeth and bear witness to changes with which they openly disagreed; at worst, like the indigenous tribes of North America, they became victims of the onslaught of progress.

CHURCH ON WHEELS

The fear of the railroad has faded over time. Paradoxically, the most influential religious associations, which were initially co-responsible for the spread of fear, were relatively quick to acquire enough knowledge to start supporting pro-development initiatives, finally realizing their possible benefits. As indicated earlier, Pope Pius IX, whose governance lasted from 1846 to 1878, changed the policy of the Papal States toward the railways. In the very first year of his pontificate, he issued a decree to build several lines. In addition to Rome–Ciampino–Frascati (1856), three others – Rome–Civitavecchia (1859), Ciampino–Cecchina (1859), and Cecchina–Velletri–Ceprano (1862) – were opened as part of the planned connection between Rome and Naples. Work was also initiated on lines running between Rome, Ancona, and Bologna. Still, they were only completed after the unification of Italy and the loss of much of the territory previously administered by the pope.[140]

With this shift on the part of the head of the Catholic Church, a new religious practice became widespread whereby the clergy blessed newly opened routes and the rolling stock that ran on them.[141] Many congregations found it easier to overcome their fears as they became convinced that the new railways were freed from demonic forces by the power of the clergyman's blessing.

In 1849, Pius IX also became the first pope in history to travel by rail, initially as a guest visiting the neighboring Kingdom of the Two Sicilies. With this mode of transport he then covered the route from Portici to Pagani. Once the Papal States had started developing their railway infrastructure, the two companies responsible for its construction (*Pio Centrale* and *Pio*

Latina) sent the pope a gift in the form of a three-carriage train set manufactured in 1858 in France. It consisted of a loggia carriage (used for papal blessings), an apartment carriage (a throne room with a sleeping compartment), and a chapel carriage. The pope made several journeys in them, visiting towns and villages along the newly established lines. The inaugural trip took place on July 3, 1859, between Rome (Porta Maggiore station) and Cecchina.[142] On another occasion, in 1863, the pope visited Velletri, as documented in a photograph taken using the then-new collotype process. This photo belongs to the collection of the Museum of Rome and can be viewed online.[143]

In 1980, 117 years later, Pope John Paul II visited the same station and, in his speech, noted the achievements of Pius IX in breaking the frostiness of the Catholic Church toward the railways.[144]

This was not the only public statement in which the Polish pope praised the railways. A year earlier, in Rome, he spoke at an event that celebrated the 150th anniversary of the opening of the first railway on the Italian Peninsula. His speech suggested that trains were no longer a source of fear, even from a philosophical and theological point of view:

> [F]or one hundred and fifty years, thanks to human 'providence,' we have had the train, which has thus become one of the many signs of human ingenuity and an ordinary component of everyday life. I will say more: this means of communication is now part of civilization and is inseparable from it, thanks also to the continuous improvement of machines and services.[145]

This was a clear change in attitude, especially when contrasted with the 1828 statement of the Ohio school board, which described the railroads as lacking even a hint of divinity and smacking of faithlessness.

John Paul II, unlike Pius IX, had direct access to a train station located on the grounds of the Vatican, which he used twice. The station is still in operation today. It was opened in 1934 and was initially used for external deliveries.[146] The first head of the Church to travel from there was John XXIII, the initiator of the Second Vatican Council. In 1962, he traveled by train to Loreto and Assisi. This was an essential signal for Catholics to make their pilgrimages in the same way.[147]

There were certain analogies to these behaviors in the activities of the Russian Orthodox Church during Tsarist times. Orthodox bishops, too, adopted the custom of ordaining and blessing new railroads and trains. In the late 19th century, moreover, they introduced their peculiar innovation – the train church. These were built to improve access to worship for migrants living in vast and sparsely developed areas along newly constructed routes, where no permanent church facilities existed. An updated version of this type of wagon is still in use in various corners of the Russian Federation.[148]

FASTER AND SAFER

Finally, let us come down to earth and defuse the myth of the dangerous railroad in the area of passenger safety. Undoubtedly, the most critical factor in overcoming this aspect of fear was the evolution of technical solutions. Technological development decreased the frequency of accidents – and, consequently, the number of casualties measured both in absolute terms and in relation to the number of passengers transported in a given period. Data from Great Britain show us that a remarkable improvement in safety levels took place in the 18 decades of railway activity, starting from the early 1850s (Table 1). The risk of death of an average passenger as a result of an accident has decreased by a factor of almost 88, and as much as 855 for railway workers. The values presented do not take into account incidents involving third parties who were in the wrong place at the wrong time through inattention or with the intention of committing suicide.

TABLE 1. IMPROVEMENT OF RAILROAD SAFETY IN THE UK BETWEEN THE 1850S AND 2010S[149]

Reference group	**1850-1860**		**2009/2010-2019/2020**		**Risk reduction rate** (1850-1860 fatality risk = 1)
	Fatalities	Relative fatality risk	Fatalities	Relative fatality risk	
Passengers	421	1:2,880,283	69	1:253,059,874	87.9
Workforce	1,365	1:888,351	23	1:759,179,622	854.6
Total	1,786	1:678,947	92	1:189,794,905	279.5
	Passenger journeys (thousands)		**Passenger journeys** (thousands)		
	1,212,599		17,461,131		

The most important technical innovation, dating back to the days of the first steam locomotive prototypes, was the safety valve installed on boilers to prevent them from exploding under increased pressure (Table 2). Unfortunately, the devices were not continuously and appropriately operated. Manual deactivation ensured better performance, so boiler explosions occurred occasionally, even in later years. The speed at which the trains moved, combined with their weight, also demanded an efficient and safe braking process. Initially, in addition to the locomotive driver, brakemen had to perform this task simultaneously, distributed along the entire length of the train. This created danger for the crew and did not allow the train to travel too fast. Ultimately, automatic air brakes that ran on compressed air proved to be the most effective solution. This made it possible to control the status of all the cars using a single valve in the locomotive.[150]

Ensuring that trains could move without colliding was a much more daunting challenge. While the traffic volume was low, an accurate timetable was sufficient, setting appropriate gaps between individual departures and arrivals. However, the system failed when trains were delayed, for instance, by breakdowns and technical failures along their route, which sometimes resulted in a standing train being rammed by another, unsuspecting train barreling down the same track.

TABLE 2. STAGES OF EMERGENCE OF TECHNICAL INNOVATIONS THAT LED TO THE CONQUEST OF THE FEAR OF THE RAILROAD[151]

<table>
<tr><th>Decades</th><th>Innovations applied to railroad</th><th>Effects</th></tr>
<tr><td>1810s</td><td>Safety valve (UK)</td><td>Protected against boiler explosion in the locomotive</td></tr>
<tr><td>1820s</td><td>Winans's friction wheel (US)</td><td>Reduced friction of rotating axles</td></tr>
<tr><td rowspan="4">1830s</td><td>Jervis' bogie or truck (US)</td><td>Enabled riding on sharp curves</td></tr>
<tr><td>Fox's switch mechanism (UK)</td><td>Improved track changing and limited the risk of derailment</td></tr>
<tr><td>Cooke and Wheatsone's electric needle telegraph (UK)</td><td>Provided station-to-station communications to support train traffic management in the event of unexpected situations</td></tr>
<tr><td>Elevated wayside signaling</td><td rowspan="2">Reduced the risk of more than one train entering a section of tracks, which created a collision risk</td></tr>
<tr><td rowspan="3">1840s</td><td>Semaphore signaling, signaling token</td></tr>
<tr><td>Electric Morse code telegraph (US)</td><td>Improved the efficiency of information transfer between railroad stations</td></tr>
<tr><td>Nasmyth and May's vacuum brake (UK)</td><td>Strengthened the train's braking force, allowing higher running speeds</td></tr>
</table>

<table>
<tr><td rowspan="3">1850s</td><td>Saxby's mechanical interlocking of signals and switches (UK), manual block system</td><td>Centralized and synchronized control of the system of devices that enable collision-free train routes, reduced the risk of human error</td></tr>
<tr><td>Steel rails (UK)</td><td>Eliminated the risk of derailment due to rails cracking under the weight of a passing train</td></tr>
<tr><td>Pullman's sleeping car (US)</td><td>Improved passenger comfort and safety during long-distance travel</td></tr>
<tr><td>1860s</td><td>Tunnel-boring machine (Alps, Italy/France)</td><td>Improved safety for railroad construction workers in mountainous areas</td></tr>
<tr><td rowspan="3">1870s</td><td>Westinghouse's automatic compressed air brake (US)</td><td>Enabled trains to brake over their entire length by means of a valve activated by the driver, without the need for crew members to simultaneously operate the brakes for individual wagons</td></tr>
<tr><td>Automatic block signaling (US)</td><td>Increased capacity while rendering it impossible for more than one train to be present on the same section and eliminating possible human error</td></tr>
<tr><td>Von Siemens' electric locomotive (Germany)</td><td rowspan="2">Reduced the disadvantages of steam traction, especially in large cities (e.g., smog, fire hazards)</td></tr>
<tr><td>1880s</td><td>Public electric railway (Berlin, Germany)</td></tr>
<tr><td>1890s</td><td rowspan="2">Wired telephony</td><td rowspan="2">Enabled the development of communication capabilities by sending voice information between railroad stations</td></tr>
<tr><td>1900s</td></tr>
<tr><td>1910s</td><td>Diesel locomotive (Switzerland)</td><td>Eliminated troublesome steam traction from non-electrified lines</td></tr>
<tr><td rowspan="2">1920s</td><td>Electrical relay interlocking of signals and switches</td><td>Extended coverage and control capabilities in each control center (signaling center or signal box)</td></tr>
<tr><td>Train radiotelephony (Germany)</td><td>Enabled communication between trains and stations</td></tr>
</table>

<table>
<tr><td rowspan="2">1930s</td><td>Inductive train protection system (Switzerland)</td><td>Enabled emergency braking, e.g., if a train disregarded a signal prohibiting further movement</td></tr>
<tr><td rowspan="2">Streamlined passenger express trains (USA, Germany, UK, France)</td><td rowspan="2">Streamlined design to reduce air resistance, further enhancing passenger comfort</td></tr>
<tr><td>1940s</td></tr>
<tr><td>1950s</td><td>Color light signaling</td><td>Improved the visibility of signals at night and in poor weather conditions</td></tr>
<tr><td>1960s</td><td rowspan="2">Cab signaling of high-speed trains, e.g., Shinkansen (Japan), TGV (France)</td><td rowspan="2">Enabled the driver to interpret signals at speeds above 200 kph correctly</td></tr>
<tr><td>1970s</td></tr>
<tr><td>1980s</td><td>Electronic interlocking of signals and switches</td><td>Further centralized train control using computers</td></tr>
</table>

The increased speed and volume of traffic on the growing rail networks compelled further innovations. The invention of the electric telegraph (originally the needle telegraph and later the Morse code telegraph) was an enormous breakthrough that enabled stations to confirm the departure or arrival of each train. Consequently, it became necessary to put up telegraph wires transmitting coded electrical impulses along the railroad lines. Communications were later improved by voice transmission, which came with wire telephony, but it was not until the implementation of radio telecommunications that direct communication with moving trains became possible. For many decades, the lack of such communication tools was the cause of many disasters.[152]

To increase the capacity of the railroad lines, administrators divided them into block sections; for safety reasons, only one train per section was allowed. Signaling, which came in many forms, prevented trains from breaking this rule. In most cases, a kind of mast was planted next to the track, with conventional signs that signaled the train was apparent to advance or had to wait in place. With time, these were replaced by semaphores with moving arms, operating according to the standards of each country. In the 20th century, these, in turn, began to be replaced by colored light signals, which were more visible. For high-speed trains, however, these are not sufficient; as a result, these trains use signals displayed directly in the driver's cab.

Token signaling is one of the oldest solutions for single-track lines and is still used sporadically. It eliminates the possibility of head-on collisions. A token is a physical object with a fixed appearance – for instance, a plate, a key, or a rod with distinct markings. Without obtaining it from the station signalman, the driver is not allowed to enter the next section, and after leaving the previous section, they must return the token they obtained.[153]

Directing the train to the correct track by means of a system of switches is no less critical than signaling. Initially, each switch was controlled independently of the signals and other switches at a given station. The lack of sufficient coordination increased the risk of dangerous situations. Therefore, as early as the 1850s, it became necessary to centralize train traffic control by means of mechanical devices located in interlocking towers (or signal boxes in Britain) designed for this purpose. The system of signal and switch dependencies that existed there no longer allowed for two trains to enter a collision course with each other. The next generations of traffic control devices made it possible to increase the range and work efficiency of any given control center, which is especially important in railroad junctions with a complicated track layout and high train traffic.

The spatial diffusion of individual improvements occurred at different times in different parts of the world. Older technologies were also progressively replaced by newer ones. When the tracks reached areas far removed from the sources of innovation, their initiators were able to immediately implement improved versions of their technologies rather than trudge through each evolutionary phase. Even within a single country, not all inventions spread equally fast. Some remained in the testing phase for a long time.

Thanks to advances in technology, today we can travel safely even on Shanghai's Maglev magnetic railroad, which travels at a daily top speed of 430 kph (267 mph).[154] This is a staggering change compared to a century and a half ago when a miniature steam-based narrow-gauge railway majestically failed to gain widespread acceptance. We are no longer threatened by the hazards that passengers faced in the past, and the railroad has become the safest means of land transport. The minimization of risk, which was possible thanks to technology honed and perfected over the years, has quelled our fears quite effectively. Today, through ubiquitous access to electronic media, we are able to learn about the accidents that still occasionally occur quickly. Nevertheless, most of us would be ready to board the nearest train at the nearest station with not a shadow of doubt or fear in our minds.

Does the Railroad Still Haunt Us Today?

From the vantage point of modern times, we can confidently argue that, for the vast majority of people in the world, the railroad as such is no longer an object of fear, and all the myths associated with it have been thoroughly debunked. However, there is a minority of people who, for various reasons, are unable to get rid of their fear, whether temporarily or throughout their lives. Some young children and intellectually disabled people, for instance, are unable to perceive the reality that surrounds them. But there are others as well. Who are these others, and what drives their distress?

First, there are those with mental disorders that trigger a fear of rail travel. Psychiatry has identified a separate condition that manifests itself in the fear of railroads and is still observed today. We sometimes meet people who have acrophobia (fear of heights), agoraphobia (fear of space), claustrophobia (fear of enclosed spaces), or arachnophobia (fear of spiders), but how often do we hear of siderodromophobia? This is a less common, pathological fear associated with travel or the external observation of moving trains and railroad facilities. The term *siderodromophobia* is a combination of the ancient Greek words *sideros* (iron), *dromos* (road), and *phobos* (fear).[155] It was first used by the German physician Johannes Rigler in 1879 to describe an affliction that, at the time, was said to affect railroad workers in particular (as opposed to "railway spine," which was thought to affect the health of passengers).[156] An English-language definition of siderodromophobia appears in a review of Rigler's scientific achievements, printed in the British journal *The Medical Times and Gazette* in 1879: "[A] more or less intense spinal irritation, coupled with a hysterical condition and a morbid disinclination for work, which, as the result of shock, occurs among railway employees, who, in consequence of their occupation, are specially predisposed to it."[157]

As the safety and comfort of rail travel have improved and knowledge about it has spread, the original understanding of the term has evolved from post-accident trauma, which was easier to explain according to the canons of today's knowledge, to an irrational aversion. Symptoms of this phobia may include seizures, sweating, gastrointestinal problems, and heart palpitations. If the sufferer chooses to undergo treatment, cognitive-behavioral psychotherapy is sometimes used with satisfactory results.[158]

The fearful few also include people whose fears are somewhat more justified, motivated by a reduced sense of security when visiting railroad stations or during travel. External factors beyond the control of the railroad itself (or which it can only control to a limited extent) play an important role. Passengers who use public transport can be easy targets for petty criminals, such as pickpockets operating at peak travel times, but also robbers and rapists operating at night. Monitoring systems, good lighting, thoughtful design, and increased security presence can significantly reduce such incidents, but they will not eliminate them.[159]

The same is true of the effectiveness of protection against terrorist attacks. The atmosphere of danger persists for a long time in places that have experienced tragic events. Many of these have a profound impact on the people who frequent the area, some of whom fear a repeat attack. Crowded trains and railroad stations have witnessed more than a dozen bloody attacks over the past two decades. These took place in locations where railroads play an important role in passenger transport – chiefly urban agglomerations and long-distance lines. The perpetrators were primarily radicalized Islamists with varying motives. In Western Europe, they were manifestations of armed jihad, among which the bombing of commuter trains at Madrid's Atocha station (2004) was particularly tragic. Since then, Spain's state-owned railway company (RENFE) has implemented additional security measures, including luggage screening before passengers can board high-speed trains that could become targets for terrorists. In Russia, North Caucasian separatism is a common motive. In India, apart from attacks by Islamists seeking to break away from the region of Jammu and Kashmir, communist and nationalist militias have perpetrated attacks on passenger trains.[160]

Today, fear of trains has taken on a form so different from its 19th-century incarnation that the use of the word "fear" to describe it is probably no longer justified. Apart from a minuscule group of people, no one today fears traveling by train. Protests against the expansion of railroads result only from the fear among certain communities that the implementation of specific infrastructural projects could cause a specific kind of damage.

The Sámi, an indigenous people living in northern Scandinavia, offer an interesting example of this. The Sámi have long-standing concerns about the construction of the Arctic Railway, which would connect the Norwegian port of Kirkenes with a station in Rovaniemi, Finland, in order to facilitate the transport of cargo from the northern sea route to Finland and further through the Baltic states to Central and Southern Europe. In view of the melting ice in the Arctic, this would provide a shorter alternative to the existing sea routes that lead from the Far East to the Old Continent. A rail tunnel under the Gulf of Finland would complement the connection.[161]

The Sámi feared that the construction of the Arctic Railway would prevent them from herding reindeer and cultivating their land, which would lower the chances of maintaining the linguistic and cultural distinctiveness of the indigenous group. Greenpeace activists became involved in the protest, organizing field demonstrations in cooperation with the local population. The slogans on the banners were economical, invoking the threat to the climate in addition to the arguments already made by the Sámi: "No Arctic Ocean track; No consent, no access; Stop CO_2lonialism; Forest is life; Choose forests; Our land our future; Respect indigenous peoples' rights."[162] Ultimately, further work on the project was discontinued, not only due to opposition by the Sámi people but also to economic forecasts that indicated the Arctic Railway would be inefficient in relation to the investment made.[163]

The public resistance to a high-speed rail project in the UK called High Speed 2 (HS2 for short) is more complex. Today, the only such line operating on the British Isles is the Channel Tunnel Rail Link (or HS1), which runs from Folkestone to London. It is served by the London–Paris, London–Brussels, and London–Amsterdam Eurostar trains. The new line, or network of lines, will connect the London metropolitan area with Birmingham, Manchester, and Leeds. The project has received government approval, and construction work is already underway.[164] However, there is still a lot of opposition from some public figures and interest groups, including political parties, social and environmental organizations, and local governments. Activists include the national action group STOP HS2, which uses a wide range of slogans that correspond to various threats, e.g.: "HS2 will cost £50,000,000,000 . . . No benefit here; 888 homes and 985 commercial buildings demolished; Your trees need you STOP HS2; Love this view! You won't with HS2."[165] These are often seen on banners during the numerous demonstrations organized by the group and in places where the future railroad will run. Let us confront these slogans with the official agenda of the project[166]:

- HS2 will form the backbone of our rail network;
- HS2 will be the low-carbon option for long-distance travel;
- HS2 will help level up the country;
- HS2 creates more space on the existing railway for rail freight services;
- HS2 is Britain's biggest environment project;
- Businesses invited to tender for £12bn worth of HS2 contracts;
- The size and scale of HS2 offers a broad range of career opportunities.

I will leave it to the reader to assess each side's rationale and determine whether there is anything to fear.

Every action we take brings change; building HS2 will too. Some are happy about these changes; others are afraid of the consequences. Who is right? It is worthwhile to imbue any assessment we make of a change or invention with some common sense, although it is said that history is the world's only objective judge. Today, we have the luxury of being able to assess the development of railroads, including the typical 19th-century fears they induced, with the sobriety that comes with our historical vantage point. Thus, it is easy for us to look critically at the naïveté of scientists, journalists, and many other representatives of the social elite of the past who were guided by erroneous premises and tried to stop the development of railroads for entirely spurious reasons. Neither their fears about adverse health effects nor their concerns about safety have come true in the long run. Even those who used to employ religious rhetoric to resist the rise of the rails have long since stopped trying to prove that trains are the spawn of Satan, simply because no sacred text from thousands of years ago mentions them.

Development, progress, the spread of education, and above all, our own experience and the passage of time purged us of our fear of trains. We already know that the fears of our ancestors just a few generations back were completely unfounded, and we recount those fears with condescending smiles. We willingly and fearlessly board the train, even if we have just learned of a train crash that resulted in dozens or even hundreds of fatalities. We are happy to hear about trains breaking speed records because it means we will reach our destination sooner, which in turn makes the journey more comfortable. We are witnessing the growing rivalry between rail and air transport for medium-distance travel. We take great interest in following the progress of Elon Musk's *hyperloop* – a cross between a train and a supersonic plane. The most important feature it shares with planes is the ability to achieve a top speed unattainable today even by trains running on a magnetic cushion; the critical feature it shares with trains is its passenger capsule, which somewhat resembles a modern railcar. We are, in a word, evolving.

Development has accompanied mankind since the dawn

of time. We have no hard evidence for the doubts that our cave-dwelling, fruit-gathering ancestors had about farming; we can only guess based on evidence unearthed by archaeologists. On the other hand, the doubts of 19th-century advocates of sticking to what is familiar and domesticated have been very well documented. Alas, progress has always had its inhibitors; they exist today, and they will continue to exist, masking their identities and pulling the wool over our eyes with supposed threats to health, life, environment, faith, or morality. We should approach such claims with caution because more and more evidence is showing up in our case files to indicate that such fears were utterly unsubstantiated. The railroad has become one of the flagship illustrations of the fact that imagined threats, while familiar in a given era and expressed jointly by elites and common folk, sooner or later end up in the dustbin of history. Let us keep this in mind the next time we feel fear bubble up inside us upon encountering the next groundbreaking invention.

TWO
CURRENTS OF FEAR: THE RISE OF ELECTRIC POWER

Dorota Dymek

Today, about 70 percent of the world's population has access to electricity. No one who uses it daily can imagine how we could have managed without it. However, the advent of electric lighting in the second half of the 19th century was greeted with concern, and the lecture halls of respected universities brimmed with experiments that demonstrated the damaging effects of electricity on human health and life. Fears ran the gamut from the impact of artificial light on the human nervous system to the welfare of farm animals. Aggravated by fatalities caused by electrocution, fear sometimes paused the progress and development of electrification – leading, for instance, to the almost complete elimination of electric street lighting in New York City in 1889. Using electricity as an instrument of execution only intensified the currents of fear. Today, paradoxically, we no longer fear electricity itself but rather the prospect of its absence through supply shortages, and modern civilization is dependent on electricity in ways we do not always fully grasp.

A FEAR IS BORN

Electricity is our constant companion. We get up in the morning, turn on the lights, turn on the radio or TV, disconnect the phone from the charger, open the fridge, make coffee, iron our clothes, and receive and respond to emails. The list of activities we perform using electricity is endless, and we can always beef it up with additional tasks requiring electrical power. Electricity plays a role in nearly everything we do and experience. We are taught how to handle it from childhood. We know we will get electrocuted if we plunge our electric blow dryer into the water while drying our hair. We know electrical current should be handled in a specific way. Of course, some people have electrophobia – the fear of electricity as a psychological disorder. This phobia may result from a combination of some traumatic event in a person's past, especially at a young age. Others, conscious of the importance of adequately handling electricity, do not fear it daily. But this was not always the case.

Until the birth of electrical engineering, electricity was known as and associated exclusively with phenomena that occurred in nature. In ancient times, Thales of Miletus noted that amber attracted small objects when rubbed against them. For centuries, however, no one understood the implications of this observation or how humanity could put it to use. Therefore, electricity was most often associated with natural electrostatic discharges, specifically lightning. Although humans did not grasp the true nature of this phenomenon for centuries, they knew it was unsafe for health, life, or property. Lightning was seen as expressing a supernatural power that brought death and destruction. According to the beliefs of many ancient peoples, lightning bolts were controlled by the gods: the Greeks had Zeus, the Scandinavians had Thor, and the Slavic tribes had Perun. Even in the Bible, lightning remains one of the attributes of a single omnipotent God. Before humankind finally cracked the mechanism governing this natural phenomenon, it lodged in our collective consciousness as a terror-inducing expression of divine anger. This image, so deeply burned into the human psyche, began to change only during the Age of Enlightenment, thanks to Benjamin Franklin.[167] In the mid-18th century, Franklin set up his famous experiment featuring a kite to which he attached a key with a metal wire. He launched the kite into the sky during a storm; as expected, the kite was struck by lightning, carrying a spark to the metal key. The experiment used a Leyden jar, a particular container made of glass covered on both sides with metal foil, and a protruding metal terminal to collect electricity. The combination of a metal wire attached to a kite and a Leyden jar enabled Franklin to famously "catch lightning in a bottle," that is, capture lightning and trap it in a Leyden jar.[168] This experiment allowed Franklin to prove his hypothesis that lightning and electricity were the same. An additional effect of the kite experiment was that Franklin invented the lightning rod, a lightning protection system typically installed on buildings to prevent the tragic aftermath of a lightning strike. This created a way for people to protect their property from the destructive force of the "Electric Fire." As Franklin himself wrote, "It has pleased God and his goodness mankind, at length to discover to them the means of securing their habitations and other buildings from mischief by thunder and lightning."[169]

Franklin's discovery was an indisputable breakthrough in the development of electricity and heavily influenced its subsequent public perception. Above all, however, it contributed to a transformation of the way people viewed lightning. The fervent prayers of the Middle Ages, the candles placed in windows, and the ringing of church bells as rituals to protect against thunderstorms slowly faded from public practice after Franklin's seminal experiment. But they are far from entirely extinct. In childhood, many of us are taught not to linger around the chimney because lightning often snakes its way through it. Some of us opened all the windows in the house to lessen the chances of a lightning strike. Today, we treat such practices as local folklore rather than a collective expression of fear of the punishing hand of God.

Of course, disconnecting various types of electrical equipment from the power supply during a storm is also widely known and applied. However, this is neither a sign of unjustified panic in the face of the destructive power of lightning nor a sign of faith in superstitions. Instead, it is a rational choice made by people who understand that electronic devices connected to the network can be destroyed due to lightning hitting the electrical system.

For centuries now, we have also known that a species of fish shocks those who try to touch them. The torpedo fish, or electric ray, can electrocute prey or predators seeking their next meal. Humans have used this unique property since ancient times when the electric current delivered by this elusive animal was used to relieve various kinds of pain.[170] Of course, at that time, nobody associated it with the electricity we know today. However, early scientists found the power of the current fascinating to explore, laying the groundwork for a body of research on animal electricity.

The experiments carried out by Italian physician Luigi Galvani were important in the context of both the development of electricity and its social perception. In his research, Galvani dealt with animal electricity or the internal electricity found in animals that connects their nerves and muscles,[171] which he explored by experimenting on frogs. He subjected dead and often skinned animals to electric shocks to prove that muscle movement is linked to naturally occurring electricity. Although they may seem revolting today, these experiments were viral. People eagerly gathered on the streets to see frogs quivering, "galvanized" muscles. Packaged and presented for mass consumption, electricity generally did not arouse fear but instead curiosity and fascination.

Sometime later, Italian physicist Giovanni Aldini rekindled these experiments. In his experiments, he went beyond using animal corpses exclusively, supplementing them with human cadavers, which he subjected to electric shocks. His most famous show took place in 1803 in London, when he used the body of the 26-year-old murderer George Forster. Using electricity derived from batteries, the scientist electrocuted Forster's corpse until it began to move. This event caused a big stir among scientists and the press, artists, poets, and writers. Some almost demanded that the experiments be adjusted to bring the dead back to life, but this Lazarus effect was never achieved. Nevertheless, the assumption that electricity could resurrect the deceased remained firmly lodged in people's consciousness. Even today, Mary Shelley's novel *Frankenstein, or, The Modern Prometheus*, first published in 1818, remains one of the most famous works inspired by those events.

MIXED FEELINGS

Initially, there was no sign that the emergence of a new technology in the form of the electric current would instill fear or horror into anyone. Initial experiments with electricity were met with curiosity rather than anxiety. Lightning shows and various spectacles that incorporated them were a popular attraction. However, only the invention of the battery (the so-called *voltaic pile*) by Alessandro Volta in 1800 opened the way for the commercial use of electricity. Thanks to the battery, electricity ceased to be simply a form of entertainment for the rich, and the range of its services began to grow briskly.

We can certainly assume that the abovementioned events impacted the public perception of electricity. On the one hand, the harnessing of electricity aroused anxiety; on the other, it beckoned the curious with the promise of breakthrough discoveries. However, as could be expected, the process of normalizing electricity was not free of complications. Technical innovations are rarely received with unmistakable enthusiasm if it ever happens. They are often met with suspicion or aversion, even if they do not trigger fear. Edward Redliński's novel *Konopielka* offers an example. In the story, an electrical engineer comes to a village in Podlasie, in north-eastern Poland, to encourage its inhabitants to build an electrical network, persuading them by offering them a glimpse of all the comforts of everyday life that electricity brings.

> And he tells tales of electric lamps in the house, in the pigsty, the barn, on the threshing floor, he talks of extending day into evening and night and braving forth till the sunrise: no more will eyes be wasted after dark, no longer will hens be our bedfellows. More than that, electricity will help us wash clothes and iron them, cook and bake, thresh and grind, separate the wheat from the chaff, saw our trees, milk our cows, cook for our pigs, hatch our chickens. Finally, he speaks of the radio, this window to the whole world, this road to happiness, reason, wealth. We listened with interest, none wishing to interrupt...

However, the costs of the new technology are enough to discourage the villagers from embracing it and even provoke resistance. One says: "I would sooner thresh by hand than pay for power and eat sand."[172] Carolyn Marvin bluntly states that the introduction of electricity has always accompanied drama. She also recalls an anecdote in which electric lighting was installed in one of the small towns of Illinois, and the local farmers, seeing the glow rising above the town, thought the town was on fire and rushed to the rescue.[173]

Today, we are accustomed to a continuous barrage of new technical solutions that invariably trigger strong emotions. For a fleeting moment, the excitement they evoke circulates through our veins. Some people are excited about the new iPhone, others worry about the effects of introducing 5G, and others are afraid of artificial intelligence. Innovations seem to unleash the full spectrum of human emotions. While we may find the fascination or even infatuation with the hot new technology of the month a little bizarre, reacting to it with fear may seem irrational.

Let us then take a moment to consider where that fear originates. A human being trying to process a complex mechanism whose actions they cannot understand often feels lost. If we add to this the unexpected effects of this mechanism, which may infringe on our life and health, what we get is an instant recipe for fear.[174] Until we get used to this mechanism and at least partially understand how it works, we cannot eliminate the accompanying anxiety. Thus, it will be challenging to accept it. So, it was the emergence of electricity that ultimately revolutionized the world. For most people, electricity was almost a magical phenomenon that could not be easily explained. How can we briefly define that suddenly, a handful of electric lamps is all it takes to turn night into day? True, gas lamps were widely known, but electricity offered incomparably more excellent brightness and did not come with the characteristic smell of burning gas. Besides, power can be such an uncertain thing. Gas was so predictable. You take a heap of coal. You heat it, filter it, pressurize it, strike a match, and voilà – a flame that will light a room. Electricity is trickier. So many different kinds of bulbs – different filaments, casings, generators, and vacuums. One malfunction and we're all thrown back into darkness."[175]

In the case of electricity, as is typical of any innovation, the initial group of insiders who understood the principles of electricity was minuscule, which was not conducive to the rapid spread of knowledge. Many of them tried to explain what electricity was and where it came from. This was no easy feat because energy itself could not be seen, smelled, or even touched. It had to be understood. As a result, they often turned their focus to technical issues, attempting to explain the mechanics of electricity rather than what it is. One could wonder whether they had intentionally forgotten that "knowing how something works and knowing what it is are two very different things."[176]

Francis R. Upton described the mechanics of electricity with poetic flair:

> The sunlight poured upon the rank vegetation of the carboniferous forests, was gathered and stored up, and has been waiting through the ages to be converted again into light. The latent force accumulated during the primeval days, and garnered up in the coal beds, is converted, after passing in the steam-engine through the phases of chemical, molecular and mechanical force, into electricity, which only waits the touch of the inventor's genius to flash out into a million domestic suns to illuminate myriad homes.[177]

This description, though colorful, is undoubtedly far from simple. Complicating matters further, the telephone and the telegraph used similar wires to those that carried electric currents, but they were completely harmless. In contrast, the current supplying energy to an electric lamp could kill. It was challenging to make people unfamiliar with technology aware of the difference. The assortment of voltages, different kinds of insulation, and other technical features were seemingly impossible to understand and must have been deeply confusing. In the end, what is electricity? How do you describe it in simple terms? The genius of electricity himself, Nikola Tesla, once said that "day after day I asked myself what is electricity and found no answer. Eighty years have gone by since and I still ask the same question, unable to answer it."[178]

Others, perhaps to more effectively reach human imagination, associated it with nature, magic, and even religion. Still others, for the sake of visualizing it for their audience, described the electric current as a liquid; this helped respond to misgivings about how energy use could be calculated, which ultimately translated into how high the bill would be. Of course, many also probed for links between electricity and the occurrence of atmospheric phenomena. At the end of the 19th century, a prominent minister of the African Methodist Episcopal Church, Bishop Turner argued that the surge of hurricanes tearing through the United States was caused by excessive use of electricity. He predicted that:

> ...the unbalancing of the air currents, which electric lights are causing, will, in a few years, if they increase as fast as in the past five years, cause whole cities to be blown away at a time, and floods unlike any save Noah's. All the floods, hurricanes, cyclones and other atmospheric disturbances taking place in the heavens and upon earth are due to the work of electric lighting companies.[179]

Turner called for the complete abandonment of electricity for the sake of humanity. Along similar lines, the Reverend A. C. Johnson preached that the unbridled generation of electricity by humans would destroy the world within 32 years. These words could have undoubtedly aroused fear in those who listened to them. What evil must this mysterious current represent that it can destroy the world? There was also an infamous comparison of electricity to Jezebel – a notorious biblical figure: "Electricity is the new Jezebel, seducing our young men into the arms of immorality."[180] This comparison was triggered by perpetually well-lit brothels whose lights beckoned passers-by to stop by and take advantage of their seductive services.

The emergence of electricity, specifically electric lighting, triggered the fundamental human fear that the world's natural order was being disrupted, upending the eternal cycle of day and night. One might have thought that the battle over using gas lighting, fought earlier following the same basic premise, had successfully paved the way, and such fears had long since been overcome. However, this was not entirely true. Some claimed that electric lighting was an unnecessary imitation of daylight and that using it was an incompetent attempt to correct Nature's mistake of delivering darkness.[181] Others were worried that artificial light might affect animals, interfering in particular with their natural circadian rhythm, throwing cattle into utter confusion about when it was time for bed.

Furthermore, the emergence of electricity convinced some people that they had superhuman skills. One woman claimed she could sniff and feel electricity when it leaked out of an outlet. Moreover, "she was afraid the electricity would drip out of the lamp sockets if there were no bulbs in them."[182] Another believed that the current flowing through telephone and telegraph wires was harmful to people because it caused ailments such as apoplexy, brain paralysis, or "nervous distress so profound that death would be a welcome remedy."[183]

THE BETTER IS THE ENEMY OF THE GOOD

Early arc lamps were already in use when electric lighting appeared and served primarily to illuminate public places. The strong, glaring light they emitted and other less prominent defects meant they were unsuitable for indoor use, making them relatively unpopular. The electric current transmission system proposed by Thomas Edison, which used light bulbs that emitted a pleasant glow and could be used indoors, offered an excellent alternative. "Arc lights flickered and hummed and were totally inappropriate for homes. For that setting, warmer and cozier incandescent light was the holy grail, the perfect replacement for smelly gaslights: no fumes, no flicker, no matches, no maintenance."[184] Initially, this solution was received with great enthusiasm. In the late summer of 1878, the *New York Sun* announced the joyful news: "*Edison's Newest Marvel. Sending Cheap Light, Heat, and Power by Electricity.*"[185] The invention also provided an alternative to the gas lighting used for years. Edison drew lessons from the stunted efforts to introduce gas lighting from Europe in the early 19th century, observing that the public was not always willing to accept new technologies. To address this problem, he cleverly designed his lighting system to resemble the familiar and time-honored gas lamp. This approach proved highly successful, and familiarizing people with the new technology was relatively fast and painless. On some occasions, the arrival of electric lighting was met with great enthusiasm, accompanied by music, joyful parades, and even ritual burials of oil lamps.[186] In Germany, an advertisement depicted the ancient philosopher Diogenes of Sinope, who, according to the tale, walked around the city looking for a man with a lit lantern in broad daylight. In the ad, an electric bulb allowed Diogenes to replace the kerosene lamp and thus save some money.

People in the Polish countryside even developed a unique custom to accompany the arrival of electrification. Just before the opening of the power line, people gathered around the transformer, smashed a kerosene lamp against it, and celebrated with dance and song.

Electricity was a potent threat to gas lighting, which was already in widespread use. Although electric power was still in its infancy, the scientific community recognized its potential, and some expressed the view that "electricity would some day become the great motive power of the world and would very soon supersede gas for illuminating purposes."[187] Such statements heralded the imminent problems of the gas giants, especially as the new lighting gained a reputation as being more pleasant and aesthetically pleasing than its gas-based predecessor. The spread of the invention was undoubtedly bolstered by the fact that it did not absorb as much oxygen as gas systems, so it did not make people feel unwell and did not cause frequent headaches. Moreover, when an electric bulb was lit, there was no smell of sulfur or ammonia in the air. The invention did not soil the walls or cause equipment to turn yellow.

Fires broke out much less frequently than gas lamps, and no explosions occurred. Electricity also had applications other than lighting. In the following years, they brought new electrical appliances for everyday household use.

Another unquestionable advantage of electricity was that access was not contingent on a collective supplier; it was possible to produce electricity independently. Anyone with sufficient capital could buy a private electricity generator – the dynamo. The dynamo used energy generated by steam engines, transforming it into electricity.[188] Initially, it was used mainly to produce energy to power lighting equipment. However, these generators were not without their disadvantages. Above all, they were loud and had vibrations that triggered a wave of complaints and the constant irritation of the neighbors. It was usually installed in the basement, gardens, and sheds to minimize the negative impacts of the generator.[189] Of course, having one's electricity generator was a show of luxury and wealth, but it was also a motivation for people who did not yet have this type of equipment to buy it.

Intense competition was an excellent stimulus for the gas lobby. The industry was aware of the numerous advantages of electricity over gas, so it began to improve its energy transmission systems, making them safer for users. Above all, it took care to maintain its advantage in the supply of gas used for heating and cooking. Nevertheless, the advent of electricity contributed to a decrease in the turnover of gas companies and forced service providers to lower the fees for the services they provided. However, they knew that people familiar with gas lighting did not trust electricity, if only because it was a poorly understood novelty. The general public knew practically nothing about it, so the gas lobby consciously took advantage of the fear it was producing. We can also presume that the gas lobby paid newspapers to publish melodramatic descriptions of accidents caused by electricity and spread rumors of frequent failures. Lobbyists were also alleged to offer the clergy a share of the profits from the sale of gas in exchange for criticizing electricity and threatening their congregation with the dire consequences of using a competing technology.[190]

The assumption among opponents of electricity seemed to be that a person afraid of something will ultimately try to avoid it. Successfully turning someone away from electricity was a badge of honor. Some may even have believed that they were doing the right thing in trying to protect others from the specter of death that lurked in electric wires. Most of them, however, probably had ulterior motives, most of which were linked to economic benefits. The circumstances were also in their favor. Accidents did happen, and the luminaries of the world of electricity were reluctant to talk about its dangers. There were at least two reasons for this. First, publicly discussing the risks people faced when using electricity did not present the product they offered in a good light, impacting profit margins. Second, these experts had some knowledge about technical solutions; however, they usually lacked knowledge about how their products affected human health. Therefore, they preferred to remain silent, not wishing to expose the fact that they sometimes had very little knowledge about the subject. Others went so far as to say that electric lighting is considered dangerous only among uneducated people,[191] which was supposed to cut off uncomfortable questions quickly. After all, who among us revels in being seen as an ignorant fool?

AC/DC: The War of the Currents

The tale of humans' fear of electricity, particularly the electric current, is impossible without recounting the famous dispute between two electro giants – Thomas A. Edison and George Westinghouse. The trajectory of their conflict and its final outcome determined the ultimate fate of electrotechnology, both in the context of its technical development and social perception. The battle unfolded in a series of events at the end of the 19th century and became known as the War of the Currents.

The seed of the conflict was planted in 1886 when Westinghouse Electric Company (WEC) debuted its *alternating current* (AC) on the US energy market. An alternating current is a type of current in which the direction of its course changes at regular intervals. In the United States, that interval is 60 cycles per second, while in Europe and most other parts of the world, it is 50 cycles. AC turned out to be very competitive with Edison's *direct current* (DC), which had been developed and sold before the rise of AC. In DC systems, the current flows constantly in one direction. Today, this type of current is used in flashlights and other electronics.

The critical difference between the two systems was that AC could be transmitted over much longer distances than DC, giving it the upper hand. It employed a system for transmitting high-voltage current that was lowered using a low-voltage transformer before it reached homes and other buildings. DC, on the other hand, was a low-voltage power transmission system whose significant transmission losses required the construction of many local power plants located at very short distances from each other – one plant per mile, on average. Another factor contributing to AC's growing popularity was the relatively fast development of transmission networks, which made it possible to connect new users rapidly. This "new" electricity was within the means of almost every citizen, as it was much cheaper than its "old" counterpart. This provoked Edison's ire and led to an open conflict on the AC/DC front. To discredit the competing current, Edison presented it in a negative light, suggesting that it posed a threat to people's lives and health. He further accused Westinghouse Electric Company of infringing his patents, including Patent No. 223,898 for the incandescent electric lamp, which Edison obtained in 1880.

The war of currents consisted of consecutive events that varied in scale and impact. However, embroiled in it were two competing companies represented by the world's top engineers, scientists, and legislators whose actions significantly influenced the development of the electrical industry.[192] The war can be described broadly as a series of attacks launched by Edison against Westinghouse and the alternating current he produced. Initially, these attacks took the form of a relatively innocuous, Edison-funded disinformation campaign in the press that described the dangers of AC. It focused on AC's alleged threats to human health and property, regularly incorporating the stories of the victims of AC to stir concern among readers of daily newspapers. In the late 1880s, Edison published a brochure titled *A Warning from the Edison Electric Light Company*. On its face, it appeared to be a list of patents Westinghouse infringed on. However, its real goal was to stoke fear, punctuated by press-style accounts of accidents caused by AC:

> Deadly Electric Light Wires. – The Shocking Sight which Met the Gaze of Passers-By on a Detroit Street. DETROIT, Mich., Oct. 4. – A corpse sixty feet from the earth hanging in a nest of wires, the arms and legs moving perceptibly, was the ghastly sight which greeted people last night at the corner of Woodward Avenue and the Campus Martius. The discoverer of this shocking sight called the fire department. The dead man was got down with an extension ladder. He had been dead for some time and his body had received the electric current of the entire Brush system, which had made his limbs move as if in convulsions. Thus perished Lineman Hiram Corliss. Nobody knows how long he had hung on the wires. The securing of the body was attended with great danger because the electric current was still on.[193]

Edison was not fully satisfied with the impact of these campaigns and decided to ramp up the conflict. Between 1888 and 1895, Edison's company launched a veritable crusade against alternating current.

Harold Brown's animal electrocutions

Edison's propaganda war coincided with the activities of one of the most ardent opponents of the alternating current of the time – Harold P. Brown. Brown rose to fame thanks to a letter published in the *New York Evening Post* in which he clearly defined his position concerning the warring currents. In his opinion, direct current was "perfectly safe as far as life risk is concerned," while alternating current was "always dangerous." Doubling down, he claimed, "Among electric lighting men it is appropriately called 'undertaker's wire,' and the frequent fatalities it causes justify the name." He described AC as "damnable" and accused the company that provided it of seeking nothing but profit, pointing to the fact that it did not invest in appropriately thick copper wires. Brown argued that, due to Westinghouse's purported obsession with the bottom line, "the public must submit to constant danger from sudden death in order that a corporation may pay a little larger dividend."[194] He expressed the view that the current should be prohibited by law.

Brown's letter echoed widely in the scientific community and the public. After a wave of criticism that followed the letter's publication, Brown was granted permission to use laboratory equipment that belonged to Edison's company. He used this equipment to conduct experiments with electricity on live animals. Shortly afterward, he began organizing public demonstrations with representatives of the scientific community, the government, and the press, during which he electrocuted animals. Typically, these were supposedly homeless dogs, but he also used calves, a lame horse, and even a circus elephant named Topsy was lethally electrocuted in public on January 4, 1903 in New York. Officially, the justification for killing the elephant was that the animal displayed aggressive behavior. The execution was even filmed by a team the Edison Manufacturing Company hired.[195] More importantly, however, the shows were organized so that the animal was killed by alternating rather than direct current. These shocks were supposed to visualize how great a threat to human life alternating current represented and thus evoke a feeling of fear of the current distributed by Westinghouse among the viewers.

But the show whose notoriety spread most widely across the United States took place on July 30, 1888 in the lecture hall of Columbia College. The organizers repeatedly electrocuted a dog with direct current, increasing the voltage with each successive test until it reached 1,000 volts. The sight of the suffering animal was described as "heartrending in the extreme."[196] Many demanded an end to the dreadful performance; some left the building. The climax, however, was a shock that used 330 volts of alternating current, which killed the dog instantly.[197] This event stirred considerable emotion among the viewers; fear and horror dominated. It is difficult to say whether this fear was primarily driven by the lethal power of the current or the ruthless behavior of Brown himself, who did not flinch as he tortured the defenseless animal. Convinced that his actions were justified, Brown concluded the show by saying that "the only places where an alternating current ought to be used were the dog pound, the slaughterhouse, and the state prison."[198] This directly tied into the vigorous discussions in the United States at the time about using electricity as a new, humane way of carrying out the death penalty. Although Brown's demonstrations aroused public opposition to the cruelty to which animals were subjected, he continued to organize them for many years, even after the war of currents ended.

The Great Blizzard of 1888

The conflict came to a head in March 1888 when a brutal winter blizzard tore down several telephone poles. In the aftermath, telephone, telegraph, and electrical wires all twisted together in a volatile, hazardous tangle.[199] The electrical wires that hung from poles mostly belonged to Westinghouse, while the more established DC wires had already been laid out underground. One may ask why this was not the case for alternating current. Despite numerous efforts, Westinghouse was not granted permission to bury his wires due to the authorities' barely concealed allegiance with Edison, for which they were allegedly generously rewarded. Edison himself claimed that burying high-voltage wires would not improve safety but "will result only in the transfer of deaths to man-holes, houses, stores, and offices, through the agency of the telephone, the low-pressure systems, and the apparatus of the high-tension current itself."[200] The tangle of snow-covered wires presented a deadly threat to human life and health. Several workers were electrocuted while attempting to clear the snow, as was a child who tragically came too close to a hidden clump of wires. This triggered the public's anxiety, as people stayed home and refrained from venturing outside, fearing for their lives.

The Electric Wire Panic

On October 11, 1889, the people of Manhattan were struck by sheer terror. John Feeks, an experienced Western Union lineman, climbed a telegraph pole to inspect the wires. As fate would have it, a crisscrossing set of electrical and telegraph wires came into contact near the pole, which caused the telegraph wire to conduct electricity – something it was not meant to do. Feeks accidentally touched the wire and was fatally electrocuted. A crowd of onlookers quickly gathered around, gaping at his smoldering, slowly carbonizing body, which hung from the wires like part of a macabre spectacle. The event shook Manhattan to the core. The next day, a can for donations to the deceased's family was placed on the death-dealing pole. Citizens came out in droves to aid the lineman's widow, so they had to wait in line to add their contribution to the can. Propaganda illustrations warning against the perils of electricity began to appear in the press.

In their panic, the owners of neighboring buildings cut the wires running across their roofs. Some threw away their phones, fearing that the wires to which they were connected would deal death through the handset. Newspapers published articles that fanned the flames of fear:

> Death-dealing currents of electricity are running all about the city over our heads, day and night, strong enough to kill any man. It is not alone the

> electric-light wires that may kill you, as was seen in the death of the unfortunate man at Chambers and Center streets today. Somewhere off in another street, perhaps miles away, the wind has blown a light wire against an iron roof connected with the telephone wire that comes into your room or your office. Death does not stop at the door but comes right into the house, and perhaps as you close a door or turn on the gas, you are killed. Likely, many of the cases of sudden death we hear of from heart disease may come about in this way.[201]

The *New York World*, a pioneer of the news industry, published propaganda illustrations against AC. One of these illustrations featured the mayor of New York City, Hugh J. Grant, standing by the tombstones of electrocuted New Yorkers. The mayor was known for his view that alternating current is extremely dangerous. His decision ultimately led to New York shutting down many of its utility lines, plunging much of the city into darkness.[202]

Within two months, outraged residents had pressured the city's government enough to persuade the Department of Public Works to start cutting down dangerous electrical wires. Nearly a quarter of all overhead wires were removed, plunging 56 miles of streets into darkness.[203] New Yorkers' growing indignation with the dangers that lurked in the city's dark alleys, and especially the rise in nighttime street robberies, led to a temporary renaissance for gas lighting.

Feeks's death is undoubtedly the most crucial factor that led the New York City energy market to collapse. In 1889, electric street lighting was almost eliminated. Torn and knocked-down wires also interrupted the energy supply to private homes and manufacturing plants. Edison's company was in a favorable position, as its wires were buried underground. Unfortunately, this made it impossible to use them for street lighting.

The gruesome accident that triggered the Electric Wire Panic was not the only event of its kind. Several other people died by electrocution in the same period. Among them was a chemist who was killed when a metal display case he was raising grazed a low-hanging lamp. This incident caused renewed public outrage, especially since it perfectly matched Edison's warning that AC would kill people during their routine activities.[204] Death by electrocution was commonly perceived as a strange new phenomenon that seemed to kill immediately without leaving a trace on the victim. Perceptions like this indicated a lack of general knowledge about electricity while subliminally communicating the vague notion of the current as a uniquely dangerous, invisible killer.

It seemed that the havoc would effectively end electricity, or at least the electricity transmitted through overhead wires. But nothing could be further from the truth. While people feared the new technology, they quickly understood that they could not do without it and began to demand access to safe electricity. Per *The New York Times*: "We are not going permanently to put up with the inferior light of gas and oil simply because the corporations have been selfish and our public servants ignorant, inefficient, or corrupt."[205] This popular view led to restoring damaged electrical wires, which had to meet new, more stringent safety requirements.

The events of 1889 in the United States went down in history as the Electric Wire Panic and represented the apogee of the fear of electricity and its consequences. Newspapers inundated readers with descriptions of tragic accidents. Headlines continuously recycled chilling phrases: "*Killed by Electricity*," "*Shock from Electric Light Wire*," "*Caused by Electricity. The Death of (...)*," "*How Electricity Kills*," "*Killing by Electricity*," "*Death by*

Electricity," "Victim to Electricity," "A Cyclist Killed by Electricity," "Lineman Feeks's Sacrifice Starts a Mighty Electric Wire Crusade."

Similar events took place in other countries that had catalyzed the growth of their electrical networks. In the United Kingdom, newspapers were keen to report on accidents involving electricity in the workplace. One magazine that focused most of its content on gas lighting described the tragic death of a worker who touched an electrical wire. The magazine stressed that its primary concern was people's health and well-being, noting that it did not aim to discredit electricity. It also reminded its readers that electrical wires appear harmless at first glance, making them more dangerous than gas, which most of us can easily detect in the air.[206]

THE KILLER CURRENT

In November 1889, Edison published an extensive article in *The North American Review* magazine about the dangers of the electric current. He made his attitude toward alternating current particularly explicit:

> My personal desire would be to prohibit entirely the use of alternating currents. They are as unnecessary as they are dangerous. In the city of New York there are many miles of conductors beneath the streets conveying a harmless continuous electric current to thousands of consumers, the maximum pressure on this vast system never exceeding two hundred and twenty volts, which will force so weak a current through the human body that it can barely be detected. Furthermore, it is found to be commercially successful, and I can therefore see no justification for the introduction of a system which has no element of permanency and every element of danger to life and property.[207]

But Edison's article was only one of many efforts to lobby against alternating current. The stakes were high. City councils, businessmen, and even private individuals saw a need to install electrical equipment that could effectively replace existing gas lighting, which could mean millions of dollars in profit for those who provided the service. However, most of those involved in these schemes were not familiar with electricity, which made their representatives susceptible to the influence of those considered to be authorities in the field. Many believed that "electricity was, after all, the stuff that lightning was made of, and it could kill you if you were struck by it."[208] At the same time, Edison's propaganda proved ruthlessly effective, and it is Edison whom we must credit for not only awakening the fear of electricity but also stoking the fire.

Westinghouse was initially passive in the face of Edison's onslaught. But over time, as his rival ramped up his attacks, he began to question his statements on the safety of AC publicly. The World's Columbian Exposition, held in 1893 in Chicago and illuminated using AC. lighting, offered powerful and widely acknowledged evidence of these systems' safety, and the exposition ultimately became one of the most important cultural events of its time.

In his crusade against AC, Edison also attempted to influence state authorities' decisions regarding laws that dealt with electricity, extending his lobbying efforts in New York, Ohio, Pennsylvania, and Virginia. In the winter of 1890, Virginia's state authorities were considering a bill, "For the Prevention of Danger from Electric Currents,"[209] limiting AC voltage to 200 volts. Edison personally attended hearings at which he explained electricity to the public in simple words and, most importantly, emphasized the harmfulness of alternating current. However, this did not have the desired effect, and the bill was not passed into law.

Another manifestation of Edison's efforts to discredit Westinghouse was his quest to lobby New York lawmakers to permit the execution of the death sentence using alternating current. This method of execution was ostensibly more modern than hanging. The proposed solution was supported by the results of the animal experiments described earlier in this chapter and the fatal accidents in Manhattan. As a result, New York's legislators were the first to legalize execution by electric current. In late 1889, this led to animal tests on a new execution tool. Many proposals were made on how the death penalty should be carried out, particularly how the condemned's body should be placed. One design involved placing the prisoner in a standing position in a special booth similar to a sentry box, while another had the prisoner positioned on a metal plate with their hands up as if for whipping, and yet another had them lying on a table. Ultimately, all these designs fell by the wayside, outperformed by the one that was deemed optimal – the electric chair.[210]

The first death sentence via electric current was carried out on August 6, 1890, on William Kemmler, convicted for the murder of his wife and imprisoned in New York's Auburn Prison. This case aroused great public interest long before its finale, fueled by two dynamics. On the one hand, the event would be a pioneering attempt to kill a man in a controlled manner using electricity. On the other, the "Wizard of Menlo Park," as Edison was often called, was personally involved in developing a system to optimally connect the electric current to the chair and advised the prison on placing electrodes on the prisoner's body. Importantly, Edison was highly regarded by government officials. His reputation as a magician of electricity meant that he was trusted almost unquestioningly, and his opinions always seemed correct. His statements on the implementation of the death penalty via electrocution should be viewed with the awareness that he did not have extensive knowledge of the biological effects of electric shocks,[211] as he admitted. Nevertheless, he argued that a 1,000-volt jolt of alternating current "would surely kill a man," this was used as a critical argument in favor of introducing the electric chair as a tool of execution in American prisons.[212] Edison further suggested that this method of execution should be called "Westinghousing," clearly intending to associate it with his stigmatized market competitor and demonize the electricity he produced.

Kemmler's trial became another battlefield in the war of the currents. Indeed, it was the site of one of its most important battles. Edison's ultimate goal was to ensure that alternating currents would be used for one purpose: to bring death to convicts. He was not looking to make these executions quick and painless. His actions seem to have been driven by the growing competition in the market for the DC electricity he produced, which significantly affected his company's income. To prevent this, Westinghouse paid Kemmler's lawyer's fees to push through an appeal that was supposed to change the sentence; this ultimately failed, and the verdict was executed.

Unfortunately, the technicians who prepared the electric chair miscalculated, resulting in the prisoner's agonizing, slow death. Reports from the event were widely distributed in the American press. Newspapers devoted much space to detailed descriptions of how the prisoner was prepared and what transpired at the critical moment. The first attempt to electrocute Kemmler failed. Moments after Kemmler was pronounced dead, it turned out that the prisoner was, in fact, alive. This was completely unexpected. Shocked spectators surrounding the chair turned their eyes away from the dreadful scene taking place before their eyes. There were several visible signs that Kemmler was regaining consciousness: hand cramps, trickles of blood, and Kemmler's own heavy, wheezing breath. Because the dynamo had already been turned off, it was impossible to administer another jolt of electricity immediately. It took 73 seconds from Kemmler's first groan to deliver a second shock, and witnesses described the time it took for the executioners to get their bearings as excruciating. The second time around, the voltage was increased to 2,000. Foam sputtered from Kemmler's mouth. The smell of burning flesh permeated the air. Frightened spectators began to leave the room. Many vomited. After the power was turned off, a member of the Associated Press stood up and tried to calm the agitated audience: "Well, there is no doubt about one thing: the man never suffered an iota of pain." Many doctors later disagreed with this assessment.[213]

The botched execution could not go unnoticed. The method used and whether the prisoner had suffered were widely discussed. The press criticized the technique of execution: "[Kemmler] died this morning under the most revolting circumstances, and with his death there was placed to the discredit of the State of New York an execution that was a disgrace to civilization. Probably no convicted murderer of modern times has been made to suffer as Kemmler suffered."[214] A few months later, Harold Brown, an ally of Edison's, spoke directly to his motivations for arguing so fiercely in favor of the electric chair:

> The majesty of the law has been vindicated, but no physical pain has been caused. Such is electrical execution. And yet strenuous attempts have been made to befog the public mind in order to prevent the use of the alternating current for the death-penalty, lest the public should learn its deadly nature and demand that the Legislature banish it from streets and buildings, thus ending the terrible, needless slaughter of unoffending men.[215]

Some believed that Kemmler's execution would be the first and last to use the electric chair. Nothing could be further from the truth. Since 1890, this method has been used numerous times in the United States and the Philippines, often with "difficulties" comparable to those that arose during Kemmler's execution. Moreover, more than 100 years later, it is accompanied by similar scenes from Dante's *Inferno.* In 1994, U.S. Supreme Court Justice William Brennan described the moment when a prisoner was electrocuted:

> . . . the prisoner's eyeballs sometimes pop out and rest on [his] cheeks. The prisoner often defecates, urinates, and vomits blood and drool. The body turns bright red as its temperature rises, the prisoner's flesh swells, and his skin stretches to the point of breaking. Sometimes, the prisoner catches fire . . . Witnesses hear a loud and sustained sound like bacon frying, and the sickly sweet smell of burning flesh permeates the chamber.[216]

Even today, four US states allow the use of the electric chair to execute a death sentence: Alabama, Florida, Kentucky, and Tennessee.[217]

ELECTRIC-LIGHT BLINDNESS

The arrival of electricity also broadened the horizons of medicine. It encouraged the development of new treatment methods but also brought further reports of the dangerous impact of electricity on human health. A group of doctors pessimistic about electric light took the lead in sounding the alarm. Dr. Henry Houghton, a well-known ophthalmologist from New York City, for instance, painted a tragic vision of the future:

> . . . the use of the present electric lamps in the office and the house will unquestionably produce weakness of the sight in the present generation, partial blindness in the next generation if persisted in, and complete blindness in the third or fourth generation . . . The persistent use of the present incandescent lamps would in a few generations produce a race of sightless beings.[218]

The development of electricity also led to more diagnoses of conditions allegedly associated with electricity exposure. The press described such revelations enthusiastically. The *Iron County Register* argued that those who come into contact with electric light and fail to shield their eyes properly may ultimately come down with electric light blindness. The symptoms of this condition ostensibly included irritation, itching pain, excessive lacrimation (production of tears), general eye pain, and foggy vision, among others.[219] *Oakland Tribune* pointed to a new threat vector associated with electric light. The stream of light waves could be so enormous that the shadow cast by the light was darker than Erebus, a symbol of underground darkness in Greek mythology. "Our eyes cannot bear it at all, and there is no reason to doubt that every nervous tissue will feel its use. We already have enough nervous stimulation in this climate and a fearful catalogue of nervous diseases arising from too much force."[220] Based on these reflections, the article argued that electric light hurts the human nervous system.

The German professor Toby Cohn, widely seen as an authority on experimental electricity and eye diseases in the same era, presented a completely different view on the impact of electricity on human health. In his opinion, "the new light is beneficial, not harmful, to the organs of vision, while letters, spots and colors are perceivable a greater distance by electric illumination than by either gas or sunlight."[221] However, given that the use of electricity by the public was only in its nascent stages, this was an isolated opinion.

In 1908, news emerged of a new eye disease that could lead to cataracts. Dresden scientists called it "electric ophthalmia" and warned that anyone who used electric lighting was exposed to it. They recommended the special yellow-green glasses to preempt the unfortunate condition.[222]

SO WHAT IS ALL THE FUSS ABOUT?

The war of the currents is a peculiar case where individual actors stoked fear of a technology that we use commonly (and fearlessly) today. Although the anti-electric propaganda outlined here concerned only one of the two currents offered on the market and was not directed against electricity, it undoubtedly delayed the process of universal electrification. The war between the two electro giants was a struggle for fame and more outstanding market share. In other words, the two titans fought over access to electrodollars. Their war led the Westinghouse Electric Company to the brink of bankruptcy. To prevent this, Westinghouse persuaded Nikola Tesla to transfer his AC patents free of charge. A license agreement was also signed with General Electric, which allowed it to use Tesla's patents, while the WEC received the rights to the electric light bulb.[223]

The fear of electricity also spread in other parts of the world besides the United States. In 1878, Robert Louis Stevenson wrote unflatteringly about the electric lighting used in Paris: "a new sort of urban star now shines out nightly, horrible, unearthly, obnoxious to the human eye; a lamp for a nightmare! Such a light as this should shine only on murders and public crime, or along the corridors of lunatic asylums, a horror to heighten horror."[224] French writers were slightly less evocative but equally pessimistic: "Well, this whole explosion of science leads directly to the crushing of what was once normal human life. Those who come will have more comfort and less joy, more luxury and less happiness. The electricity that makes life so much easier also takes away its charm."[225]

However, the fear of electricity does not seem to be a significant factor in the development of electricity networks and the electrification of the world today.[226] Even the climactic moments of this fear, which probably occurred during the Electric Wire Panic, could not interrupt the electric current's forward march. While it may have been one of the factors that slightly delayed the distribution of energy to households, the costs associated with bringing the network to end users were the decisive factor.

Electricity is not that bad

Electricity had many opponents from its inception, but it enjoyed an even larger circle of enthusiasts. Soon after developing the electricity transmission system, Thomas Edison embarked on a promotional campaign in which he persuaded the public that electricity was not a threat to people's lives and health. He also distributed specially prepared leaflets that ran along the same lines.

Although numerous concerted attempts were made to present electricity in a favorable light, its widespread use provided the best testimony in its favor. Theaters played a considerable role here, to the point where one could view them as the pioneers of molding public opinion about using electric power. In 1881, the Savoy Theatre in London became the first public building in the world to be illuminated by electricity. The decision to use the new technology was justified: "The greatest drawbacks to the enjoyment of the theatrical performances are, undoubtedly, the foul air and heat which pervade all theatres. As everyone knows, each gas burner consumes as much oxygen as many people and causes great heat beside. The incandescent lamps consume no oxygen and cause no perceptible heat."[227] Other theaters soon followed suit, including the Bijou Theatre in Boston in 1882.

Numerous public shows and demonstrations also accelerated the normalization of electricity. On New Year's Eve, 1879, Edison organized a public demonstration of the electric light bulb in Menlo Park, which drew crowds interested in the spectacle, undeterred by the stormy weather. The show was such an essential event that additional trains were scheduled to accommodate potential onlookers. The audience was ecstatic.

Just as electricity use grew in scale, so did the expectations for its potential applications. The technology was expected to bring many benefits. In the early 20th-century Warsaw, the current was sometimes described as the harbinger of innovation: "Like a horn of plenty, this 'new' force of nature has become a source of countless, increasingly diverse, strange, and unexpected discoveries and applications."[228] Meanwhile, Edison claimed that "[t]he one great value of the electric light – and the electric railway too – is that they expand mankind's 'day.'"[229]

In 1882, New York City's Christmas tree was decorated for the first time with colorful electric lamps connected with a single wire at the behest of inventor Edward Johnson. More than that, the tree was rotating. Though revolutionary and certainly much safer than traditional wax candles, the idea did not immediately catch on. The high cost of the lights, lack of access to the electric grid, and general distrust toward electricity were not conducive to the spread of this manner of decorating Christmas trees. Only at the dawn of the 20th century did the idea truly gain traction, mainly among the affluent segments of the American populace. Soon afterward, General Electric began to produce and sell electric Christmas lights for home use. Due to the high market price of the product, it was also offered as a service where one could borrow a set of lights temporarily. This was accompanied by an intensive advertising campaign highlighting the advantages of decorating trees with electric lamps.

Before it entered private homes for good, electricity was developed primarily for use in public spaces. In its infancy, it was mainly used to illuminate streets, public squares, and stores. Dazzling electric lights also added splendor to the world's great industrial exhibitions, which showcased the latest developments in science, technology, culture, and art. The most famous of these illuminations include those used at the Columbian Exposition in Chicago in 1893 and the Paris Exposition in 1900. This allowed the public to become accustomed to new, unknown technology, which some attributed almost mystical properties.

The global publicity that accompanied the beginning of electrification was a source of pride for Americans as proof of their nation's technological capabilities. Some even believe that significant cultural events, national celebrations, and grandiose political gatherings spurred Americans' love of electricity.[230] Electricity gradually entered high society.

Sophisticated interior lighting was a luxury that not everyone could afford and imbued events with gravitas and prestige. At the same time, it was a marker of the hosts' openness to new technology. No self-anointed member of the urban elite wished to be seen as someone who could not afford electricity. This brought the latest technology into the household. Thus, human envy was one of the factors that contributed to the lightning-fast adoption of the magical current. Rumors about how valuable electricity was in various domains of domestic life circulated from house to house. Lady Churchill – Winston Churchill's mother – resided in one of the first houses in the United Kingdom to be equipped with electricity and became a vigorous promoter of electricity in the home. She recalled, "light was such an innovation that much curiosity and interest were evinced to see it, and people used to ask for permission to come to the house."[231] At the same time, advertisers trumpeted the benefits of electric lighting and lured prospective customers with the promise of all the time they could save. The modern housewife had a wide range of devices to support her daily work, which feminist circles enthusiastically perceived as the first sign of relief from the burden of housework.

The beginning of the 20th century brought intensive advertising campaigns organized by energy distributors. The press routinely published ads that rattled off the benefits of electricity, precisely the benefits of using electricity-powered equipment. Others emphasized that electricity was cheaper than other products available on the market, such as the kerosene needed to power an oil lamp.

Is electricity a woman?

The electric lobby, wishing to build people's trust in the technology it offered, tried to spruce up its image. One of its tactics was to associate electricity with the image of a beautiful woman. Following the era's aspirational portrayals of the ideal woman, they linked electricity to charm and a sense of safety. It was also supposed to arouse longing and desire.

The discoveries that took place in the 18th and 19th centuries were a catalyst that greatly expanded the number of applications of electricity. In France, electricity was presented as an almost mystical, obliging electric fairy that brought people light. One only had to ask her for a miracle, and she will deliver immediately. This romantic picture was meant to encourage people to use electricity. In 1937, during the World Exhibition in Paris, the Parisian Electricity Distribution Company commissioned Raoul Dufy to paint a mural on a 600 m2 stretch of curved wall in the exhibition hall, on which he presented the history of electricity and its applications. The image of an electric fairy is surrounded by the most cutting-edge technological achievements of the day, accompanied by images of people who influenced its development. At their side are the gods of Olympus, including Zeus himself.[232] This painting is entitled *La Fée Electricité,* The Electric Fairy. Over time, this image came to be adapted in other countries. Various depictions of electric fairies advertising the latest achievements in electrical engineering increased in the United States, Great Britain, Denmark, and Germany. The electric fairy was often portrayed as a winged woman wearing an airy dress, holding an electric lamp and a lightning bolt. Sometimes, she is also surrounded by numerous electric devices.

A USEFUL TOOL

The business world quickly realized that electricity could bring significant windfalls to another growing sector: industry. The electric current could increase the efficiency of industrial production and sometimes even automate it. One account stated that "[t]he electric light installation at the Mechernich Mines in its once volcanic Eifol district in Rheinish Prussia has now had a fair trial for more than three years and has proved a complete success. The expectation that it would both facilitate the operations and increase their security has fully been realised."[233]

Electricity opened the way for new inventions, like mushrooms, which sprang up on the market. Countless electric appliances were produced. The vibrating electric belt, which was to be a panacea for almost all known diseases and ailments, was a real hit. Many believed that the weakness of the human body resulted from disruptions to the flow of its natural energy and that electricity could bring it back to its proper state. The belt was a feature of various methods of curing human ailments using electrotherapy, which experienced its heyday at the turn of the century. Advertisements published by the device's manufacturers encouraged customers to purchase the belt, reminding them that

"All sufferers should know that Electricity is now recognised as a valuable curative agent in all forms of disease."[234]

Over time, electrotherapy became very popular among physicians, who eagerly used it to treat illnesses and mental disorders. Its effects were sometimes auspicious, which only galvanized the method's spread. However, some embraced the rapidly spreading belief in the usefulness of electric energy as a tool to treat diseases while remaining mistrustful of its use for other purposes. A reporter's notebook from 1900 contains an entry that validated the fear of electricity: "Despite the vaunted medical benefits of electrotherapy, can we be assured of its true safety? The untapped electrical fluid leaking from these outlets and wires, we are told, may cause serious bodily damage and – with prolonged exposure – possibly death."[235]

In the first half of the 20th century, the electric current expanded into global markets. Electrification progressed apace, and with it came new lessons on how to handle electricity. Posters and brochures educated regular people about the potential perils of improperly using electricity and the devices that it powered. In 1931, physician Stefan Jellinek, inspired by his experience treating victims of electric shock, published a book that used 132 illustrations to vividly showcase how everyday human behavior could lead to electric shock or another accident involving electricity. In the Netherlands, Evert Möllenkamp designed a poster that called for caution when working near electrical wiring using a memorable warning: "One touch! There are monsters lurking in electric cables."

A FEAR EVOLVES

Over time, the fear of electricity has been overcome, and the global dissemination of electricity has made us deeply familiar with it. The gradual expansion of electric networks greatly facilitated this. As science evolved, human experience was enriched by direct contact with electricity, which unlocked new chapters in our understanding of the current and our ability to pass it on through education. Insurance companies, which initially stood alone in the struggle for safe transmission networks because it was in their interest to reduce the number of accidents, eventually gained strong support and leverage from the scientific community and technical experts. As a result, the security of transmission networks and the equipment used constantly improved. Government actors responsible for issuing permits to conduct business related to electricity transmission also played a significant role here.

Over time, electricity demand grew, and private suppliers who dominated the market ceased to be able to supply the right amount of electricity at prices that were acceptable to consumers. This increased the interest of state authorities in controlling energy production and sales, ultimately catalyzing government-led electrification campaigns in Great Britain, France, Germany, Switzerland, Italy, Soviet Russia, Canada, and other countries shortly after World War I. In the United States, the share of energy produced in publicly owned power plants in total industrial energy consumption quickly reached half of the country's total consumption.[236]

In the Kingdom of Poland, then a polity subordinate to Tsarist Russia, one of the factors that significantly accelerated the expansion of the power grid was the numerous attacks on Tsarist officials in 1905. These took place mostly under cover of darkness. To frustrate these efforts and increase the level of security on the streets, the Russian authorities ordered city authorities to electrify their streets.[237]

The first significant breakthrough in how electricity was perceived was undoubtedly the New York blackout of 1889. The event gave Americans a tangible idea of how badly they needed electricity. The fear of a potentially lethal technology quickly proved much weaker than the fear of the consequences of not having it. To reduce the risk of power outages, cities worldwide began drawing large-scale plans to build power grids. In 1930, at the International Energy Congress in Berlin, German engineer Oskar Oliven presented a plan for an international power grid. He proposed building five main power lines totaling 9,750 km, connecting Oslo with Rome, Calais with Lisbon, Warsaw with Elbasan in Albania, Paris with Katowice, and Rostov with Lyon. This would link areas with high energy consumption with efficient hydro or coal power plants. This approach would minimize the risk of a situation in which excessive energy consumption interrupted the supply of energy by exceeding the available energy resources.[238] President Franklin Delano Roosevelt was another staunch supporter of electrification in the United States, proclaiming, "Electricity is a modern necessity of life and ought to be found in every village, every home and every farm in every part of the United States."[239]

The electrification of city streetcars was another watershed moment. Between 1887 and 1888, Frank J. Sprague developed the first successful electric streetcar in Virginia. His prototype was quickly adopted, electrifying 16 percent of American streetcar lines only two years later. By 1902, 97.5 percent of all streetcars in the United States were powered by electricity. The same technology quickly gained recognition in France and Germany. Electric propulsion also gained sway in subway systems, and the turn of the 19th and 20th centuries brought about intensive electrification of primary railroad lines, both in the United States and Europe.[240]

Meanwhile, electricity demand continued to skyrocket. People had already learned to love electricity and its benefits so much that they began to feel the need to use it whenever they pleased. Thus, it quickly became apparent that increased production volume was not keeping up with the growing demand. World War II became a pivotal turning point, as the fluctuations in the electricity produced were considerable, depending on the ongoing military operations. Since a large part of the power plants and transmission networks of many countries were destroyed during the war, governments introduced special regulations that aimed to reduce electricity consumption. For example, on January 13, 1945, the governor of Białostockie Province in Poland issued an order prohibiting the use of electricity by persons and institutions who did not hold a permit, "even if the premises of such persons and institutions were connected to the grid and equipped with meters or limiters, and even if these meters drew electricity." After the end of the war, production began to grow more steadily.

A surge in the number of electric devices available on the market accompanied the development of electricity. While washing machines and fridges gained a foothold in people's homes with no major complications, the vacuum cleaner and the radio faced more significant challenges. Some were terrified of vacuum cleaners, believing little demons dwelled in the wicked household appliance. Radios were thought to awaken people's hidden murderous instincts, while television sets earned a sordid reputation as weapons of the surveillance state. Thus, the fear of electricity took on a new shape, transforming into the fear of specific types of electrical equipment. However, some ways to produce electricity turned out to be much more severe and durable sources of anxiety than any one appliance. Nuclear power rapidly emerged as the most widely feared method of energy production, but every technique has raised fears in various communities, some of which escalated into fierce protests.

In 1985, a study was conducted in the United Kingdom on students' knowledge of electricity. The study examined two groups. The first comprised children aged 11 to 12 who had not yet learned about electricity during their school education, and the second included young people aged 13 to 14 who had already been exposed to the subject. In both cases, the students most frequently associated the electric current with danger, using phrases such as *dangerous, shock,* and *kill/die*. This study confirmed that the knowledge, experience, and warnings about the dangers of using electricity that we absorb as children significantly influence how we perceive electricity and what associations it evokes. Of course, knowledge about potential risks is essential to navigate the world of electricity properly. Today, we can hardly fathom life without electricity, so educating the public on how to handle it is necessary so that no one gets hurt.

However, the average person today is so familiar with electricity that they are afraid not so much of electricity itself as of the consequences of its absence. According to a survey conducted by TNS Polska 2015, 84 percent of Poles fear losing access to electricity through power outages and other unforeseen circumstances. It is impossible to disagree with the statement that "... modern society has come to depend on reliable electricity as an essential resource for national security; health and welfare; communications; finance; transportation; food and water supply; heating, cooling, and lighting; computers and electronics; commercial enterprise; and even entertainment and leisure – in short, nearly all aspects of modern life."[241] Electricity accompanies us at every step, whether at home, work, school, or on the bus. Some of us carry power banks every day to charge on the go. Others buy stun guns, using electricity to defend themselves from danger. The technology that enables the production of light from various sources keeps improving, decreasing energy consumption without compromising brightness and encouraging us to illuminate almost everything we can. One scholar said, "It is no longer necessary to write about how important electricity is; everyone sees it, knows it, and feels it. Electricity is everywhere and used for everything."[242]

But have we ever imagined a situation where the world suddenly plunges into darkness? A moment in time when we flip the switch, and nothing ever happens again, when we look out the window in the evening and see nothing but pitch blackness? We drain the last of our phone's battery, and there is no Internet. Suddenly, we realize that we can only talk to the people in our immediate vicinity. We have no idea what is going on, and our subconscious delivers nothing but darker and darker thoughts. In addition, we have taken advantage of the benefits of electricity to binge-watch films and TV shows where something similar happens – such as *Into the Forest* (2015), *Revolution* (2012-2013), or *Blade Runner 2049* (2017) – we know that we are standing before an indescribable tragedy. We feel the fear creeping up from deep down. Or perhaps we have read Marc Elsberg's *Blackout*, where chaos takes over in a gridless Europe. Whatever our consumption of apocalyptic fiction, we know the situation is dire. According to the World Bank, 8.6 percent of the world's population had no access to electricity in 2021. We certainly wouldn't want to be in this group, would we?

Electricity has shared the fate of hundreds of other inventions and new technologies. In the 19th century, humanity feared electricity, just as it now fears 5G technology. Today, when we think about the fear and panic that electricity caused a hundred years ago, it is hard not to feel slight bemusement. After all, if we know how to use it, is there anything left to fear? Who knows – perhaps in 50 or 100 years, there will be those who will think back to our concern about 5G or artificial intelligence in precisely the same way.

In the case of electricity, reason scored a decisive victory over faith and the erroneous beliefs about its harmfulness that skeptics peddled in the technology's infancy. The stoking of fear by the gas lobby, which aimed to nip its emerging competitor in the bud, was mainly driven by economic interests, as were the manipulations and fraud of actors in the electricity market. Of course, we cannot rule out that some honestly believed that electricity posed an enormous threat to human life and health. However, the rationality and particularly the usefulness of this technology prevailed. Our fear was tamed and neutralized relatively quickly. The culmination of the panic in 1889 was probably one of the turning points in human history. Depriving people of electricity immediately made them realize that the current was something we needed in everyday life – a force without which further social and economic development would not be possible. Looking at how many areas of life depend on electricity as a lifeline, we cannot doubt that the original fear of electricity has been eradicated, and what remains can be described as a healthy fear of the effects of improperly using it. This allows us to function correctly in a world built on electricity. The awareness of the potential repercussions of handling electricity without proper care helps us minimize the risk of its occurrence through rational behavior. Our experiences with electricity and its development show that "there is no turning back from electricity because, so far, mankind has not invented anything better."[243]

THREE
APOCALYPSE NOW?

Jolanta Jóźwik

If you are reading these words, the world has not yet ended. The Earth continues to spin around its axis, even though doomsday prophets throughout history have predicted at least several hundred world-shattering catastrophes that were supposed to end life on Earth as we know it. One of the earliest prophecies of this kind estimated that the world would end no later than 634 BC. Since then, similar predictions spanning thousands of years have been made, each time with absolute seriousness, and educated adults took them to heart just as much as did illiterate people and children. Only a select few would be able to escape Judgment Day, alien invasions, celestial bodies slamming into the Earth, and other global catastrophes – those who embraced the guidance of a self-proclaimed prophet who could guarantee their followers safety and sometimes even lead them to another dimension. The fact that none of these predictions ever came true does not bother true believers who continue to cling to every new prophecy, often supporting their preferred soothsayers with generous donations. The myth of the end of the world is alive and well, permeating even the societies of highly developed countries, in some of which every third adult citizen expects the apocalypse to arrive during their lifetime.

Nothing lasts forever

Humans are prone to dichotomous thinking and perceiving the world as a set of contradictions that are mutually exclusive but form a cohesive whole. For most of us, this regularity makes the world more precise, simpler, and more complementary on the one hand. Still, on the other hand, it triggers internal conflicts in which we are condemned to constantly put our faith in choices we consider to be better and fear those we believe to be worse. Since there are no half-measures, there is no room for ambiguity, and one choice will always appeal to us more than the other. This duality is ubiquitous: good versus evil, peace versus war, day versus night, up versus down, light versus darkness, sacred versus profane, and friend versus foe are only the tip of the iceberg. All these polarities reinforce humanity's belief that the same is true of our world; if it had a beginning, then it must also have an end. We live with the knowledge that nothing will last forever, and Earth will be no exception. As the late Frank Kermode wrote, "even when we hear something as trivial as the ticking of a clock, we ask what it says, and we agree that it says tick-tock. By this fiction, we humanize it, make it talk our language . . . *tick* is our word for a physical beginning, *tock* our term for an end . . . Tick is a humble genesis, tock a feeble apocalypse."[244]

Everybody knows that none of us has ever seen the end of the world, and no one can predict it. It is also clear that the end of the world, as its name suggests, is a story with no epilogue. If so, then what is there to dwell on? If all apocalypses were made equal, this chapter could begin and end in the span of a single page. But the end of all things is constantly delayed; countless theories surround it; apocalyptic and catastrophic themes pervade artistic works with broad and foreboding interpretations, and each era brings a number of new, self-proclaimed prophets. Given the rich tapestry of doom before us, it would be a shame not to take a closer look at it.

Why enter this sad world of bad omens? To understand what is happening around us. In keeping with our nature, we often take shortcuts, fail to examine details, generalize, and remain reluctant to analyze and process the information that reaches us. We voraciously consume the jumble of signals served to us by the world of information around us. All this leads to prejudice and common subconscious cognitive distortions, which more impartial outsiders can identify as fallacies and faulty conclusions. The most common of these include dichotomous thinking, catastrophizing, excessive generalization, and personification. Importantly, these examples are not disconnected categories but form a "thought jumble." Such thinking characterizes us all, and it is completely normal if it is not used excessively in our lives. This reality is slightly different for people with mental disorders, such as depression, eating disorders, social phobias, or personality disorders. In their case, fallacies and erroneous thinking occur much more frequently. Aaron Beck first observed cognitive distortions in the 1960s in patients suffering from depression.[245]

Time-honored and established stereotypes make us think that if the creation of our world were a wonderful, exciting, solemn, and truly extraordinary moment, then the end would surely be a terrifying, bloody, chaotic, and tragic event. A wide variety of people, ranging from clergy to scientists, have delivered a steady stream of relatively plausible End Times scenarios that fuel this phobia of the destruction of the world as we know it. One might think that with our capacity and propensity for abstract thinking and creating grim scenarios in our minds, we will never get rid of our anxiety about the end of the world.

The end of the world, which we often view through the

lens of faith, usually refers to the second coming of the Messiah, the Great Tribulation, Judgment Day, the resurrection of the dead, and eternal punishment for sinners combined with eternal reward for true believers. These events and the signs that precede them are described in detail in the holy books of each religion. All of them speak of terrible corruption, chaos, natural disasters, a sweeping tide of death, wrath, and the deliverance of God's ultimate justice.

Over the years, periods of intense development in technology and science have prompted us to reframe the end of the world thoroughly. Increasingly, we look to the sky and ponder whether the actual existential threat to humanity, our planet, or the entire Universe lies somewhere in the vast expanses of space. The collapse of the Universe, an asteroid impact, the expansion of the Sun, a gamma-ray burst, a supernova explosion, a black hole swallowing up the Earth – these phenomena are so abstract to regular people that they can barely imagine how they could happen. On the other hand, humanity possesses such extensive knowledge and advanced technology that we can eradicate our planet with atomic energy, invisible microbes, nanotechnology, or artificial intelligence – intentionally or by complete luck. We may not actually destroy the earth in the physical sense, but we could easily deprive the human species of its continued privilege to exist on this planet. Some of us undoubtedly believe that the best way to tackle this problem is from multiple perspectives at once, combining an element of faith with an aspect of science. That is, we can pin our hopes on theories regarding the end of the world drawn from prophecies as well as stories about aliens and zombies but combine them with the hypotheses of astrophysicists and cosmologists.

Of course, we can also perceive the end of the world in a completely different way; the range of possibilities is extensive. For example, it can have a dimension that is intimate, private, and personal. Many of us have experienced our micro-scale apocalypse: the death of a loved one, a failed relationship, or a job we abruptly lost. These are, after all, traumatic experiences that affect our physical and psychological condition, often serving as critical points or even turning points in our existence. Our death can also be classified as a private end of the world – as we leave our mortal coil, the world behind us lives on, and where we will be after that depends mainly on what we believe.

We can also speak of the end of the world in a purely symbolic sense. Events we know or hear about often seem to indicate or confirm that the world is so morally corrupt that it cannot get any worse. The end of the world is also an undefined and forlorn point in space, somewhere far away – in the wilderness, at sea, in the desert, at the South Pole, or anywhere else – or, on the contrary, a very precisely defined location, such as a town in Brazil, Australia, or England; a scenic spot in Norway; a precipice in Sri Lanka; a Chelsea neighborhood; a pub in London; or a park in Pennsylvania.

In this chapter, the end of the world is understood as a future apocalyptic event, representing some turning point that will lead to the destruction of humanity, the Earth, or the entire Universe. Given also that we will consider the end of the world as a story with no epilogue and no sequel, we will avoid discussing "new beginnings" and what life might be like for the chosen ones in heaven or survivors in a post-apocalyptic world.

Outlooks on the End of the World

When will the end of the world occur? Is it possible to predict it? Is it close, or do we still have some time? And what will ultimately trigger the end of all things? Perhaps it will be something so small as to be invisible to the naked eye, or maybe something enormous that will cast its shadow on humanity long before it arrives. Perhaps it will even be a being from another world?

Humankind has been trying to answer these nagging questions for centuries. Who among us hasn't heard of the biblical apocalypse, the Y2K bug and the panic that accompanied it, the end of the Maya calendar, the predictions of Nostradamus, or other apocalyptic scenarios involving a buffet of disasters such as black holes, nuclear wars, large asteroids, and climate catastrophes? Every theory has its believers and its opponents. You may ask which one is correct or most likely. The answer is that it depends on what you believe, how you were raised, and how you look at the world. The pages that follow are a snapshot of the most popular and perhaps lesser-known perspectives on the end of the world. It is up to the reader to judge for themselves which one speaks to them the most. Maybe all of them are equally probable, and perhaps you will see some of them as myths, or . . . maybe it is futile to dwell on it since the end is the end, and nothing will matter if or when darkness comes.

Verily I say unto thee: The grim visions of faith

Since the dawn of humankind, people have passed down stories and prophecies about where we came from and what fate awaits us. The Book of Daniel in Judaism, the Apocalypse of St. John in Christianity, and the final suras of the Qur'an in Islam are just a few illustrations of holy books conveying records of what may occur to the followers of a particular religion when the Final Day comes. But what do we really fear? The Book of Daniel actually says very little about the dire circumstances that will catalyze Judgment Day. It mentions a long, bloody, and vicious war between rulers (Dan 11), which is to be followed by "a time of trouble, such as never was since there was a nation even to that same time" (Dan 12:1), and finally the Day of Judgment, when "every one that shall be found written in the book" (Dan 12:1) will be saved. The dead will awaken, "some to everlasting life, and some to shame and everlasting contempt" (Dan 12:2). All this is to last until an unspecified moment, which is described as "a time, times, and a half." (Dan 12:7).

In contrast, in the New Testament, the Apocalypse of St. John contains perhaps the most frightening and resonant vision of the end of the world and humanity of any prophetic work. In this depiction, apocalyptic events are set in motion when Jesus Christ removes seven seals securing a tainted book or scroll. The opening of each seal is associated with specific events happening on Earth: the first four releases, the Four Horsemen of the Apocalypse. The first horseman – and the most mysterious, according to Bible scholars – is a figure on a white horse wielding a bow and a wreath and is most often identified with Jesus, the victorious march of the Gospel, or false Christianity. The second, riding a red horse and holding a great sword, heralds war and the destruction of much of humanity. Another figure, sitting on a black horse and with a pair of weighing scales in his hand, is supposed to bring famine, which is also portrayed in the context of war. The last rider, Death, is the only one mentioned by name. Accompanied by Hades, Death rides a pale horse, which may represent further calamities descending upon sinners in the form of wild animals and worldwide pestilence.[246]

Here, let us deviate briefly from our story. The tale of the Four Horsemen of the Apocalypse was modernized and linked to our modern-day reality by John Hogue, an expert in the field of prophecies and predictions. He portrays the first horseman as a pregnant and starving beggar woman, calling her Overpopulation. She symbolizes the human drive for procreation, leading to growing masses of hungry people in the world. The next horseman is a priestess named Earth Trauma, who hurls volcanic fire and lightning. She heralds the destruction of humanity through climate change and the food chains it has disrupted. The third horseman, wielding a syringe, is a rodent-like creature known as the Lemming Syndrome. He is associated with the plague of modern life, which is the ubiquitous stress that adversely affects people's physical and mental health. The last rider symbolizes terrorism and is known as the Third World War. His attributes include a halo of phosphorescent light hovering over his hooded head and representing atomic energy, a nuclear missile on his shoulder, a shield in the form of radar, and a yellow pin on his chest. These objects point to the future destruction of humanity through nuclear holocaust.

But returning to the Apocalypse of St. John, the opening of the fifth seal unleashes the souls of the martyrs, who come to claim justice for the blood they shed. After the next seal is removed, a series of natural disasters and frightening anomalies in the cosmos begin: a great earthquake, a blackened sun, a blood moon, falling stars, vanishing skies, and the displacement of mountains and islands. When the last seal is opened, for a brief moment, there is silence supreme. However, this is not the end of the sinners' torment. These terrifying events are followed by seven more disasters with even more tragic consequences: scorched vegetation and earth, bloody seas, waters as bitter as wormwood, a partial eclipse of the sun, moon, and stars, monstrous locusts attacking only humans, riders on horses sowing death with mouths filled with fire, smoke, and brimstone, and a great battle pitting Saint Michael and a host of angels against a seven-headed dragon with ten horns.

Here again, let us take a brief side road. All these cataclysms will kill one-third of the human race, burn one-third of the earth, and empty one-third of the oceans. In terms of the current population of our continents, this would mean that the equivalent of the entire population of Africa, Europe, and Latin America would die, almost all of Africa and North America would be burned, and the Atlantic Ocean would be hollowed out, as would half of the Indian Ocean.

Next, in the biblical depiction of the end of the world, a

Beast with an unspecified name (corresponding to the number 666) crawls out of the sea. Through another Beast, identified with the False Prophet, it gains power over humanity. This might seem like the culminating point of the suffering that will befall the sinners of the world – but it is not the end. Seven angels pour out seven bowls containing more plagues on the wicked and the faithless: painful wounds for the worshippers of the Beast, bloody seas, bloody springs, and rivers, unbearable heat, darkness in the kingdom of the Beast, the drying-up of the great river Euphrates, a great earthquake, and a punishing hailstorm. And birds called by the angels gather to "eat the flesh of kings, and the flesh of captains, and the flesh of mighty men, and the flesh of horses, and of them that sit on them, and the flesh of all men, both free and bond, both small and great" (Rev 19:18). These events are followed by the Last Judgment, in which everyone is judged "according to their works" (Rev 20:13): sinners are cast down to Hell, and God's faithful people are given the honor of entering the city of God – the New Jerusalem.

Once again, you may ask: When will this happen? The Bible does not offer a precise timeline. The only pointed indication of when we might expect it is contained in the word, "Indeed, I will come soon" (Rev 22:20). This warning, much like the entirety of the Apocalypse of St. John, has had such an impact on believers over the centuries that the book has become the main subject of numerous works of art.

Let us take another look at what the Day of Judgment will look like, this time according to the holy book of Islam. As in Judaism and Christianity, the critical accounts of doomsday can be found in the final suras (chapters) of the Qur'an. Among scholars of the holy book, Mohammad Humayoun Khan has presented a relatively comprehensive interpretation of the Muslim end of the world, including how it relates to the world of science. In his interpretation, the Qur'an depicts a long-lasting event involving the entire Universe. Thus, a nuclear war, a natural disaster, a plague, or a falling meteorite, constrained by their localized nature, can only lead to the destruction of the world and cannot be treated as signs of the apocalypse. Instead, the end of the universe will be a science-bending catastrophe in which "time and gravity will reverse when the universe begins to contract. Reversal of time will bring about the resurrection from the grave. In this time and gravity reversed and transformed world, we will come across all the good and evil that we did in our lives."[247] This reversal of time and gravity will bring about an unfathomably powerful earthquake, transforming our globe into a hollow sphere with the sky inside it. All this will lead to the opening of portals leading to higher dimensions, flanked by angels – messengers of God – who will shepherd humanity through. After this escape from a dying Universe, everyone will answer for their actions, and once again, only the deserving few will enjoy paradise. At the same time, the rest will suffer the eternal torments of Hell. Of course, we find no notion in the Qur'an of when precisely the Universe will begin to shrink and when the end of all things will arrive. The holy book itself drives that point home: "Men ask you of the Hour, Say the knowledge of it is with Allah only, What can convey to you that may be the Hour is near." (Qur'an 33:63) and "The threatened hour is near; none beside God can disclose it. Are you surprised then at this statement?" (Qur'an 53:57-59).

Among fervent believers, regardless of what religion they follow, there is a shared conviction that the world is so broken that they are awaiting doomsday with impatience rather than trepidation. One might venture to say that they have overcome their fear of the end of the world, as they have shifted their focus to preparing for that day as best they can, and sometimes even try to make it happen themselves. In this unpredictable, uncertain world rife with economic and political crises, environmental contamination, and natural disasters, the only thing that is certain for them is the apocalypse. This is clear proof of the victory of faith over reason. Very often, apocalyptic movements offer an answer to the turmoil of the modern world, enticing lost and frightened people with promises of revealing the "truth" and the "right path" while rejecting information from the outside world that could change their point of view. Examples of attempts to initiate the end of the world abound; here are but a few.

THE FAMILY *(THE APOCALYPSE OF AUGUST 1969)*

The founder and leader of this sect, Charles Manson, has been counted among "the most serious and influential terrorist personalities."[248] The inspiration for the founding of this new movement came from the Beatles' *White Album* and the message of rebellion by blacks against whites that it allegedly contained. Its actions were driven by the "Helter Skelter doctrine," whose core idea was an Armageddon involving a bloody racial battle in which whites would be annihilated. When it became clear that the world was not plunging into chaos on its own, a self-proclaimed guru decided to initiate the event. As a result, the world witnessed eight brutal murders committed in a Los Angeles neighborhood that are still a subject of public debate, not only in the United States but all over the world. Among those murdered were actress Sharon Tate (Roman Polański's wife) and her unborn child, Polish actor Wojciech Frykowski, well-known activist Abigail Folger, and Hollywood stylist Jay Sebring.[249]

THE PEOPLES TEMPLE *(THE APOCALYPSE OF NOVEMBER 1978)*

> At the lectern stands a handsome man in an elegant suit . . . "I love you, and more importantly, Jesus loves you!" he says. To prove it, he begins to heal those in attendance. A blind woman regains her sight, another regains feeling in her fingers. The building

> fills up with cheers and applause, and people weep with emotion. After a moment, the gaze of the man in a suit falls on a paralyzed old woman ... "Come closer, my dear. Stand up, take this step, I accept my blessing," he says in his melodious voice. Supporting herself with her hands, the old woman slowly rises from the wheelchair. The crowd goes wild, people scream, jump, and run, together with the healed woman. "Long live Jesus, long live Jim Jones!" they chant. They feel that they have participated in something special, that they have witnessed a real miracle ... They don't know that the blind black woman has been able to see since birth and that the wheelchair-bound old woman is Jones' entirely healthy secretary ... Nor do they know that the day will come when Jim Jones will tell them to swallow a deadly poison. And before they take it themselves, they will administer it to their own children.[250]

This is how one online source describes the activities of cult leader Jim Jones. In its glory years, his sect could count on the support of up to 20,000 people.[251] The self-proclaimed Messiah, plagued with delusions about the impending end of the world, did not shy away from using tranquilizers and drugs. Ultimately, he decided end the Peoples Temple in what became known as the Jonestown massacre. More than 900 bodies of cult members were found in the Guyanese village of Jonestown. Most of Jones's followers had drunk a lethal concoction of potassium cyanide; the rest were either shot or injected with poison.[252]

THE SOLAR TEMPLE *(THE APOCALYPSE OF 1994-1997)*

The Order of the Solar Temple presented a shocking vision of the end of the world prompted by an ecological disaster that resulted from human irresponsibility. It was led by Grand Master Joseph Di Mambro (a jeweler) and guru Luc Jouret (a homeopathic doctor). The sect's followers were convinced that extraterrestrials would relocate the order's chosen ones to a planet near Sirius, creating a new divine state. However, the condition for achieving the reward of eternal life was to commit suicide under the full moon. This is how Di Mambro spoke of the preparations required for the "cosmic transit": " . . . we are at the point of exhaustion of our moral, physical, and even our spiritual resources . . . Not everybody has a seat at this table, but I believe that we represent them and that by embracing our responsibility, we embrace theirs, in everything we do, in everything we say."[253] A total of 74 people died between 1994 and 1997 as a result of ritual murders and suicides in the name of the cosmic transit as a means of escaping this broken world, most of whom were shot, laid radially with their heads together, and then burned.[254]

Aum Shinrikyō (The Apocalypse of March and April 1995)

Led by Shōkō Asahara, the Aum Shinrikyō religious cult in Japan offered the fulfillment of a spiritual mission and the chance to experience the actual end of the world in a highly material world. The group, which targeted young and educated people (primarily biologists, chemists, doctors, and computer scientists), held beliefs that blended Buddhism, Christian apocalypticism, Nostradamus' prophecies, esotericism, and science fiction. It is estimated that the sect had about 10,000 followers in Japan and 30,000 in Russia. Its self-proclaimed "last messiah" predicted an impending Armageddon sparked by a nuclear attack on Japan by the United States and the United Nations between 1996 and 2000, as well as his leading role in these cataclysmic events. The secretive sect, threatened by the prospect of public exposure, was not content to wait for End Times and decided to take action to allow their leader's prophecy to come true. The first terrorist attack took place on several lines of the Tokyo Metro, while the second occurred at a train station in Yokohama. The weapon of choice in this "final war" was sarin, a highly poisonous gas used in combat. The group's first act of terrorism was of gigantic proportions, with about ten dead and more than 5,000 injured, while the other injured approximately 300 people. The cult was planning another attack, which was expected to collect its most grievous harvest – up to 10,000 dead – but luckily, it was foiled.[255]

HEAVEN'S GATE *(THE APOCALYPSE OF MARCH 1997)*

Heaven's Gate is another classic example of an apocalyptic collective. It was founded by "The Two" – Marshall Applewhite, also known as "Do," and Bonnie Nettles, also known as "Ti." Their mission was to fulfill the prophecy contained in the Book of Revelation (11:3-13) in which they would be resurrected three and a half days after being killed, thus ending the perpetual cycle of reincarnation of their souls. They believed they would subsequently be escorted to the Kingdom of God in space by a convoy of UFOs. All they were waiting for was a sign that the apocalypse was upon them; that sign appeared in the form of the Hale-Bopp comet. When the spaceship that purportedly followed the comet had come close enough to Earth, the 39 members of the cult, aged 26 to 72, decided to hitch a ride on it to God's kingdom. Clad in black t-shirts, sweatpants, and black and white Nike shoes, they ingested a concoction that included a high dose of a drug used to treat epilepsy and chased it down with vodka.[256] One of the group's members left an "Earth Exit Statement," dated March 19, 1997, that explained why the cultists had to go:

> We do not identify ourselves as the body, as almost all humans mistakenly do, but rather as the soul that occupies the body it is temporarily using as a "vehicle" or "suit of clothes." Furthermore, as Members of the Next Level, we do not think or act as humans think and act. However, because we are occupying human vehicles for the duration of this task, the inhabitants of this planet insist upon identifying us as what they see – human vehicles – and therefore demand that we conform to their standard of thinking and acting as the 'vehicles' and not as who we truly are . . . We have, through Do (our Older Member), a very active and current means of communication with the Next Level, through Ti (Do's Older Member). Ti occupied a human vehicle for the first 10 years of this task but is currently in a Next Level vehicle overseeing this task from a Next Level spacecraft [Bonnie Nettles died of liver cancer in 1985]. Thus, we receive continual instructions from Ti, which we must be free to follow from moment to moment. It is therefore imperative that we live as nomadics, free to go wherever we are led on short notice.[257]

SCIENCE IN THE SERVICE OF HUMANITY?

In modern times, all it takes is one small, inconspicuous button to ignite the world and end humanity's existence. In a fraction of a second, an atomic missile releases so much energy that it can kill hundreds of thousands of people, cause severe injuries, generate harmful gamma radiation, cause serious damage to infrastructure, and even raze entire cities to the ground. It took only a few years to discover that nuclear fission had the potential to release large amounts of energy and to turn an experimental weapons program into a weapon of mass destruction. Fear of nuclear war and atomic energy undoubtedly ranks high among ideas for the End Times, but since fear of atomic power will be the focus of the next chapter, we will not address them here.

Just as it is impossible to see an atom with the naked eye, it is impossible to pinpoint the cause of an epidemic, another much-discussed vision of the end of the world. Diseases have accompanied us since the inception of our species. The transition from a nomadic to a sedentary lifestyle, rapid population growth, poor sanitary conditions, close contact with livestock, the development of trade, globalization, air transport, and the increasing concentration of people in cities all create ideal conditions for the transmission of pathogenic microorganisms.

Pandemics such as plague, smallpox, cholera, typhus, tuberculosis, the Spanish flu, Ebola, and now the coronavirus have left their mark on history. Each epidemic is potentially dangerous and has the potential to reap hundreds of thousands or even millions of human lives in the space of a few years. It is estimated that the Black Death of the 14th century claimed as many as 150 million lives worldwide, killing about 60 percent of the total population of Europe alone. The Spanish flu, which raged through the world for just two years (1918-1920), affected more than 500 million people worldwide, of whom 50 to 100 million died. HIV contributes to about one million deaths per year, and smallpox may have caused several hundred million deaths in the 20th century.

In most cases, you don't even have to have physical contact with an infected person – breathe the same air. Worst of all, people can become infected without developing any symptoms of the disease. Asymptomatic spread makes it difficult to take any action to control the epidemic. Often, no one knows how to treat or prevent the disease or how to avoid death. Everyone becomes a potential source of infection, and everyone is treated as such.

Interpersonal relationships begin to degenerate, and those we are close to can turn into strangers of sorts when infected.

Pathogenic microorganisms can be used deliberately as massive biological weapons. History already knows of such cases. Even in ancient times, contaminated clothing and the bodies of sick people were used to poison sources of drinking water during military battles. The largest medieval plague epidemic in Europe also began with the deliberate use of biological weapons. During the Tatars' siege of the city of Kaffa on the Crimean Peninsula in 1346, the attackers threw the bodies of their plague-stricken dead over the city walls, and this was enough to spread the disease throughout Europe. Biological weapons were also used during the conquest of the Americas. Indigenous people were sometimes given gifts contaminated with smallpox, including blankets that were then used to cover the sick. It is estimated that imported epidemics killed up to 95 percent of the indigenous population in those areas.[258]

During World War II, Japan's Unit 731 conducted top-secret, large-scale biological weapons research; their war crimes and human experiments are compared to those that occurred in German concentration camps. The Cold War and the arms race contributed to growing interest in these types of weapons. Still, it quickly became apparent that they were not as helpful as nuclear weapons and could even threaten the societies that held them. Therefore, a convention was passed in 1972 that banned the research, production, use, stockpiling, and acquisition of biological weapons. Of course, this convention did not prevent even those states that signed the document from continuing to work on such weapons.

Then there remains the question of madmen, criminals, and terrorists, in whose hands illegal biological agents become a tremendous threat. Here again, history provides us with interesting examples: the multiple biological attacks carried out by the Aum Shinrikyō sect described above, the neo-sannyasin sect's attempt to poison the residents of the American town of The Dalles, Oregon, and the terrorist attacks carried out after the World Trade Center attack in 2001 in which anthrax-laced letters were sent by mail to essential people and institutions such as the Senate, the U.S. Embassy in Vilnius, NBC, the *New York Times*, and Pakistan's *Daily Jang* newspaper.[259] As if that weren't enough, despite orders to destroy biological samples, the United States (in Atlanta) and Russia (in Novosibirsk) have a stockpile of smallpox viruses – just in case they ever need to use them. Of course, other samples may be stored in hidden locations unbeknownst to almost anyone, and this creates the possibility of accidentally releasing a deadly weapon that will threaten all of humanity. Additionally, scientific research is helping to decode the genome sequence of viruses; since virtually anyone can find out the order of all the amino acids that comprise them, such pathogens can technically be recreated or modified.

Let us now zoom out and examine the topic at the macro scale. The bane of our existence may also come from outer space, where many secrets and dangers dwell. Just look at the Moon, pockmarked as it is with numerous impact craters of various sizes. From the earliest years of our schooling, geography teachers tell us that the Earth is also hit regularly by objects from space, but most of them are unnoticeable, small, and burn up in the atmosphere. Still, according to the Earth Impact Database, to date, 190 impact craters have been confirmed on the surface of our planet.[260]

In 1908, an asteroid the size of a giant skyscraper disintegrated over uninhabited areas of central Siberia, north of Lake Baikal, about 10 kilometers above the Earth's surface, knocking down trees within a 40-kilometer radius. In 2013, the Chelyabinsk meteor disintegrated nearly 30 kilometers above the

Earth's surface, causing damage to more than 7,500 buildings and injuries to more than 1,500 people, primarily due to shards of glass from windows shattered by the shock wave. These two relatively well-known examples show the enormous scale of destruction caused by objects that never even touched the Earth's surface. By extension, the consequences of a collision would be monumental. Scientists believe that a celestial body about 10 kilometers in diameter struck the Earth 66 million years ago, creating the Chicxulub crater on Mexico's Yucatan Peninsula, which contributed to (if not single-handedly caused) the mass extinction event at the end of the Cretaceous period. Approximately 75 percent of all species found on Earth went extinct, including (but not exclusively) non-avian dinosaurs – animals that were uniquely adapted to life on land, in water, and in the air. The collision released vast amounts of sulfurous compounds that obscured the Sun, which led to a rapid drop in temperature and slowed photosynthesis. Admittedly, this was more than 65 million years ago, but what if it happened again in the near future? Humanity would not even have the slightest chance of survival.[261]

Another theory of cosmic annihilation was popularized in 1995 by Nancy Lieder, a self-anointed "contactee" who, per her claims on her website, receives telepathic signals from the Zeta Reticuli star system through alien genetic material implanted in her brain.[262] Lieder, whose theory is known as the "Nibiru cataclysm," contends that the actual threat to humanity is called Planet X. As she claims, the celestial body is an enormous magnet, four to five times the diameter of the Earth. As it passes our planet, its magnetic field will overpower ours. As it approaches, its north pole will be facing the Earth, and our planet's poles will move to avoid collision. The shift will occur with such violent force that the Earth's crust will move, and the core will have to realign accordingly. Then, the north and south poles will swap places.[263] In other words, believers in the Nibiru cataclysm expect that the world will turn upside down during Planet X's brush with the Earth, accompanied by earthquakes, droughts, tsunamis, and volcanic eruptions.

Astrophysicist Ethan Siegel presents the coming end of the world in a very different way. He distinguishes four stages of doom for our planet. The first is the extinction of the population due to the inevitably slow evolution of humans. In straightforward terms, all life on Earth boils down to the emergence of new species, their transformation through forced changes within living organisms, and their complete disappearance due to the inability to survive or reproduce in a given environment. This is the future of humans on Earth. In a billion or perhaps two billion years, the second stage of extinction will arrive, during which the oceans will boil. The area where nuclear fusion occurs inside the Sun is constantly expanding, increasing its brightness and the amount of solar energy produced. At some point, the amount will be so significant that once it reaches the surface of the water, the water will boil. The temperature on Earth will rise to such levels that we will not find suitable conditions for the existence of any further life on Earth. The next stage of the solar apocalypse will occur in five to seven billion years and will reduce our planet to barren rock. Hydrogen, as the driving force of the Sun, will be ultimately used up, and the core will begin to shrink, heat up, and start burning helium. Turning into a red giant, the Sun will increase in brightness and size, devouring Mercury and Venus along the way. Consequently, the Earth will be roasted, and the Sun will slowly end its life in the white dwarf stage, its exposed core cooling over time. The final, fourth stage of the Earth's destruction can unfold in several ways: the planet's skeletal remains will either be destroyed by a collision with another object from space, doomed to wander eternally in space after being gravitationally ejected from the galaxy by another entity, or absorbed by a black dwarf – the cold, exhausted, radiation-less remnant of the Sun.[264]

Prophets and alien encounters

If none of the above scenarios for the end of the world appeal to you, there are several more that are located on the frontier between science and faith.

Prophets have played and continue to play a huge role in stoking fear of the end of the world. Their task has always been primarily to communicate the will of God, explaining the past and the present, and predicting the future. One of the most globally famous prophets was Nostradamus. Many people have forecast the future, and many will do so in the future. Still, he was the historical figure who ultimately gained fame as the one who predicted, among other things, the fire of London, the French Revolution, World War II, and the assassination of John F. Kennedy. So why not assume that his prediction about the end of the world is also accurate? Nostradamus was undoubtedly an educated and knowledgeable man. He spoke many languages, including Greek, Latin, and Hebrew, studied botany, learned astrology and occult practices, traveled, studied medicine, and used ancient natural healing methods. His career as the supreme visionary began with a successful prediction about King Henry II of France.[265]

> The young lion will overcome the older one,
> In a field of combat in single fight,
> He will pierce his eyes in their golden cage,
> Two wounds in one, then he dies a cruel death.[266]

Indeed, the King of France was killed during a jousting tournament by Count Montgomery, who was younger than him. His opponent's broken lance pierced the king's golden helmet, entering the back wall of his eye socket. After ten days, the king died as a result of sepsis, which was practically untreatable at the time. It seemed that Nostradamus' prediction had come true.

How did the prophet see the end of our existence? Initial interpretations of his prophecies led to the conclusion that 1999 would be humankind's final year. The end of the world was to come as a result of a lunar or solar eclipse, an attack by a Soviet space probe, the second coming of Jesus and the Last Judgment, the destruction of Paris and London, an invasion by an Islamic leader, a battle between God and the Antichrist, a meteor shower, nuclear war, or the outbreak of World War III. Whatever the vehicle of destruction, it was inevitable that the cataclysm would spare few lives.[267]

> The year 1999, seventh month
> From the sky will come a great King of Terror
> To bring back to life the great King of the Mongols,
> Before and after Mars to reign by good luck.[268]

After the prediction failed, it came back in full force after September 11, 2001, when it was reframed as presaging the attack on the World Trade Center.[269] Today, those who believe in Nostradamus' prophecies claim he placed the end of the world in the year 3797 – his last prophecy – and claim that the catalyst will be the outbreak of World War III, initiated by an attack on New York City. These events are to be preceded by a series of economic, spiritual, ecological, and social disasters, such as the assassination of the Pope, the coming of the third Antichrist (after Napoleon and Hitler), the collapse of Christianity, the breakdown of social relations, terrorism, gravitational disturbances, meteor showers, great floods and fires, climate change, the evaporation of the oceans, and nuclear and biological warfare.[270]

Of course, the end of the world can and has been associated with intelligent extraterrestrial threats. Outside our solar system, there are many stars similar to the Sun and many planets similar to the Earth. And if there is life here, why shouldn't there be life on other planets? The universe is too large for the Earth to be the only planet to host intelligent life.

While no life has been found in space so far, that does not automatically mean that there is no life there at all. But if there is, do we really want to find it? As Elisabeth and Mark Neila write, "Governments do not care to confirm the existence of extraterrestrial civilizations, as this could significantly change the way we think about the Universe, not to mention the fact that people would have to reject a selfish vision of themselves as the only chosen rational beings in the world . . . Then there is the Church, which probably does not care much about confirming the existence of rational alien civilizations either."[271] In addition, could well-known and respected celebrities such as Muhammad Ali, Victoria Beckham, Tom Cruise, Mick Jagger, Will Smith, and Robbie Williams be lying when they say they have seen UFOs? Could hundreds of similar descriptions depicting spacecraft sightings and alien encounters be the figments of the imaginations of ordinary people?

Let us consider what the end of the world could look like if it were to be wrought upon us by extraterrestrials. The age of the Universe is estimated at nearly 14 billion years, while the Earth is only 4.5 billion years old. Therefore, any alien civilization that mounts an invasion of our planet must be at a much higher level of civilizational development than humans; after all, we are incapable of and insufficiently advanced to carry out the invasion of another planet. Going further, if aliens do reach the Earth, they will probably do so using some awe-inspiring vehicle that can travel faster than the speed of light, which would dynamite all of the laws of physics that we know. How could we possibly oppose such a force? If their vehicles use technologies that we did not believe were possible, what about their weapons? We can't imagine what they might have, and the defense of our planet would likely be akin to throwing rocks at tanks rather than a natural, balanced struggle.

Furthermore, considering that for centuries, some cultures have sought to eliminate others and that the winners are usually not more advanced but rather more aggressive (take Genghis Khan and the Khwarazmian Empire as examples), we must assume that the human race would come to an end. To claim that we will triumph in our defense against such an extraterrestrial foe would be to embrace a naïve belief. We can attempt to negotiate, but what are the chances that the aliens will listen to us? There will be chaos among humans, the boundaries between Americans, Europeans, and Africans will collapse, and there will be only Earthlings at the mercy of their new extraterrestrial overlords.

Another alien-related theory on how humanity might end involves an insidious, ongoing colonization of the Earth by visitors from other worlds. The first recorded case of alleged alien contact, or rather an alien abduction of humans, is that of Betty and Barney Hill in 1961. The Hills claimed they had been stopped by a UFO during an overnight trip in their car and abducted by unknown beings. According to their account, they were subjected to medical experiments on board the ship and subsequently released. Neither of them had any memory of the incident except the landing of the ship until they refreshed their memory with hypnosis. Since then, the "alien abduction syndrome" – the personally held conviction that extraterrestrials have abducted a person – has followed nearly the same story and still arouses considerable controversy.[272]

THE FINAL COUNTDOWN: 100 DOOMSDAYS, 100 REASONS TO FEAR

If you are reading this, then the end of the world has not happened yet, and you are still alive. That is excellent news. Newspapers, the internet, social media, and news channels bombard us time and time again with insight into when and how our lives will end. Earthquakes, volcanic eruptions, asteroid impacts, zombie attacks, nuclear war, and rebellious artificial intelligence systems routinely receive coverage as threats to our very existence. Of course, the predictions of all sorts of "experts" do not appear out of thin air. Many of them are supported by diligent calculations and exhaustive reviews of secret codes embedded in holy books, others are predicted by observing the sky and the cosmos, and still others emerge in the form of visions inspired by extraterrestrials or directly triggered by purported alien contact. Here, even more good news awaits: to date, no prophet has managed to pinpoint the day the world will end correctly.

It is impossible to come up with an exact count of the dates that have been indicated so far as potential Armageddons. The complete list is extremely dynamic, and it is futile to try to explore the full breadth and depth of the predictions, mainly since many of them have stayed local and never received wider exposure. Nevertheless, for this chapter, we were able to track down approximately 360, counting from the beginning of our era to the year 2020. A table with a selection of a hundred predicted ends of the world can be found in the appendix at the end of the book.

Statistically, this gives us one prediction every 5.5 years or so. The average American can expect to live 78.9 years; the average German or Englishman 81.2 years; the average Australian 83.3 years; and the average Japanese national 84.5 years.[273] Assuming that a person will live an average of about 80 years, that means they will experience 15 ends of the world in their lifetime. This is not too many, considering that the number of predictions has increased with each century. In this respect, the most fruitful period was the turn of the new millennium – that is, 1999 and 2000.

Considering who has been making predictions about the end of the world, you might think that everyone would be up to the task. All you have to do is find an excuse, set a date, and add an evocative background to the story, whether based on global events or calculations that even the prophet does not need to understand. Once doomsday comes and goes, it becomes necessary, as has happened very often in history, to (a) admit the mistake and set a new date, (b) declare that the prophecy was fulfilled and support it with examples from around the world, where natural disasters happened at precisely the right moment, (c) state that the events in question were not physical, but somewhat spiritual, and those who experienced them are already on a higher plane of existence, or (d) end your fortune-telling career.

Over the years and with the development of scientific thought, more contemporary predictions have been based on knowledge than on faith. Today's predictions for the future are primarily hypotheses based on scientific discoveries and theories. Professor Anthony Aveni states that:

> The medium for conveying the divine message also has changed. The complex mathematical calculations behind fixing the date of the end of the world were worked out with pen and paper . . . Today the revealed word is conveyed via the Internet – that leveling agent of legitimacy – and via film media. Scientific-sounding warnings of fire in the Earth and erupting volcanoes . . . are replaced by today's magnetic field reversals, sunspots, and planetary and galactic alignments.[274]

Ultimately, it is extraordinary that, even though all the holy scriptures underscore that no one knows the day or hour of the Last Judgment, many members of the clergy and religious organizations that base their entire faith on these scriptures often point to a specific date for the end of the world, claiming they are the true keepers of this arcane knowledge.

It's (Not) the End of the World

You probably have mixed feelings after reading this far into this chapter. On the one hand, your head may be spinning with questions: Are these people crazy? Are they the chosen few? Are they incorrigible visionaries who have learned a supposed inscrutable truth? Or perhaps we are simply talking about charismatic leaders with mental disorders who strive for fame, recognition, and wealth?

On the other hand, you may wonder if what they have said over the centuries carries more than a grain of truth. After all, we read newspapers, watch the news, and see that the world we observe around us is constantly changing, often not for the better. Add a cocktail of worldly woes such as social, political, and economic crises, poverty, and natural disasters verified by studies published by eminent scientists from all over the world, and we may conclude that maybe we really are approaching doomsday. Whom should we trust? Where should we seek knowledge? Regrettably, we cannot delve into all these questions in this section. However, I will try to soothe your mind and persuade you that the disaster we fear is not as terrible as it may seem.

A Game of Faith

Let us start with religion. Faith holds great power, and in the hands of unaccountable people, it can prove to be very dangerous. As long as we are talking about a handful of self-proclaimed visionaries who seek the truth about the end of the world at any cost by cracking codes purportedly contained in the holy books, we can afford to pay them no mind. But some among them take pains to turn the prophecies they developed into reality, and that is where things get thornier.

Building our fear of the end of the world on religious foundations is somewhat problematic. First, the belief in gods, deities, and supernatural forces has existed since the beginning of our species. In fact, religion is instilled in us in the first years of our lives by our loved ones, and we accept its principles, take them for granted, and submit to them. It is only later, in adulthood, that a small number of us independently verify the religious beliefs that we have learned from our parents and stand up for what we really believe. The remaining majority preserves their faith until they die. At this point, perhaps without even knowing it, many probably make a choice based on Pascal's famous wager that if one must choose between faith and lack of faith, it is better to choose faith. If God really exists, then the believer will attain eternal life by devoting only a small portion of their mortal life to prayer, so the risks run low. The alternative is much more sordid.[275] Second, no one who has died has risen from the dead and told us whether there is an afterlife. Thus, we don't know for sure, but we believe it just in case. The apocalypse follows a similar mental trajectory: no one has experienced it and reported back, so we don't know for sure that it will happen – but we believe it will because the belief is inscribed in the holy books and fostered in us by the clergy, self-proclaimed and often very convincing prophets and other members of our community.

To take a somewhat more objective approach, in principle, we should not be surprised that people feel fear when reading religious texts. Virtually all of them portray the end of the world as a tragic event that will bring an end to all things temporal. They are filled with vivid descriptions of the bloody struggle of evil against good, the destruction of the world, the disruption of the natural order, great suffering and oppression, and all sorts of cataclysms that rain down on the Earth. These descriptions, enriched by ever more works of art and cinematic megahits featuring dazzling special effects crafted by Hollywood film studios, strongly affect our imaginations, intensifying the fear of a new, unknown, unexplored phenomenon. This is only fueled by the fact that no one has experienced a catastrophe of this kind to date. But new artistic creations are not the only vehicles of this messaging.

A good example is the series of 15 woodcuts titled *Apocalipsis cum figuris*, created by Albrecht Dürer in the 15th century and considered to be one of the most outstanding works of European art. Equally significant is the fresco depicting the Last Judgment on the altar wall in the Sistine Chapel, created by Michelangelo in the 16th century. The fresco portrays Jesus as a judge surrounded by a heavenly order of righteous souls ascending to heaven, which stretches above an Earth swarming with a chaotic mass of human bodies being thrown into the abyss of Hell.

Yet we must recall that apocalyptic visions of the end of the world should not be read literally. The language of symbols plays a vital role in all these depictions, often retaining highly mystical, esoteric, and ambiguous qualities. One symbol can take on several meanings, and several symbols can refer to a single thing. Despite this, religious visions of the end of the world are still deeply entrenched in many people's consciousness. Of course, one must not forget that these visions expect severe punishment to be meted out to sinners. Frightened by their earthly guides, sinners become more obedient and put in their best effort to attain the honor of entering the Kingdom of God:

> The end of the world was first predicted for the year 1000. Mankind, shrouded in the darkness of the

> Middle Ages, fanaticized and rendered insensible by the vapid clergy of the time, exercised extreme piety for months before the expected Day of Judgment, repented, and bequeathed their estates and priceless jewels to the monasteries. The end of the world did not come, nor did the Church's legations lose their legal force.[276]

Fear is a powerful trigger of fervent faith and increases our level of reverence for the deity we believe in, while supernatural figures and events we can hardly fathom create feelings of terror in the face of divine wrath. The fear of God's wrath, of pervasive evil, and the end of the world lends itself perfectly to being used in this "game of faith."[277]

It is unlikely that a religiously motivated fear of the end of the world will ever be disproved. Fervent believers will not disavow it because their faith derives from emotions and the needs of the heart, not necessarily from reason. Those who harbor doubts or feel lost in what they believe and what they fear might experience a slightly different path. Since people are social creatures, they default to looking for others with similar problems who can help them out of such existential quandaries. In some cases, they turn to sects and cults whose charismatic leaders paint themselves as sources of support and relief, which is precisely what the lost souls were missing. Suddenly, their problems are no longer problems; they put their complete faith in their new mission on Earth and are ready to sacrifice their lives to fulfill it. They are born again as devout believers, but this time, they are not waiting for the end of the world like the rest of us but instead want to make it happen. Unfortunately, history shows that craving the apocalypse can cause people to trigger times of turmoil, and they are perfectly capable of doing so without the intervention of a divine force or other supernatural being. Belief in the prophesied end of the world has only led to tragedy and suffering for the loved ones and families of those who died in one of its many supposed iterations while padding the bank accounts of their spiritual shepherds.

THE PANDEMIC OF FEAR

Global diseases are another catalyst of fear. Epidemics are an inherent component of human life on Earth, whatever their geographic range. At this very moment, each square centimeter of the skin on your hand is swarming with tens of thousands or even several millions of bacteria cells, and you suffer no harmful effects because most of them belong to the physiological microflora of the skin. Even if some undesirable pathogen appears within it, this does not immediately mean that we are a step away from a global pandemic. To eliminate the danger, all we need to do is wash our hands with soap and water for 30 seconds, which allows us to get rid of pathogenic microorganisms completely. You must admit that this is not a particularly demanding task.

Fortunately, we also have our immune system waging a perennial war against attacking intruders. In the history of humankind, medical advances have allowed us to dispatch previous pandemics effectively, so there is no reason to assume that we will fail to find a way the next time around. Unfortunately, it takes time – and sometimes scores of victims – before we see a remedy for the disease and a vaccine to prevent the spread of the disease, but in principle, we are able to do it. Science is constantly evolving. New research is being conducted, better technologies are emerging, more effective drugs and vaccines are being produced, and the Internet, mass communication, and globalization facilitate and foster the exchange of views and experiences of scientists from all over the world. All of these dynamics only sharpen our capacity to respond.

Improved sanitation and hygiene, combined with increased

public awareness, are also non-trivial. Medieval Europe did not know antibiotics, so it took a long time before the cause of one of the most effective mass killers in history – the plague – was definitively established. Medieval physicians attempted to treat plague patients with herbs, poultices, and bloodletting while advising terrified patients to flee to safety and immerse themselves in prayer, as one theory held that the plague was God's punishment for their sins. Today, thanks to cooperation between governments, trained personnel, rapid technological progress, and medical advances, we can gain a much quicker understanding of specific facts about diseases. It took several years to identify the AIDS pathogen, but only a few weeks to identify the pathogen responsible for the severe acute respiratory syndrome (SARS) outbreak of 2003. In rapid succession, scientists determined its cause, tracked its spread, and decoded the genome of the virus, which enabled rapid coordinated action to stem the epidemic.

But viruses carry another risk – the risk of being deliberately used as biological weapons, which could also bring us closer to the extinction of the human species. Let us remember, however, that the threat of bioterrorism is not high due to the technical difficulties involved in such attacks, the need to work in secrecy, the barriers to obtaining pathogenic microorganisms, the need for specialized knowledge and equipment for mass production, the danger to the attackers themselves, and the low level of precision that is possible in striking a specific target. These factors combined explain the small number of cases in which biological weapons have been used to date. According to the National Defense University, there have been only 180 cases of illegal use of biological weapons in the 20th century, of which only 21 involved such weapons actually being deployed. The vast majority is composed of threats to use, such as them or simply false alarms.[278]

The pandemic of fear of a doomsday event triggered by

some infectious disease is continuously fueled from all sides. On the one hand, we have numerous biblical descriptions of plagues, beginning with the plagues of Egypt and ending with the plagues that are supposed to be delivered in the Apocalypse. On the other hand, the media, state institutions, and even the World Health Organization, engage in a manner of reporting on successive epidemics that severely exacerbates the fear about what is to come.

Cosmic deception

The fear of annihilation by forces from outer space is also unfounded. The Earth was formed 4.5 billion years ago and has been hit by objects from space on a fairly regular basis ever since, but impacts by things that have real global implications are extremely rare. According to experts, on average, an object the size of a grain of sand approaches the Earth every 30 seconds. This is what we observe when we watch shooting stars sail across the night sky. As the size of the objects increases, the average time between their collisions with the Earth also increases. It is estimated that an object with a diameter of 1 meter falls to the Earth once a year, one with a diameter of 100 meters falls once every 10,000 years, and an object with a diameter of 10 kilometers reaches us every 100 million years. Only objects with a diameter of at least 1 kilometer could have a global impact, but they hit the Earth once in a million years, on average.[279]

Of course, there are potential threats to us and our planet lurking in the Solar System and beyond, as there are many unexplored and even undiscovered celestial bodies out there. Indeed, it's just a matter of time before we will find out what other phantom menace lies in the endless void of space. But whatever the threat, we can be sure that it is not Planet X. Why? Because there is no reliable evidence that such a body even exists. Amateur pictures purported to show it are taken with very low-quality cameras and are not fit for thorough analysis. The results often indicate that the alleged Planet X is just a reflection on the lens. Moreover, as NASA pointed out in the wake of the 2012 end-of-the-world commotion, if the planet were visible to the naked eye, astronomers with specialized equipment would have quickly discovered it long ago. There is also no scientific basis for believing that some mysterious planet might be interfering with the orbits of other worlds, as the effects of such an interference would be easy to observe and prove today.

The notion that a passing planet could cause a physical change in the Earth's poles is also the stuff of fiction. Supporters of this theory erroneously associate it with the reversal of the Earth's magnetic field, which has indeed occurred in the past and is unlikely to happen again in the next few thousand years.[280] The date of our destruction by Planet X is constantly being postponed, and supporters of this theory are busier preparing for its arrival than seeking hard evidence to verify its very existence.

Most times, we fear what we do not understand and often what we cannot control. Both of these statements prove true in the case of cosmic-scale events, which serve as excellent vectors for the hypothetical destruction of life on Earth. On top of that, the discovery of more and more large celestial bodies stimulates our imagination and keeps us in a state of fear of what might come. But even if the Earth will die in a few billion years, do we really not have more severe worries? By that time, our species will have long since evolved beyond recognition or become extinct. In the meantime, we will have copious opportunities to annihilate ourselves through our stupidity, national selfishness, or simple lack of imagination.[281] Of course, there is also a chance that, in the meantime, we will find a way to move to other previously uninhabited parts of space.

In 2016, NASA established a particular unit under the Planetary Defense Coordination Office whose tasks include early detection, tracking, warning, and response to potentially hazardous objects such as asteroids or comets with a diameter of 30 to 50 meters that orbit close to Earth, that is, within a radius of no more than 5 million miles from Earth's orbit.[282] This project is part of NASA's more extensive Near-Earth Object Observations Program, which aims to find, track, and characterize even larger objects. Currently, these are objects that are 140 meters and more significant in diameter within 30 million miles of our planet's orbit.[283] To date, 23,846 near-Earth objects have been discovered, the vast majority of which are asteroids.[284] Just over 2,000 objects have been identified as potentially hazardous celestial bodies that might eventually come dangerously close to the Earth. Still, they account for less than 9 percent of all cases. Once again, thanks to our scientific, technical, and technological progress, we observe the sky more rapidly, more thoroughly, and in ever-higher resolution, and we can take specific actions to neutralize a potential threat from space. Thus, we do not have the slightest reason to fear a celestial body colliding with our planet, mainly since we will detect any such object far in advance.

SHOW ME YOUR HAND, AND I WILL TELL YOU THE FUTURE

"Some new information about an interesting field could have you browsing the web and looking through books to learn more about cancer. This could involve law, philosophy, history, or spirituality. You could find so much that you want to take notes or make a lot of photocopies. Don't tire yourself out, and try to keep track of time. You might miss dinner or get to bed very late."[285] This is one of many daily online horoscopes. It is always lovely to hear that we can expect a good day ahead. It is also handy to know what decisions we should make to ensure the best future for ourselves and when we should make those decisions. However, upon closer inspection, it is easy to see that this horoscope is virtually devoid of content. It is impossible to tell whether it is true or false. So why do we read it and accept it as truth when we are aware that it constitutes the essence of superstition?

Scientists have observed this effect since the first half of the 20th century. In 1948, Bertram Forer conducted an interesting experiment on his students. Their task was to complete a personality test, based on which a psychologist would give each of them a personalized interpretation of the results. When asked to evaluate the accuracy of his analysis, the students gave him a score of 4.26 on a 5-point scale, where 0 meant very low accuracy, and 5 meant very high accuracy. In fact, all the students were given the same set – 13 generic statements about human personalities drawn from an astrology book:

> 1. You have a great need for other people to like and admire you. 2. You have a tendency to be critical of yourself. You have a great deal of unused capacity which you have not turned to your advantage. While you have some personality weaknesses, you are generally able to compensate for them. 5. Your sexual adjustment has presented problems for you. The most common problem is that you are not able to compensate for it, but you are able to do so. At times you have serious doubts as to whether you have made the right decision or done the right thing. 8. You prefer a certain amount of change and variety and become dissatisfied when hemmed in by restrictions and limitations. 9. You pride yourself as an independent thinker and do not accept others' statements without satisfactory proof. 10. You have found it unwise to be too frank in revealing yourself to others. 11. At times you are extroverted, affable, sociable, while at other times you are introverted, wary, reserved. Some

> of your aspirations tend to be pretty unrealistic. 13. Security is one of your major goals in life.[286]

In this way, Forer confirmed, among other things, that the human brain tends to look for information that will confirm its views and that we accept general sets of characteristics that apply to a broad group of people as truth. This phenomenon is now known as the Forer effect, after the scientist who discovered it.

The same is true of prophecies and their tendency to be viewed as fulfilled by those who believe in them. The vast majority are formulated comprehensively, often inspired by well-known events, and written by cautious observers of reality. Ray Comfort puts it bluntly:

> I decided to delve into the famous prophecies of Nostradamus. After comprehensive study, I began to see a peculiar pattern. Nostradamus warned that the future would bring signs in the sun. Interestingly enough, so does the Bible. He forewarned of earthquakes. So does the Bible. He spoke of the earth being round. So does the Bible. He warned of a coming world leader - the anti-Christ. So does the Bible. He speaks of the dead coming out of their graves. So does the Bible. He prophesied that the Jews would get Israel back. So does the Bible. To my amazement, I uncovered documented evidence that Nostradamus read the Scriptures in secret, stole Bible prophecies and claimed them as his own. That's why he is so famous. Anyone who is ignorant of Bible prophecy will be impressed with the prophecies of Nostradamus.[287]

Nostradamus's "Centuries," or groupings of prophecies, are so ambiguous that anyone can match them with countless past and future events. This makes them highly malleable, manipulable, and primed for retroactive application. It is also easy enough to predict specific broad trends in the world, including perpetual conflicts between countries over land, resources, markets, or ideologies. This is a constant cycle, an endless rollercoaster of humanity's ups and downs, of peace and war between states. Moreover, the original writings of Nostradamus have not survived, and we can only rely on works distorted by transpositions, changes in spelling and punctuation, typographical errors, and even forgery. With all this in mind, interpreting his prophecies becomes a monumental challenge. Successive translations and interpretations over hundreds of years have imbued his visions – recorded in the form of unrhymed poems, four verses each – with a wide variety of meanings. The quatrains were written in French, Latin, and other languages, shuffled around to blur their chronology, and permeated with anagrams, obscure terminology, and coded versions of places, names, and dates.[288] Nostradamus's work was written after the loss of his wife and two children in a plague epidemic – undoubtedly a harrowing experience. According to some, it was written: "on pieces of paper during trance sessions, mostly in the middle of the night and with the help of occult magic and large quantities of nutmeg, which affects the body and mind in a way similar to modern ecstasy drugs – though the quantities of nutmeg required were ingested over long periods and in enormous amounts."[289] Do the predictions of Nostradamus still come across as reliable in light of these revelations?

Now, let us tackle another one of the prophecies described above – the one about the 112 popes. It is generally accepted that the list is a Renaissance forgery created in 1590 – 451 years after the purported date of its creation – to suggest a "suitable" candidate for the papacy to the conclave. Cardinal Girolamo

Simoncelli of Orvieto (Latin: *Urbs Vetus*, meaning Old City) is believed to be the actual author of the prophecy, purportedly identifying himself as the 75th pope, associated with the motto "*De antiquitate Urbis*," or "From the ancient city." Ultimately, despite the prediction, Simoncelli was not elected to the papal office. Malachy, on the other hand, is revered in the Church as a man who could predict the future, and given that he had stayed in Rome between 1139 and 1141, he was the perfect potential author of the prophecy.[290] Again, upon closer examination, we see that the descriptions of the popes are so general, laconic, and ambiguous (often comprising two or three words) that they are entirely open to interpretation. For example, the term "glory of the olive" could be matched with practically any pope, as in liturgical symbolism, olive oil is associated with the Holy Spirit – and the Spirit, after all, chooses the successor of St. Peter through the cardinals in the conclave. It could just as well apply to a cardinal who comes from Italy, a country where olive trees are abundant; a Hispanic with olive skin; a Dominican whose monastery is located among olive trees; or a black cardinal, as olives can take on darker hues. But then again, an individual with a dark complexion or a cardinal from the East could technically be described with the words "from the labor of the Sun." Leaving aside the fact that the prophecy is a forgery, this is another illustration of the Forer effect: we accept a generic term as accurate, and our brain finds some explanation for it that reinforces our belief that it is true.

Furthermore, lest we forget, prophecies and the activities surrounding them can bring considerable financial benefits. Consider the example of Poland. Astrologers and fortune tellers are both in the Polish government's official registry of professions. They provide personal services, just like tour guides, cooks, waiters, bartenders, hairdressers, salespersons, firefighters, or driving instructors. The astrologer's duties include: "giving opinions on selected matters, problems, predispositions, and events relating to an individual or society, to a given moment, year, or age, on the basis of the alignment of the planets of the solar system and the stars; to draw up horoscopes; to advise on specific matters, such as the choice of a life or business partner, favorable moments for a transaction, the use of talents or professional opportunities, etc." The fortune teller's duties are outlined as follows: "making statements about the future or past relating to people or events; giving advice about missing persons or things; using methods appropriate to astrology, numerology, psychographics, among others."

On the one hand, one can argue that this is a profession like any other, which allows those who exercise it to earn income from the services provided. On the other hand, giving legal force to an activity that contributes to beliefs in superstitions defies common sense. There is reason to believe that Nostradamus, too, may have undertaken to provide such services for profit: "[Nostradamus] set up for a gift that he did not possess, and soon found the imposture was far more lucrative than the dull routine of medical practice, as in those times the superstition of the public was unlimited. The ignorance of the Middle Ages is pointedly contrasted for us now with the wisdom and knowledge of our day."[291]

Nowadays, in the age of the Internet and social media, the number of likes, shares, comments, and page views one receives has become extremely important. Therefore, it is hardly surprising that aspiring global influencers have taken to making new predictions or modifying existing ones to boost their popularity. Regrettably, the COVID-19 pandemic is a excellent contemporary example of this. Outlandish theories that the pandemic had been predicted in 1551 by none other than Nostradamus circulated online from the very outset of the crisis.

Of course, it is easy to mock and ridicule predictions that

failed in the past from the vantage point of the present. When the forecast is made, especially when its disseminators are prominent and influential, it is common practice to bake in a hint of uncertainty about tomorrow. However, we should be conscious of the tricks that self-proclaimed prophets have used in the past, continue to use today, and probably will use in the future:

- Countless predictions: perhaps one of them will come true, and then it can be amplified and deemed a great success. People tend to remember the hits more than they do the misses, so it doesn't really matter how often the prophet is wrong;
- Vague and ambiguous statements that can be assigned an appropriate interpretation in the future, using phrases such as "it could be that," "I feel that," "perhaps," etc.;
- An overabundance of symbols that can be adapted to many things and situations;
- Claiming that their prophecies are a message from God, and the prophet can, at worst, misinterpret them, which makes them less effective and prone to error;
- Predicting disasters that are common and easy to predict and remember;
- Providing little detail when they predict an event after it has already occurred – otherwise, they might arouse suspicion.[292]

Uninvited guests

The fear of an apocalypse initiated by an alien invasion is also unjustified. In fact, there is no scientific evidence whatsoever – nothing that can be seen, measured, touched, felt, or smelled – that could objectively verify the hypothesis. Skeptics who doubt the existence of extraterrestrials would probably be persuaded by evidence in the form of a UFO landing on the front lawn of the White House, in the middle of Red Square, or a central square of even a mid-sized city. There are also no photographs that depict aliens, and the current appearance of aliens described by abductees appeared after 1961, following the heavily publicized case of the Hills. Before that, aliens were green human-like creatures, then creatures with a beautiful human appearance, and later even hairy dwarfs. All of this may be rooted in our tendency to imitate television images, the written word, and radio messages that have become firmly entrenched in people's collective consciousness.[293]

Where do we go from here? Astronomers who spend all day and night scrutinizing the sky have never seen an alien spacecraft, yet reports of flying saucers have circulated since ancient times. Modern science has dealt with this problem and convincingly explained previously unexplainable astronomical and weather phenomena, indicating that what people thought were UFOs were actually celestial bodies, satellites, meteorites, probes, kites, rockets, clouds, light, and other optical phenomena, or the hallucinations and visions of fanatics. Nor do we have any objects, records, or traces that would unequivocally point to the presence of extraterrestrials. We could also speculate that alleged alien abductees tend to have mental problems, but psychologists have not observed a higher-than-average propensity for such disorders among this group. Instead, they noted that what connects them is low self-esteem, and they are more prone to daydreaming, have a more vivid imagination, and can temporarily lose touch with reality more readily than others.

In addition, our perception, memory, and vision are far from perfect, and people may only think something happened when, in fact, it did not. By opting for hypnosis, which often manipulates human memory, they wonder if it even actually happened. What's more, accounts of being "taken" by aliens can be linked to what is known as sleep paralysis, in which the muscles are paralyzed and unpleasant mental sensations and hallucinations of various kinds can occur.[294] Susan Clancy, a Harvard psychologist, notes that faith and popular culture also play a considerable role, as "nobody reported being abducted before they actually saw it on TV or in the movies" and "in the same way that people find meaning in their religious beliefs and experiences, these people find meaning in their alien abduction beliefs and their alien abduction experiences."[295] In the end, can we really believe that, if we were to observe something that provided irrefutable proof of the existence of extraterrestrials, it would be kept secret? After all, the discovery of something so extraordinary would undoubtedly be a big deal!

We all await something

But what if it is not the end of the world that we fear, but rather the feeling of being powerless to predict when it will happen and to prepare for our final day as best we can? Who among us has not eagerly awaited Friday, our next payday, or another event imbued with its unique meaning? Just like the end of the world, these moments contain a promise that, at some point in time, something better awaits us and that it will be its breakthrough of sorts. Recalling the words of the fox from his conversation with the Little Prince:

> If, for example, you come at four o'clock in the afternoon, then at three o'clock I shall begin to be happy. I shall feel happier and happier as the hour advances. At four o'clock, I shall already be worrying and jumping about. I shall show you how happy I am! But if you come at just any time, I shall never know at what

> hour my heart is to be ready to greet you . . . One must observe the proper rites . . . [296]

The fox's point about the anxiety of being unable to make a prediction is highly relevant, even in the context of the end of the world. We yearn to know the day and the hour so that we can best prepare to make our final stand, whether physically (by finding shelter, water, food, and other resources that will help us survive) or spiritually (through confession, prayer, or making up for wrongs we have committed). In truth, we will probably never know the actual date. Fear of the end of the world, whether triggered by an alien invasion or any other event, affects the socio-economic lives of not only individuals but often larger groups of people as well.

Monetizing the End of the World

All believers in the various theories of the end of the world have one thing in common: a profound belief, bordering on conviction, that they are the ones who will survive the coming cataclysm. Consequently, they take every step imaginable to ensure that this happens. The will to survive and live in a post-apocalyptic world can be seen most clearly in the measures they take to provide shelter for themselves and their loved ones. Some religious organizations hold annual gatherings for their members to prepare for the horrors of the Great Tribulation. Another popular option is to build shelters with stockpiles of equipment: water supplies, food and medicine, communication equipment, air filters, and more. South Dakota boasts a neighborhood with 575 private bunkers that were used initially as an ordnance depot. Today, they are a potential shelter for 5,000 people. One of the largest shelters in the world is located in Rothenstein, Germany, and includes 34 private apartments in addition to a common area. This shelter was used as a storage facility for military equipment and ammunition during the Cold War, after which it was converted into a huge bunker with over 5 kilometers of interconnected tunnel chambers.[297] Another equally famous nuclear shelter called Ark Two is located in Horning Mill, Ontario. It can accommodate up to 500 people. Interestingly, it was built using 42 school buses, which were then poured over with concrete and covered with soil. According to the shelter's designer, children would be the intended occupants of the Ark, as they would be able to rebuild society after the apocalypse.[298]

Social isolation can be another repercussion of our fear of doomsday. Those around them may perceive people who are passionate about a particular end-of-the-world theory as having a mental disorder. Such individuals often lose their jobs, become increasingly alienated from family and friends, and even spiral into depression. They try to find others who think the same way, have had similar experiences, and will help them find their way through a complicated reality. This situation creates ideal conditions for the creation and growth of sects. What is more, if the sect is apocalyptic, it may strive to bring about the end of the world at any cost, which may lead to murder or collective suicide.

One can also seek help in online forums, social media, support groups, social movements, or even with scientists themselves. One good example is NASA's Ask an Astrobiologist website. The peak volume of inquiries submitted to this website came before the purported end of the world in 2012. Dr. David Morrison, who led the agency's efforts to control public anxiety about the impending apocalypse, received more than 5,000 emails inquiring about doomsday. Here are two of them: [299]

> I know that everyone has been asking you the same question, but how do I know the world is not going to end by a planet or a flood or something? I'm scared because I'm in 10th grade and I have a full life ahead

> of me so PLEASE I WOULD REALLY LIKE AN ANSWER TO MY QUESTION.

> I am really scared about the end of the world on 21 December. I'm headed into 7th grade and I am very scared. I hear you work for the government and I don't know what to do. Can someone help me? I can't sleep, I am crying every day, I can't eat, I stay in my room, I go to a councilor, it helps, but not with this problem. Can someone help me?

In a radio interview, he described the kind of people from whom he received these messages.

> They include some young people who say they're contemplating suicide. A friend of mine, a teacher in Stockton, had two parents come saying they were planning to kill themselves and their children before December 21st. And another extreme one; the early questions I got was quite touching. It was: My only friend is my little dog. When should I put her to sleep so she won't suffer in the cataclysm?[300]

Fear of the end of the world and how to deal with it is also a widely discussed issue on Internet platforms. Anxiety-laced reactions have led to the creation and development of new professions, including ufologists and bunker maintenance personnel. Some of them, in an effort to increase demand for their services and products, are cranking up and fomenting fears of the apocalypse. The effects of their activities on the market are plain to see: people buy up candles and flashlights to guide them through the approaching darkness; they stockpile food, water, and medicine (just think back to the beginning of the COVID-

19 pandemic, when grocery stores ran out of food and toilet paper); they launch flash sales of electronic equipment for the end of the world (as was the case with the German multinational consumer electronics chain Media Markt); they promote products such as Armageddon-themed beer; they manufacture "thought-screen helmets" made of Velostat and marketed as a means of defense against alien telepathy; they churn out souvenirs such as t-shirts, caps, and mugs; they organize concerts, shows, and performances to commemorate our final destruction; they coordinate "survival adventures" (for example, the 2012 Survival and Revival Group trip cost 10,000 euros per person); they build bunkers (the average cost of a 200-square-foot shelter, usually excluding transportation and installation costs, is about $50-60,000, but customizing it to your preferences can cost several million USD); and they collect donations for awareness campaigns, of which the most famous, led by Harold Camping, cost more than $100 million.[301]

Likewise, we should not forget that the obsession with the end of the world is also a bonanza for the tourism industry. People choose a place to visit because it may be the last trip of their lives; some go on pilgrimages to religious sites; others see areas once inhabited by the Maya civilization, places where UFOs have been sighted, and crop circles or other paranormal phenomena have been observed. Additionally, the places that various prophecies claim will be spared from the flames of doom experience significant increases in real estate prices. Books, movies, and other cultural products become bestsellers due to the apocalyptic themes they proudly tout. Books about Nostradamus are perennial favorites; the Roland Emmerich-directed disaster film *2012*, bursting with special effects, earned almost $800 million on a $200-million budget. Other examples include television shows about preppers – people who prepare for various complex circumstances, including the end of the world.

The National Geographic Channel, for instance, has broadcast a series of specials titled *Doomsday Preppers*.

Such media messaging plays an influential role in shaping people's ideas about the end of the world. Indeed, in life we imitate art and vice versa, and the narratives we adopt are based on the experiences and emotions we undergo when we absorb them. We should always treat them with a grain of salt when we consume them, knowing that their primary purpose is to provide viewers with intellectual entertainment and force them to reflect on a given topic – not to tell a truthful story about the future, which is how we sometimes perceive them.

THE MYTH IN THE NUMBERS

We should stop and ask ourselves: Has the myth of the end of the world been broken? As indicated earlier, the end of the world was supposed to happen on at least 360 different days identified by past prophets. Given that it is impossible to reach all sources, the actual number of prophecies and dates is undoubtedly higher. New prophecies continued to emerge, providing tangible proof that the issue is alive and well in our minds. One look at a list of books and movies with an apocalyptic theme is enough to see that Armageddon is also a hot topic among artists. On Amazon alone, the search term "Nostradamus" brings up more than 2,000 books. More than 330 apocalyptic films can be found on the Internet, more than a hundred of which were made in the last decade. Since 1947, the board of the Bulletin of the Atomic Scientists at the University of Chicago has maintained a symbolic "Doomsday Clock" that counts down the time to midnight – the moment humanity will end. Its setting is determined by the situation in the world and the threat of nuclear war. The initial position of the clock was at seven minutes to midnight; as of 2023, it is at a mere 90 seconds to midnight due to global climate change, the war in Ukraine and the risk of using nuclear weapons (Fig. 1). But is it really sensible to fear an apocalypse predicted by a symbolic clock?

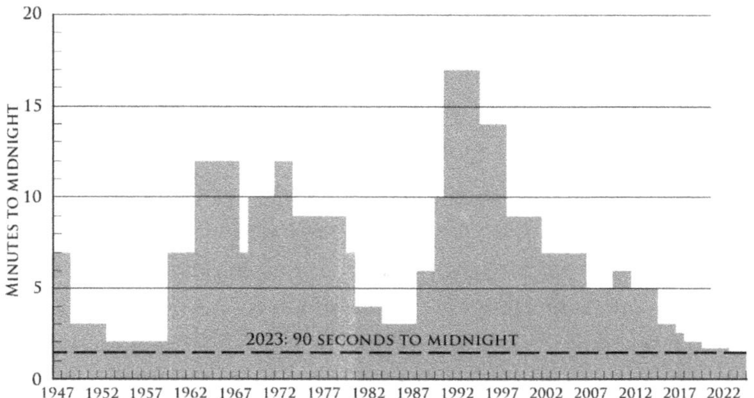

Fig. 1: Doomsday Clock readings between 1947 to 2024.[302]

Another indicator that can indirectly point to social attitudes toward the end of the world is the number of reported UFO sightings, which the National UFO Reporting Center logs. The data shows that the number of reported sightings increases every year, so we can assume that more people embrace theories about alien beings visiting our planet. The past decade alone saw more than 62,000 such sightings. In contrast, more than 4,000 were reported in 2023. Most of these reports have come from the United States, primarily in major metropolitan areas. Apparently, other countries are not as attractive as destinations for our extraterrestrial guests as the United States are.

Another data point is the relative global popularity of the Google search term "end world" between 2004 and 2020. The scale of the data is 0-100, with 100 indicating the highest popularity of the time in the analyzed period, which was observed in December 2012. A value of 50 indicates that the keywords were half as popular as they were at their peak, while a value of 0 indicates low interest in the topic. As we can see, internet users continue to be interested in the end of the world (see Fig. 2).

The myth is doing quite well; it fades away for a while and then resurfaces, depending on how widely publicized and likely the event is considered to be. As one can guess, the two highest peaks correspond to the doomsday predicted by Harold Camping in May 2011 and the doomsday associated with the end of the Maya Long Count calendar that was supposed to occur in December 2012. Another peak in early 2018 may be related to the unusual appearance of the two full moons that occurred in a single month. The chart also does a relatively good job of capturing the sentiment surrounding the COVID-19 pandemic, which has also been named as a sign of the coming apocalypse. If we consider the region in which the most queries originated, New Zealand, the United Kingdom, the United States, and Australia are the top countries. This is hardly surprising, as English is the most commonly spoken language by an overwhelming margin in these countries. Still, if we tracked queries in other countries in languages that are common there, the charts would look similar.

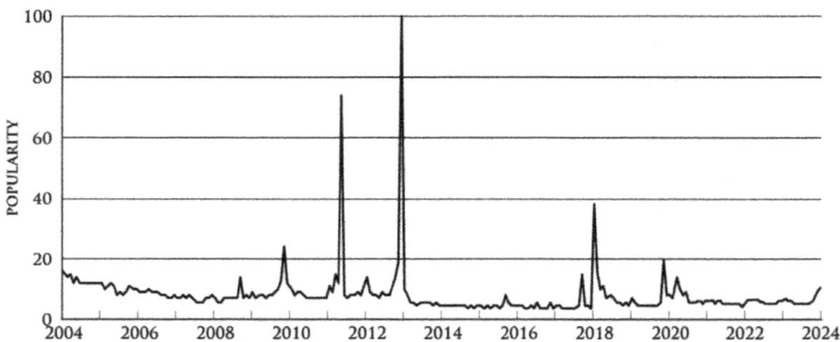

Fig. 2: Worldwide popularity of the search term "end world" on Google between 2004 and 2023.[303]

Survey results are another excellent encapsulation of how we view the end of the world. In 1979, 54 percent of French people surveyed expressed fear of the year 2000. In 1999, about

40 percent of Americans and 78 percent of American evangelicals stated a belief that the end of the world would come as a result of a battle between Jesus and the Antichrist. In the same year, 18 percent of French respondents indicated that they feared the apocalyptic predictions of Nostradamus. A 2010 Pew Research Center study showed that 58 percent of Americans surveyed expected World War III to break out by 2050, 53 percent expected a nuclear terrorist attack on the United States, and 41 percent believed Jesus would return to Earth by mid-century. A 2012 study conducted by Ipsos in 21 countries indicated that one in seven people thought the world would end in their lifetime (ranging from 6 percent in France to 22 percent in Turkey and the U.S.). Globally, 10 percent of all respondents believed in the Maya prophecy, with percentages ranging from 4 percent in Germany and Indonesia to as much as 20 percent in China. Elsewhere, 14 percent of Russian, 13 percent of Polish, 12 percent of Chinese, and 11 percent of Turkish and Japanese respondents expressed feelings of anxiety or fear about it. The prophecy caused the most miniature panic among the people of Germany, Canada, Australia (5 percent), and the United Kingdom (4 percent). The study also found that younger people with less education or lower income were more likely to believe in the coming apocalypse.

According to a YouGov poll, in 2015, 23 percent of Britons surveyed thought it was quite likely that they would live to see an apocalyptic disaster. Interestingly, more than half of those surveyed (54 percent) thought they would survive more than a week if the apocalypse started the next day. In terms of potential causes, 37 percent cited nuclear war, 13 percent cited climate change, 5 percent cited global revolution, zombies and doomsday both captured 3 percent each, 1 percent cited an alien invasion, and 8 percent opted for another reason. Only 31 percent did not think doomsday would occur. A similar study conducted in the United States found that 31 percent of respondents expected an apocalypse in their lifetime. A whopping 83 percent of those surveyed had thought about preparing for a natural disaster, and 55 percent had considered preparing for an apocalypse. Under apocalyptic conditions, 46 percent of Americans stated they would survive longer than a week. Nuclear war was considered the most likely catalyst (28 percent), followed by climate change and global calamities described in the holy scriptures (16 percent each), global revolution (9 percent), zombies (2 percent), and alien invasion (1 percent). Another 8 percent cited another reason. Only 20 percent did not believe the apocalypse was coming.

Apocalypse Forever

The myth of the end of the world is alive and well; thus far, we have not managed to overcome it. A large proportion of respondents in societies that are considered to be highly developed and educated believe that, sooner or later, perhaps even in their lifetime, a terminal catastrophe will be unleashed. Interestingly, trends in attitudes toward this idea indicate that this myth is not likely to be stamped out in the coming years. In highly developed societies, the importance of science and the established knowledge that derives from it is much greater than ever before, and both the social role of religion and the percentage of people declaring participation in religious practices are declining. Yet, as long as we exist in this world, we will continue to fear the end of the world. Although it is rational to view death as inevitable, our obsession with the impending apocalypse is another matter altogether. Scientists do their best to disprove and debunk catastrophic visions, many of which are not based on any rational premises, but the success of their efforts has been limited at best. Admittedly, their task is challenging and arduous because of the pervasive misinformation that circulates in society and the enormous commitment of conspiracy theorists who devote their whole lives to confirming their theses despite clear evidence to the contrary.

Many modern visions of the end of the world are based on strictly scientific premises, but the conclusions we draw tend to go in the wrong direction. Of course, we can all believe what we want, but we must remember that, since the Enlightenment, truth is not decided by voting or wishful thinking but by the intelligent eye of science. We want to be scared, we adore horror movies, and we want to believe in the impending end of all things. That is human nature. Perhaps it's easier that way? Maybe we seek to understand ourselves, and therefore, we imbue all the frightening and seemingly strange things that happen to us, as well as the evil that surrounds us, with a deeper, metaphysical dimension. We seek comfort in it, we long to feel special, and we yearn to be part of a larger plan precisely because it happened to *us*. And in some twisted way, the myriad predictions add magic to a world devoid of it. Ignorance is our greatest enemy, which heightens our feelings of fear and undermines our physical and mental stability. Whenever we don't know what's coming, we imagine the worst. These images lie deep in our subconscious. And, as you will likely agree, this mysteriousness is highly appealing. However, we should not be afraid. On the one hand, they say we live in apocalyptic times, but on the other, we must look at the challenges we face with a critical eye.

As history shows, with the passage of time and progress, visions of the end of the world take on different forms. In the beginning, we derived them from religion and the fear of unexplainable natural phenomena. Today, with the development of science, we are increasingly looking for explanations that do not contradict our knowledge and experience. The conclusion is that what we already know does not scare us, and what is still unexplored will always inspire us to unearth new reasons why the world must end.

What does the future hold? We do not know, but one thing is sure: humankind has already survived more than one end of the world, and there are many more to come, and our faith in the apocalypse will not fade away. The constellation of prophets, saints, charlatans, and scientists we already know will be enriched by new ones who will reveal our next date with doomsday to the world, which will inevitably turn out to be just another ordinary day of the week. And thus, the fear of the end of the world will accompany humanity forever. What we should really fear is not so much the end of the world as the side effects of fearing it. As Franklin Delano Roosevelt said, "Let me assert my firm belief that the only thing we have to fear is fear itself – nameless, unreasoning, unjustified terror which paralyzes needed efforts to convert retreat into advance."[304]

FOUR
NEVER TRUST AN ATOM: THE HARNESSING OF NUCLEAR ENERGY

Grzegorz Iwanicki

Humanity has been harnessing the energy that dwells in atomic nuclei in various ways for more than a century. This period can be divided into several distinct phases, taking into account both technical aspects and the prevailing mix of public sentiment at any given time. The proportions of this mix have varied from time to time. Still, its ingredients have remained the same from the beginning: an assortment of views that stem from current knowledge, the effects and impact of various incidents, and the emotions that accompany these incidents. The latter can be placed on a scale that ranges from full approval to categorical opposition to the use of atomic technology. The era of full approval, which lasted roughly until the end of World War II, was characterized primarily by lofty hopes associated with the various ways of exploiting the phenomenon of natural radioactivity and with vague visions of an inexhaustible source of energy that would be available to all. It is notable that the world's elite scientists of the era almost unanimously tried to dampen the enthusiastic attitude of a large part of society and rejected the possibility of harnessing nuclear energy for practical use.

The second period, which kickstarted the atomic age proper, was ushered in by the detonation of a new kind of deadly bomb at Hiroshima and Nagasaki in 1945. On the one hand, it heralded the triumph of man over nature; on the other, it set a tragic precedent that left a lasting mark on our perception of nuclear technology. The fear and dread of the power of the atom, previously manifested mainly in science fiction literature and films as well as in dubious pseudo-scientific articles published in the press, gained a firm foundation in the form of tangible evidence: a single bomb can destroy tens of thousands of human lives, in addition to polluting the local environment with radioactive elements. Due to a lack of knowledge among the general public, this well-founded fear of nuclear weapons also extended to the operation of nuclear power plants and all that it entailed.

Although many detailed technical reports already existed in the burgeoning days of nuclear power, early publications on the ins and outs of generating and harnessing this power for civil uses were too complex for most of the public to digest. In the foreword to *Nuclear Power, Today and Tomorrow* (1961), one of the first books on the subject aimed at a wider audience, Roger Makins, Chairman of the United Kingdom Atomic Energy Authority, justified that this kind of publication was needed to "give the layman a better understanding of the nature of nuclear power and to explain some of the major problems which have to be overcome in making practical use of it."[305] The need for an objective and straightforward explanation of the intricate processes surrounding the production of energy through nuclear reactors became crucial, given the emergence of a public trend toward mass and organized resistance to investments in nuclear power. These tendencies became the dominant strand of public sentiment in the third era discussed here, which we will call the period of vigorous debate.

The exact date when the third era began cannot be determined because it is not tied to any specific event. Increased skepticism toward nuclear power development emerged in different countries at different times, just as the ideas of the Renaissance or the Industrial Revolution once had. However, while authors have generally placed the start of this era in the 1970s, the social implications of the flourishing anti-nuclear movement, which was bolstered by celebrities from the world of show business, are more critical than its development timeline. At some point, the media began to give as much of a voice to experts as it did to emotional speeches by actors and singers and systematically whittled away the former in favor of the latter. Mass protests in local communities resulted in many investments being withdrawn, many power plants unbuilt, and nuclear waste dumping sites left on the drawing board. Unfavorable public sentiment intensified after the Chernobyl accident in 1986, which triggered a fourth period of increased fear of nuclear energy that continues to this day, reinvigorated by the Fukushima Daiichi accident following the 2011 earthquake in Japan.

The events at the Ukrainian and Japanese plants, and especially the media coverage that accompanied them, turned the public perception of the civilian nuclear industry more strongly toward disapproval and fear of another accident. The staunchest opponents began to perceive nuclear power plants and nuclear waste sites as ticking time bombs. Did they have a point? If we look at the official data contained in reports published by the United Nations Scientific Committee on the Effects of Atomic Radiation (UNSCEAR), the accident in Chernobyl resulted in 31 direct casualties. At the same time, in Fukushima, there were no casualties from excessive exposure to radiation.[306] The data cited in these reports also show no massive increase in cancer cases among the local population as a result of the incidents. Long-term estimates of the health of the people at risk also gave no basis to the concerns brandished by supporters of the anti-nuclear movement. Traditional methods of generating power based on coal or hydroelectric energy have so far resulted in many times more direct and indirect casualties, some of which were caused by air pollution from the burning of energy resources.[307]

But if there is no clear and present danger involved, why do nuclear power plants evoke such terror while other forms of energy production generate much less excitement? After all, thousands of reports, books, and articles on nuclear issues have been published in the past few decades, many of them dealing with issues of safety, reliability, and the role of the human factor in the civil nuclear industry.[308] Pro-nuclear publications abound, as do texts with neutral overtones. However, it is the anti-nuclear attitudes that seem to dominate today, as highlighted by Jerry W. Manfield's 1984 book *The Nuclear Power Debate: A Guide to Literature* published two years before the Chernobyl accident. Manfield pointed out that "in the last few years more books have been written against nuclear power than for this energy source," perhaps because "nuclear advocates seem less vocal because they are lost in the din of the ignorant. . ."[309]

The fear of one of the safest technologies for generating energy has been the subject of much research and scholarship, including Spencer R. Weart's seminal *Nuclear Fear: A History of Images*, published shortly after the Chernobyl accident, and its somewhat abridged version, *The Rise of Nuclear Fear*, updated to encompass later events, including the Fukushima accident.[310] This fear is fueled by publications and media material created not only by laypersons prone to using catchy titles and illustrations but also by established academics. For example, the cover of one version of *The Legacy of Nuclear Power*, written by esteemed professor Andrew Blowers, features a little girl blowing the seeds off a dandelion that is emitting a radioactive glow. In the background is a dirty brick wall with a sign bearing the well-known black and yellow trefoil symbol.[311] The same distinctive black and yellow color scheme was used on the cover of *Fallout: Disasters, Lies, and the Legacy of the Nuclear Age* by noted popular science author Fred Pearce.[312] This time, barrels of radioactive waste serve as the backdrop for the evocative title. These are just two of many examples of emotional appeals. It is hardly surprising, then, that some materials and publications by authors with much less renown who are negative towards nuclear energy are almost overflowing with symbolism that imposes an alarmist point of view from the get-go. After all, pulling people's emotional strings is a well-known method of manipulation, especially when the arguments and information presented lack authenticity and sufficient resonance.

This chapter is not an attempt to provide a comprehensive description of the phenomenon of nuclear fear since such a study would require at least several thick volumes, if not more. Instead, this chapter is an attempt to confront the dominant media reports on nuclear technology development with facts to demonstrate that some of the opinions expressed in anti-nuclear circles have more in common with myths than with the truth.

ROUGH BEGINNINGS

According to the International Atomic Energy Agency (IAEA), at the end of 2022, there were 438 nuclear power plants in operation worldwide, spread across 32 countries, producing about 10 percent of the world's electricity.[313] We owe the current state of the nuclear power industry to several generations of scientists and engineers: from the pioneers working on radioactivity at the turn of the 20th century to the builders of the first nuclear reactors in the 1950s, to the specialists designing the sophisticated safety measures and control systems in the newly built reactors. Each of these generations faced numerous problems and occasional unexpected accidents, which are normal in the course of designing and launching new technologies. Some scientists of the early 20th century, including Marie Skłodowska-Curie, experienced the harmful effects of radioactive elements firsthand. The sacrifices they made through their tenacity contributed to the development of safe standards and more accurate estimates of safe dosages of radiation, not only for medical procedures but, above all, in the further development of nuclear technology.

Every accident recorded in nuclear power plants in nearly 70 years of their operation – even the smallest one – has brought similar progress. Both the experiences of Chernobyl and Fukushima and a number of other mistakes and accidents over the years have led to improvements in reactor technology and the elimination of weak points in safety systems. Only an incorrigible optimist would think that such advanced technology would be not just impeccable from the outset but also immune to errors, often caused by a faulty human factor. Some industries, however, somehow enjoy a much higher level of public confidence despite suffering near-cyclical incidents that claim far more lives than all the direct victims of nuclear power plant accidents combined. One example of this difference in perception is the airline industry. After all, no one in their right mind would call for a ban on air travel because of the many thousands of victims of numerous plane crashes around the world.

Another example is road transport. Approximately 1.19 million people worldwide die in car accidents each year, and between 20 and 50 million are injured, often becoming permanently disabled.[314] This does not, however, trigger ubiquitous panic, massive fear of cars, or organized protests at the gates of car factories. Unforeseen accidents and errors are, after all, impossible to decouple from the natural course of development.

EINSTEIN AND THE KINDLING OF AN INVISIBLE FORCE

"There is not the slightest indication that [nuclear energy] will ever be obtainable. It would mean that the atom would have to be shattered at will." Albert Einstein made this statement in an interview in 1934.[315] Over time, his erroneous assertion became more widely known and, to this day, remains one of the famous scientist's most commonly cited blunders. However, Einstein was not the only one who incorrectly predicted the future of atomic research. Another great physicist, Ernest Rutherford, voiced a similar opinion repeatedly, including when he stated in a 1933 interview with the *New York Herald Tribune* that "The energy produced by the breaking down of the atom is a very poor kind of thing. Anyone who expects a source of power from the transformation of these atoms is talking moonshine."[316] Robert Millikan, one of the world's preeminent experimental physicists, struck a similar chord in October 1928 in a speech to members of the Chemist's Club in New York: "There is no likelihood man can ever tap the power of the atom. The glib supposition of utilizing atomic energy when our coal has run out is a completely unscientific Utopian dream, a childish bug-a-boo."[317]

When reading such historical statements, one is struck by their authors' unquestioning certainty about the impossibility of harnessing the atom and forcing it to obey human commands. These claims quickly became outdated and were refuted just a few years after they were made. From today's vantage point, is it fair to consider these luminaries' prophets of the myth that it is impossible to extract energy from the atom? This kind of judgment would certainly be unfair and unjustly damaging to their renown. After all, at the time they made these statements, all three scientists were respected Nobel laureates and the planet's most outstanding authorities in the field of physics. In expressing their opinions, they were guided by the knowledge they possessed and the latest experimental results. Thus, they had the right to put a damper on what they perceived to be whimsical visions of taming the enormous energy hidden in the invisible bricks that build all matter. They differed from true propagators of myths because facts guided them. The facts at that time were unambiguous: energy cannot be drawn from the atom in a controlled manner – end of story. Whoever believed otherwise was treated as a fabulist.

However, such fabulists existed among the figures of the era who brought science to the masses, as well as among the scientists themselves. One example is Frederick Soddy, a radiochemist and later a Nobel Prize winner. At the beginning of the 20th century, heartened by the discovery of radioactivity and particularly radium, Soddy began promoting a vision of unlimited energy obtained from the decay of elements, which would ostensibly make it possible to bend and shape the human environment to our will almost effortlessly "and make the whole world one smiling Garden of Eden."[318] His prognoses were part of a current of thought among parts of the elite of the time who followed the lines of renowned chemist Marcellin Berthelot in believing that the scientific discoveries of the early 20th century would lead humanity to universal prosperity and fraternity, ending the era of wars and competition for material goods.[319] But these utopian visions came in tandem with dark prophecies. As early as 1903, the controversial scientist Gustav Le Bon threatened to construct a device that would require merely one push of a button to destroy the entire world.[320] The editors of the *New York Times* went a bit further and, in 1929, published a text about the possibility of accidentally blowing up not just the entire planet but the entire universe with atomic energy.[321]

Newspapers voraciously picked up any fantastical mention of the potential benefits or dangers of radioactivity, guided mainly by sensationalism, much like today's tabloids. Reports that described an unknown, invisible force tickled the imagination. When a radium sample was put on display at the Museum of Natural History in New York in 1903, record crowds of onlookers were reported to be huddling together to get a glimpse of an inconspicuous pinch of radioactive powder.[322]

The newly discovered phenomenon stimulated human minds. Writers raced to outdo each other in creating stories that described the use of atomic energy in instruments of mass destruction capable of wiping out entire cities, if not all, of humanity. One example of such a story was the 1913 novel *The World Set Free by* H.G. Wells, in which miniature atomic bombs dropped from airplanes wreaked unprecedented panic and havoc. The end of our civilization or its complete reconstruction due to the conscious or unconscious use of the energy trapped in atomic nuclei began to gain enormous traction in the literature on disasters, unseating the numerous prospects for one or several apocalypses unleashed by natural processes. However, the real fear of nuclear Armageddon was yet to come – and what's worse, this time, it was justified.

However, it took almost half a century of intensive research and media coverage before atomic energy was truly harnessed. And it all started, one could say, with the discovery of radioactivity in 1896. Initially, the invisible, unexceptional radiation emitted from elements such as uranium was merely a curiosity to the general public. It was not until the discovery of radium by Marie Skłodowska-Curie and her husband – and, in particular, the first presentation of a sample in Paris at the Inaugural International Congress of Physics in 1900 – that the breakthrough was fully recognized and widely covered in the media. The properties of radiation and the secrets of atomic structures unearthed in the following years catalyzed the imagination of not only journalists but also famous scientists and classical scientists alike. The aforementioned Gustave Le Bon, bursting with enthusiasm for the scientific achievements that were unfolding before his very eyes, predicted that the moment humankind learned how to use radioactivity, civilization as we know it would come to an end, and "the poor [would] be equal to the rich and there [would] be no more social problems."[323]

Today, we are enriched by the lessons of hundreds of unproven predictions about the end of the world, erroneous demographic projections, and many other incorrect forecasts about the future. This experience has taught scientists to avoid tenaciously holding unambiguous, uncompromising opinions. However, Einstein and his colleagues should be excused for their firm yet misguided statements for at least one reason: the time in which they lived featured a galloping pace of scientific progress, but this progress was only in its infancy when it came to the internal structure of the elements. After all, neutrons were only discovered in 1932, and scientists had all the right to believe that taming the atom was a distant prospect.

But the war changed everything. As is often the case in times of conflict, the strenuous efforts of scientists and engineers to tip the balance of victory to one side significantly accelerated technological progress. The fear that Nazi Germany would harness the process of nuclear fission and build an atomic bomb pushed Einstein to engage in determined diplomacy. An indirect result of these efforts was the famous Manhattan Project. It began with a famous 1939 letter, which the great scientist addressed to President Roosevelt at the behest of Hungarian physicists Leo Szilard, Eugene Wigner, and Edward Teller. However, several months passed before the letter reached the White House, as no government advisor – and not even Roosevelt himself – took the possibility of building this mysterious bomb seriously. A surge of research and funding in this direction only began after the Japanese attack on Pearl Harbor. It took two years for the main cogs of the administrative machine to start to build the new weapon envisioned by Einstein.

Thus, propelled by the fear that Nazi evil would triumph, a declared pacifist, who only a few years earlier had unequivocally mocked those expressing the hope that humanity would successfully split the atom, became one of the chief proponents of research on the atomic bomb.

THE MILITARIZED ATOM: FROM SCIENCE FICTION TO AN INSTRUMENT OF DEATH

Until the late 1930s, both the hopes and the fears surrounding the use of atomic force were mainly linked to radioactivity. Although there were known cases of increased incidence of cancer among workers in uranium mines and people working with luminescent paints, the thousands cured of cancer through brachytherapy (treatment through direct exposure of affected body sites to radiation) provided hard evidence that continuing research on the atom was the correct path to follow.[324] A series of films shown in theaters in 1935 even featured a device that brought a dead character back to life through the power of radium.[325] Some creators across the artistic spectrum expressed high hopes for the role of radioactivity in the future of art.

Catastrophic predictions, including visions of deadly weapons based on radioactive decay, were relegated to science fiction films and literature. These visions often came accompanied by the stereotype of the mad scientist who constructed horrific devices or bombs to control humanity or carry out his nefarious plans. Examples of such maniacs included the depressed scientist from the novel *The Doomsday Men*,[326] published in 1938, or the insane and dangerous Professor Radium from a 1941 edition of *Batman* comics.

What still seemed like pure fantasy in the mid-1930s had become reality by 1938, after German scientists managed to unexpectedly split a uranium atom in half using a neutron beam, and other teams replicated their experiment. The result of this breakdown was termed fission, a term from biology. The media responded instantaneously, unleashing a torrent of sensationalist reports and foretelling the coming atomic age in hundreds of articles published around the world.[327] However, despite the significant research breakthrough, there was still a long way to go before the uranium nucleus could be tamed, and scientists were well aware of the challenges ahead. For a controlled nuclear chain reaction to be possible, scientists at the time believed that at least two things needed to be done: slowing down the neutrons in some way and obtaining sufficient quantities of the uranium isotope U-235.

Why was fulfilling these two conditions so important? Although the shattered uranium nucleus generated additional neutrons, these were moving at too high a speed to split subsequent nuclei in a controlled manner, so a safe chain reaction could not occur without slowing these particles down. Another problem was the availability of research material. Of the two significant isotopes of uranium found in nature – U-238 and U-235 – the latter proved far easier to break down, but it accounted for less than 1 percent of mined uranium by weight. In addition, it wasn't easy to separate on an industrial scale from its slightly heavier variety.

To make matters worse, some of the public and some scientists were not only skeptical but even frightened by the possible ramifications of the research, which could blow up entire laboratories. Hans von Halban, Jr., a French physicist, was among those who raised this flag; the editors of *Reader's Digest* went somewhat further in 1941 and inquired whether a chain reaction could start a process that would ultimately ignite the entire globe.[328] Not all editors let their imaginations run so far; some took a more pragmatic approach. For example, *The New York Times* presented a more sober view in an article that raised the question of what would happen if a hypothetical nuclear power plant were to explode and complicated the scenario further by pointing out that the parallel spread of many kilograms of radioactive substances would potentially contaminate the environment. The author concluded that he would much prefer the sight of smoke rising from the chimneys of a traditional coal-fired power plant to the risky gamble of nuclear energy.[329]

However, all the theoretical musings that appeared in the press at the time had little effect on the course of history; the decision had already been made. As mentioned in a previous chapter, diplomatic efforts to get the United States deeply involved in the race for victory by developing an atomic bomb had already resonated thoroughly. Nonetheless, as it turned out, the effect was not immediate. After initially demonstrating interest in the subject, Roosevelt changed course and froze all efforts to develop the bomb; the project did not get off the ground until 1942. Manufacturing the bomb required several years of hard work by thousands of scientists and support staff led by J. Robert Oppenheimer, the project's scientific director. Overseeing everything was the US Army. After all, the main goal of the project was a military one: to build an atomic bomb before Germany did.

As late as the end of November 1944, *Time* magazine described Londoners' fear that Hitler would ultimately drop an atomic bomb.[330] Today, we know that the progress that American and British military intelligence made in reconnoitering the nuclear activities of German engineers did not keep pace with the progress of the scientists working for the Manhattan Project to build a new type of bomb. None of the experts within the ranks of the US Army truly knew that the German atomic program was, in fact, in its infancy. In the minds of military strategists, the race continued. Only later did it become clear that the Americans, in cooperation with their British and Canadian counterparts, had reached the finish line first, while the Germans had barely crossed the starting line.

The top-secret part of the Manhattan Project culminated in the first detonation of an atomic bomb in human history at the Trinity test site on July 16, 1945. It proved to be a complete technical success, and Oppenheimer, when asked by a reporter how he felt at the moment of the explosion, famously responded: "I am become Death, the destroyer of worlds."[331] After that test, it was clear that the effort scientists and engineers had put into atomic research had brought to life H.G. Wells's extravagant 1914 vision of aircraft dropping city-leveling atomic bombs on population centers. Reality contradicted even predictions made a mere several months before the Trinity test: Admiral William Leahy, one of President Truman's chief military advisers, when asked about the prospects of ever utilizing the atomic bomb that was under development, said that "that is the biggest fool thing we have ever done. The bomb will never go off, and I speak as an expert in explosives."[332]

First Blood

But it happened. A great flash, followed by a devastating shock wave accompanied by a speeding fireball, began a new era in the history of humankind: the atomic age. In August 1945, the world, and none more so than the people of Hiroshima, learned what a handful of scientists, soldiers, and officials at the highest levels of government in the United States and Great Britain had known for nearly three weeks: man had once again tamed nature. Unfortunately, the prophecies of science fiction literature had come true. The new weapon wreaked havoc, fear, and unprecedented destruction. Within seconds, both in the Hiroshima explosion and three days later in Nagasaki, tens of thousands died, many of whom were literally vaporized. Tens of thousands more died mere days after the explosions from wounds, burns, and radiation sickness. The enormity of the destruction, which reached hitherto unknown proportions, shocked everyone, especially as both cities were blown off the face of the earth with a single blast.

Not surprisingly, the press revived fears and myths that had been reproduced for decades, culminating in a radio program on NBC in which the host discussed the atomic bomb using an evocative literary reference later repeated *en masse* on the streets of the United States: "We have created a Frankenstein."[333] During another broadcast on French radio in early 1946, a story was aired in which listeners heard that "atoms from radium used for research in America have broken loose," resulting in a terrible atomic storm engulfing the globe. This triggered terror among Parisians, evoking the panic in New Jersey by Orson Welles's famous 1938 radio play about a Martian attack on Earth, and cost the manager of the French radio station his job.[334]

Contrary to other myths, including that of *The World Set Free*, the invention of the atomic bomb did not end wars between states, nor did it lead to global unity and fraternity. Admittedly, it accelerated the end of World War II by forcing the unconditional surrender of Japan. After the establishment of the United Nations, it enabled a more civilized dialogue not only between the superpowers but also among the other members of that organization. However, this was merely an expansion of the idea driving the League of Nations, the discredited precursor to the UN. Not only did the atomic bomb fail to end the age-old uncertainty associated with future wars, it actually rekindled the fear of the future. While those who believed in an impending nuclear Armageddon before the outbreak of World War II were in the minority, the tragic events of Hiroshima and Nagasaki compelled even the leaders of the superpowers and heads of state in the developed, democratic world to speak with apocalyptic overtones when referring to possible future military disputes.

Fear of the power of the atom made its way from books, comic books, and science fiction movies into everyone's living rooms. As one American sociologist put it, the atomic bomb was a bridge over which the "phantasies of apocalyptic visionaries" entered the minds of society.[335]

Another myth – this time a wholly original one – was that Albert Einstein was the father of the atomic bomb. It does not matter that the famous physicist had little to do with the actual development process, that he wasn't invited to participate in the Manhattan Project, or that his research virtually never involved investigating the structure of the atom or any laboratory experiments.

It turned out that Einstein's primary problem was that he was perhaps the most famous scientist in the world, a physicist, and the creator of the most renowned formula related to energy. In the minds of many, he would forever remain the father of the atomic bomb. It is worth noting that some scientists did not entirely reject the blame laid upon them for the post-war fear of the atom and the possibility of a nuclear conflict threatening to annihilate our civilization. After all, Oppenheimer himself compared the process of figuring out the basics of physics and finalizing research on the atomic bomb to committing a sin on the scale of plucking an apple from the biblical tree of wisdom.[336]

The image of a hyper-focused scientist who sees nothing beyond their experiments in the laboratory would undoubtedly be damaging if it took root, and some in the community were well aware of this. One example was Leo Szilard, the originator and co-author of the famous 1939 letter to President Roosevelt. The Hungarian physicist's initiative was not the result of an irresistible desire to take part in groundbreaking research but rather a sign of great concern for the fate of civilization, which would undoubtedly suffer if Hitler acquired the formula for constructing an atomic bomb. After the bomb was built in 1945,

Szilard vigorously opposed using it against Japanese civilians. He launched a petition that would later bear his name, featuring the signatures of nearly 70 scientists working on the Manhattan Project.[337] The document reminded President Truman that the bomb was created so that the Allies could defend themselves and strike back in the event of a nuclear attack by Germany. According to the signatories, once it had become clear that neither Germany nor Japan had been able to develop the new weapon, its use, especially against civilians, was highly immoral. The petition went unheeded, but it planted the seed for what later became the Emergency Committee of Atomic Scientists, established just after the war by Szilard and Einstein to promote the peaceful use of atomic energy and to alert the public to the dangers of nuclear proliferation.

Although atomic bombs were never used in warfare again, nuclear energy would forever be associated with danger and devastation. In the years following the war, bomb tests conducted in remote locations made the world community increasingly familiar with the new dealer of death. When the Soviet Union successfully conducted its test in 1949, it became patently clear that a rivalry between superpowers would ensue. In the years that followed, they were joined by Great Britain, France, and China, and ultimately by states whose nuclear arsenal had a more limited range, such as Israel, India, Pakistan, and North Korea. Weapons of mass destruction evolved into thermonuclear and neutron armaments of annihilation, and warning and automatic response systems evolved along with them. To many, it became clear that, given the level of technological development humanity had achieved, only a madman who cared nothing for his own life could willingly provoke a war – one after which the world would be relegated to fighting with sticks and stones. The two significant powers clashed on several occasions during the Cold War alone, and the world held its breath every time. The most famous of these was the Cuban Missile Crisis of 1962 – but even then, Soviet leader Nikita Khrushchev, facing accusations of provoking a nuclear war, replied: "Only lunatics or suicides, who . . . want to destroy the whole world before they die, could do this."[338]

CHERNOBYL: THE WORLD'S NUCLEAR SCARECROW

In the first decade after World War II, many societies suffered energy shortages due to the scarcity of traditional energy resources. Atomic physicists proclaimed that an effective solution to these problems was to produce electricity in nuclear reactors. However, the technology of the time allowed only for bold promises without much payoff. In addition, most of the public associated atomic energy exclusively with bombs, and the only enthusiasts for the peaceful use of nuclear energy were a handful of scientists and politicians enthralled by the idea. In parallel with research on increasingly advanced types of atomic bombs, governments conducted classified research on the civilian uses of nuclear energy. After many years of strenuous effort and innumerable projects, they succeeded. The first nuclear power plants were built in the 1950s. They set a trend that continues to this day, with nearly 450 power plants operating around the world supplying about 10 percent of humanity's total production of electricity.

Fear arose alongside the first power plants, but this fear revolved not so much around the potential for horrifying explosions as around the danger of contaminating the environment with radioactive isotopes if the reactors failed. Shortly after the twin bombs hit Japan, there was a widespread view that both cities would remain contaminated for several decades and no plants would be able to grow there.[339] Fossilized ideas about the mystical, supernatural properties of radioactivity also resurfaced, an iconic example of which was Japan's *Godzilla*, the movie monster from the deep whose birth was described in the 1954 film as the result of atomic testing in the Pacific. These alleged effects of radiation, in addition to many others, stimulated people's imagination. Had it not been for the subsequent accidents that occurred in nuclear power plants, they would have mainly remained as cautionary tales told on movie screens or in the pages of science fiction books.

But there were also positive visions. Initial fears notwithstanding, there was no shortage of experts who, like Frederick Soddy and his followers half a century earlier, enthusiastically believed in the ultimate triumph of scientific discoveries in the field of radioactivity. Famous scientists and some journalists, like their colleagues in the days immediately following the discovery of radium, also heralded the imminent arrival of a glorious new era. Even their rhetoric did not change in any profound way. In 1947, *The New York Times* told its readers that "Africa could be transformed into another Europe."[340] All that was needed was to learn how to draw energy from the decay of atomic nuclei. To achieve this, large amounts of money were needed for scientific research, which in democratic countries meant gaining the support of voters and funding. The propaganda machine was in full swing.

One of the watershed moments in the history of the pro-atomic movement was President Eisenhower's famous speech at the United Nations in 1953, titled "Atoms for Peace." After this event, enthusiasm for atomic development spread around the world, with hundreds of newspaper articles, radio broadcasts, and specially made propaganda films.[341] The promotional efforts were successful and kindled a desire in many countries for their reactors. Among them was the Soviet Union, which had been pursuing its nuclear program since 1943. Several renowned scientists channeled their nuclear fantasies in this period. They included John von Neumann, a respected physicist and chemist who had worked with the Manhattan Project and the Atomic Energy Commission. In 1955, von Neumann argued that "there is little doubt that the most significant event affecting energy is the advent of nuclear power. . . . [A] few decades hence, energy may be free – just like the unmetered air."[342] As we know, he was as wrong in his prediction as Einstein or Rutherford once were when they publicly asserted that one could not simply extract energy from an atom.

As attitudes toward building nuclear power plants grew more favorable, the scientific community issued its first warnings. Edward Teller, widely seen as the father of the hydrogen bomb, warned at a meeting of nuclear experts in 1953 that "a runaway reactor can be relatively more dangerous than an atomic bomb."[343] In a similar vein, as co-author of a paper presented at the 1955 Conference on the Peaceful Uses of Atomic Energy in Geneva, he argued that operating a nuclear reactor could be equated to "conducting both explosive and virulent poison production under the same roof."[344] However, the media did not pick up such statements too excitedly, tempering their urgency and focusing their coverage on the hard work that scientists were putting in to minimize the risks associated with electricity production. This was exemplified by the title of an article in *Popular Science*: "Experts bare the weird hazards of nuclear-electric stations and tell of the measures being taken to protect you."[345]

The experts were right. Introducing a new technology always entails potential mistakes, along with all their consequences. Unfortunately, Murphy's Law has not spared nuclear reactors. The first accidents in military facilities and submarine engine rooms resulted in the first direct casualties. However, these incidents were covered by a confidentiality clause and thus did not affect public perception to any great extent. The contamination of an area with radioactive waste as a result of a disaster in a nuclear plant – the exact situation predicted by the aforementioned *The New York Times* reporter in 1941 – did not happen on a larger scale until March 1979, at the Three Mile Island power plant in the United States. Although no one died in the incident or even received a life-threatening dose of radiation, there was local environmental contamination, the effects of which were only cleaned up entirely in 1993. The incident had a severe economic and social impact on the entire nuclear power industry in the United States.[346]

A similar accident, though on a smaller scale, occurred at the Windscale reactor in England in October 1957. Staff managed to contain the crisis, and there were no casualties, but the area around the plant was contaminated by radioactive fallout. This prompted the government to intervene – for instance, by destroying milk produced by local farmers.[347] In the following years and decades, there were up to several hundred cases of cancer among local villagers that could be linked to the accident, dozens of which resulted in the death of the patient.[348] However, because there was no precise methodology to study the impact of the accident on the health of the local population, these data may not be reliable. The Three Mile Island incident, in turn, had no significant impact on the health of the local population.[349]

In the Soviet Union, power plants were mainly built for the dual purpose of producing electricity and supplying plutonium for atomic bombs, in accordance with the Communist Party's policy. For economic reasons, they were often built with relatively cheap but also outdated high-power channel-type reactors (known by their Russian acronym, RBMK). One of the sites equipped with this type of reactor was the Chernobyl plant, which in April 1986 suffered the worst accident in the history of nuclear power. The accident itself was a veritable media and emotional bomb, and the echoes of its detonation can still be heard today.

While the chain reaction in an atomic bomb was triggered by accelerating beams of neutrons, the "chain reaction" that resulted in the power plant disaster in Chernobyl consisted of a series of significant omissions and a sequence of poor choices. These began when the plant's crew turned off the heat-sensitive reactor's emergency core cooling system and continued with a whole series of commands that violated the safety rules that were in place. The root causes were human error, routine, and incorrect assessments of facts. This cost the lives of 28 emergency personnel, who died within four months after the accident as a result of exposure to excessive doses of radiation. In addition, two members of the plant staff died as a direct result of the burns they suffered when the reactor exploded.[350]

The number of direct victims of the Chernobyl catastrophe is usually estimated at 30 or 31 people and does not elicit powerful emotions. Some estimates add a small number of people who died during efforts to extinguish the flames and secure the remains of the damaged part of the power plant, such as the crew of a helicopter whose rotor got caught in one of the steel ropes during an attempt to throwing sand on the smoldering reactor. However, the incidence of cancer among people evacuated from the affected area, personnel working on cleanup operations around the power plant, and residents of regions adjacent to Chernobyl is a different story. There are significant discrepancies between information presented by various organizations and entities in this respect.[351] Data released by Soviet authorities and later copied by Ukraine put the estimated number of victims at 125,000. In contrast, estimates presented in a report by Greenpeace suggest that 200,000 people died between 1990 and 2004 as a result of the Chernobyl accident.[352]

The most precise and authoritative data, provided by UNSCEAR in a 2008 report, states that 19 people died between 1987 and 2004 among the 106 plant workers and emergency personnel who received high doses of radiation on the day of the accident. However, this figure includes all deaths, not necessarily those related to radiation exposure. More than 6,000 cases of thyroid cancer have also been reported among people under the age of 18 at the time of the accident in Belarus, Ukraine, and several regions of Russia adjacent to these countries. A significant part of these cases is likely linked to the consumption of milk that contained a high dose of radioactive elements. Of these cases, only 15 ended with the death of the patient by 2005. Apart from a slight increase in reported cases of leukemia and eye diseases among Russian workers who cleaned up around the plant, there are no other proven correlations between radiation released from the Chernobyl accident and increased incidence of disease.[353]

The panic created by the media, however, had multiple strongly adverse effects among the local population and even in countries nowhere near Ukraine, as did the impact of the preventive measures taken by the authorities of the USSR, which were disproportionate to the scale of the threat. More than 300,000 people were evacuated and resettled, not only from the immediate vicinity of Chernobyl but also from regions deemed to be at risk of excessive radiation. Over half a million "liquidators" took part in cleanup operations in the contaminated areas. Together with those who had been displaced, they were exposed to enormous stress, which was intensified by unconfirmed media reports on the effects of radiation. The results were unsettling: depression, alcoholism, and, in some extreme cases, suicide.[354]

These indirect effects of the panic must be supplemented with the thousands of abortions performed after the incident for fear of giving birth to mutants or children with serious illnesses caused by the radiation that their mothers had been exposed to during their pregnancy. This fear spread to countries that had received doses of radiation that were much lower than the natural radiation that occurred there. For example, about 2,500 abortions in Greece and about 400 in Denmark were reported to have been motivated by fear of the fallout.[355] In post-war Japan, where radiation doses were many times higher, there were no reports of massive genetic defects among newborns, so many abortions performed in Western European countries in the period immediately after the Chernobyl accident can be viewed as a direct result of the hysteria triggered by mass media, which shaped public sentiment based on unconfirmed information.

The catastrophe has been so deeply engraved in the minds of societies around the world that almost everyone is familiar with the approximate course of the accident and its consequences, including a radioactive cloud threatening nearly all of Europe for days after the explosion and large swathes of land closed to human settlement in the immediate vicinity of the plant. Chernobyl became an illustration of fears and anxieties that had been germinating for decades, only to blossom in the wake of the Ukrainian disaster fully. At almost every demonstration against the construction of new nuclear power plants since then, one can find banners among the protesters that say, “We don’t need another Chernobyl” and various references to the disaster, like posters with images of “Deceased Liquidators” from Chernobyl cropping up on the streets of Geneva during anti-nuclear protests many years after the disaster.[356]

On the other hand, how many people can say anything about the Bhopal disaster in India, which happened two years before Chernobyl? A gas leak at a pesticide plant in Bhopal killed 4,000 people almost instantly; some estimates state that 8,000 died within two weeks of the disaster, and 8,000 more perished because of further medical conditions linked to the incident. In total, more than half a million people suffered varying degrees of health damage as a result of the Bhopal accident, many of whom were left permanently unable to work.[357]

The Bhopal disaster is often considered the worst industrial disaster (or one of the worst) in history. Why, then, has it not generated as much attention and raw emotion as the Chernobyl accident? Why do people remain unafraid of pesticide factories, and why are they not protesting their existence or the construction of more? Perhaps Bhopal's perceived remoteness from the societies of the Western world is the culprit. After all, the deadly gas cloud had no chance of reaching Europe or the United States. The way in which the disaster was covered in the media is another possible reason. A gas leak is much less evocative than radioactivity, which is not detectable to the senses in any way. After all, anyone can imagine the stench of gas, and most of us are familiar with the sight of factories. Many of us have family members or friends who work in one factory or another. However, not everyone has seen a nuclear power plant with their own eyes, let alone know how it works. These factors, plus the fear of radioactivity that has accompanied people for more than a hundred years, undoubtedly had a significant impact on public perception of the Chernobyl accident.

We saw just how great this fear can be after another major accident at a nuclear power plant, that is, the Fukushima disaster in Japan in March 2011. The front pages of newspapers around the world featured news that we know today was clearly exaggerated. A headline in the *Daily Mail* read, "Japan's nuclear disaster spirals out of control amid warnings it could end in apocalypse." The editors of *The Sun* plastered its front page with a headline that read "Exodus from Tokyo," which covered almost the entire page and came with the familiar yellow-and-black symbol of radioactivity.[358] Anti-nuclear protests held in the following years added a fashionable new slogan: "No more Fukushima." However, official, widely accepted data from a UNSCEAR report published in 2014 show that there were no direct fatalities or cases of acute radiation sickness resulting from the accident. The radiation doses that the population of the surrounding area received (and continues to receive) were considered low or very low. Additionally, and from a public health perspective, most importantly – experts contended that "no discernible increased incidence of radiation-related health effects are expected among exposed members of the public or their descendants."[359]

As with the Chernobyl disaster, most of the harmful effects of the accident are related to the mental and economic fallout of the decision to resettle more than 100,000 people from the areas surrounding the plant. Although there were no direct casualties, more than 2,200 people – mostly the elderly and those suffering from various illnesses – died from a variety of non-radiation-related causes during the evacuation, many of them sequestered in places of temporary residence far away from their homes. These victims are commonly regarded as "disaster-related deaths," which clearly distorts the accurate picture of the Fukushima accident.

An additional media narrative that contributed to the negative perception of the scale of the catastrophe was the linking of the Fukushima accident with the number of dead and missing solely as a result of the earthquake and tsunami. This included misleading messaging circulated by broadcasters such as the BBC, which implied this link through its phrasing: "the Fukushima meltdown was the world's worst nuclear accident since Chernobyl in 1986. Around 18,500 people died or disappeared in the quake and tsunami. More than 160,000 were forced from their homes."[360] Meanwhile, a local news portal reported that "deaths directly related to the disaster that triggered a triple meltdown at the Fukushima No. 1 nuclear power plant came to 15,899 with 2,529 people missing, according to official records."[361] Many other broadcasts and articles with similar overtones continue to perpetuate an exaggerated image of the accident at the Fukushima power plant.

Tough decisions

Regardless of whether the economic arguments for building nuclear power plants are correct or off the mark, the decision to create a new plant is often met with protests from anti-nuclear groups and local communities, driven by the fear of their distinctive chimneys and the reactors that operate in their shadow. Each investment of this kind brings with it the clash of several distinct interest groups. Today, the two main stages for these clashes are media and social media platforms.

Traditionally, politicians decide whether to accept or reject a given investment plan. Generally, they must either side with the nuclear lobby and the balanced voice of experts or, out of sincere concern for the environment or to score political points, follow the will of people and circles that are opposed to nuclear energy. One alternative way to shift the responsibility for this decision from the shoulders of politicians to the people would be to hold a referendum. But would this kind of choice be optimal in the case of such a long-planned, expensive, complex, and emotionally charged topic as nuclear power? If not, then who should be the one to make the decision?

Nuclear investments: Who should decide?

In an ideal world of free markets and consumption, demand for products (and the competition that comes with it), coupled with strong safety standards and regulations, would be the critical factors in any decision to invest. In democratic countries, this approach works successfully in many industries, from discount stores in attractive locations to private nurseries and kindergartens in newly built housing developments. Granted, problems sometimes arise when the investment may interfere with local customs or religious sentiments, among others. However, the most significant protests are related to those new investments that may disturb the harmony of the local landscape and potentially have a negative impact on the environment. Especially in the latter case, people often fear the effect that the project may have on their health – a fear usually driven by a lack of knowledge or understanding. Protests against the construction of cell phone towers, including the widely covered global resistance to 5G technology, are an emblematic example of this fear.[362]

There is always a lot of emotion among local communities surrounding the construction of new landfills and sewage treatment plants. Everyone would like to quickly dispose of their waste and garbage and live in a world with clean streets and near-sterile public spaces, but it would be best if such installations were far from their place of residence and the waste fee was as low as it could be. Investments in energy follow a similar pattern. It is much easier to convince residents to accept new coal-fired power plants in areas associated with coal or lignite mines or to drum up support for hydroelectric power plants near locations where they are convenient. On the other hand, nuclear power plants generate massive resistance. Leszek Kołakowski perfectly sums up the demands of anti-nuclear groups in a somewhat ironic tone in a quote that already appeared in the introduction to this book: "You, those in power, are to give us as much electricity as we desire, but without nuclear reactors, without harming the environment, and without spoiling our beautiful landscape. You have to come up with something – and what that something will be is your problem."[363]

Are the politicians in power really the right people to make decisions on long-term investments in nuclear energy? Initially, the view (or at least the hope) in elite circles was that experts – scientists – should be the ones responsible for implementing new technologies, including those based on radioactivity. Only they could then fully understand the possibilities and dangers that arose from attempts to harness atomic energy, as no layperson could grasp their full extent. With science and scientists in mind, Frederick Soddy preached that the most sensible solution was "for the public to acknowledge its real master" and place power in the hands of "those who are concerned with the creation of its wealth."[364] Over time, the idea of an alliance between scientists and businesspeople, with an eye toward meeting community and consumer needs, found its expression in the slogan "*Science Finds – Industry Applies – Man Conforms.*"[365]

The stereotype of the detached scientist holding little consideration for anything but their research was not conducive to building public trust in experts. The association of nuclear science with massive casualties certainly did not help: the public was fully aware that, had it not been for the scientists, there would be no destructive atomic bombs, as the cover of *Time* emphatically implied on its 1946 cover, overlaying an atomic mushroom with $E=mc^2$. Some scientists' misguided and ultimately erroneous visions of the future – including both the skepticism of Einstein and Rutherford and the enthusiastic and utopian fantasies of Soddy and von Neumann – did little to help. Even today, similar opinions from decades ago are quoted in the media to discredit scientists and argue that experts are not worth listening to. The faulty prophecies of esteemed figures were listed along with other off-target predictions in a 2018 article in the *Arkansas Democrat Gazette* titled "Can We Trust Experts?" by economics professor Walter Williams. The author summed up his doubt-ridden text by stating that "the point of all this is to say that we can listen to experts, but take what they predict with a grain or two of salt."[366]

In totalitarian regimes, decisions regarding nuclear investments appear to be easier to make. Their utter disregard for the voice of the populace, coupled with massive propaganda efforts and untoward consequences for those who dare to dissent, make it easier to implement such plans. However, in normal countries, decision-making processes at least partially take into account the viewpoints of the electorate. The public, distrustful of experts and assurances and equally distrustful of politicians they often deem to be corrupt, is thus left to take matters into its own hands. There have been many examples of such decisions being made with regard to nuclear investments, from blocking the construction of a plant by local communities (as in the case of the famous 1971 protests in Wyhl, Germany) to nationwide referendums and protests. In most cases, the leaders of these protests were successful.

The beauty of democracy, however, has its downsides. Driven by unfounded fear, anti-nuclear movements have indirectly promoted existing energy sources – in most cases, coal power – thus exposing themselves further to the detrimental effects of burning conventional energy resources. Suppose we are to entertain the idea of leaving critical issues such as energy and its future development in the hands of society. In that case, the only way to do so with a clear conscience is to promote responsible education. After all, those who believe (among other things) that Bill Gates promoted the development of the COVID-19 vaccine in order to implant microchips hidden into people's bodies also vote in referendums, even if we may hope that they are a small minority.[367] We should also remember that voters are often unstable in their views, and occasionally, their pattern of voting changes entirely in a short period. The victories of post-communist parties in countries that once lay behind the Iron Curtain and the cyclical transfer of power between Democrats and Republicans on the American political scene are two clear examples of the fickleness of voters' preferences.

As long as a large part of the public is guided mainly by emotions in making decisions, the debate about nuclear energy will be based primarily on myths instead of complex, factual arguments. This leads us to a simple conclusion: education is the key.

Education is the Key

Devastated by the loss of a friend during World War I, Frederick Soddy lamented that "governments and politicians, or man in general, was not yet fitted to use science." In later statements on the prospect of nations building atomic bombs, he argued that society had to be reformed through education before governments acquired the technology to produce them. Otherwise, we risked total annihilation.[368] Newspaper and magazine editors of the day followed a similar line of thinking, employing educated science editors with the requisite knowledge to critique information that came down from laboratories. The world was galloping headfirst into great discoveries, and older journalists were unable to keep up, often reproducing far-fetched ideas and unnecessarily firing the imaginations of readers who devoured utopian or sensationalist articles on radioactivity and other news from the world of science.

Even top-ranking scientists sometimes displayed shortcomings in areas unrelated to their research specialty, rejecting facts or falling out of step with the latest expert consensus. One compelling example is Marie Skłodowska-Curie, who did not believe, or refused to believe, that the same radium that had cured thousands of patients of cancer could at the same time be dangerous to her health. Thus, she consistently rejected most of the basic safety measures in her work on the elements and deteriorated further with each year, ultimately dying in 1934 with symptoms of radiation sickness.[369] Nonetheless, most scientists, especially those working on atomic energy, followed widely accepted recommendations and performed their duties with extreme caution.

Casual observers and health and safety professionals alike would be undoubtedly impressed by the safety procedures that were in place during the construction of the first-ever nuclear reactor in Chicago.[370] The team responsible for conducting the first fully controlled uranium chain reaction preferred to play it safe, not only because they were conducting their experiment in a major metropolitan area but also because they were aware of the possible dangers inherent to working on a force that was not yet fully understood. Procedures far beyond the safety precautions that were strictly necessary soon became a hallmark of the nuclear industry, setting standards that were not just unknown in other industries but sometimes downright unfathomable.[371]

Of course, after the experiences of Hiroshima and Nagasaki, the fear associated with the use of nuclear energy was understandable. However, once the US Atom for Peace program kicked off, efforts began to familiarize the public with the newly developed energy production technology. The proponents of these programs used an array of channels to try to reach a variety of social groups, including children and young people. Case in point: Walt Disney's 1957 animated film *Our Friend the Atom*, which was widely played on television and in schools. The cartoon certainly had an impact on children's imagination by referring to well-known fairy tales and emphasizing the productive and valuable role of scientists in taming the magical energy associated with radioactivity.[372]

Familiarizing adults with the atom was much more difficult. Tours of nuclear power plants were organized for schoolteachers to prove that such plants were much safer than any other production facility. Dozens of scientists and experts strained their vocal cords for hours at a time at public meetings to explain that reactors could not explode like atomic bombs, dispelling widely held doubts. President Kennedy also leaped into the fray in January 1962 by drinking a glass of milk from a local store in the company of reporters while highlighting that dairy products were served daily in the White House. This sounds somewhat ridiculous today, but after Hiroshima, there was considerable fear stemming from the belief that cows were eating grass contaminated with radioactive fallout from nuclear reactors and bomb tests.[373]

Over time, sociologists concluded that a specific part of society takes a pro- or anti-nuclear stance by default, regardless of the knowledge it absorbs and guided primarily by its own previously acquired beliefs.[374] It is virtually impossible to change these beliefs, as some of us are so convinced that our views are correct that we do not accept any arguments to the contrary. For most of us, however, education remains crucial. But this is where we encounter a significant hurdle: the knowledge that is conveyed in schools about radioactivity and nuclear energy is, in fact, relatively sparse. It would take very little to increase this knowledge, even if schools limited themselves to providing compelling examples. After all, no one needs to encourage patients and recreational bathers to visit spas offering radon baths as treatments. The many people who indulge in such treatments every year to rest and regenerate do not fear them in the slightest.

Poland, which has been planning to build the first nuclear power plant on its territory since the 1980s, is an interesting analytical case, as its negligence in terms of educating students about natural radioactivity and safety issues in nuclear power plants is easy to demonstrate. One would imagine that since the country is trying to initiate its nuclear program, those in power would care about promoting reliable information related to nuclear energy. However, if one were to leaf through the high-school geography textbook that shaped many of today's middle-aged population, they would mostly read about the consequences of major accidents and the problematic issue of radioactive waste but otherwise find no more than a few terse paragraphs with a handful of statistical data points related to world nuclear power production. The textbook's authors wrote that the Chernobyl disaster "caused the deaths of several thousand people, and hundreds of thousands of residents of surrounding villages and settlements were irradiated." How high were the doses of radiation that these unfortunate souls received? This we will not glean from the text. The authors only add that, in a similar accident in Windscale, there were 100,000 cases of radiation sickness.[375]

Of course, these figures have zero support in official research results, but the message burrowed its way into the minds of millions of Polish children in the 1990s and early 2000s. Have things improved? In one geography textbook for secondary school students, nuclear energy is only mentioned in a single paragraph in the chapter devoted to the energy industry. It says, among other things, that building a nuclear power plant is very expensive, and many European countries are planning to abandon their nuclear programs.

But perhaps we should look to physics textbooks instead of geography textbooks for some semblance of support for reasonable discourse. Maybe the physics curriculum, seeing as it represents a discipline more closely related to the subject of nuclear energy, will explain its possible pros and cons in more detail. Let's take a look at a physics textbook intended for the final year of technical and vocational high schools.[376] This textbook was the essential book for many Polish secondary school students in the mid-to-late 1980s and 1990s, that is, for groups whose support was particularly pivotal in building the country's fledgling nuclear program. The natural radioactivity of different elements, nuclear reactions, and nuclear energy are described in considerable detail in over 40 pages. However, not a single sentence outlines the doses of natural radiation we receive from the nature that surrounds us. There is also no mention of safety measures in nuclear power plants. The text is merely a technical explanation of the phenomenon of radioactivity and the technologies that lead to nuclear reactions.

More recent publications have embraced a distinctly different approach. Already in the standard-level version of the primary physics textbook for high schools, students can learn about the natural radiation that has accompanied our species since the dawn of time.[377] The issue of nuclear energy is also explained in an accessible way, with a basic description of risks and safety measures that are typically applied, including an accurate account of the causes of past power plant failures and the consequences of these disasters. The textbook explains nuclear physics in a way that is far from frightening, presenting a relatively optimistic picture of nuclear power plants. It also conveys information on the role of coal-fired power plants in the spread of radioactive elements. The overall impression this gives is that the younger generations of Polish students are leaving school with a basic but solid understanding of nuclear energy. However, it will take another generation before they join the ranks of nuclear-conscious voters and start making up a significant part of that cohort.

Older generations, deprived in their school years of access to objective and balanced information, may be surprised to learn that all forms of life as we know it on Earth exist thanks to two sources of nuclear energy: energy produced by the Sun and energy produced by the decay of radioactive elements deposited in the interior of our planet. Ultimately, we must accept that we go through our lives surrounded by radioactivity. One of the world's most eminent physicists expanded on this in vivid detail: "Every falling raindrop and snowflake carries some radioactive matter to earth, while every leaf and blade of grass is covered with an invisible film of radioactive material."[378] Reading statements like this, one might think that the cause of such widespread environmental contamination is the dozens if not hundreds of atomic bomb tests that have been held over the decades, coupled with the accidents at Chernobyl and Fukushima. But this esteemed physicist was Ernest Rutherford, and the quote is from 1905 – long before the atomic age began. Rutherford was right, of course, and some level of radiation is present in every particle of matter around us, from the walls of the buildings we live and work to the food we eat every day.[379]

THE ATOM AT THE MERCY OF POLITICIANS

Government intervention in the unrestricted use of radioactivity and nuclear energy in the broad sense of the term had clearly become necessary by the 1930s, when fashionable products based on radioactive substances, often manufactured by home-made businessmen in garages and sheds, conquered several markets at once, from cosmetics to dietary supplements and all sorts of "miracle cures," including potency enhancers and youth potions. Had these products only been advertised as containing radioactive admixtures, the only damage dealt would have been to the wallets of those who purchased them. However, there were cases in which these magical concoctions caused actual bodily harm to casual practitioners of alternative medicine and sometimes even led to death from radiation sickness.[380]

The ban on the free sale of products containing radioactive elements was the first salvo to the monopolization of decision-making by politicians on issues related to nuclear technology. Subsequent decisions were often the result of cold calculations based on current military or political needs, both in international relations and in their backyards, and did not necessarily follow expert opinion. A glaring example of such political cynicism was President Jimmy Carter's visit to the site of the Three Mile Island power plant disaster. Carter was a nuclear physics engineer by training and had military experience serving on a nuclear submarine. After returning from the accident site, he told members of his cabinet that the accident had had no severe impacts but did not repeat this line in official interviews and public speeches, not wishing to harm the Democratic Party.

In some countries, politicians initially did not have to worry about the voters when implementing plans to build nuclear infrastructure. Besides communist states, among such countries were France and Japan. The fear of becoming dependent on imported energy resources proved stronger than the fear of nuclear technology. The French and Japanese public stood with their leaders on their road to energy independence. This was a difficult choice, especially for the Land of the Rising Sun, where the tragic experience of 1945 was still fresh in people's minds. After the Fukushima disaster, however, the Japanese government acted too emotionally, shutting down almost all operating reactors and leaving it up to local governments to turn them back on. This was not just a temporary sign of weakness imbued with fear kindled by anti-nuclear protests. A single accident at a single plant compelled Japan to turn its entire energy development plan on its head and move away from nuclear reactors, opting for alternatives such as coal-fired power plants and drawing up blueprints and schematics for dozens of them.[381] A few years after the disaster, however, the government reversed course, and the nuclear program was revived with a simultaneous plan to modernize the existing infrastructure.[382]

The Japanese government was not the only one to be seemingly gripped by inexplicable fear after the Fukushima disaster. German politicians did the same by announcing the closure of the country's nuclear reactors.[383] The Italian government shifted the responsibility for this challenging decision onto the voters, who overwhelmingly voted against the construction of new plants in a referendum.[384] Interestingly, the countries closest to Japan, including the Philippines, China, and Taiwan – theoretically those most threatened by the relentless wave of fear, did not give up their nuclear power plans.

Activism Rising: Emotions vs. Reason

The first protests against nuclear power were linked to a legitimate fear of the uncontrolled growth of nuclear weapons arsenals. In later years, the energy of the protesters spilled over into all other uses of nuclear power. At first, this resistance mainly operated on a local scale, but from the late 1960s onwards, it gained momentum. As early as 1947, farmers were organizing protests against the construction of an experimental reactor near Paris, fearing damage to their crops and other woes, while in 1956, the Belgian government agreed to a proposal to build a power plant near Brussels on the condition that the installation be located as far as possible from the royal palace.[385] However, the anti-nuclear movement recorded its first significant success when it blocked the construction of a nuclear power plant in Wyhl, Germany, in 1971, following protests that were widely reported around the world. The organizers' success set a precedent and practically every nuclear construction project and investment that has occurred since then has attracted groups of disgruntled citizens – some small, others imposing.[386]

The widespread popularity of anti-nuclear movements became a thorn in the sides of people associated with the nuclear industry, with some describing such protests as "attended by a number of hippy characters professing no knowledge of nuclear energy."[387] This contemptuous phrasing carried more than a few grains of truth about the anti-nuclear movement. One of the first leading environmentalists to join the protests confessed that, even if nuclear power plants were safe and more economically viable than other plants, "it would still be unattractive because of the political implications of the kind of energy economy it would lock us into."[388] Robert Jungk, another virulent opponent of nuclear power and author of a famous late-1970s anti-nuclear manifesto titled *The New Tyranny: How Nuclear Power Enslaves Us,* likened the new energy industry to a dangerous ideology that could soon transform humanity into a society of enslaved people, creating an empire more threatening and deadly than Hitler's grand project.[389] Some circles almost began to personify nuclear energy as evil incarnate, practically divorced from the human factor.

Such controversial comparisons would not be possible without the evolution of fear associated with nuclear power. Surging investment in nuclear energy and the lack of serious accidents and incidents over more than two decades were not just a testament to the safety of this technology. Still, they had also gotten the public primarily accustomed to the new power plants. Reactors were not exploding, the Earth had not been blown to smithereens, and people were not dying en masse from cancer induced by radiation sickness. It was only a matter of time before a new trigger for fear was found that could continue to unite the disparate anti-nuclear movements. The radioactive waste produced in the reactors turned out to be the perfect bogeyman. According to surveys and research at the time, the issue of nuclear waste did not occupy much space in the public debate until the mid-1970s. Still, it came to the forefront after that period, pushing other concerns about nuclear power to the sidelines. Fear of the waste grew to the point that most people surveyed said they would rather live near a nuclear power plant than near a site where radioactive materials were stored.[390]

Were it not for the extraordinary precautions put in place at power plants and waste disposal sites, one might be suitable to express concern about radiation emissions in their surroundings. However, nuclear facilities operating in accordance with top-down safety requirements often emit volumes of radioactive material that are comparable to or even smaller than those of coal-fired power plants and their accompanying coal-fired waste dumps.[391] Interestingly, however, this does not trigger widespread fear of coal dust and fails to generate any strong emotions. Much like other significant accidents – such as the pesticide mentioned above plant disaster in India or the 1979 freight train accident in Ontario that resulted in a deadly poisonous gas leak – these sites and the dangers associated with them produce limited public outcry. After the Ontario accident, a quarter of a million people in the surrounding communities had to be evacuated. Still, journalists' interest in this event was short-lived and did not result in protests against the transporting of hazardous substances.[392] Dam breaks in Asia in the 1970s received similarly scarce media coverage. In 1975, a typhoon destroyed dozens of dams in Henan province, flooding many cities and killing at least 26,000 people (with some sources claiming a death toll of more than 220,000) and directly or indirectly affecting more than 10 million.[393] Four years later, a similar catastrophe took place in neighboring India, but with a smaller scale of destruction, killing between 1,800 and 25,000 people.[394] These events left no trace in the public consciousness of societies in Europe or the United States.

Despite these accidents and disasters, it is Chernobyl and Fukushima that will remain synonymous with the fear of technological progress for many years. They caused relatively few casualties but, to this day, arouse extreme reactions among opponents of nuclear energy – reactions that are sometimes incomprehensible even to many ecologists. When asked about the impact of the Fukushima accident on the future of the nuclear industry, James Lovelock – creator of the famous Gaia hypothesis, according to which the biosphere is an enormous, self-regulating body – said the following: "The business with Fukushima is a joke. Well, it's not a joke; it is severe – how could anything like that have misled us? Twenty-six thousand people were killed by the magnitude-9 earthquake and tsunami (that caused the nuclear meltdown), and how many are known to have been killed by the nuclear accident? None."[395] He spoke in a similar vein about the emotions that continue to churn in people's minds about the Chernobyl disaster: "The most amazing lies were told, still are told and widely believed . . . Despite at least three investigations by reputable physicians such as those of the UN agency UNSCEAR there has been no measurable increase in deaths across Eastern Europe."[396]

Grains of truth, particles of falsehood

Most of the radiation we all receive during our lives comes from natural sources, and only a small fraction is linked to radioactive emissions from the nuclear industry in the broadest sense. As we already know, the coal industry is hardly free of radioactive elements. Coal, however, is no exception in this respect since other rocks, the ground, the water in the oceans, and the air we breathe all have low amounts of naturally occurring radiation. This was true long before humans appeared on Earth, and the knowledge of these processes should come with primary schooling. With this in mind, the reactions of certain activists who are vehemently opposed to nuclear power may seem hysterical and incomprehensible, especially considering the impact of other types of power plants. The only effective tool to combat such misguided perspectives appears to be increasing public awareness and knowledge of nuclear technologies, in addition to improving technical solutions to minimize people's fear of how nuclear reactors operate and how the dumping grounds for nuclear byproducts are kept secure.

The atom is not your nemesis

Nuclear energy has been part of the fabric of our planet since the dawn of time in the form of radioactivity that results from the decay of elements buried deep within the Earth as well as our planet's proximity to the largest reactor available to us – our Sun. We also come into contact with radioactivity on a daily basis, and not just by visiting spas that offer radon baths. Nor is this contact limited to those who live near nuclear power plants, military training grounds, or locations where atomic bombs were detonated in the past. Simply enough, we are bombarded with radioactive material and breathe in radioactive air every single day. However, these are usually small doses that can vary depending on the region in which we live. For example, people in the state of Colorado are exposed to slightly higher-than-average levels of radioactivity, mainly due to the geological structure of the ground and the uranium-rich rocks that abound in Colorado. This was the subject of a radio program in 2011, where a lecturer from the Colorado School of Mines educated and reassured his listeners that there was nothing to fear.[397]

The citizens of the United States are generally exposed to an average of about 2.2 millisieverts (mSv) per year. This is similar to most of Europe but almost twice as high as most of the United Kingdom, several times lower than some areas of Spain and Finland, and dozens of times lower than the parts of the world that hold the record for the lowest exposure to radiation. A whopping 90 percent of this amount comes from natural sources, that is, from the never-ending decay of elements in nature and the cosmic rays that reach the Earth's surface. The rest is made up of medical sources such as X-rays and CT scans (6 percent) as well as remnants of past nuclear tests (1.8 percent), air travel (0.24 percent), and others. Current nuclear power infrastructure accounts for only 0.1 percent of the dose of radiation that Americans receive each year.[398]

The data cited are not forbidden knowledge and have been published many times to educate a public that is highly sensitive to reports about radioactivity. But perhaps what may shock us more than this array of percentages is the fact that we are a source of radiation. Every hour, our bodies decay several million atoms of the potassium isotope that we ingest with our food. The same goes for the 7,000 atoms of uranium that also come from our daily meals. In addition, 30,000 atoms of radon, polonium, and lead are decayed every hour in our lungs, and we introduce them into the body with the air we inhale.[399] As a result of the decay of these elements, we emit alpha and gamma radiation throughout our lives. Does this mean that hugging another person is dangerous? Of course not. Well, unless someone decided to carry a lump of radium in their pocket, as some did in the early 20th century.

In addition to emitting radiation ourselves, when we walk around outdoors, we are bombarded with millions of gamma rays that emerge from the ground and the materials that make up the buildings around us, penetrating our bodies continuously. In addition, neutrons fall on us from the sky because of cosmic radiation. We receive hundreds of thousands of them during an hour's walk.

Although these numbers may seem high, they are no reason to panic; we receive the same doses of radiation from the day we are born. We would do well to remember this and continue to spread knowledge about the natural radioactivity that has surrounded people for centuries. Only then can we render young people and adults less susceptible to the catchy yet dangerous slogans of the opponents of nuclear energy – slogans that should not trigger our fears. As one expert from the nuclear industry points out, it is only a matter of time until most countries accept nuclear energy as the core of their energy systems: "After all, the future belongs to them. But we can't wait too long and keep putting off decisions until tomorrow."[400]

ATOMIC ENERGY AND THE ENVIRONMENT

One unquestionable advantage of nuclear power plants is that they do not emit pollutants that are typical of the combustion processes of traditional fuels such as coal, gas, or oil. According to estimates, this simple fact has allowed nuclear power plants to prevent the death of nearly two million people around the world thus far.[401] These pollutants consist of various substances that can be roughly divided into particulate matter and gases that primarily trigger or exacerbate respiratory and cardiovascular diseases. The chimneys of power plants that burn fossil fuels (especially coal) emit soot and fine particulate matter known as PM 10 and PM 2.5 that constitute essential components of smog, which mainly poisons our cities. At the same time, these chimneys emit large amounts of sulfur dioxide (SO_2), which transforms into sulfur trioxide (SO_3) through chemical reactions and combined with water, forms sulfuric acid (H_2SO_4). Sulfuric acid is a component of acid rain, which lays waste on mountain forests and many other landscapes. Another gas that is a mass product of coal and oil combustion is nitrogen oxide (NO_x). Like sulfuric acid, nitrogen oxide contributes to the formation of acid rain in the form of nitric acid (HNO_3), which it transforms when it reacts with air and water. Millions of tons of these varieties of particulate matter and gases are belched out into the atmosphere every year. Still, we must also count the other substances that are released as a result of combustion, such as carbon monoxide (CO), carbon dioxide (CO_2), or elements that are hazardous to human health, such as arsenic, mercury, cadmium, nickel, lead, and chromium.

The construction of nuclear power plants, the process of producing the materials that make up the plants, and the mining of uranium ore all generate large volumes of greenhouse gases indirectly. Still, overall, nuclear power is one of the most low-carbon energy sources available, along with wind power. For this reason, many closures of operational nuclear power plants are met with petitions from groups concerned about global warming.[402] In addition, both the power plants themselves and uranium ore mines – not to mention radioactive waste dumps – are usually located far from human settlements. In contrast, many coal mines exploit the raw material from deposits located directly under cities. This causes dangerous subsidence that sometimes reaches several meters, creating cracks and fissures on the surfaces of roads and buildings. At the same time, coal-fired power plants and the waste dumps that come with them are often located close to mining sites for purely logistical reasons.[403]

The oft-cited nuclear disasters at Three Mile Island, Chernobyl, and Fukushima provide fuel for anti-nuclear organizations. Still, paradoxically, they have significantly contributed to the creation of safer technologies and more efficient procedures for obtaining energy from nuclear reactors. After all, mistakes are best thought of as learning opportunities. Nuclear energy has become so safe that the daily operations of a nuclear power plant result in lower radiation doses reaching people living nearby than those emitted by a typical coal-fired power plant located at a similar distance. In both cases, these doses are a tiny fraction of the overall radiation our bodies receive from the environment. Research to date has not confirmed the harmful effects of either living near nuclear power plants or working there – or, for that matter, of living in areas with naturally high radioactivity.[404]

If we consider the cumulative number of deaths that result from direct accidents and air pollution per unit of electricity produced by each kind of energy source, nuclear energy places below almost all other sources, at 0.03 cases per TWh of electricity supplied. By comparison, the figure for lignite-based power generation is more than 1000 times higher (Fig. 1). Only solar power plants have a lower rate. Still, the difference between their results and those attributed to nuclear power is tiny.[405] As the saying goes, waiting for death can be more frightening than death itself. And many in the anti-nuclear movement believe that radioactive waste dumps are significant death dealers. Even statements by industry experts suggesting that "in over 50 years of civil nuclear power experience, the management and disposal of civil nuclear waste has not caused any serious health or environmental problems, nor posed any real risk to the general public"[406] fail to alleviate their fears.

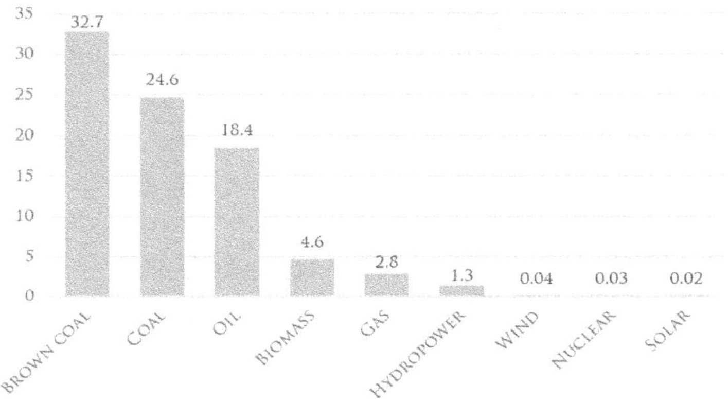

Fig. 1. Mortality rates calculated as deaths from accidents and air pollution per terawatt-hour (TWh).[407]

While it is true that many tons of radioactive waste are produced every year by more than four hundred active sites around the world, this waste is stored with the highest safety standards for hazardous materials in mind. Their longevity is a much bigger problem. The half-life of most isotopes generated in reactors ranges from several thousand to several million years. For this reason, they are stored in the safest locations possible from a geological standpoint. The chances of these dangerous materials escaping into the environment are minimal, – comparable to the chances of naturally occurring radioactive ores and elements that have been deposited in the depths of the Earth for billions of years.

On the other hand, the storage of waste in the coal industry remains consistently underexplored. This waste also contains large amounts of radioactive material, as coal deposits are never 100% clean. For this reason, radiation levels at coal-fired plants are sometimes several times higher than at nuclear plants. In addition, the spoil heaps from the excavations are generally left unsecured, unprotected, and often wholly uncovered for many years. Thus, the fine dust that forms them is usually carried by the wind and rainwater and blankets the surrounding area. The waste rock that is left on the ground after being separated from the much more valuable coal is the primary source of radioactivity here, together with the ash left over from burning fuel. To give an idea of the scale of the problem, 600,000 tons of ash produced in the aftermath of burning coal contains an average of 3 tons of uranium and 7 tons of thorium. Unlike nuclear radioactive materials, which are stored according to strict rules in designated areas, radioactive elements deposited in open spoil heaps can easily penetrate the environment.

Interestingly, countries that are rich in coal deposits are often the scene of vigorous protests against planned investments in nuclear energy. However, these pickets and rallies are not driven by fear of the unknown and purportedly radioactive technology but mainly by the careful calculations of groups connected to the coal industry. [408] For instance, in mid-2020, demonstrators in Poland held a banner that said "No to the atom. We have coal." One would be forgiven for thinking that those holding it were environmental activists; in reality, they were members of unions representing the interests of Silesian black coal mining operations. The opening of a nuclear power plant would bring significant job losses, and there are whole regions where working in the mines is almost considered a family tradition.

As we have seen, the opponents of nuclear energy do not treat the waste generated by different types of power plants in the same way. For some reason, well-protected waste buried deep underground and securely cushioned by geological features is viewed as deadly in comparison with the spoil heaps that people have coexisted with since the beginning of the industrial era. It turns out that, once again, what is new but less familiar can frighten us more than the old problems we have faced for years. Perhaps this is yet another instance where the old familiar adage rings true: "Better the devil you know than the devil you don't."

FUTURE TRENDS: SAFETY FIRST

Nuclear power is constantly evolving, and the plants that are built today have little in common with those whose walls went up 70 years ago. The scientific world has long been waiting for further progress in civilian nuclear power. Even at its very outset in the 1950s, scientists predicted that nuclear power plants that used fusion as an energy source would start appearing by the 1980s, heralding the long-awaited and strongly hyped "atomic golden age."[409] But nothing of the sort has transpired. The commissioning of conventional fourth-generation nuclear reactors, which are safer and produce less waste, is not expected until later this decade, and it is unclear whether this will even come to fruition at all. The blueprints for such reactors were first drawn around the early 2000s, but the first experimental plants are relatively young, with construction dating back only to 2018.[410] Although commercial power plants of this type are only expected to become fully operational in approximately a decade, they are worth a closer look.

The most important advantage of the new generation of reactors, from the point of view of the widespread fear of nuclear technologies, is the significant reduction in the life cycle of the radioactive waste they generate. This would only be hazardous for a few hundred years, which marks a substantial improvement over current numbers. Another no less significant improvement is that these reactors enable much greater efficiency in the production of electricity from the same amount of raw material used, including the possibility of using existing waste as fuel in some types of reactors. Finally, designers are working to automate specific safety procedures. The new plants will be less susceptible to human error than their present-day counterparts, which means that human error may not result in the severe accidents we know from the past.[411]

The design changes that are expected in next-generation reactors are closely related to the idea of passive nuclear safety, which has already been implemented to a limited extent in older plants. The passive protection of procedures such as cooling and shutting down reactors, as well as automatic responses to emergencies, are intended to reduce the probability of the disasters that we know from previous decades. Paradoxically, the automation of such operations through advanced technology will almost entirely remove the need for human intervention, which may also be a magnet for future criticism in anti-nuclear circles. If a malfunction were to occur in such an automated power plant, many would fall back on a familiar, comfortable line: "We have created a Frankenstein."

THE REAPPEARING MYTH

Why is conducting a rational and honest public debate on issues related to nuclear energy such an uphill struggle? Why do we perpetuate the myth of a highly hazardous method of producing energy that societies should abandon as soon as they can? The popularity and ubiquity of the Internet have led to thousands of self-proclaimed experts speaking out on all sorts of issues. Thus, people probing the Web for objective and verified information have to wade through a dense web of dubious material. This is all good and well if these seekers are persistent enough to reach the facts they seek, undeterred by the trivia they encounter along the way. Their only loss will be a small amount of precious time in the process of verifying the materials they find. However, some of those who are less patient will likely stop at an article or film with one or more exclamation marks in the title and fall into a trap set by those driven by a desire to lure readers or viewers with cheap sensationalism – or worse, to stoke unfounded fear and propagate myths still smoldering on a bedrock of ignorance.

I'M NO EXPERT, SO HERE'S MY TWO CENTS

We live in a time of widespread access to the Internet. Almost anyone can feel like an expert and write their commentary, post a video they recorded on YouTube, or create a blog where they can post virtually anything. This has made a new quasi-profession: the influencer. Influencers, as their self-appointed title suggests, influence other people with their opinions, primarily on social networks.

The lack of demand for objective expert opinion is not a new phenomenon. A new class of opinion shapers emerged in the early stages of the development of modern media, especially in TV commercials. Today, celebrities and respected people smile down at us from thousands of billboards, from the covers of newspapers, and from the packaging of everyday products. Debates on environmental issues, too, are often driven by the voices of famous actors and singers, whose reflections are constantly recycled in the media. One of the most famous examples of such activity in recent years is Leonardo DiCaprio's speech on global warming at the 2016 Academy Awards gala.[412] It no longer matters whether the person speaking on a given topic has an education that entitles them to make authoritative judgments or whether they have knowledge or experience of any kind. What matters is that they are the darlings of cinema and television screens – a surefire guarantee that they will attract many viewers, who in turn will bring in a new batch of advertisers.

DANGER LURKS IN THE DARK

Despite the best efforts of the personnel of nuclear power plants and the safety procedures that have been in place for years, an accident could always occur at any of the more than 400 nuclear power plants currently in operation, resulting in widespread contamination. Such accidents could be triggered, for instance, by a terrorist attack, for which we can never be 100% prepared. Back in 1908, enraged mobs in Anatole France's science fiction novel *Penguin Island* took revenge on cities by destroying them with small atomic bombs.[413] The September 11, 2001 attacks have also persuaded some that it is theoretically possible for extremist groups to hijack planes and crash them into selected targets, such as nuclear installations. After all, there is never a shortage of lunatics or religious extremists willing to take lives other than their own. But would such an event lead to widespread destruction and the contamination of a vast area? Unlikely.

The Fukushima disaster drew many people's attention to the fragility of our technology in the face of nature's leviathan forces. One cataclysmic earthquake and the resulting tsunami were enough to lead to the greatest accidental nuclear catastrophe in Japan's history and the second one in history after Chernobyl. If something like this happened even in Japan, despite the country's high levels of technological advancement and social discipline, then an earthquake or meteorite could cause a similar disaster in another power plant when we least expect it. Some activists believe that it's only a matter of time. However, what they fail to understand is that were it not for the confluence of inevitable procedural and technical missteps, the damage would have been much smaller. Unfortunately, the human factor and the simple errors that come with it cannot be effectively eliminated, not just in nuclear facilities but in any area of human activity.

Finally, there is the fear of another possible technical failure compounded by previous disasters. After all, the Three Mile Island incident sparked additional restrictions and safety measures that were put in place across many other facilities, but this did not prevent the Chernobyl disaster. The incident in Ukraine was supposed to be the last severe calamity to involve a nuclear reactor – and yet, a quarter of a century later, another one struck in Fukushima. Who can guarantee that the next one will not happen in the next year or the next five years and that it will not be at a power plant close to where we live? Of course, none of us are crystal ball-bearing clairvoyants with a perfect record, and thus, it is impossible to rule out such events unequivocally. As history has shown, even the greatest sages can be seriously mistaken in their judgments from time to time. In such cases, however, we must strive to ensure that all proper procedures are followed and for technological improvements to reduce the risk of serious fallout from such failures continually. On the other hand, if another catastrophe did happen – even one as big as the one in Ukraine or Japan – would humanity be unable to cope with its consequences? The practice has shown that the big, bad wolf is not always as bad as some choose to paint him.

Fear is easier than seeking knowledge

From the very dawn of atomic research, knowledge was amalgamated with fear and fantasy. Some, like Frederick Soddy or John von Neumann, proclaimed the coming of a utopian world with free energy for all; others warned of an impending nuclear holocaust. However, on both sides of the equation, at least some voices came with solid expertise in the structure of the atom and the phenomenon of radioactivity. It was much worse when hapless journalists or writers of fiction took on the task of describing the nuclear world. The latter, of course, deliberately wrote various scenarios that depicted the positive or sinister use of atomic energy, and we can assume that their audience treated such works as pure entertainment. Perhaps some of the fear that accompanied successive fictitious Armageddons and assorted apocalyptic events remained somewhere in the subconscious of those who were prone to believing in them. However, the actual harvester of mental havoc was – and still is – the media.

Type in a search term related to nuclear power or a past nuclear disaster, and thousands of articles and reports will pop up in your favorite search engine. Their narratives are so varied that a person who wishes to form an opinion based on them will undoubtedly find it very difficult to do so. Nuclear-friendly authors often include references and footnotes to the information they present, but this is not the rule. Reliable descriptions are sometimes mixed with utopian enthusiasm for further development of atomic energy, which sometimes harkens back to similarly glowing articles from before World War II. On the other hand, sources that project a negative mental image of nuclear power are usually accompanied by graphics intended to evoke and reinforce unfavorable associations with such investments, including towering steam-belching chimneys or bright symbols associated with radioactivity. The very titles of these materials are often designed to arouse negative emotions. Strong emotions are what people usually need and expect in a world filled with information. Netflix knew this when it recorded a hit 2019 miniseries that bore a deceptively simple title: *Chernobyl.*

Using only the name of the power plant, which became synonymous with the fear of radioactivity, was a marketing success for the producers. This one word was enough to reel viewers in and glue them to their computers and TV sets. Viewers were hungry for emotions, craving the chance to experience this most famous of disasters together with the characters. After all, few (if any) of those who tuned in to the first episode did so with an educational purpose. Most wanted sensational entertainment rooted in facts, which heightened the excitement of watching a disaster unfold.

Stirring, overcharged YouTube videos with titles such as 3 Reasons Why Nuclear Energy Is Terrible! (which has been viewed by 4.6 million users)[414] or the equally popular 88,000 tons of radioactive waste – and nowhere to put it (4.3 million viewers)[415] do not aim to contribute to the debate on the merits of investing in nuclear energy. They seek to impose the narrative that the atom is dangerous and it is wiser to invest in other energy-providing technologies. Such scaremongering can be found not only in semi-anonymous YouTube channels but also in reputable newspaper articles written by purported experts. One example is a December 2011 piece in *The New York Times* by Australian physician Helen Caldicott, who wrote that "By now close to one million people have died of causes linked to the Chernobyl disaster" and that the disaster in Fukushima "far exceeds Chernobyl in terms of the effects on public health."[416] The very title of her article – *After Fukushima: Enough Is Enough* – betrayed the purpose of conveying scientifically inaccurate information.

All media enjoy scaring their readers. In 1979, after the accident at the Three Mile Island power plant, the cover of *Time* magazine attracted readers by plastering the words *Nuclear Nightmare* over a menacing image of power plant chimneys.[417] As we know from U.S. President Jimmy Carter's visit to the site of the disaster, the incident was no nightmare. Disappointingly, however, the President bought into the newspaper's narrative. Instead of reassuring his citizens by explaining the causes and consequences of the accident, as befitted a true statesman, he let unfounded fear run amok in the name of specific political interests.

WHAT WILL WE FEAR NEXT?

The difficulties inherent in understanding nuclear energy inevitably drive the emotions of people who are not familiar with physics and indirectly influence the creation of myths. In antiquity, every lightning storm conjured the image of Zeus, the god of thunder, whose ire not only explained all that was undesirable, dangerous, and threatening but also aligned well with the religious inclinations of the day. Despite significant scientific progress, similar myths remained very much alive in Christian cultural circles as recently as the 20th century, manifesting themselves in subtle everyday rituals such as placing votive candles or images of the Virgin Mary in windows during storms. These measures were supposed to protect the inhabitants from being struck by lightning. Ancient societies interpreted energy derived from the sun (which was of *de facto* nuclear origin) somewhat differently.

On the one hand, it was seen as a desirable, safe, and beneficial energy source that allowed vegetation to flourish and provided heat and light. Still, it also evoked fear, as vividly emphasized in the mythologies of desert-dwelling peoples such as the ancient Egyptians. Nuclear power plants have inherited a similarly ambiguous character. By providing electricity, they play an undeniably positive role. But their frequent association with nuclear weapons and the media's powerful amplification of the few accidents that have occurred in recent decades are enough to persuade part of the public to look at nuclear energy through the lens of emotions and myths, which render it dangerous and unpredictable.

Given that the world's leading politicians immediately surrendered to fear after the Fukushima accident, we can expect further protests against the development of nuclear power, not just in highly developed countries such as Germany and Japan. Radioactive waste dumps will continue to frighten us as they expand. We can also expect protests against overly autonomous fourth-generation reactors and other machines, such as proton and hadron colliders, which smash the most miniature known bricks of matter into dust. These and other technologies will continue to elicit claims among influencers that such dangerous experiments could blow up our planet and create a black hole. Or perhaps we genuinely enjoy being afraid – after all, in normal times, we routinely line up to see the next blockbuster horror film on the big screen, overwhelmed with both fascination and fear. Perhaps "the only thing we have to fear is the 'culture of fear' itself."[418]

FIVE
IS THE EARTH BIG ENOUGH FOR US ALL?

Jolanta Rodzoś

Even in antiquity, in the age of Confucius, when fewer humans lived on the planet than there are today in Bangladesh alone, concerns circulated about whether there would be enough space and food for everyone if the population grew. For centuries, eminent scholars and political figures alike argued with conviction that the struggle for space, food, and other resources would unleash an imminent catastrophe, often urgently calling to limit the rate of population growth in a variety of ways. Even today, this current of thought about the finite capacity of the Earth continues to dominate, and fears that the Earth will not be able to sustain us all are widespread.

The question of how many (or how few) people inhabit the Earth or parts of it has always been a pesky problem for humanity. It was and is important for many reasons, but two stand head and shoulders above the rest: the space a growing population needs to live and the amount of resources it needs to survive. Put simply, some may argue that population growth inevitably leads to shortages of both space and the resources that are necessary to stay alive, not to mention other problems that arise along the way. Nature provides numerous examples that the unfettered growth of a species can lead to terminal consequences, both for the species itself and the environment in which it lives. After all, we have all heard of lakes, once filled with crystalline water, that, through the constant growth of plants, have irreversibly turned into quagmires. These simple comparisons to the natural world lead humans, as rational beings, to reflect on the consequences of human population growth and to fear for the future of both humanity and the planet that nourishes it. They also give rise to various theories and generate actions aimed at halting the suffocating sprawl of humanity on the lake that is Planet Earth.

It is said that human history is a story written by humanity's successive achievements. Still, it is also the story of how our species has struggled with its growth processes to reach a state we consider optimal. If we look into the past, it is easy to see that the fears associated with the size of the human population have been bi-directional. We have feared both population surpluses and population shortages. We have taken measures to suppress population growth as well as to increase population. It all depended on the goal. For more than 200 years, however, an anti-population trend – one that seeks to halt the process of population growth – has prevailed. It is accompanied by hostile rhetoric towards population growth, which evokes many fears and anxieties and perpetuates negative ideas about population processes. It has virtually become a binding doctrine in modern social policy. Elements of it have entered permanently into school and university curricula and constantly appear in the social debate occurring at the institutional as well as the private levels. Nearly everyone has heard that the Earth is overpopulated and, therefore, in grave danger.

Where do these tendencies to demonize demographic phenomena and create a negative atmosphere around them come from? They stem from the simple fact that we live in times in which the world population is growing rapidly. In just two or three generations, our species has grown by the billions. Currently, the population of all the continents put together is estimated at over 8 billion, while only half a century ago, we numbered just over 3.5 billion. According to the United Nations, in 2050 there will be about 9 billion people on Earth, and we might hit 10-11 billion by the end of this century. Although it is not clear what this really means, it is straightforward to accept the notion, once expressed by Anne Ehrlich, that the expansion of the human species is the most spectacular event of the current geological epoch, the Holocene.[419]

Debates about human population growth often touch on the alarming notion that while our population grew slowly during the first few millennia of our existence, the rate of growth has accelerated significantly in modern times. After all, it was not until the 19th and 20th centuries that the world population began to be counted in billions. We reached our first billion around 1804, our second in 1927, and topped it off with another five billion in just the last hundred years.

Another common concern is that, as our population grows, the volume of the Earth's resources available to each human inhabitant shrinks, and, above all, the amount of land available to humans decreases. This is because human settlements are still concentrated in the regions of the Earth that offer the best and most ample mix of natural resources. For the most part, these are relatively flat areas with fertile soils, a long growing season, and access to water. As it turns out, in general, settlement preferences have changed little since ancient times. Our habitable zone is indeed expanding gradually, but there are still natural and non-natural settlement factors that prevent us from making use of the Earth's entire surface. This triggers anxiety about the living space that will be available for future generations. At the same time, many believe that population growth that inflates the population density in areas suitable for human settlement generates negative socio-economic and environmental processes. In a word, it harms both humanity and the planet and is a straight road to extinction.

Since the world's population has been growing for as long as the world has existed, but this has not yet led to our total annihilation as a species, it is reasonable to ask: To what extent are the fears justified, and to what extent are they imaginary?

Exponential growth, or the power of the human imagination

How the world's population has grown

According to international statistics, in 2022, 8 billion people were living on Earth. Although the history of our species is very long – scientists estimate that *Homo sapiens* appeared on this planet at least 200,000 years ago – it was only recently that the Earth's population began to balloon. Scientists assume that the first noticeable increase was associated with the Neolithic agricultural revolution, which took place between around 10,000 and 8,000 BC. The transition from hunter-gatherer societies to a sedentary way of life and the birth of farming and animal husbandry generated food surpluses. It translated into a marked increase in the human population. If modern statistics are to be believed, at the dawn of this revolution, only a few million people lived on the entire planet.[420] In that period, an average person needed several square kilometers of space to stay alive. In ecosystems with ample natural resources, 2 square kilometers were enough; where food was scarce, every human needed more than 10.[421]

The scientific community believes that, in the first year of the Common Era, the Earth may have been able to host only

150 to 400 million people across all continents; the Earth would have been simply unable to support a larger population.[422] These figures are, of course, imprecise due to the lack of reliable and consistent sources of information that far into the past, but all historical analyses and mathematical models point to similar values.

In the first centuries of the modern era, the human population grew slowly. The world reached a population of 600 million around 1700. The 18th century was a watershed period, as it saw a record population increase of 400 million people. It was then that the first theory on overpopulation was developed. Around 1804, humanity hit another milestone: 1 billion humans on Earth. The next billion took much less time to incubate. However, the most significant population increase occurred in the second half of the 20th century. Between 1960 and 1970, the human population increased by a whopping 700 million, then again by 740 million between 1970 and 1980, and by 840 million between 1980 and 1990. The time required to reach each additional billion shrank significantly over time.

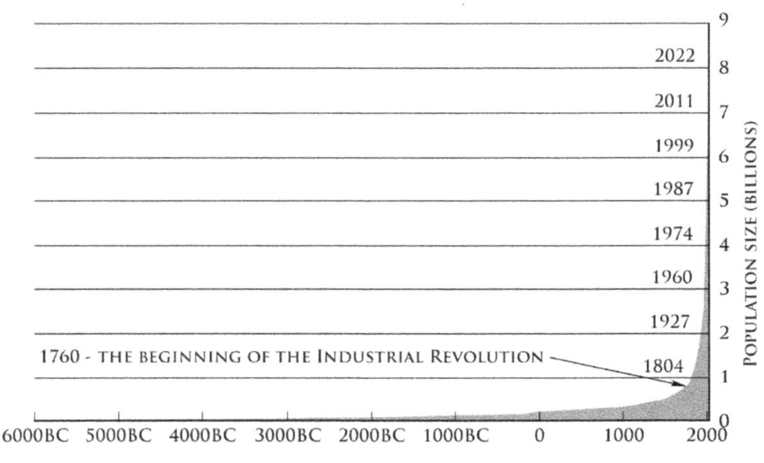

Fig. 1: Change in world population over time.[423]

This simple analysis alone indicates that the growth of Earth's population has not followed a linear pattern. However, it is possible to identify a period of significantly accelerated growth that sent the total number of people in the world skyrocketing. That period encompasses the last three centuries, with an apparent surge in the 20th century, particularly in its second half.

WHAT IS EXPONENTIAL POPULATION GROWTH?

Humans, like many other species, tend to expand in numbers through a formula described in mathematics by the exponential function. This happens when the rate of change is relatively constant for a prolonged period; that is, in successive units of time, the values change by the same percentage. Keeping the rate of population growth constant, however, means that in each subsequent unit of time, there is a more significant increase in population than in the previous one. This may not seem very logical at first because our instinct tells us we should equate a constant percentage with a continuous number. However, a continual increase by the same rate does not mean a boost by the same number because in each successive year, the base from which we calculate the percentage increase becomes larger and larger.

Imagine town X with a population of 1,000. If the number of inhabitants was to increase by 20 percent a year for several years in a row, then after the first year, the town would have 1,200 inhabitants (1,000 + 20 percent of 1,000), but after the second year, it would already have 1,440 (1,200 + 20 percent of 1,200), not 1,400. In the third year, it would have 1,728 inhabitants (1,440 +20 percent of 1,440), not 1600, and so on. The longer the period of steady percentage population growth, the more rapidly the population expands. This can be seen in the graph below. At first, the line showing the change in population size is almost horizontal. Still, as the population increase in successive years becomes larger and larger, the growth curve, though previously running almost parallel to the timeline, suddenly begins to shoot upward and takes on the shape of the letter J.

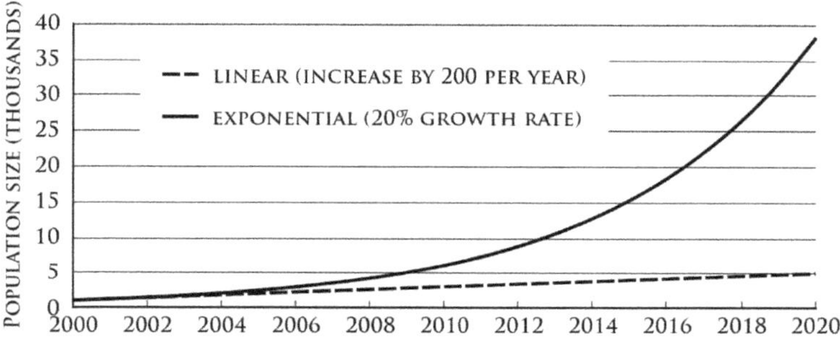

Fig. 2: Linear vs. exponential growth.

The second feature of exponential growth is that the higher the rate of change, the faster the population grows. If we assume that the annual growth rate for a population of 1 million people is 1 percent, then after 100 years, the population size will be 2.7 million people. If the rate is 2 percent, the population will grow to 7.2 million people in the same period. And if the rate of growth is only 0.1 percent, in 100 years, the population will grow to only 1,105,000. This shows how much exponential growth differs from linear growth. Small changes in the rate of growth cause significant changes in population growth.

EXPONENTIAL GROWTH AS THE BEDROCK OF FEAR ABOUT OUR FUTURE

The rate of human population growth throughout history has been variable. It is estimated that in the first centuries of the modern era, harsh living conditions, epidemics, and wars – all of which underpinned high human mortality – kept the annual population growth rate at no more than 0.1 percent. That is, if the human population at one point was 1 million people, then in 100 years, there were only 105,000 new human specimens.

As civilization developed, especially in response to medical advances, access to a variety of goods, and improved living conditions that reduced mortality, the rate of population growth increased. By the middle of the 20th century, it had already reached an average of 1 percent on a global level. This seemingly low rate produced significant real increases in population. If we go back to the example of a population of 1 million people, then at an annual growth rate of 1 percent, the community will have 2.7 million people after 100 years. This centennial surge far exceeds the initial population size. This is the essence of the exponential function.

In the second half of the 20th century, the rate of population growth began to increase even further, exceeding 2 percent at its peak in 1965-1970.[424] This was in response to continued medical advances, improved living conditions around the world, and demographic processes to compensate for the population losses that occurred during World War II. With such a high growth rate, the actual population growth was tremendous. Our model population would grow from 1 million to 7.2 million in a mere century. As we can clearly see, the number we end up with is much higher than our starting point. Suppose in 1970, the population of the Earth was about 3.5 billion. In that case, it is easy to calculate that, a 2 percent rate of growth, the annual numerical increase worldwide would be 70 million people. In the following years, at the same rate of growth, the figures for actual annual increases were even higher as the baseline for the calculation became larger and larger. This phenomenon, because of its incredible scale, was called the population explosion.

This is when alarm bells started ringing. Not for the first time, but this time, they rang out with unique urgency. The unprecedented phenomenon stirred people's imaginations, and catastrophic visions soon flooded in, along with pessimistic forecasts of how the situation would develop. The skyrocketing numbers, combined with uncertainty about the future, led to the adoption of a distinct research philosophy and justified the omission of alternative options for how events would unfold. Fear of impending doom overwhelmed all other emotions. People began to compare the time it took for the population to double and the time that elapsed between each additional billion humans. The conclusions were sobering. While it took humanity several hundred thousand years to reach the first billion, the increase from 1 billion to 2 billion took only 123 years, and the jump from 5 billion to 6 billion took only 12 years. Such comparisons obviously imposed a narrative of imminent demographic disaster.

However, it also took 12 years for the seventh billion people to be born, which means that the rate of world population growth had slowed somewhat. It turns out that, as for other living organisms, exponential growth in the population of humans has its limitations. First, the natural rate of change is high when there are favorable conditions for people to grow. As studies of other species show, any environmental constraints slow down developmental processes. Second, the rate of population growth also depends on cultural and economic factors, which generate separate constraints. Third, and finally, humans may consciously control their developmental processes. Thus, a logarithmic model, in which a deceleration follows a period of dynamic growth, becomes a more appropriate approach to describing these phenomena.

At the time when the growth curve was rising fastest (in the 1960s and 1970s), it was difficult to predict whether this deceleration would occur, and even those who expected it did not know when it would come. This was a classic example of what the social sciences call *present bias*, which is the tendency to attach too much importance to phenomena occurring in the present and to extrapolate them into the future. This underlies the emergence of alarmist demographic theories. Many of their theses concerning the way we use nature's resources are not unfounded and deserve attention. However, how we exploit our environment and population growth are two very distinct issues.

Is more better than less?
Population and the world's great religions

The development of the human population is not only a theoretical issue but, above all, a practical one, as it has a direct relationship with social, economic, and cultural development, sometimes going as far as to determine the fates of countries and nations. At the same time, it is an essential phenomenon from a regular person's perspective, as the size of the community to which they belong partially determines how they function and act. It also affects their quality of life and determines possibilities for further development. For these reasons, demographic growth has commanded our attention since ancient times. It has been a component of both the social policies of specific countries and regions and the religious systems that flourished in different cultural areas.

The vast majority of the "great religions" of the world, which germinated in the first stages of human development, have strongly emphasized the need to procreate and perpetuate the human race. However, the strength of this imperative has varied. In Judaism, Yahweh addressed the first humans with the words, "Be fruitful and multiply, and fill the Earth."[425] One of the most essential divine commandments, its fulfillment was a key manifestation of fidelity to God. It was subsequently codified and expanded in both state and customary law and became an inseparable part of the moral framework of Jewish communities. It unequivocally obliged the followers of Moses to procreate. It obliged men to marry and leave behind at least one daughter and one son who would be able to produce their offspring.[426]

In Judaism, having many children was seen as a sign of

God's special favor. Childlessness, on the other hand, was considered a punishment and a misfortune, and women without offspring were considered cursed. The Talmud compares childless people to inanimate beings. Many women known from the pages of the Bible – Sarah, Abraham's wife; Rachel, Jacob's wife; and Samson's mother – went down in history because they experienced God's special grace: they were purportedly cured of infertility. Despite the vast civilizational changes and the relaxation of many social norms that have occurred since then, Judaism continues to embody an unequivocally pro-fertility culture.

Hinduism carries a similar message. Today, Hinduism is estimated to have some 1.3 billion followers. Both marriage and producing offspring (especially male offspring) have always been viewed as the sacred and inalienable duties of every man, regardless of his social status. This obligation is based on two foundations: one's commitment to their ancestors and the desire to preserve the prevailing socio-religious structures and traditions. For followers of Hindu sects, the lack of children is a confirmation of sins committed in the present life or previous incarnations, as well as a severe and legitimate reason for social rejection.[427] For a woman, historically, motherhood was the primary way to gain the respect of family and society, if not the only way. Since Hindu religions are also a philosophy of life for their followers, their influence on the realities of social life was and still is very strong. Traditional Hindu families have always strived to have numerous children as a way of fulfilling their religious obligations, a ticket to better incarnations, and a guarantee of respect and recognition in their earthly life. For this reason, demographic processes in India have been and continue to be more dynamic than in other cultural systems.

The cult of fertility is also very pronounced in Islam. The Qur'an, the religion's central holy book, very clearly encourages believers to marry and have children. It outlines a system of norms and values, including the role of women in the family and society, that incentivizes high fertility.[428] Islam even embraced polygamy among men because it was beneficial to the demographic development of Muslim communities. This was an excellent solution, especially for times of war, which periodically thinned the ranks of the male members of the community and lowered widowed women's chances of procreating. In Islam, religious doctrine has become the basis of law and a universally binding form of social education. Fertility rates in Muslim families have always been higher than those in Western religions; countries that are built on the Islamic tradition are populous and continue to grow at an exceptionally rapid pace.

The Christian religion is less firm on the issue of procreation despite having grown out of Judaism. The New Testament, which provides an interpretation of the faith and formulates moral and ethical principles that the followers of Christ consider binding, emphasizes married love and fidelity rather than the need to deliver a large number of offspring. Placing women in a position more equal to that of men is an expression of a less decisive approach to fertility than in Judaism. Having children has traditionally been understood as one of the purposes of marriage, but it has never been treated as an inalienable obligation. Christianity has even elevated celibacy to a sacred status and Catholics have made it obligatory for its sizable clergy. Nevertheless, in the Christian tradition, the family has always been treated as the embodiment of the highest values of faith, and having numerous offspring was seen as a manifestation of acting for the glory of God.

Buddhism has the most casual approach to demographic issues and one that rests upon achieving long-term goals that transcend temporality. The central axis of this system is the spiritual development of the human being and achieving a state of liberation of the mind from worldly worries and desires. Thus, there is no unconditional mandate to start a family and give birth to numerous offspring. Buddhist religious law does not impose any templates for procreation, just as it refrains from imposing other social obligations.[429] And as in Christianity, celibacy is a virtue and is obligatory for monks. Yet Buddha's teachings very clearly underscore the importance of perpetuating life, with a focus on the value of life.[430]

Despite differences, all religious systems are focused on increasing the number of their followers. If for this reason alone, they would likely favor fertility.

Population in Historical Social Doctrines

Aspirations toward a large population can be found above all in the philosophical doctrines of agrarian societies and those with grand military ambitions, which required a large base to achieve an adequate level of agricultural production and to maintain a sizable army. The currents of demographic thought in ancient China and India illustrate this trend. The best-known evangelist of the former was Confucius, who lived between 551 and 479 BCE. Confucius praised the notion of a large family with numerous offspring in each generation. His teachings clearly stated that having a large number of children, especially sons, was a condition for happiness and prosperity, as well as a duty to one's ancestors and to society.[431] This conviction has clear cultural and economic underpinnings. Having many offspring provides the family with a cheap labor force, ensures the continuity of the bloodline, and guarantees that the parents will be taken care of in their old age.[432]

The entire philosophy of Confucianism, developed by the Master's disciples after his death, was filled with references to the family and its duties. In China and other parts of East Asia, it gave rise to a system of values in which large numbers of children were held in esteem, respect, and social prestige. On the other hand, Confucius recognized the dark sides of overpopulation in some areas. In particular, he saw the prospect of poverty and famine, especially in periods of prolonged crop failures.[433] His concerns probably stemmed from the realities of social life in China at the time. Confucius recommended that the authorities move citizens from overpopulated regions to areas with lower population densities that could feed a larger population. He also gave guidelines on the optimal relationship between the size of an area and its population.[434] However, he never advocated limiting population growth.

A similar approach is found, among others, in the socio-political thought of ancient India. This is conveyed in high relief by one of the most distinguished and influential representatives of philosophical thought of that period, known as Kautilya, Vishnugupta, or Chanakya (375-283 BCE). A longtime imperial advisor and author of social and political strategies, Kautijya strongly emphasized that a large population was one of the sources of a state's political, economic, and military strength.[435] He, therefore, held that the goal of the state should be to pursue population growth, and to provide human settlements with enough support to enable them to maintain a robust size, which in turn allows them to defend themselves. His views and approaches to state governance, recorded in the form of political treatises, influenced the culture of ancient India and the canons of state governance.

Population concerns were also one of the cornerstones of ancient Greek social thought. The most comprehensive discussion of the subject can be found in the philosophy of Plato (423-347 BCE) and Aristotle (384-322 BCE). They lived somewhat later than Confucius and, unlike him, represented a highly urbanized part of the world that was at the peak of its cultural and demographic development. It is estimated that, between 1000 and 400 BCE, the population of Greece may have increased as much as threefold, and the rate of growth may have periodically reached 2-3 percent per year.[436] The city-states of Greece may, therefore, have been intimately familiar with the scarcity of consumer goods and the social problems that resulted from it.

Both thinkers argued that a large population was a net negative for the state. In their view, ballooning populations are negatively correlated with prosperity and the level of social satisfaction and inhibit economic development. They also hinder efficient and effective state governance. Therefore, they postulated that population processes should be supervised, and the state should maintain a kind of population optimum, that is, the most appropriate people for a given area. Plato even indicated specific optimal population numbers for the Greek city-states of the time. In the case of population surpluses, he suggested establishing colonies and delegating some of the population to the territories they comprised. Both philosophers advocated birth control, including the use of abortion. In Aristotle's view, overpopulation was more threatening than invasions from the outside world, given the social ills it purportedly brought: misery, depravity, social unrest, and internal wars.

The currents of thought that flowed in ancient Rome presented a completely different approach whose most famous and influential spokesperson was Cicero (106-44 BCE). Guided by the political goals of his empire, he argued that the more Romans there were, the better, for an empire needs men to conquer territories and women to feed them.[437]

Regardless of the positions each of these cultures and governments espoused, all of them were guided by pragmatic concerns.

Population in Modern Social Theories

One of the first modern socio-economic doctrines to present a clear position on population issues was mercantilism. This doctrine emerged in Europe and filtered across borders between the 16th and 18th centuries, synchronizing with scientific and technological progress and geographical discoveries that significantly expanded the frontiers of the known world, thus opening up new prospects for economic development.[438] Mercantilism was full of optimism and faith in the possibility of using these unprecedented opportunities to build new economic powers, primarily by increasing the production of various goods and spurring international trade. When it came to population issues, the theorists that represented this economic philosophy believed that, from the point of view of the state, a large population was a valuable asset. A large population meant a more extensive and less expensive labor force, a larger market, larger trade volumes, and a stronger army for both defense and expansion.[439]

Mercantilists looked at society in a multidimensional way, seeing it not only as an economic and military resource but also as consumers driving demand for goods, stimulating innovation and progress along the way. They, therefore, advocated increasing population growth by promoting procreation-friendly policies, prohibiting emigration, and discouraging celibacy and childlessness. In some states, this doctrine was pursued so doggedly that unmarried men were not given government positions, while those who married before the age of 25 received tax exemptions. Despite this general fertility-friendly stance, mercantilism also included a more restrained current that more carefully assessed the possibilities and consequences of population growth. It was represented, among others, by Niccolò Machiavelli and Giovanni Botero, two Italian thinkers who argued that regardless of the development of manufacturing and trade, land resources and their productivity were essential factors that limited the possibilities of population development.[440]

In the mid-18th century, a school of thought opposed to mercantilism was born in France. It was called physiocratism, a name that came from the Greek *physiocratie*, which meant *the rule of nature*. The founder of this school and one of its leading representatives was François Quesney, court physician to King Louis XV. The physiocrats' opposition to the theses put forth by the previous system was driven by the simple observation of its effects.

Mercantilism put the welfare of states and nations first and promoted solutions that were good from that point of view. This included keeping wages as low as possible and artificially regulating the prices of manufactured goods, including grain. Consequently, as particular social groups (such as the merchant and banker classes) got more affluent, the lower classes suffered extreme pauperization, exacerbated by the fact that it was among them that the most significant population growth occurred. Primitive agriculture was not able to meet the nutritional needs of the entire society. Therefore, physiocratism, as a new socio-economic trend, accepted the thesis that, while a large population was a positive phenomenon from the economic point of view, all human beings must be provided with decent living conditions. Therefore, population growth should be allowed only when it is possible to increase agricultural production. According to the Physiocrats, an adequate level of agricultural development and a sufficient amount of agricultural output were the prerequisites of prosperity.[441]

Another theory with 18th-century origins and specific views on population issues was the economic doctrine of liberalism, which promoted the concept of the free market as the best regulator of all economic and social processes. This idea, developed over the following centuries, has become a permanent feature in modern economics and politics, both in the theoretical and practical sphere. One of its most recognizable representatives is the Scottish philosopher Adam Smith, who is also considered the father of modern economics.

The main principle of liberalism is that demographic processes should occur naturally, without state interference, because it is very difficult or even impossible to determine the optimal population.[442] The market, together with the supply of jobs, specific salaries, and consumer goods, should be the factor that regulates population growth. Society functions much better when the state does not interfere in the decisions of individuals.[443] Individual actions lead to a state of equilibrium, seeing as the laws of the market dictate them.[444] Their profound faith in the activities of the market allowed representatives of the liberal doctrine to remain optimistic about population growth. A large population was considered beneficial, if only because it allowed for the efficient division of labor and progress in the economy.

Toward the end of the 18th century, Utopians took an even more optimistic view of population growth. They believed that the primary source of all evil, including food shortages, was mismanagement and inadequate distribution of resources. In the abolition of the institution of the state and the abandonment of government and the standardized form of marriage, they saw a chance to push for the unencumbered use of the Earth's resources. William Godwin, a member of the Utopian school of thought, argued that without government or any form of governance, the resources of the Earth would be more accessible, especially since three-quarters of the Earth's surface is uninhabited. Besides, humans are capable of unlimited development in various spheres of life as long as their reason guides them. Therefore, there will come a time in the development of humankind when reason will prevail over libido. Godwin, therefore, formulated the conclusion that the Earth will not be threatened by overpopulation, even in a billion years.[445]

MALTHUS'S POPULATION THEORY

However, the most significant and influential current in the following centuries was the theory formulated by Thomas R. Malthus. In its heyday, it dominated scientific theory and found its way into the social policies of many countries; its coherence and relative completeness have prompted some to call it the first demographic theory. Malthus presented it in 1798 in *An Essay on the Principle of Population.*[446] It is a pessimistic theory whose core prediction is that population growth will have catastrophic consequences.

Malthus's theory assumed that there is a negative relationship between the growth of the human population and the Earth's resources and, more specifically, food production. Malthus observed the reasonably rapid rate of population growth that was typical of early-stage industrialization and concluded that the dynamic population processes were not going hand in hand with dynamic surges in food production. Analyzing the demographic statistics of several countries, he estimated that the population was increasing at a geometric rate of about 3 percent per year. In contrast, the rate of growth of agricultural production was defined by a much slower arithmetic growth rate.

An arithmetic rate represents an increase by some fixed number in each successive period. Using the example of our fictional town, this could be an annual increase in the population by, say, 200 people. Malthus treated both characteristics as invariant over long periods. Despite the fact that a technological revolution was taking place before his eyes, he underestimated the importance of progress in increasing agricultural productivity. He stubbornly clung to the belief that food production was strictly dependent on the amount of land cultivated. He did not, therefore, consider the possibility of increasing food production to meet the needs of an expanding population.

On the contrary, he foresaw an inevitable moment of over-population, that is, a situation in which the population would prove far too significant in relation to the amount of food produced, and it would not be possible to feed everyone. This was to lead to famine, wars fought over food resources and widespread armed conflict. Malthus predicted that this could happen very soon – within 50 years of his prediction, by the middle of the 19th century.

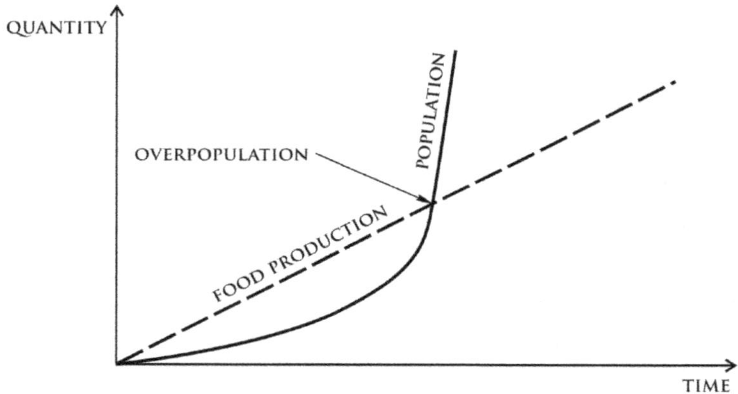

Fig. 3. The essence of Malthus's theory

A description of Malthus's theory cannot be complete without noting that it identified both the factors responsible for significant population growth and the means of reducing it. This element of the theory proved to be highly durable. Malthus considered excessive fertility to be the leading cause of rapid population growth. Harnessing and regulating fertility, in his view, was instrumental to solving the problem. As humankind was becoming increasingly successful in overcoming the natural forces that had previously controlled the human population by maintaining high mortality rates (such as epidemics and crop failures), he proposed a whole suite of preventive measures. These included delaying the decision to start a family, rejecting marriage, and sexual abstinence, especially among the lower classes. Going even further, Malthus believed that all aid to the lower classes was a factor in their population growth, which should ultimately be avoided.

Malthus believed that the looming catastrophe was a consequence of prosperity. Improving quality of life led to increased fertility, which in turn led to increased demand for food, and thus indirectly to famine, wars, and epidemics, all of them resulting from a shortage of means of subsistence. He argued that the poor, hungry, and sick should not be helped. Interestingly, Malthus was an Anglican minister.

Many elements of this theory were very controversial, if not unethical. The concept was severely criticized even during Malthus's lifetime. As Ronald Bailey put it, the way Malthus framed reality implied that "human beings are no different than a herd of deer when it comes to reproduction."[447] However, his pivotal argument lit up people's imaginations and continues to do so in the modern age. Evocative and persuasive, they had a profound impact on the way later generations thought about population processes, and they resonate loudly to this day.

Standing room only: Alarmist population projections

The birth of neo-Malthusianism

It was during Malthus's lifetime that the Earth's population reached its first billion. Any data for this period are estimates, of course. Malthus's theory caused a profound stir in the British Parliament and, in fact, contributed to the decision to conduct Britain's first census in 1801.[448]

In the 19th century, when agricultural progress significantly increased the food supply, the world dropped the subject of overpopulation for a while, and Malthus's theory fell into relative oblivion. It returned with a vengeance in the mid-20th century, when the population growth rate increased dramatically, and old fears about the future of humanity were revived.[449] Malthus's thesis that consistent population growth was a threat to the world and that it was necessary to introduce limits to it proved highly appealing. A veritable raft of Malthusian-style theories followed. Because they significantly expanded the range of measures proposed to solve the problem, they came to be called neo-Malthusian.

Neo-Malthusian theories have maintained the belief that humans live thanks to the Earth's resources, which are limited and exhaustible. Therefore, there may come a time when there are too many people and a shortage of what is necessary for life: space, water, food, and raw materials. It has become quite common to compare the Earth to a pond in the process of being rapidly overgrown by water lilies or to a spaceship hurtling through the cosmos. The latter analogy was proposed in 1966 by the American journalist Barbara Ward and suggested a way of looking at the Earth as a body seen from space, that is, a fragile object with a finite size and resources that cannot be expanded or replenished. In a book titled *Spaceship Earth,* Ward wrote: "Our planet is not much more than the capsule within which we have to live as human beings . . . We depend upon a little envelope of soil and a rather larger envelope of atmosphere for life itself. And both can be contaminated and destroyed."[450] In this way, population growth became a bogeyman for many years, and the word "overpopulation" became one of the chief markers of the era.

THE DEMOGRAPHIC EXPLOSION THEORY

The 1960s were particularly conducive to the framing of population growth as a serious problem. Over the decade, the world population exceeded 3 billion, and annual population growth was greater than 60 million. In 1968, Paul Ehrlich, an American biologist working at Stanford University, published *The Popu-*

lation Bomb, a book whose impact mirrored that of Malthus a century and a half prior.[451] It shook both the scientific world and numerous broad social circles while imposing a way of looking at population processes that would prove highly persistent. The book's impact was all the greater because it was written in an era of dynamic media development. Ehrlich was often featured on television, gave interviews, and placed articles in widely read newspapers. By virtue of this constant exposure, the book became incredibly popular, and the topic of overpopulation sailed into the mainstream.[452]

The publication cooled the fascination with technological progress and rising living standards in Western societies. Already in the first paragraph, the author of the book retraced the value of all these achievements and assessed the direction in which humanity was heading, stating:

> The battle to feed all of humanity is over. In the 1970s and 1980s hundreds of millions of people will starve to death in spite of any crash programs embarked upon now . . . although many lives could be saved through dramatic programs to "stretch" the carrying capacity of the Earth by increasing food production and providing for more equitable distribution of whatever food is available.[453]

According to Ehrlich, the cause of the impending cataclysm, as in Malthus's earlier work, would be overpopulation resulting from uncontrolled population growth and the consequent depletion of the planet's resources.

Ehrlich had so thoroughly succumbed to the lure of the rising numbers that he refused to believe in the power of civilizational development. He argued that increasing food production was too costly to be successful. In subsequent editions of the book, he even claimed that the success of the Green Revolution in agriculture – based on the introduction of more prolific crop species and saving the lives of millions of hungry people in India, among other places – did not exist. He attributed the increase in crop yields that occurred in the mid-1960s to favorable weather conditions rather than to agricultural progress. He, therefore, predicted that, as a result of uncontrolled population growth, the number of people in the world would increase dramatically, especially in the poorest parts of the globe.

Ehrlich also made irrational predictions. For example, Calcutta would have a population of 66 million in the year 2000; today, the city has a population of just over 5 million and less than 15 million if we include the surrounding metropolitan area.[454] Assuming that it takes 35 years to double the world's population, he calculated that in 900 years Earth could be inhabited by 60,000,000,000,000,000 (60 quadrillion) people, or about 100 people per square yard. Earth would become a standing-room-only planet.

Ehrlich's handling of the numbers revealed the same mistake that Malthus and many other prognosticators had made earlier. He assumed that trends that are typical for a given moment in history would persist in the long run or even intensify. In calculating the growth of the human population, he assumed a two percent annual growth rate. This was the rate that prevailed in the mid-1960s, in the middle of a population boom associated with the wide dissemination of medical innovations and the effort to compensate for losses after World War II.

The perspective adopted by Ehrlich omitted authentic scenarios of development, such as a future decline in population growth. It was also full of exaggerations when it came to interpreting data.

The Population Bomb also predicted an increase in deadly epidemics. Its author estimated that more than a billion people would die from Lassa fever alone, and another 300-400 million would die from other pandemics, famines, and wars sparked by competition for food, water, resources, and living space.

Ehrlich clung to his views, even though none of the predictions came true at the time he specified. He reiterated his warnings in his book *The Population Explosion*, published in 1990, where he defended the claims made 20 years earlier. He predicted, among other things, that the population of India would reach 2 billion in the 21st century, even though the rate of population growth in that country had been declining since the 1980s, and everything seemed to indicate that it would slow down even further in the following years.[455] Even the rather crude projections made based on World Bank data were more restrained. They predicted that, in 2050, the population of India would be 1.6 billion and grow only slightly (to 1.7 billion) by 2100.[456]

THE LIMITS TO GROWTH

Another major study published in the second half of the 20th century struck a similar alarmist tone. *The Limits to Growth*, published in 1972 by the Club of Rome, had four primary authors: Donella H. Meadows, Dennis L. Meadows, Jørgen Randers, and William W. Behrens.[457] This report heightened fears about the future of the Earth and the people who inhabit it by advancing the thesis that the Earth's resources are finite and the consequences of exceeding its productive capacity would be dire. In relation to Ehrlich's theory, the focus here shifted from social problems to environmental problems. The main message of this report can be summarized as follows: population growth threatens the very life of our planet and the people living on it. In view of the severely limited and constantly diminishing supply of natural resources and the finite size of the Earth, population growth will bring irreversible environmental degradation and lower the standard of living to the point of disaster. The only way to stop this process is to slow down the growth of the human population.

The authors of this world-renowned report argued that the world was already very close to the tipping point. They projected that the time required for the population to double would continue to shrink and that by roughly the year 2000, the world's population would be about 7 billion. They were wrong on both counts. At the turn of the millennium, the world population was just over 6 billion, and humanity would only reach the projected seventh billion in 2011. Similarly, the population of the Earth reached double its 1972 size (3.8 billion) in 2018, after 46 years. Although in 2023, the size of the population living on Earth exceeded 8 billion, the world has not imploded.

The Club of Rome's report also predicted that the production of increasing amounts of food would consume significant capital and lead to a situation in which all available financial resources would have to be directed to this sphere of economic activity, which would obviously limit the development of other areas of manufacturing. In the first half of the 21st century, around 2025, population growth would collapse as a result of resource depletion and stalled industrial and food production.

The law of increasing costs formulated by the report's authors, which states that each successive increase in crop yields will be much more costly and more economically unviable than the previous one, does not work. There has also been no depletion of natural resources, no collapse of industrial production, and no decline in the overall quality of human life. On the contrary, the percentage of people on Earth suffering from hunger and malnourishment has fallen significantly. In 1970, 941 million people, or 25 percent of the total population of the Earth, went hungry daily.[458] By 2019, according to the United Nations World Food Programme, this had fallen to 821 million, or 10.5 percent of the world's population.[459] Their errors stemmed partly from faulty assumptions and partly from the application of historical population data to the future.

In the summary of the Club of Rome's report, there was a proposal to strive for zero growth of both population and industrial production, as the latter was a sphere of human activity that led to the depletion of resources and degradation of the natural environment. Such a solution was considered necessary to postpone the moment when the capacity of Earth's environment would be exceeded, irreversibly destroying the natural world and catalyzing social and economic collapse.[460] But the consumption of resources and the amount of pressure we put on the environment is determined not so much by the number of people on Earth as by our lifestyle and the strategies of managing natural resources adopted around the world.

The authors of the Club of Rome report maintained their core theses in a slightly modified form in a book published 20 years later, titled *Beyond the Limits: Confronting Global Collapse, Envisioning a Sustainable Future*.[461] Only the moment of collapse of the global economic system was slightly shifted in time. In another update to the book, published in 2004 and titled *Limits to Growth: The 30-Year Update*, they did not retreat from their conclusions about humanity heading in the wrong direction, although they dropped the population projections.[462] In analyzing existing threats to the Earth, they acknowledged that world overpopulation and the depletion of resources, while continuing to be a problem, are not front-and-center risks. They turned the spotlight to global climate change.

Pessimistic theories continued

Another pessimistic and ultimately influential study was the *Global 2000 Report to the President: Entering the Twenty-first Century*, published in 1980 by the Council of Environmental Quality and the Department of State on behalf of the US government under President Jimmy Carter.[463] It was widely distributed, translated into more than a dozen languages, and had a circulation of 1.5 million copies. The report outlined prospects for world development until the year 2000, with particular emphasis on three elements: population, resources, and the environment. Its conclusions were very similar to those presented in *The Limits to Growth*, although they contained slightly different arguments, more attuned to the knowledge and realities of life in the 1980s.

These types of studies shaped the views of millions of people and built stereotypes about population dynamics that made their way into scientific studies and educational resources. Even today, some school textbooks are permeated with simplified images of an overpopulated world headed for extinction. Overpopulation, which is sometimes wrongly identified with high population density, is presented as the cause of serious social and environmental problems.

Population projections created by respected international institutions such as the World Bank and the United Nations have also brought much anxiety. These institutions have been systematically preparing them since the 1950s, estimating the population of the world and its regions and describing the basic parameters that make up population growth over reasonably long periods. Although they adopted a scientific methodology that has been constantly verified and improved, they also contained somewhat exaggerated results, especially in relation to distant points in time (that is, more than 20 years into the future). The challenges they have faced in assessing these processes only reinforce a phrase attributed, among others, to the famous physicist Niels Bohr: "Prediction is difficult, especially about the future."

These forecasts, which over time have become increasingly accurate and elaborate, played an essential role in the planning of development processes and were extremely important for the economic policy of countries and regions. However, they provided materials that were also used for propaganda purposes. They presented, for example, different variants of population development depending on an assumed fertility rate. The "highest" variants, while highly unlikely or even virtually impossible, provided ample fodder for grim development scenarios. The power of these forecasts also lay in the fact that they were made at a time when the population growth was high. By their very nature, forecasts of the distant future indicated large numbers that could seem frightening.

In the UN's 1957 forecast, the high scenario assumed that 6.9 billion people would be alive in the world by the year 2000.[464] The low estimate was 4.8 billion, but the magic of statistics is that the most extreme projections are the ones that command the most attention. Imagine, then, a society of fewer than 3 billion people that suddenly finds out that, in just forty-odd years, the population of the world will more than double. This was very impressive and gave rise to much speculation about the future of the world.

For this reason, these otherwise useful predictions became a source of anxiety, as reflected in the scientific literature and media coverage. This fear has often led to fatalistic predictions that are far from the truth.

Both print and broadcast media, later joined by the Internet, became virtual emissaries of agencies involved in forecasting demographic phenomena. They took on the role of interpreters of the forecasts they published. As the hot topic aroused great public interest, it was discussed vigorously. Naturally, most regular citizens formed their opinions about population dynamics not on the basis of a thorough analysis of published data but precisely on the basis of this often distorted media message.

THE LABYRINTH OF POPULATION DATA

Population phenomena fall into categories that, at first glance, are simple to interpret. An increase is an increase, a decrease is a decrease, and we know where it all leads. Besides, we believe that numbers are objective and impartially describe reality. However, to understand population forecasts and formulate correct conclusions about them, it is necessary to know their broad determinants and interdependencies between individual elements. Suppose we approach population data in a mechanistic and shallow way. In that case, we can easily conclude that the population is growing at dangerous rates, and nothing is slowing it down.

Calculations based on reliable data, such as those from statistics published by the United Nations, show that the world's population has increased every year since the 1960s by roughly the same number, or about 80 million people per year. One can quickly draw a hasty conclusion – and many do – that we are simply experiencing a perpetual population explosion. Population Matters, a world-renowned population charity, states on its website that "[g]lobal population is still growing by more than 80 million a year, however, and is most likely to continue growing for the rest of this century unless we take action."[465] Meanwhile, the truth is that an increase in numbers by the same amount means that the rate of growth is *decreasing*. If it were not, the absolute rate of growth would be greater every year since the total population continues to grow. This was the case, for example, in the 1950s and 1960s. Nowadays, annual population growth even exhibits the beginnings of a downward trend.

The decline in the rate of population growth, in turn, means that demographic processes are slowing down. Unfortunately, this cannot be viewed as an unmitigated success. It means that societies are aging. The world may soon lose the balance between the number of working people and the number of retirees and older adults. Therefore, alarmist forecasts presented by the media or the scientific world that are based on the mere notion of population growth are not accurate. Using only selected elements of statistics is misleading and leads to false conclusions. To properly assess the dynamics of demographic phenomena, one must look at other parameters than just the absolute population, including, first of all, the population growth rate. As it turns out, this rate is steadily declining. Ignoring this fact is either a simple misunderstanding of the essence of the matter or a manipulation.

We often make this kind of mistake when evaluating population processes that take place in developing countries. Analyzing raw population size in particular years can easily lead us to the conclusion that their birth rate is always too high and that these countries have a problem with excessive population growth. Using simplistic logic, we expect that if birth rates are falling, population growth should immediately fall or at least stop. We conclude that if this does not happen, it means that nothing is changing. However, it is changing; it is simply that this kind of process always involves some delay before the effects take hold.

One illustration of this is India. For years, it has been treated as an example of uncontrolled population growth that was destined to culminate in tragedy. But the annual rate of population growth has been steadily declining since the mid-1980s, indicating that the country's total population is stabilizing. Between 1985 and 1990, the annual growth rate was 2.31 percent, while in 2020, it was only 1.04 percent.[466] The real fertility rate, which is the number of children a statistical woman gives birth to during her lifetime, has also decreased significantly.

India also provides the perfect example of demographic hysteria. First, the projections of both the United Nations and the World Bank have always underscored the enormous population of this rapidly expanding country. Second, they have almost always been highly pessimistic about the consequences of this growth. As early as the 1960s, when India's population growth rate was reaching a high point at over 2 percent, Paul Ehrlich predicted the imminent collapse of the country's social system if the population continued to grow.[467] The population of India at that time was about 500 million.

Further population growth provoked scientists and columnists to publish even more gloomy predictions. When in 1997 India surpassed 1 billion inhabitants, they predicted widespread hunger, poverty, depletion of resources, including drinking water, and the eruption and spread of social conflicts outside the country due to lack of necessities of life.[468] Today, India has a population of nearly 1.4 billion people, and despite a steady increase in population, poverty rates are declining.[469] In India, as in the rest of the world, in parallel with population growth, there has been a substantial increase in food production. India is even an exporter of cereals.

Boserup and Simon: A breath of optimism

Necessity is the mother of invention

In 1830, Thomas B. Macaulay, a British historian and politician, asked an engaging and inspiring question: "On what principle is it that when we see nothing but improvement behind us, we are to expect nothing but deterioration before us?"[470] Let us try to find an answer to this question, as, in fact, this is the dilemma to which most of our demographic reflections can be reduced.

Much of the population pessimism we have seen seems to be rooted in the fear of exceeding certain limits of Earth's resilience as a planet. Sometimes, this is framed as uncertainty about our ability to maintain an adequate quality of life, especially for those who have already achieved a certain level of prosperity. In more modern times, ecological considerations have also come into play, stemming from concern for Earth's environment. Anxieties about securing human lives and livelihoods derived from the conviction that both resources and the ability to multiply them are limited in relation to the needs of an expanding population. After all, one of the critical assumptions of Malthus' theory was that the world population was growing at a geometric rate while food production was growing at only an arithmetic rate.

Ester Boserup, a Danish economist and activist who worked with many international organizations, including the UN, exposed how false these assumptions were. In the 1960s, she presented a theory further developed by other researchers in the following decade, in which she proposed a different view of the relationship between demographic processes and the development of agriculture and food production. Following in the footsteps of her great predecessors, such as Adam Smith and Émile Durkheim, she assumed that population growth could be a catalyst for progress. She argued that an increase in population, already by the mere fact that it stimulates changes in the way work is organized, contributes to the rise in the productivity of that work. Additionally, she proved that the increase in demand for products that are necessary for life and the vision of their scarcity triggers creativity in people and directs them toward innovative solutions. Thus, she put forward the thesis that population could be a factor that stimulated technological development in agriculture and increased the productive capacity of resources.[471]

According to Boserup, agricultural progress since the beginning of human history has been closely linked to population growth and increasing demand for food. In her view, had it not been for surging demand for agricultural products, humans would never have abandoned practices such as fallowing. They would have never developed plowing techniques, fertilizers, or irrigation. Successive population increases triggered ever more perfect ways to manage the land.[472] The concept of the Green Revolution, which significantly increased world food production in the 1960s, was born in response to the food crisis in developing countries.[473] Ester Boserup's framework offers an alternative configuration of three factors: population, technology, and resources. While Malthus assumed that population growth was the result of technological progress and improved livelihoods (invention-pull population growth), Boserup embraced a different perspective: invention-push agricultural change.[474] She, therefore, took a broader view of the developmental processes that were taking place in 18th-century Europe. According to her, population growth was one of the main factors behind the agrarian and industrial revolutions that took place at that time.

Boserup's theory, published in her book *The Conditions of Agricultural Growth*,[475] shed new light on population dynamics and brought some optimism to the scientific and social debate that took place in Europe and around the world in the 1960s, fueled by the intensified dynamics of demographic phenomena. She saw humans not only as consumers of Earth's resources but also as creative beings capable of creating solutions to meet the needs of a growing population despite limited natural resources and even protecting those resources. The concepts put forth in her book break down the notion of the Earth's "carrying capacity" and move it away from the starring role it played in previous frameworks. What humanity has at its disposal ceases to be finite. The Earth is no longer seen as a static system with a set amount of goods but as a space of many possibilities. As development continues, the capacity of the Earth increases enough to allow us to dismiss the thought of a population catastrophe. This progress will be in perpetual motion because necessity is the mother of invention.

POPULATION GROWTH IS A GOOD THING

In the 1980s, as the field of economics reaffirmed the importance of capital accumulation and technology in socioeconomic development, the optimistic approach to the population question gained more adherents. As early as the 1960s, Simon Kuznets, winner of the 1971 Nobel Prize in Economics, supported the idea that a large population could be an asset. He argued that large communities are more capable of development than smaller ones because they have more power to multiply, disseminate, and exploit accumulated knowledge. He also assumed that the percentage of brilliant people in the population remains at a constant level, so the more significant the population, the greater the chances that individuals will be born whose inventions will allow us to reduce the imbalance between the needs of people and the capabilities of the planet, that is, to prevent a demographic catastrophe.[476]

Julian Simon, an American professor specializing in economics and business, often considered one of the greatest minds of the late 20th century, was a perpetrator of this vision.[477] He shared the belief that population growth stimulates socioeconomic development because, as the population grows, so does intellectual capital and the power of creative problem-solving. This thesis was convincingly articulated in his famous book *The Ultimate Resource*.[478] Walking through the history of civilization, Simon argued that humans facing difficulties creatively use the intellectual capital accumulated over generations and create increasingly efficient ways of production, exchange, and consumption of goods and services to meet the needs of a larger population.[479] While Boserup's approach is often abbreviated with the adage "necessity is the mother of invention," the central tenet of Simon's theory may be that the larger the population, the more likely it is to have reformers who will come up with solutions to new challenges. Simon argued that "[w]riters about population growth usually mention a greater number of mouths coming into the world, and sometimes note more pairs of hands, but never mention more brains arriving."[480]

Simon's interest in the population question grew out of the expansion of the neo-Malthusian movement and its dissemination of views about the limited opportunities for development due to world population growth. Reading anti-population studies and analyzing their conclusions provided him with both inspiration for profound analyses of the relationship between population growth and economics as well as evidence of how mistaken the tenets of neo-Malthusianism were. Simon became one of the leading figures in the movement against the rhetoric of publications like *The Limits to Growth* or *Global 2000.* Together with Herman Kahn, he fact-checked the latter of the two and, in *Resourceful Earth*, exposed all of its errors and flawed interpretations, beginning with the fact that even if there are more people in the year 2000, that would in no way mean that the world would be more crowded. He outlined a more optimistic vision of a future in which, despite population growth, the prices of goods fall, and prosperity rises.

Simon's views, supported by solid analysis, theoretical arguments, and empirical evidence, have had a significant impact on the scientific debate about demographic dynamics as well as on policy practice. They alleviated the atmosphere of fear about the demographic development of the world. His books, however, did not achieve as much publicity as those that chose fatalism, and the ideas they conveyed were not as widely disseminated in the media as the opinions of Ehrlich or the Meadows team.[481]

HOW TO CURB POPULATION GROWTH – AND WHY?

TWEAKING THE SIZE AND FEATURES OF A POPULATION

The population is a strategic element that participates both in the production of various goods and benefits and in their consumption. Hence, since ancient times, rulers have tried to shape population processes in order to achieve the desired size of the population in relation to specific goals. To influence population size, one must regulate births or deaths or initiate population flows, that is, migration. The first of these methods seems to be the easiest of the three and is, therefore, the one that is chosen most often. State-driven birth control relies on encouraging the population to have many children or on preventing too many children from being born. Population policies are, therefore, most often pro-natalist when they aim to increase the number of births or anti-natalist when they seek to restrict childbearing. There is only one way to regulate deaths effectively, and it requires much more radical measures, all of which culminate in the killing of people. Such cases are known in history, but modern societies strongly reject them.

The third way to regulate population sizes is population displacement, which aims to shape the population of societies and to enforce a certain kind of distribution or structure. This is also a problematic issue for several reasons. Its extreme variant, mass population transfer, was infamously implemented under the Stalinist system in the first half of the 20th century. The history of how the Europeans settled Australia is another illustration of this population policy. Sending prisoners from Great Britain to the newly discovered Australian continent in the second half of the 18th century was nothing more than an effort to relieve Britain's territory of its excess population, especially those who were socially inconvenient. The pro-immigration policies of such countries as the United States, Canada, Australia, Brazil, and Argentina are examples of non-coercive actions along similar lines. However, in the context of overpopulation on Earth, population movement has not become a panacea. Instead, it is one way to supplement the population deficits of specific regions, as well as to shape their desired social structure.

More is better: Pro-population policies

It is not difficult to imagine that societies may consciously strive to increase their population, whether for economic or political reasons or even out of sheer will to survive. This was the policy of ancient Rome, which pursued an active strategy of territorial expansion. Conquering vast territories and maintaining control over them required a sizeable army of soldiers and officials. During the reign of Augustus, laws were enacted that penalized celibacy and childlessness while granting numerous privileges to families with at least three children. To increase the birth rate, marriage was made compulsory for both men and women. Widowers were obliged to remarry immediately, while widows had to do so within two years at the latest. They could only be exempt from this obligation if they had already had at least three children. Married people could not receive their entire inheritance and those without children were granted only half of it.[482]

Until the second half of the 18th century, most states applied a pro-natalist policy based on a system of incentives to increase the size of their populations. In particular, absolute monarchies strove to increase their demographic potential, not only in order to retain their sovereign power but also to strengthen their military and economic power. They, therefore, looked to the population factor as a pillar of state power. Only strong demographic potential offered hope of securing development and maintaining absolute control. It was also a testimony to the strength and importance of the monarch in the international arena. Therefore, as early as the 17th century, France and Spain began to introduce laws to encourage population growth. In Spain, tax exemptions were used for couples who married young and for large families. In France, in addition to tax exemptions, pensions were introduced for fathers with at least ten children born in wedlock.[483] This pro-natalist policy, however, was selective and did not extend to the lower strata of society.

In Europe, France was the first to adopt a pro-natalist policy in a widespread and highly consistent manner. Its defeat at the hands of Prussia in 1870 and the resulting loss of Alsace-Lorraine vividly demonstrated the dependence of a country's military and economic potential on population resources. This provided the impetus for planned measures to increase France's demographic potential. These measures gained momentum after the end of World War I, as a result of which France lost a large part of its population. The government's policy to rebuild this potential was based on limiting the promotion of contraception and on establishing an array of family benefits.[484]

In reviewing the history of planned efforts to increase countries' populations, it is impossible to ignore the policies of Nazi Germany in the 1930s. What characterized and distinguished this policy was not only the drive by the Third Reich authorities to spur population growth but, above all, the drive to increase the subset of the population that represented the "pure Aryan race," which the regime considered the German people to be the sole embodiment. Thus, every effort was made to make the German "master" race more numerous and more robust than any other. Probably no other country in the world expended such resources to increase its population as Germany did during the Third Reich. The key measures introduced included an extensive system of incentives for marriage and large families aimed exclusively at the pure-blooded German population. These comprised marriage loans that were canceled after a family had its fourth child, various material aids for families with many children, and allowances for young people taking up education.[485] The authorities in Berlin offered free education and priority access to state jobs to the fourth and every subsequent child born into a German family. Mothers with many children were awarded medals. In addition to these measures, more sophisticated steps were planned to foster strength in numbers among the "pure"

Aryan race that was expected to dominate Europe. In 1936, the Lebensborn (source of life) association was founded to organize a network of centers that were to be "factories" for children of "pure" Aryan blood. They aimed to select racially suitable women to produce more offspring for the citizens of the Third Reich who were considered valuable: soldiers, SS officers, and police officers.[486]

Before World War II, family-friendly policies were also adopted in Finland, which had been plagued by a drastic decline in the number of births and high infant mortality since the early 20th century, especially in the lower social strata. In 1938, the government introduced a so-called starter kit for young children, targeting Finland's poorest families. It contained the basic things needed to care for an infant in the first months of their life: clothes for sewing, diapers, cleaning products, and care accessories. The box in which mothers received these supplies could also serve as a crib for the newborn. In accepting this aid, the mother-to-be also accepted an obligation to report to the doctor and remain under their care for the duration of the pregnancy, which significantly reduced infant mortality. In 1949, the kit became available to all pregnant women, regardless of their social status.[487] Interestingly, this form of support has survived until the present day, despite the introduction of other, more modern forms of assistance, such as paid parental leave or subsidized childcare at home.

Pro-natalist policies in developed countries became quite common in the second half of the 20th century in connection with the progressive aging of their societies. Economic development, women's equality, and their greatly expanded access to education and the labor market significantly reduced fertility. To prevent depopulation, a number of initiatives to increase birth rates emerged. Currently, most European countries have implemented such measures, as did Japan, South Korea, Russia,

Canada, Australia, and Israel, which are also threatened by depopulation.

Economic incentives are used in the form of extended and paid maternity leaves, tax breaks, or direct financial support granted in the form of baby bonuses, birth grants, or lump sums. In Russia, where the one-child family model has become quite common, a "maternity capital" was introduced in 2007. This is a one-time, non-cash benefit given to mothers to encourage them to give birth to another child. It can be received only once in a woman's lifetime. It may be used to contribute to a pension fund or for specific purposes, such as buying or renovating an apartment, paying off a mortgage, or educating a child.

Social practice shows that financial incentives only marginally increase birth rates. They may accelerate the decision to have a child, but they do not fulfill their role in increasing female fertility. Therefore, some countries apply more sophisticated family policy approaches, including solutions that allow women to reconcile their family and professional responsibilities and compensate for earnings lost due to childbearing and childrearing. It is, therefore, increasingly common for fathers to be granted leaves of absence to relieve women of their child-rearing duties and allow them to pursue professional careers despite having children.

But small is beautiful! Anti-population policies

At their core, intentional measures to reduce the population of a given area may appear incompatible with nature. However, they have come to dominate the most recent pages of history.

Anti-population policies come in two guises. The first is action against other societies, which, for one reason or another, are treated as a threat and are therefore subjected to planned persecution and extermination. Mass persecution has deep roots: the Bible, for instance, speaks of the Egyptian pharaoh's intention to destroy the nation of Israel. Many of the wars that have taken place in the long history of humankind are precisely wars against other nations. An integral part of World War II was Nazi Germany's desire to exterminate the Jewish people and other peoples of Central and Eastern Europe who occupied the space designated by the ideologues of the Third Reich as belonging to the German people. World War I, in turn, is historically linked to the slaughter of more than a million Armenians by neighboring Turkey. In terms of more recent history, the genocide perpetrated by the Hutu people against the Tutsi population in Rwanda and the ethnic cleansing in parts of what had previously been Yugoslavia that took place in the 1990s stand out as prominent examples. Such dark moments can be found at every stage of human history. They are part of the struggle for space, resources, or the age-old animalistic desire to dominate individuals who belong to groups other than one's own. Although humans have primarily been able to curb that desire thanks to the development of culture, its natural force, arising from the characteristics of evolutionary processes, sometimes bursts to the surface and leads to more or less sophisticated actions against other groups, from gradual discrimination to slaughter.

The second type of anti-population policy includes actions that limit population growth within one's community. Their basis is usually the fear of excessive population growth in relation to the environmental resources and economic opportunities of the state and the belief that a significant population limits further development opportunities. Scientists assume that the desire to limit one's population was already a feature of primitive tribes thousands of years back. To ensure an optimal population in relation to their ability to feed themselves, they killed both children and the infirm, seeing them as a burden to the community. However, these were spontaneous actions aimed at group survival and do not fit into the framework of contemporary demographic policy.[488]

An example of a country taking steps against excessive population growth was ancient Greece, where several independent, though small, city-states developed. Their economic and social balance, in addition to income from trade, was largely dependent on local environmental resources. The specter of overpopulation, so powerfully articulated by Plato and Aristotle, prompted many of these mini-states to adopt solutions to limit population growth. In classical-period Athens, both the law and religion permitted people to abandon their children, especially disabled and illegitimate children, as well as girls.[489] Disposing of offspring who were deemed to constitute a burden on society was a way of maintaining balance in relation to the environmental capacity of the area and the economic capacities of the group. At the same time, it was a method of qualitative selection.

The real, deliberate development of anti-population movements did not begin until the 1950s, which saw the first signs of hypercharged population growth around the world, especially in developing countries. This was seen as a global problem in urgent need of a solution. Under the aegis of international organizations dealing with population issues and international aid, including the United Nations and the World Bank, programs to control population growth were implemented in many countries on various continents. In the 1990s, such policies were applied in a total of 115 countries out of a total of about 200 that existed in the world.[490] It is striking, however, that with few exceptions, the impulse to introduce measures limiting population growth in individual countries came from outside. They were not the result of internal social reflection or grassroots development movements. The idea of restricting population growth was born at the supranational level as a result of cooperation between organizations dealing with the problems of social and economic development in the world.[491]

Where did the idea of drastically limiting population growth come from in the 20th century and on a global level? One could understand that population control was necessary for societies at a lower level of technological development because of their limited capacity to produce the goods needed to sustain an ever-increasing population. But the middle of the 20th century was a time of extraordinary technological progress and great opportunities to solve the challenges of food security, so that one would expect a very different line of action. Undoubtedly, the two most important reasons underlying the dominance of population-curbing policies are the actual rapid growth of the world population and the dominant neo-Malthusian interpretation of statistical data.[492]

In the 1950s, a comprehensive count of the world's population was made for the first time in human history, and the results were made available to a broad audience. In addition to population data and annual growth rates, these published reports included numerous comments and projections. It was also customary to add regional breakdowns, highlighting the situation in developing countries, especially the most populous ones, such as China and India. In this way, governments, international organizations, politicians, scientists, columnists, and other audiences received material that enabled them to analyze and discuss population processes. A global discussion on the future of the world began. Data showing rapid population growth fired up people's imaginations and prompted them to treat population expansion as a problem. The impact of population statistics on the state of consciousness was aptly summarized by Theodore W. Schultz, winner of the 1979 Nobel Prize in Economics: "We extrapolate global statistics and are horrified by our interpretation of them, mainly that poor people breed like lemmings headed toward their destruction."[493] Contemporary statistics produced a similar effect, especially when they were programmed to impress the viewer. One example is population clocks, which, as they note the birth of every new citizen of the Earth, show how many people are born every minute or even every second.

The adoption of a catastrophic narrative and the Malthusian message that each new birth was a threat to the world was another significant element that weighed on the outcome of this debate – taking such a perspective led to the simple conclusion that there is an unconditional need to stop the growth of the human population. In addition to a lack of faith in the power of technological progress and human adaptability, a rather simplistic logic was at work here, according to which the only way to ensure stable economic development and avoid demographic disaster was to reduce consumption, and this goal can only be achieved only by reducing the number of consumers.[494] The conviction that the growing population was a barrier to economic development became powerfully entrenched. Thus, in the second half of the 20th century, a kind of anti-population movement was born that involved many international organizations, such as the International Planned Parenthood Federation, United Nations Population Fund Activities, and the World Bank. These organizations developed programs to halt population growth, especially in developing countries. The period that was most rife with anti-natalist programs was 1974-1994.[495]

Birth control became the primary tool for reducing population growth. Of all possible methods of influencing the size of the population, limiting the number of children born was considered the most effective and appropriate. This was a classical, direct interference in demographic processes, which today is seen as somewhat out of step with modernity. Two bestsellers of the time, *The Population Bomb* and *The Limits to Growth,* which we have already covered, exerted a powerful influence on both the understanding of the problem and the direction of measures taken towards birth control. Such publications, which raised so many factual and methodological doubts, became fuel for the global anti-population policy promoted by serious international organizations, including the UN, until the mid-1990s.

India is often considered to be the first developing country to implement policies aimed at curbing population growth in the post-war period. As early as 1951, India introduced its first measures aimed at reducing the birth rate: voluntary contraception and sex education. In the 1960s, under pressure from international organizations, birth control measures were intensified and turned into a condition for receiving food aid from the United States.[496] To increase the effectiveness of the process, the government decided to introduce sterilization programs targeting men and women – initially on a voluntary basis and then, in some cases, on a forced basis.[497] These mass sterilizations have become perhaps the most recognizable and unquestionably negative symbol of India's anti-population policy. On a smaller scale, this method is still used today.

Beginning in the 1960s, a large number of developing countries, under international pressure, undertook to implement programs aimed at reducing births. While it is difficult to imagine today, both politicians and scientists of that era called for uncompromising solutions. For instance, Garett Hardin, an American biologist, called for a firm stance on reproduction, writing in the prestigious scientific journal *Science* that "Freedom to breed will bring ruin to all."[498]

The most infamous anti-natalist policy of modern times was a program implemented by China known as the "one-child policy." It was developed in the 1970s by a team appointed by the State Council called the Birth Planning Leading Small Group, working under the supervision of members of the Political Bureau of the Communist Party of China.[499] This policy was introduced in 1978 as a short-term program aimed at reducing the annual rate of population growth to below 1 percent and, in effect, stabilizing China's overall population. The implementation of this program was a reversal (and thus, in a way, a consequence) of the pro-natalist policy pursued previously by Mao Zedong in connection with the realization of China's aspirations to become a Great Power. That program contributed to an increase in the population of the Middle Kingdom from 540 million to almost 1 billion between 1949 and 1976.

Under the one-child policy, 95 percent of families living in cities and 90 percent of families in rural areas would only be permitted to have one child. It was predicted that thanks to this solution, the population of China in 2000 would be 1.2 billion people and decrease to 700 million within one hundred years.[500] The projected fertility rate in China would also drop to 1.5 children per woman by 2080.[501] This was an extreme approach, as a fertility rate below 2.0 does not ensure the replacement of generations and leads directly to the depopulation of the country. In communist China, however, this program, like many others, was not subject to discussion. It was imposed by the central authorities and strictly implemented. It is estimated that the one-child policy prevented the birth of between 100 and 400 million children.[502]

The policy has had dramatic ramifications for society as a whole. Chinese culture, built on the bedrock of the centuries-old Confucian cult of the large and extended family in which children provide for their parents in their old age, experienced a traumatic shock, and people suffered many personal misfortunes. The implementation of the program required the use of previously unknown coercive measures. Families were deprived of their right to decide for themselves and were subjected to total surveillance. Many millions of forced abortions were performed. Failure to comply with the limits imposed led to severe financial penalties and social and professional degradation. As a result, children born outside the limits the plan imposed were killed or hidden. The program was terminated in 2015. It was replaced by a two-child policy, which loosened the restrictive procreation ban to an extent.

One instructive example of steering population processes to achieve specific socioeconomic goals is Singapore. This small city-state underwent a major baby boom in the early post-war period, as did other countries around the world. By the late 1950s, the fertility rate was over six children per woman.[503] A decade later, in line with worldwide trends, an anti-natalist program was introduced to curb the high rate of population growth, encouraging delayed marriage and limiting the number of offspring. Its goal was to achieve zero population growth. A number of campaigns, mainly in the media, were carried out to promote the 2+2 family model. Abortion laws were liberalized, and a system of financial reductions for families with no more than two children was introduced. The policy proved so effective that, by the early 1980s, the fertility rate was already 2.0, and women (especially educated women) were marrying less and less frequently. As a result, the segment of the population that had a higher social status began to shrink.

In 1984, therefore, a new policy was adopted, this time with a pro-family bent. To ensure both a higher population growth rate and a "proper" social structure for future generations, the government introduced incentives for families with higher education to have more children. In contrast, the lower social strata were offered financial benefits for having fewer children and undergoing sterilization. In 1987, when it became clear that the program was not working, a pro-natalist policy was introduced based on a system of incentives encouraging people (including singles) to have more children regardless of social status. The advertising campaigns for this program featured such slogans as, "Why Build Your Career Alone? Family Life Helps, or Children - Life would be empty without them."[504] In 2001, an additional system of financial incentives was introduced in the form of the Baby Bonus program, under which families were given large amounts of money to give birth to and raise a second and third child. However, these actions have not brought any visible effects; the female fertility rate in Singapore in 2020 is only 1.22, and Singapore is among the top five countries with the lowest values of this indicator in the world.

Do population policies work?

It is often claimed that the effects of population policies have a poor record of effectiveness. There are indeed many examples where measures taken to motivate people to have more children, as well as to discourage procreation, have failed. The pro-natalist policy of the Third Reich is an illustrative example. Between 1933 and 1939, as a result of its intensive pro-family policy, Germany's fertility rate increased from 1.47 to only 2.03 children per mother.[505] Considering the extensive incentive system, this was really not much. India's anti-natalist program also failed despite the use of coercive measures. In the 1970s and 1980s, several million sterilizations were carried out annually. Until the end of the 1980s, it proved impossible to reduce the annual rate of population growth to less than 2.1 percent.[506] The rate only began to decline in the next decade. Currently, raw population growth in India is still higher than it was more than half a century ago, amounting to several million people per year.

However, it is not entirely correct to say that natalist policies are completely ineffective. There are many examples of success among both pro-natalist and anti-natalist policies. Mao Zedong's Communist China, which treated population as capital necessary for economic development and banned contraception, was unquestionably successful. In just five years after 1949, the population grew from 500 to 600 million.[507] At the time of Mao's death, China's population was already 950 million. Thus, it is safe to say that the adopted program to stimulate population growth met its objectives. But this effect was not at all desirable from the standpoint of the global community at the time. Therefore, the regime introduced the inverse of the Mao-era policy, reducing the dynamics of demographic development.

The effectiveness of an adopted program as measured by specific indicators is one thing, and its social or economic value is another. The success of a given policy in the sense of achieving a given result (for example, a target fertility rate or annual growth rate) does not necessarily spell success for society, especially in the long run. This is, in fact, the main problem with natalist policies. Their goals are usually formulated in relation to a specific situation, but when the effects and impacts come around, it turns out that the plans were inaccurately defined.

How do we stop previously initiated processes when they are no longer socially and economically beneficial? Governments often take countermeasures to reverse demographic trends, but this is not easy. Prescribed or enforced procreational behaviors become part of the culture over time. When the one-child program was abandoned in China, and married couples were allowed to have second offspring, it turned out that there were not many people in urban areas willing to change the prevailing family model.[508] When Singapore introduced an incentive system to encourage families to have more than two children after years of encouraging women to delay the decision to start a family, it turned out that more than half of the women in Singapore did not want to start a family at all.[509] Procreational attitudes cannot be changed within a year and in isolation from socio-economic and cultural realities. When smaller families become the norm, it is tough to restore old patterns. In Taiwan, a pro-natalist policy was introduced as early as 2008, with new elements added in subsequent years to encourage families to have children. Unfortunately, they did not work. The high cost of living and education and an open labor market for women against a backdrop of low economic stability in the region have successfully kept the birth rate down.[510] Population policies assume that demographic processes will follow a set scenario; that scenario is often difficult to fulfill.

The ethical dimension of these activities is a separate issue. As history shows, anti-natalist programs can be fierce. They interfere directly with family decisions and go against tradition. They permanently disrupt the cultural patterns chiseled out over the centuries. They often deprive the individual of their agency. The implementation of the one-child policy in China involved total surveillance of women, tracking their biological cycle and private life, and required them to register these personal details in a centralized database. The authorities knew everything about their citizens and made the most critical decisions in their lives for them. The use of coercive measures such as compulsory abortions or sterilizations, as in India, Vietnam, Indonesia, and Peru, was an extreme violation of human rights. In many cases, due to the unsatisfactory sanitary conditions of the units where these procedures were carried out, people lost their lives.[511] These tragedies had a profound negative impact on the moral state of society.

Interference with natural demographic processes also has notable side effects. The demographic explosion of the mid-20th century resulted primarily from a reduction in the number of deaths and the extension of human life. Adopting an anti-natalist policy based on limiting the number of births triggered the rapid aging of societies and an avalanche of unfavorable economic phenomena, undermining the foundations of pension systems built on the basis of generational solidarity and contributing to rising costs of health care. In China, the one-child policy disrupted the country's gender structure. Since male offspring are considered more desirable in the Chinese tradition, when female children were born, they were often killed so that the parents could have a son instead. Abortions were also common when prenatal tests indicated a female fetus was developing. As a result, China's sex ratio at birth in 2010 was 120:100 in favor of boys, compared to 104-107 in other societies around the world.[512] For a country of more than one billion people, this means that 20-30 million men will never find a female partner to start a family, which will translate into a declining birth rate.

For years, it was believed that, in order to achieve a high level of economic development, it is necessary to reduce population growth. Still, history has proven that precisely the opposite is true. It is economic development itself that reduces the fertility rate. Perhaps, then, the 18th-century liberals were right when they said that demographic processes regulate themselves by responding to social and economic changes, so in order to achieve specific demographic effects, one should focus on the economy and not try to control demography manually.

A WORD ON OVERPOPULATION

WHERE DID THE FEAR OF OVERPOPULATION COME FROM?

The fear of overpopulation has been present in the population debate since time immemorial. Ancient thinkers, starting with Confucius, Plato, and Aristotle, recognized the risks of overpopulation. It was this problem that turned their attention to population issues, and this was at a time when Earth as a planet was nearly empty. At the time of Plato and Aristotle, the average population density of the world was only one person per square kilometer, and in Attica – one of the most densely populated areas on Earth at the time – it was only 100-130 people per square kilometer.[513] This translates into 0.75-1 hectare of land for every statistical inhabitant of the region. This is high for the ancient world but still comfortable enough to feed the entire population.

Addressing the problem of overpopulation at a time when population density, both globally and locally, was negligible indicates that it is a concept that has little to do with actual population density. In the 1960s, when the topic of global overpopulation took on particular importance, the average population density on Earth was only 20 people per square kilometer, India and China, which analysts claimed were the drivers of global overpopulation, had an average of 150 and 75 people per square kilometer, respectively. This was considerably less than in Belgium or the Netherlands at the time, where no alarm bells rang even though the population density was about 300 people per square kilometer.

It follows that the concept of overpopulation is, to some extent, an emotional one; it expresses not so much fear of lack of adequate space but concern about providing for the population. Currently, it is defined as a state of surplus population in relation to the resources available in the area – resources that every individual needs to survive. The problem, however, is that it is unclear what we mean by this. Is it a certain number of calories, water, clothing, and a roof over one's head to provide shelter from the cold and the threats that lurk outside? Does it also include access to education, culture, and a high quality of life? Is it possible to compare human needs in the times of Malthus to those of modern societies? Is it legitimate to equate the basic needs of people living in highly urbanized areas with those of the keepers of the Amazon rainforest? All these nuances make it difficult both to use the concept of overpopulation and to assess the phenomenon objectively. Instead, they make it easier to generate anxiety about population growth.

Throughout history, the problem of overpopulation has usually arisen in the midst of a significant increase in population. That is why both Confucius and Plato and later Malthus, expressed concern about the substantial population. The same was true in the second half of the 20th century. The vision of an increase in the number of people who participate in the consumption of manufactured goods and services set in motion the narrative of overpopulation and contributed to the entrenchment of anti-natalist movements. It is often said that the problem of overpopulation is the result of fear among the rich that a growing population will diminish their prosperity. It is also not uncommon to think that it is a pretext for criticizing developing countries and imposing development paths on them that are favorable from the point of view of rich countries.[514]

The limits of the Earth's carrying capacity

Many of those interested in the problem have tried to determine the maximum size of the human population on Earth that can be sustained and fed. The first calculations of this kind date back to the 17th century. In 1679, a Dutch merchant and naturalist named Antonie van Leeuwenhoek estimated the upper limit of Earth's carrying capacity at 13.4 billion, basing his calculation on the population density of the Netherlands at the time (120 people per square kilometer).[515] Gregory King, who lived at the turn of the 17th and 18th centuries, assumed that the Earth would be able to accommodate 20 times more people than Earth's population at the time – that is, about 12 billion. Based on his knowledge of demographic processes, he calculated that it would take humanity about 8,000 years to reach that number.[516] Gianmaria Ortes, an Italian industrialist and economist living in the 18th century, estimated the capacity of the Earth at 3 billion. It is interesting that, despite living almost contemporaneously with Malthus, Ortes did not see overpopulation in the world that surrounded him, which at the time had less than 1 billion people. He rightly assumed that geometric population growth was only a short-term trend. He expressed his position vividly, arguing that, since humankind had existed for several thousand years, considering a constant geometric increase in population, "the human population would have grown not only beyond the number of people that could breathe on the Earth, but to more than could be contained on its entire surface, from the lowest valleys to the highest mountains, crowded and packed together like dried herrings in a barrel."[517]

The world reached a population of 3 billion in the 1960s. Paul Ehrlich wrote at the time that this already constituted a state of overpopulation and that the size of the human population on Earth should not have exceeded 1-2 billion.[518] David Willey, co-founder of the Optimum Population Trust, held a similar view. In 2000, when the world had just surpassed 6 billion citizens, he argued that the optimal population was 3 billion.[519] Almost ten years earlier, in 1991, John Holdren estimated that the capacity of the Earth would be exceeded with a population above 10 billion.[520] Joel Cohen, one of the most prominent researchers of the problem, considered different levels of human needs and estimated that to be compatible with American standards of living, only 1 billion people could live on Earth, or 5-7 billion according to the standards of less developed agrarian societies.[521] Other estimates were much higher. Some, for instance, estimated the maximum capacity of Earth at tens of billions of people[522] or even at 1 trillion.[523]

The overarching conclusion that emerges from all this is that views on the overpopulation of the Earth changed with time, depended heavily on the assumptions made, and were highly diverse in the estimates they generated. Since many supposed limits of Earth's capacity were exceeded with no population Armageddon in sight and the human species, defying gloomy predictions, continued to exist, the practice of numerically estimating the Earth's capacity fell into disuse.

In 2004, however, a duo of Dutch economists, Jeroen C. J. M. van den Bergh and Piet Rietveld, did it again. They conducted a meta-analysis of the factors that determined the maximum capacity of the Earth and produced a new estimate of the maximum sustainable human population. Their calculations suggested that the Earth could accommodate between 0.7 billion and 98 billion people. The availability of water and forest resources proved to be the most restrictive factors. If the capacity of the Earth were to be determined solely on the basis of those two resources, van den Bergh and Rietveld claimed the carrying capacity of the Earth was 2 billion people.

On the other hand, land and related food production would be capable of supporting as many as 62 billion people, and energy resources could secure the lives and livelihoods of a population of more than 100 billion.[524] Since the range of extreme values in this model is enormous, the median value of 7.7 billion was used as the most appropriate number. The world reached this number in 2019. Clearly, life on Earth continues and nothing has happened that would indicate that the planet's capacities have been exceeded. This should not prompt us to disregard social or environmental problems; instead, it is an observation that reality defies mathematical rules and is challenging to forecast due to myriad factors that we cannot predict.

Just as attempts have been made to estimate the maximum population of the world as a whole, researchers have embarked on similar quests in relation to specific countries. At a demographic congress in Berlin in 1935, the representative of the British Population Society, Sir Charles Close, stated that a population size of 46 million would already be too large for Great Britain. The country reached this population size in 1939, but of course, it did not provoke any negative consequences. Instead, World War II wrought severe economic devastation and whittled down the country's population. In 1969, at a population symposium organized by the British Royal Geographical Society, some expressed renewed concern about what would happen once the population of the United Kingdom exceeded 66 million.[525] The UK reached this milestone in 2016 with no additional economic or environmental imbalance.

In 1939, an American demographer named Pascal K. Whelpton declared that the United States, with a population of 130 million, had already reached a state of overpopulation. He believed that the optimal number would be 100 million inhabitants.[526] Ehrlich, whom we already know well, argued that the optimal number of people for everyone in the United States to have a decent quality of life was 150 million. The authors of the book *Too Many Americans*, Lincoln H. Day and Alice T. Day, estimated that surpassing 200 million would be dangerous.[527] In 2020, the U.S. had a population of 330 million. It remained a global economic powerhouse with one of the highest per capita GDPs in the world, signaling the high standard of living of its citizens.

One might ask why all these estimates of overpopulation have proved to be utter failures. So many attempts have been made to define the limits of the Earth's capacity and to indicate specific population numbers that should not be exceeded. Still, none of these predictions have proven accurate. Humanity continues to exist, and the specter of global malnutrition is not a significant source of concern. The answer is simple. In each case, the prophets of the Earth's reckoning made a mistake that is typical of classical economic theory: they overestimated the value of the Earth's natural resources and underestimated the importance of human capital.[528] Estimates and calculations of the maximum sustainable size of the Earth's population were based on a static theory of resources and the logic that, since natural resources are limited, the number of people living on Earth must also be limited. They overestimated the importance of arable land in food production and assumed that it would always be the limiting factor in population growth.

The critical error of these projections was that they underestimated the creative capacity of human beings. They assumed that the level of human knowledge, skill, and technological know-how would be the same as it was when the forecast was made.

Overpopulation as a Cause of Hunger

The existence of hunger in the world is a fact. As we cross the threshold of the third decade of the 21st century, quantitative or qualitative food shortages affect more than 800 million people in the world. The idea of linking hunger to population growth stems from the simple principle that whenever we are faced with the scarcity of a given resource, we get the irresistible urge to point to too many people taking part in its distribution as the culprit. Statistics show that, in spite of dynamic population growth, food production has also been steadily increasing, both overall and per capita.

The link between famine and overpopulation is based on this assumption, derived from Malthus's theory that an increase in Earth's population is an increase in the number of people using up limited food resources. It was this assumption, among others, that led Adolf Hitler to adopt the policy of territorial expansion that we know as *Lebensraum* – living space."[529] Hitler sought to expand the borders of the Third Reich because he believed that the implementation of his grand plan to expand the German population required new spaces capable of feeding all citizens. He argued: "Germany's population growth is 600,000 new heads every year. That's six million in ten years. How can Germany continue to feed her people? That is only possible if we acquire new territory-and we must get that by brute force."[530] As we know from history, Germany ultimately acquired no new territories, but this did not prevent the economic and population growth of post-war Germany, which today is the undisputed economic leader of Europe and one of the most significant economic powers in the world.

The perception of the Earth's resources as too small in relation to the needs of an expanding population was characteristic of the entire Malthusian and neo-Malthusian movement, which flourished after World War II. The famous Club of Rome report from 1972 mined this position extensively. It concluded that the world would soon be threatened by mass starvation due to the depletion of land available for agricultural use. The report's authors assumed that its area was limited to 3.2 billion hectares at most – that is, 32 million square kilometers, or just over 21 percent of the Earth's land area. Since they estimated that half of this land – the most fertile and accessible portions – were already being cultivated, they expected a severe shortage of arable land before the year 2000 and by 2010 at the latest, as a result of which food prices would have risen so much that a large part of the world's population would starve to death.[531] At the beginning of the 1980s, the United Nations Food and Agriculture Organization (FAO) also pointed out that the populations of some developing countries had already exceeded their food-growing capacities and that, by the year 2000, many more regions would find themselves in the same situation, despite squeezing as much as they could out of their agricultural land.[532] In 1966, Lester Brown concluded that "[f]ood scarcity will be the defining issue of the new era now unfolding, much as ideological conflict was the defining issue of the historical era that recently ended."[533] These assessments primarily underestimated the amount of land resources available for agricultural use. They failed to predict the actual increase in yields that makes it possible to secure food production at an adequate level without expanding the area of cultivated land.

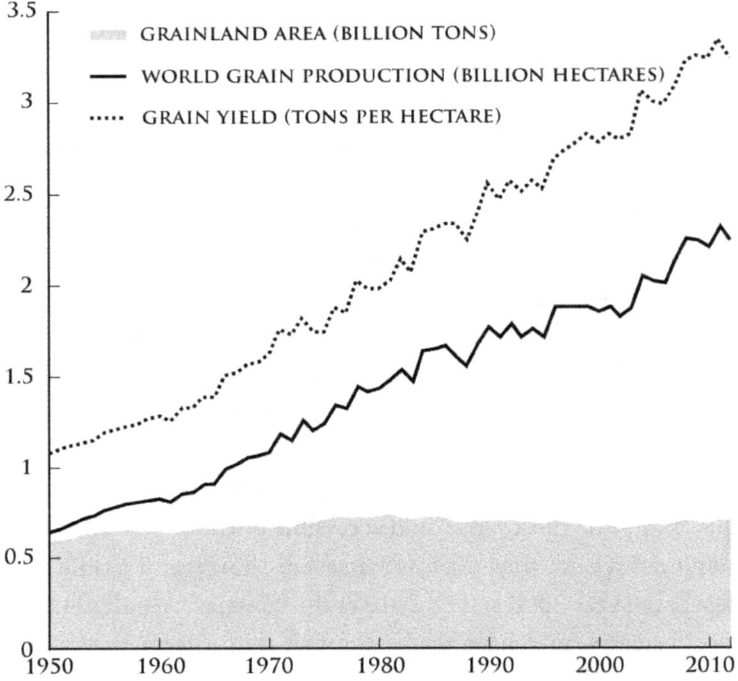

Fig. 4. World Agriculture Development: 1960-2012.[534]

Statistics show that, despite the increase in the world population, the number of people in the world who suffer from undernourishment is falling. The phenomenon still exists, but its scale is smaller than a few decades ago. The growing population does not appear to be a causal factor. First, it is difficult to find any consistent trend in long-term statistics regarding hunger and malnourishment – periods of very high death rates from malnutrition alternate with less dire years. Second, there has clearly been a significant improvement since the 1970s. While in the years 1940-1970, several million people died of starvation each year, since the 1980s, these numbers have been significantly lower. According to Alex de Waal, who analyzed the causes and trajectories of hunger in the world, the risk of death due to starvation has fallen in the last 30 years to a level never before recorded in history. Most of the victims of the great famines in the world in the previous half-century died before 1980.[535]

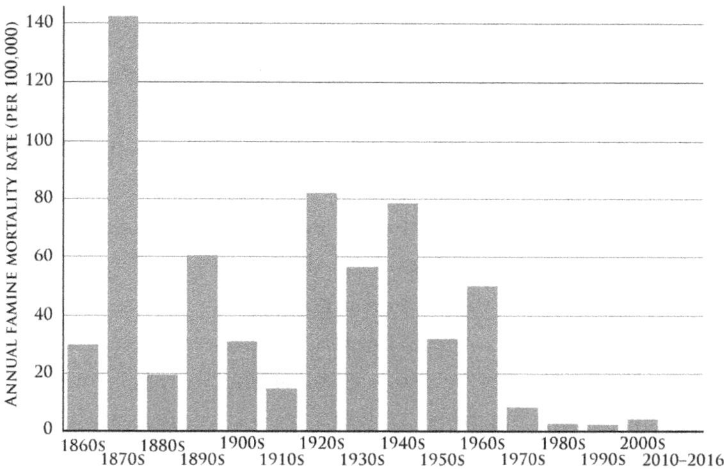

Fig. 5: Famine mortality rate: 1860-2016.[536]

Let's look at the spatial distribution of famines: We can see that the majority of those that have occurred in modern times were related to political systems that pursued completely irrational economic policies. Totalitarian systems create particularly favorable conditions for the spread of famine, limiting the financial freedom of individuals and imposing national income redistribution schemes. Enormous food shortages that led to the death of millions of citizens occurred, for example, in countries that implemented the communist system by force. In the 1930s, famine broke out in Russia, Ukraine, and Kazakhstan, among others. This was not a result of sudden population growth but instead of the nationalization of the economy, forced collectivization of agriculture, and mandatory food deliveries to the state. The authorities confiscated grain and all food produced, and ordinary people died en masse. In China, a similar scenario unfolded in the years 1958-1962, during the reign of Mao Zedong, whose implementation of an ideological, economic program called the Great Leap Forward led to the collapse of China's agriculture and the death of tens of millions of people by starvation. A similar situation occurred in Cambodia in the 1970s and in Ethiopia in the 1980s. The use of irrational solutions in agriculture, combined with the emergence of a repressive political regime and the bloody suppression of opposition to the new locus of power, brought famine to these countries.[537]

In contrast, recent famines in Nigeria, Somalia, Sudan, Yemen, and Syria are the result of devastating civil wars. Religious and ethnic conflicts, prolonged military operations, and the accompanying economic devastation are responsible for the severe food shortages in these parts of the world. Citizens of these countries suffer from hunger for political reasons because they are cut off from the world, and their economies collapse. This is often compounded by unequal distribution of wealth among certain social groups. It is worth noting that famine does not affect well-managed, democratic countries, where the free market regulates the relationship between demand for food and its supply. Well-administered domestic and international policies are the best way to avert famine.[538]

Although the leading causes of hunger lie in politics and the flaws of economic systems, it is hard not to notice that widespread malnutrition occurs mainly in countries that have a high birth rate. However, this does not mean that the former is a simple consequence of the latter. In the late 1980s, Frederick Buttel and Laura Raynolds conducted studies in 90 countries on the relationship between population growth, food consumption, and other elements of the economic system. The study found no relationship between population growth and hunger, instead showing that both occur where there is poverty and social inequality.[539] The relationship between population growth and food shortages exists, but it is not a relationship of dependence. Both phenomena are parallel effects with a common root in low levels of economic development and unequal distribution of resources.

In addition, the Global Hunger Index (GHI), when analyzed across time and space, shows us that although the highest levels of hunger occur in some countries with high population growth, these relationships are not directly proportional. Despite growing populations, almost all countries for which data exist between 1992 and 2017 have reduced overall levels of hunger, the only exception being war-ravaged Iraq. In China, this period saw a 16 percent increase in population, while the GHI has decreased by 18 points on a 100-point scale. In Bangladesh, despite a population increase of 44 percent, Bangladesh's score on the GHI has declined by 27 points. Angola, Niger, and Mozambique, despite more than doubling their population, saw their GHI decline by more than 30 points.[540]

Food crises or even famines occurring in various parts of the globe have nothing to do with surpassing the carrying capacity of the Earth in terms of its human population. Famine has loomed over humanity since the dawn of time and occurred even more frequently when the population was many times smaller. One example is China, which, despite devoting vast acreage to urban and communications infrastructure in recent years and maintaining a population of 1.4 billion, has an overall food surplus. The famine of 1959-1961 occurred with a population of 650 million – less than half the size it is today. This proves that the occurrence of famine does not simply flow from a large population but instead depends on the level of technology employed and the ways in which both resources and the entire socio-economic system are managed.

OVERPOPULATION AND POVERTY

It is quite common to use the concept of overpopulation to explain unfavorable economic phenomena, such as the low level of development in specific countries and regions. This way of thinking, as well as the issue of malnutrition, has its roots in Malthus, who presented population growth as a negative phenomenon that leads directly to the impoverishment of societies. By the mid-20th century, the belief that population growth hampers economic development and condemns societies to poverty had become so entrenched that it became common lore. Many people accept as a universal truth that when the population is large, financial resources are diverted from investments in infrastructure and new ventures and used to meet the current living, health, and educational needs of a growing population. Thus, the economy cannot grow, and the standard of living remains low.

We do not need to conduct a thorough analysis to conclude that this is not the case on a global level. Even cursory knowledge about the economic situation of the world is enough to understand that, despite a persistently increasing world population, the overall level of prosperity is growing. World Bank data show that, between 1960 and 2022, the GDP per capita of the Earth increased from $450 to $12,650.[541] Even if we consider the change in the actual purchasing power of the dollar, the increase is still unquestionable. If we adjust the data over this entire range to the 2015 dollar value, we get a boost from $3,600 to $11,300. This development came in parallel with a significant increase in the world population, which shot up from 3 billion to 8 billion. If there were an unconditional dependence of the level of economic development on the rate of population growth, there would be a decline in GDP, not a multifold increase.

Similarly, we cannot credibly establish a correlation between poverty levels and population density. In Chad, which had a GDP per capita of just $709 in 2019, the average population density is just 11 people per square kilometer, among the lowest in the world. In many other countries where GDP is less than $1,000 per person (for instance, Afghanistan, Liberia, and Mali), the population density is also low. Thus, we can hardly claim that poverty is the result of an excessive concentration of population in a given area. On the other hand, many countries with high population density are highly developed. The two countries with the world's highest population density, Monaco (over 18,000 people per square kilometer) and Singapore (over 7,000 people per square kilometer), are also among those with the highest GDP per capita ($185,000 and $65,000 in 2019, respectively).[542] Many other rich countries in the world, such as the Netherlands and Japan, also have large populations and high population densities. However, they do not reveal the purportedly distinctive symptoms of overpopulation, be it socially or economically.

Statistics also show us that the increase in Earth's population that we have recorded since the end of World War II does not translate into an expansion of poverty. The level of poverty – including extreme poverty, which is understood as the number of people who live on less than $1.90 per day – is clearly decreasing. While 1.9 billion people were in this group in 1990, by 2015, this had been truncated to only 730 million – two and a half times less. Furthermore, this period saw declines not only in the absolute number of people living in extreme poverty but also in the percentage of the total population they comprised, which fell from 36 percent to 10 percent.[543] This means that, despite the growth of the world's population, an ever-smaller proportion of humanity is experiencing poverty. This contradicts the thesis that population growth promotes the spread of poverty.

However, analyzing the spatial distribution of national income and population growth shows a convergence of the two. Indeed, the most economically developed countries show little population growth or even experience population decline. On the other hand, countries with the lowest values of GDP per capita and a large share of the population that suffers from poverty record significant population increases. This pertains primarily to African countries, especially Congo, Niger, Mali, and Somalia. In these regions, the annual rate of population growth exceeds 3 percent, and GDP per capita is only a few hundred dollars. Some regions that have managed to contain rapid population growth have seen economic growth and poverty reduction. One example is China, whose economy skyrocketed in the 1990s. But here, the same question arises as in the case of famine: does the convergence of these phenomena mean that the size of the population or its rate of growth are the cause? Research casts doubt on this claim.

The one-sided and unconditional understanding of the relationship between high birth rates and poverty has been questioned since the 1980s.[544] Micro-level studies have shown that the relationship between these elements is bidirectional. High population growth does indeed reinforce poverty and make it more difficult to escape from it. However, reinforcing a process is not equivalent to causing it. In low-income families, many offspring will, to some extent, hinder material improvement. This is because the family uses its income to meet its basic needs, which prevents them from creating surpluses that could be used for investment and development. A high fertility rate, therefore, raises barriers to growth, but in economically underdeveloped regions, reducing the number of offspring does not change much since deficiencies in infrastructure and limited access to the labor market will not allow families to improve their material situation even if the fertility rate is reduced.

In fact, quite the opposite is true. Suppose the only possible source of income is agriculture due to poor economic development in the region. In that case, many children may even be beneficial because by engaging more hands to work on the land, it is possible to obtain more abundant harvests. In addition, a large family is a source of security for parents when they reach their twilight years, seeing as it serves as a kind of makeshift pension system. Therefore, poverty, underdevelopment, and lack of access to the labor market contribute to high fertility rates, not the other way around.[545] This means that lowering fertility and reducing population growth is not enough to get out of poverty.

Instead, what is needed is new investment as well as better access to education and the job market. China has strengthened its economic position not because it has reduced family fertility but because it has introduced a number of economic reforms. First, it implemented a market economy focused on urbanization and the development of modern industry, as well as a well-developed education and health system. It expanded the non-agricultural labor market, including for women, and opened itself up to the world. In China, the extreme poverty rate has decreased from 66 percent in 1990 to 0.5 percent in 2016.[546] If the state had continued to pursue Mao Zedong's irrational economic policies, reducing population growth would have done little to reduce poverty. It is also essential to know that population growth during Mao Zedong's reign entailed a substantial decline in living standards because it was accompanied by a significant economic downturn due to the dysfunctionality of the communist system. Under other economic conditions, the effects of population growth probably would not have been so dramatic.

Modern economists do not doubt that the best-substantiated finding in the relationship between population phenomena and living standards is that economic development is a factor in both reducing poverty and reducing family fertility. The development of human capital is a crucial component of this, as rapid population growth can have a negative impact on the standard of living of the population only in countries where human capital is low.[547] The education of women and their inclusion in the labor market is essential. Taking up education and professional activity postpones motherhood and shifts the family model toward a smaller number of offspring.[548] Therefore, investing in human capital while strengthening the economy and developing the labor market solves the problem of poverty better than forcing a reduction in the fertility rate. It is the low level of economic development and deficiencies in social and technical infrastructure that cause poverty and drive population growth, not the other way around.

OUR FUTURE HOME

ARE WE RUNNING OUT OF LIVING SPACE?

In a book published in 1970 under the telling title *The Doomsday Book: Can the World Survive?*, Gordon Rattray Taylor told the story of James Island in the Chesapeake Bay on the Atlantic coast of the United States. In 1916, several deer were relocated there. Within 40 years, the population had grown to 270 individuals, after which all of them died out. Taylor's diagnosis was that the extinction occurred due to a lack of food and the burden that the high density of the animals placed on their population. He speculated that the same fate awaits humans on Earth due to excessive population growth.[549]

The story is moving and evocative. It also perfectly illustrates exponential population growth and the clash of its effects with nature's limited resources. People who are sensitive and keenly aware of their decisions as far as starting a family is concerned may be discouraged from having children. But is it entirely valid? First, it compares a planet with a land area of 510 million square kilometers to a small, narrow, one-mile-long island; second, it juxtaposes humans and their ability to adapt to their environment with those of hoofed ruminants creatively.

Meanwhile, humans' creative potential is the potent ingredient that has allowed civilization to develop for millennia, even if our species has come to a crossroads more than once.

First, we must address the question of whether Earth is overpopulated in the physical sense and whether humanity is in danger of running out of surface area for further development. If one considers the entire land area of our planet, then with 8 billion people, the population density is 139 people per square mile. This means that there are almost 2 hectares of land area for every inhabitant of the Earth. Even if we subtract the 29 percent of this land that is unsuitable for settlement, such as mountains, deserts, and swamps, the average population density in habitable areas remains very respectable, at 1.3 hectares of habitable land per capita. Obviously, this is not an accurate distribution, nor is it possible to implement it due to pre-existing settlement networks. However, it shows that there are still considerable reserves of space.

It should also be noted that uninhabitable areas, such as areas occupied by ice sheets, dunes, mountain ranges, or swamps, are not useless from the point of view of general human needs. They are naturally active areas, provide ample resources, and, when equipped with infrastructure, serve as recreational areas. Therefore, they are part of the overall space that humanity can use productively.

That the Earth is far from physically overpopulated is also clear from the data we have on the actual distribution of the human population. Currently, 55 percent of the world's population lives in urban areas.[550] These cities occupy no more than 3.5 million square kilometers or about 2.4 percent of the Earth's land area.[551] This leads to two conclusions. First, more than 97 percent of the land area of our planet is populated by only 3.5 billion people. Thus, there are significant reserves of space not only for settlement purposes but also for maintaining natural ecosystems and securing food production. Second, humans can live in a heavily populated area. One can even venture to say that this is a natural human preference. Nobody forces people to live in a city. Billions of people consciously agree to live surrounded by a denser-than-normal concentration of humans because such spaces offer better material and social infrastructure and more excellent opportunities for development. Besides, this developed infrastructure compensates for the inconveniences of urban areas. Access to health, education, culture, running water, and a variety of services not only improves our quality of life but also extends it. Residents of urban areas experience more significant stress and a more polluted environment but ultimately live longer than their counterparts in rural areas.[552]

However, even if the problem of overpopulation is overblown, this does not undermine the validity of the discussion about the pressure we put on the environment. Still, habitat destruction is more a result of certain lifestyles and ways of managing space than of the population itself. Putting all the blame for pollution and environmental degradation on population growth is detrimental to ecological causes because it diverts attention from the main problem, which is the irresponsible use of resources.

WHAT ABOUT ALL THE FOOD?

With all that said, we still have to tackle the question of providing food security to a growing population. Anti-populationists frame the problem of food as one of the central issues in the debate on population processes. They argue that because of population growth, more food will have to be produced on less land using less water and energy without upsetting the fragile ecological balance.[553] This problem, too, appears to be solvable. We should distinguish two levels here: the production of food in quantities adequate to the growing population and the elimination of economic barriers that prevent the entire population from using the resources produced. Poor people will starve without means of subsistence, even with surplus food available on the local market. The Green Revolution that took place in the 1960s, while significantly increasing grain production, did not eliminate hunger in developing countries for this very reason. Economic barriers have prevented the poorest parts of society from participating in the distribution of the goods produced. This problem, however, remains completely detached from demographic processes. It is a problem whose root lies in states' economic policies, both at the national and international levels.

There are still many ways to achieve the goal of securing enough food to feed a growing population. Global food production is already sufficient to feed the entire world population hypothetically. There are large surpluses of food in highly developed countries that go to waste. In addition, world agriculture is still far from reaching maximum productivity, especially in the underdeveloped regions most affected by hunger and exhibiting the most significant population growth. In many regions, there is still a large gap between potential and actual yield.[554]

All that is needed to achieve greater productivity is to invest in agriculture. Above all, this entails making changes to the way in which farmland resources are managed, equipping rural areas with adequate infrastructure, and, most importantly, providing farmers with access to education. It is these factors that can unlock humanity's great potential to increase food production. The use of modern technologies of land cultivation and animal husbandry also yields positive results. Introducing high-quality seeds, fertilizers, plant protection products, and mechanized production technologies also plays a significant role. This is more important than the question of soil fertility itself. Western European soils are much weaker than in Eastern Europe yet yields there are much higher. For example, the average yield in Ireland is nearly 10 tons of wheat per hectare, whereas, in the Czech Republic, it is less than 6 tons; in Poland, it is around 4 tons; and in Kazakhstan has an average yield of only 1 ton.[555] This shows that there is still a lot of potential for growth in yields and that agricultural culture is a crucial determinant of agricultural productivity – and, thus, the production of food.

In times of climate change and unstable weather conditions, it is also vital to introduce and cultivate plant species that are more productive and, at the same time, more resistant to extreme weather conditions and pests. Research teams around the world are currently working on innovative solutions for "climate-smart agriculture" in order to reduce the adverse effects of climate change on food production and ensure food security. Work is underway on a range of issues related to improving agricultural efficiency in least-developed countries, including crop physiology and genetics, adaptation for livestock, the flow of ecosystem services, and climate risk management.[556] After all, the last green revolution also started in laboratories. High-yield cereal varieties were the result of work conducted in an international research center. Scientific research in the 21st century is much more sophisticated than it was in the mid-20th century. Suppose we can create artificial organs and retinal implants, and we have harnessed the power of sequencing long strands of DNA. In that case, the prospect of developing innovative solutions to increase plant resistance to pests and improve agricultural productivity without additional pressure on the environment seems quite realistic.

There is also great potential to reduce food waste at the production and delivery stages. Eliminating errors during harvesting, processing, transportation, and storage of produce throughout the farm-to-table process can result in lower and more efficient food production, even in the case of ever-growing increases in demand for food. FAO estimates from 2019 indicate that about 14 percent of the food that is produced on a global level is lost, just between the farm and retail stages (but excluding the latter). In sub-Saharan Africa, which is most affected by famine, these losses are even higher, and in Central and Southern Asia, they exceed 20 percent.[557] Additionally, many food losses occur at the household level, for example, due to poor planning of purchases or a consumer lifestyle in which purchasing products and services becomes an essential human need. Reducing these losses requires complex and challenging measures, including technological investment in the processes of production, transport, and storage. These solutions can support the fight against hunger in a growing population.

Another answer to the food needs of a growing population is the concept of vertical farming, proposed at the end of the 20th century by scientists from Columbia University under the leadership of Dickson Despommier. It has been implemented in the United States with satisfying results. It constitutes an example of human creativity in solving problems and, at the same time, proves that creating simple and highly adaptable solutions is just as important a marker of human progress as the exploration of outer space.

Vertical farming is a method of multi-level plant cultivation that saves space in the process of food production. It takes place indoors, with adequate lighting, irrigational, and thermal conditions.[558] It is essentially an intensified version of greenhouse cultivation, but one that can be implemented in former factories, warehouses, or even shipping containers. Its great advantage is that it is entirely invulnerable to weather conditions, and it can be strategically implemented in the immediate vicinity of places with high food demand or even within them, significantly reducing transportation costs and environmental pollution. Since the method is based on renewable energy sources, it is even more eco-friendly. Vertical farms are being tested in various locations around the world and are constantly being improved in terms of production efficiency and reduced environmental impact. In the context of population and environmental problems, they seem to be an extremely beneficial solution.

There are endless possibilities for solving the problems of the modern world, ranging from the use of modern technologies to changing political and economic systems. Many solutions require financial resources and education, as well as a change in mentality, attitudes, and even the abandonment of tradition. We can insist that these are insurmountable barriers, but it would look a little as if we were clinging to the idea that the world should not change at all, whatever the costs. The price we would pay for this immutability and continued adherence to the old order would be the halting of natural demographic processes. The more realistic approach is to change our ways of doing things, our lifestyles, and our economic mechanisms, even if it takes a monumental effort, in order to make room for future generations. This is the best way to solve the problems of human population expansion. We have so many ways to make space for all of humanity and guarantee everyone a decent standard of living.

Why do we panic so easily? Why do we prefer to sound the alarm rather than think constructively about the future? There is a principle at work in our perception of reality that German philosopher Martin Heidegger put so succinctly: people view new things through the lens of what they know.[559] Not only is it difficult for us to imagine solutions that did not exist before, but we also perceive new phenomena through the smokescreen of previously acquired experiences. If we are soaked in knowledge about the disastrous effects of population growth, the prospect of the continued growth of the human population will arouse fear in us, and catastrophic visions of the future will speak to us. In mastering this fear, it may help to know that our goodwill, combined with our creativity, has helped us resolve many challenges, and the story of humanity is a story of how successive generations have climbed to heights that their predecessors never even dared to dream of.

SIX
DOWN TO THE LAST BARREL

Wojciech Janicki

Every day we take a step closer to the end. To the end of everything: to the day our universe fizzles out, to the moment our sun dies, to our own demise, to the last day of work before retirement, to an explosive New Year's bash, to the moment we run out of our favorite beer that we are stocking in our pantry. As we read in chapter 3, nothing lasts forever and everything that had a beginning must also have its end.

But what do we mean by "the end?" Even if our universe expires in a few billion years' time, all we can do is spend a moment pondering the vastness of space and time and raise a glass in appreciation. If we learn that in about five to ten billion years the Sun will devour all the hydrogen in its nucleus and inflate into a red giant (absorbing the Earth along the way), we will probably have a similar reaction. If I am 52 years old today and the average male in my country can expect to live until the age of 80, then chances are I have almost three decades to live before I clock off for good. If I plan to retire at 65, then I have 13 years of work ahead of me. If today is the 31st of July, then in 153 days the year 2024 will be over. If we have three crates of beer in the pantry with eight bottles per crate and we drink one beer with dinner every day, then in 24 days' time we will deplete our supply.

The common thread connecting all the above scenarios is that each is an attempt draw up a timeline and pinpoint the moment at which an event will occur that will alter the reality around us – or the reality of our descendants. However, each scenario is completely different. Some endpoints are very uncertain and the chances of empirically verifying our thesis are negligible. After all, we cannot be certain that there are no other universes parallel to ours in which life and time will continue flowing, as Hugh Everett visualized in his famous quantum theory of many worlds.[560] In these other worlds, which branch out infinitely like the arms of an enormous tree, we exist as well, branching off continuously as individuals and collectives – and so do our alter egos, who live out their lives while choosing different roads than the ones we took. If the Sun swallows the Earth and everything on it, the human species, if it still exists, will probably be able to observe it from a different vantage point in the universe that it will move into in the meantime. If I can be considered a statistically representative inhabitant of my country, then I will live another 28 years, but no one will be surprised if I fail to follow the statistical calendar. I may retire earlier, using the bridging pension that some future government will offer to scientists, or perhaps later, because the same government will have raised the retirement age instead. The beer in the pantry will last me 24 days, unless one evening a neighbor visits me and we power through my entire weekly supply.

What these simple examples show is that it is inherently difficult to precisely indicate the moment a certain event will occur. Pinpointing this moment requires us to adopt certain preliminary assumptions and parameters that define the variability of the phenomenon whose end point we want to predict. Out of all the snapshots presented above, only the arrival of New

Year's Eve and the transition to a new year require no additional assumptions, which makes them relatively safe from the follies of the future.

Just like we can try to forecast what the future may hold from the examples above, so can we attempt to predict the moment Earth will run out of mineral resources. This is no easy feat: to approach this task in a responsible way, we must take many different variables into account, starting from the choice of raw material we will analyze. Some substances are so common on Earth that, in practice, we will never be able to deplete them, regardless of the rate at which we exploit them and regardless of the population of our planet. According to the most widely accepted theory of the origin of the Earth, the current shape of our planet is the result of millions of years of collisions of meteorites moving chaotically in space. Each subsequent collision gradually increased the mass of the primordial Earth, expanding its gravitational field, which in turn pulled in even more meteorites even more effectively. The chemical composition of the Earth should therefore correspond to the typical chemical composition of the meteorites that built it. To take this line of reasoning further, iron is a very common element in our planet because it is abundant in meteorites, forming 40 percent of their mass, on average. Even after making the necessary corrections to account for the differing structures of the Earth's nucleus and crust, we can assume that iron constitutes about 5 percent of the latter's mass. Silicon, aluminum, calcium, sodium, and others are also common. Simply put, we will never run out of sand, aluminum, cement, or salt. The only problem may be the availability of a specific raw material in a specific location. It is for this reason that trade emerged as one of the most basic forms of human economic activity several millennia ago and continues to operate in the same vein today. Even iron, though common, is often a key object of trade and sometimes political engagements, as it was during World War II, when the Third Reich offered Sweden a guarantee of neutrality and security provided that the Scandinavian country export iron ore to the Reich, which was in dire need of it.

Among the raw materials that are much less common (and thus theoretically depletable) is the substance that has virtually become the poster child of research about the exhaustion of raw materials – crude oil. Like most substances used by humankind, oil is a non-renewable raw material. Once used up, it cannot be replenished for generations.

Scientists are not certain about the precise processes that lead to the formation of oil. The most widely accepted theory in the scientific world today is the organic theory, which states that oil is formed in the sediments of the seabed as the endpoint of millions of years of transformation of plant and animal remains occurring under high pressure and temperature, with bacteria facilitating the process. An alternative theory is that oil is the product of the transformation of inorganic substances located in the upper part of Earth's mantle, directly below the crust, the outer rocky shell of our planet.[561] However, this last theory has few supporters in the scientific community.

Though it may appear otherwise, the debate over the origin of oil is not simply academic in nature. And for us to unlock the future possibilities of using oil, it is a critical debate to settle. If the organic theory is true, then not a single barrel of oil used today will ever be replenished, except perhaps if we extend our timeline to millions of years into the future. If, on the other hand, the few supporters of the "inorganic oil" theory are right, then we will never run out of oil, because it is constantly being produced in the depths of the Earth. However, let us take the more challenging road and assume that this time the majority is right, even if, quite often, it is wrong. This would mean that every barrel of oil that is processed into fuel, heating oil, solvents, lubricants, paints, candles, plastic bags, bottles, clothes, car bumpers, asphalt, fertilizers, explosives, medicines, tires, toys, and thousands of other products brings us closer to the final and irreversible exhaustion of our oil supply.

In our collective imagination, this moment of terminal depletion has become synonymous with a catastrophe of unimaginable proportions, nearly amounting to the end of the world. For how to imagine a world where none of the products mentioned above are being produced anymore? After all, oil is the lifeblood of modern economy; without it, we do not exist.

This is our first waypoint and our first opportunity for serious reflection. Are our struggles to fathom such a world truly dictated by the fact that it is impossible for modern society to function without oil? Or do they stem from the limitations of our imagination, which alarmist currents have shaped into accepting only one possible scenario? Perhaps our fear of the day when oil runs out is akin to children's fear of darkness, a perilous void where child-eating wolves dwell, as in Charles Perrault's *Red Riding Hood*? After all, darkness is everywhere: in the street, in the park, even in one's own bedroom, where the child hides under a comforter, looking for shelter from the monsters beyond.

Is this an exaggeration? Perhaps. To balance the dominant belief that a catastrophe is imminent, it may be worth exaggerating a little in the other direction so that we can start thinking again about whether what threatens us is truly a catastrophe. This requires us to take a step back and re-examine our assumptions without the static of emotions, without reverence for single sources of truth, and without the conviction that we already know everything there is to know. We may even have to consider the possibility that we were wrong, even if that is always a bitter pill to swallow. If we assume our own infallibility in advance and block out every attempt to question challenges to established conclusions, we will never move forward. What else did Copernicus do if not contest the state of contemporary knowledge? What about Newton? Einstein? As the saying goes, the greatest discoveries are made by those who do not know that what they plan to achieve is impossible. Trying to overcome the barrier of impossibility is therefore in itself a valuable scientific method, thanks to which our understanding of the world around us can ascend to new heights.

Any attempt of this kind should be built on a firm foundation of knowledge. Whatever baseline knowledge we pursue, we should not undervalue or obscure its meaning, nor should we disingenuously style it as a kind of omniscience whose claim of superiority over folk wisdom is unjust. Otherwise, we run the risk of concluding that science, too, is infallible by design, which would create an opening to place it in the same box as dozens or hundreds of other (actual) myths.[562] Boiling science down to incontestable truths was not the goal of the 17th- and 18th-century European thinkers who spearheaded the aptly named era known as the Enlightenment, where reason became the basic means of explaining and comprehending the dynamics of nature, society, and the economy. The advances of that age and the ones that followed it would have been in vain if we were to return to a path where we are guided purely by emotions and infinite faith in truths once revealed. The narrative of the impending oil and energy catastrophe has long since escaped the confines of reason and safely lodged itself in a place where it is extremely difficult to eradicate – our emotions, beliefs, and deepest convictions. Along the way, it has morphed into an unquestionable truism, a truth so evident that any attempt to classify it as a myth exposes everyone who attempts to do so to accusations of ignorance at best. Oftentimes, it also places them among a group of lunatics and conspiracy-mongers who should be pitied and ignored because discussing established science with a madman is a waste of everybody's time.

However, in the previous chapters, my co-authors have shown how deeply all the most powerful minds of each era were mistaken in matters we find mundane today, from the rise of iron railways to electricity. Armed with this knowledge, you are well prepared to face the myth of the depletion of oil. This myth has planted itself firmly in our minds, and the voices of those swimming against the current of common beliefs and deeply rooted knowledge have barely been able to make a dent in its hardened shell. Yet there is reason to believe that our fear is futile and no catastrophe looms over the horizon.

Why don't we listen to such voices? Why does the narrative of impending doom dominate in popular messaging? Because we enjoy being afraid. We react much more strongly to negative reports describing situations and events we fear than to positive messaging. The mass media are filled to the brim with snippets about assassinations, explosions, accidents, shootings, crimes, conflicts, tornadoes, volcanic eruptions, floods, and fires. All these calamities are the core of the message around which the tension and attention of the recipient is built. Positive messages do not carry the same emotional charge: they do not involve or affect us, like a news chyron informing us that nothing of any importance happened today. The myth about the depletion of resources fits perfectly into the general narrative of doom. It is well-constructed, giving us information while building tension. It is almost like the tanker truck from Steven Spielberg's *Duel*, constantly accelerating to push the protagonist's car off the road – only that, for much of the film, the car is driving at the same speed and the tanker trails the protagonist at an unchanging distance. Our interpretation of the depletion myth perfectly complements this script. For myths are not only lies or invented stories; they are also powerful networks of symbols that suggest certain ways to interpret the world around us.[563] And it is extremely easy to be convinced by the simple and common-sense narrative that every barrel of oil that we use up is one barrel fewer that we can use in the future, and that therefore the end is nigh.

In October 1938, CBS broadcast the radio drama *The War of the Worlds*, directed and narrated by Orson Welles. Some listeners panicked, believing that the story was an account of an actual Martian invasion of Earth. This episode shows how poorly our societies are immunized against manipulation (including unintentional manipulation), how naive we are, and how we like to be afraid. If the preceding chapters on the atomic energy that should not trigger our anxieties and the overpopulation of the world that will never happen were able to provoke some opposition in our readers (at least in the beginning), this chapter on the exhaustion of raw materials is even more challenging. I know that I risk rejection and opprobrium from faithful defenders of the myth. However, I assume that we use the same tools, and that ironclad logic can persuade anyone who is not absolutely convinced of their own infallibility. In this chapter, I ask the reader for the chance to make that case.

Why we should be afraid

Aunt Bessie's birthday bash and the story of the vanishing cheesecake

Let's begin with a simple scenario. Imagine that we are going to our Aunt Bessie's birthday party. She places a freshly baked cheesecake on the table and offers us tea or coffee. The cheesecake is large, weighs five pounds, and each of the five ravenous guests gets a solid helping of one-half pound. After a while, only half of the original weight of the cheesecake remains on the table. Does this stunningly simple logic, which would be understandable even to a three-year-old child, apply to minerals on Earth? Do we have less oil, coal, iron ore, and other substances when we consume a slice of each of them than we did before? Yes, of course we do. But with one important caveat.

Earth has a limited volume, like the cheesecake. If we assume that the average radius of Earth, which is not a perfect sphere, is about 3,959 miles, then its volume is $^{4}/_{3}\Pi r^{3}$, which translates into about 260 billion cubic miles. Most of this volume is out of our reach and will remain so for a long time; as depth increases, so does the temperature, at an average rate of roughly 4.5 degrees Fahrenheit for every 100 yards – a little less than the length of a football field. This means that, already at a depth of about a half mile into the bowels of the Earth, we can expect the temperature to be more than 40 degrees higher than the surface of the Earth in the same location. There are places where the rate at which the temperature changes is lower, but in other places, the temperature rises faster with increasing depth. For the sake of simplicity, let us limit ourselves to a surface layer roughly half a mile thick, which we have a chance to penetrate almost entirely. This layer has a volume of just almost 200 million cubic miles. It is difficult to imagine and visualize this volume, so we need some reference points. Our small slice of Earth's crust corresponds to nearly 200 billion Great Pyramids of Giza.

Of course, a considerable majority of this volume is composed of substances that will never be of any use to us, with exceptions that include building materials such as sandstone, clay, or granite. Exactly how much of the total they comprise remains a mystery – probably one that we will never solve. To calculate this proportion with precision, we would have to blanket every mile of the Earth with boreholes and analyze the samples excavated from the depths below. The costs of drilling a single exploratory well, depending on its location, depth, purpose of exploration, and other parameters, typically run into the hundreds of thousands of dollars,[564] which nobody is ultimately prepared to spend without a clear need for it. Therefore, the wells are drilled progressively, when the company that bears the costs of the operation needs new fields. For some natural resources, it is possible to use remote techniques. Such methods can be used to search for iron, significant volumes of which can change the course of the lines that define Earth's magnetic field; they are also useful in pinpointing larger quantities of radioactive elements. We also know that a portion of the Earth's surface is excluded from future exploitation because it stretches over accessible mountainous areas (about 1.5 percent of the Earth's land area), areas covered with ice (11 percent), forests (31 percent), areas used for agriculture (36 percent), and urban areas (1.5 percent). Even if we assume that just one thousandth of the volume calculated above contains any substances that are both obtainable and useful for humans, we will still have to dig through 200 million Great Pyramids – a staggering number by any count.

Indeed, it may be overly stringent to narrow our lens to one thousandth. In Poland, a series of maps commissioned in 2019 by the country's chief geologist highlighted known deposits and areas of potential mineral occurrence in Poland. If one were to overlay the maps showing the country's energy, chemical, metallic, and rock resources – including those already exploited today, those fully documented, and prospective resources – the various colors indicating the presence of some raw material in a given location would spread over more than 90 percent of the country's surface.[565]

Though it may not seem obvious yet, these calculations are a critical, solid foundation for the main argument distilled in this chapter. Returning to Aunt Bessie's cheesecake, one could say that there is a cheesecake on the table that weighs not five pounds, but five hundred tons. Every bite we take from the cheesecake reduces the size of the cake that remains on the table, but its gigantic starting mass renders the timeline for the last guest to finish the last bite and exhaust the cheesecake unimaginable.

EXPONENTIAL GROWTH – WHAT COMES NEXT?

Nonetheless, our fears about the impending depletion of resources are growing. To some extent, this is due to the rapid increase in Earth's population, as described in the previous chapter, and to an improved standard of living around the world, which has been associated with increased consumption (including consumption of raw resources) since the dawn of time. Global carbon dioxide emissions from burning fossil fuels have grown at an average rate of 3.3 percent per year since the beginning of oil production in the mid-19th century, and experts expect similar rates in the near future.[566] At first glance, this growth rate might not seem significant. The world economy is developing at a similar pace and the Gross Domestic Product of many countries is rising at a similar rate if we follow annual economic reports and forecasts. We are used to such single-digit numbers and they do not make a great impression on us.

But what does a steady rate of annual growth really mean? To answer this question, let us take a closer look at the well-known example of a water lily in a pond. Imagine a genetically engineered lily growing at the edge of a pond, doubling the number of its leaves every 24 hours. On the first day of our experiment, the lily has one leaf floating modestly near the banks of the pond. It has two leaves on the second day, four on the third day, eight on the fourth day, and so on. We also know that, after 30 days, the leaves of our water lily will cover the surface of the entire pond. On which day will we be able to observe with the naked eye that we are close to the final stage of growth that the lily will reach on Day 30? Let us take a look at the following graphic.

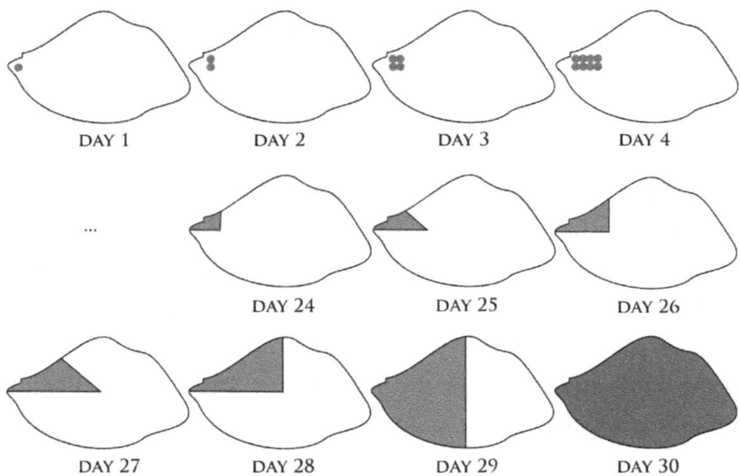

Fig. 1: A lily growing in a pond.

In the first few days, there are so few leaves on the water's surface that we need no more than a glance to count the leaves and correctly indicate the day. After only a few days, this becomes an impossible task. Let's take the opposite approach and look at the last day instead. On Day 30, the pond is entirely overgrown with leaves; we know it is the last day because that was our starting assumption. On Day 29, only half the pond is overgrown, which means that there are half as many leaves as on the last day. The day before that, once again, there are half as many leaves as on Day 29, covering a quarter of the pond. If we go back to the 24th day, we will see very few leaves on the pond and understand that we cannot see with the naked eye how close we are to the last day without having the faintest idea about it. This last day may represent a catastrophe whose onset will be completely unanticipated if we do not understand the basic dynamics at play here – exponential growth – and fail to prepare accordingly.

What does our lily have to do with GDP growth or a 3.3 percent annual increase in carbon dioxide emissions? They are exactly the same thing. In the case of the lily, the multiplier (the number by which we multiply the number of leaves every day) is 2, and in the case of carbon dioxide, it is 1.033. Although this may seem negligible, it only takes about 22 years for emissions to become twice as high as they were, so our consumption of this group of resources doubles every 22 years. This means that, over less than the last quarter of a century, we have used up the same volume of fossil fuels as humankind used from the dawn of our species to 1999! The data for the actual consumption of oil are similar. Since we began exploiting it (1860), we have extracted about 1.4 trillion barrels of oil worldwide (1 barrel is 159 liters or 42 gallons), almost exactly 700 billion of which was extracted in the last 25 years.[567]

A quarter of a century corresponds to one generation. Simply put, each generation consumes as many resources as all previous generations put together. If this trend holds, then our 200 million Great Pyramids will also run out surprisingly quickly.

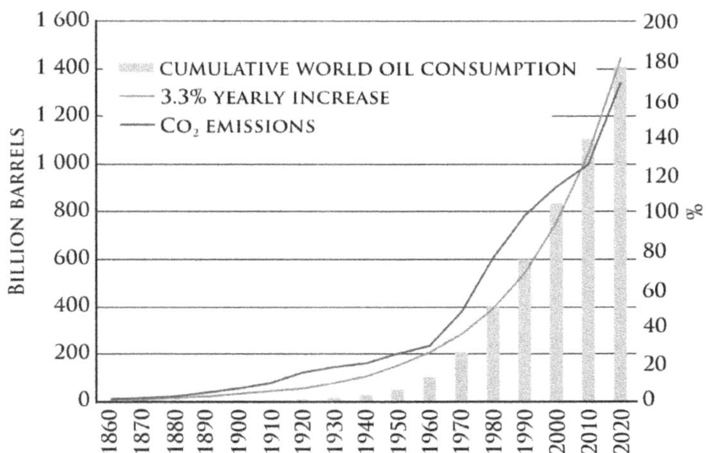

Fig. 2: Global growth rate of CO_2 emissions and global oil consumption.[568]

Everything's eventual: The theory of linear resource growth

The exponential increase in the consumption of mineral resources, as described above, is a powerfully evocative picture. It almost hurts us to realize how rapidly we are draining Earths resources and where it might lead us. After all, resources are limited, our consumption and the pressure to use them are growing at a rapid pace, so it stands to reason that they will soon run out. Let us try to visualize this relationship on a graph.

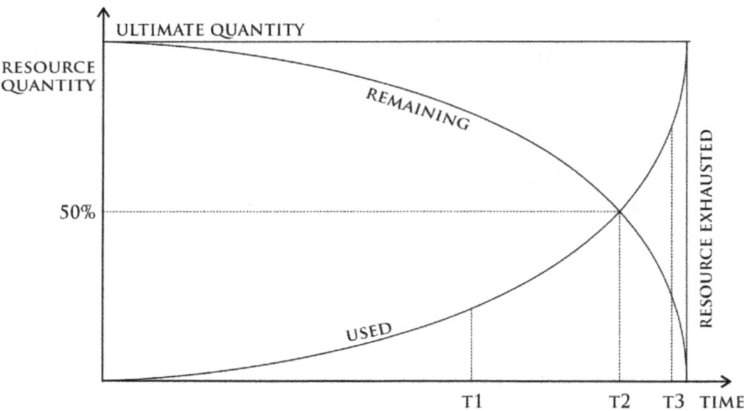

Fig. 3. Resource size as a function of time.

At first glance, one key question appears to emerge from this graph: Where are we in this process now? Are we at some hypothetical point t_1, at which we haven't used up half of the available resources yet, but some smaller portion? Or maybe we are at the midpoint, that is, at point t_2? Or perhaps we have already breezed through the checkpoint and barreling toward the end at t_3? Given that we consume as much oil in 25 years as in all the preceding centuries combined, if we are at t_2, then we have 25 years left until there is no trace of oil left on Earth. If we are at t_3, we have even less time and are even closer to the precipice. If we are in t_1, however, the clock still works somewhat in our favor.

At which of these points are we right now? Nobody truly knows. Why is this? Let us recall what circumstances prompt us to drill new exploration wells that will allow us to find new deposits. We do it when we need new fields to exploit, when the forecasts tell us that, in light of what we have exploited thus far, at some point we will have to start extracting more. In practice, this means that the line of known oil reserves on the graph above climbs upwards with each subsequent discovery. A correctly constructed chart should therefore look a little different:

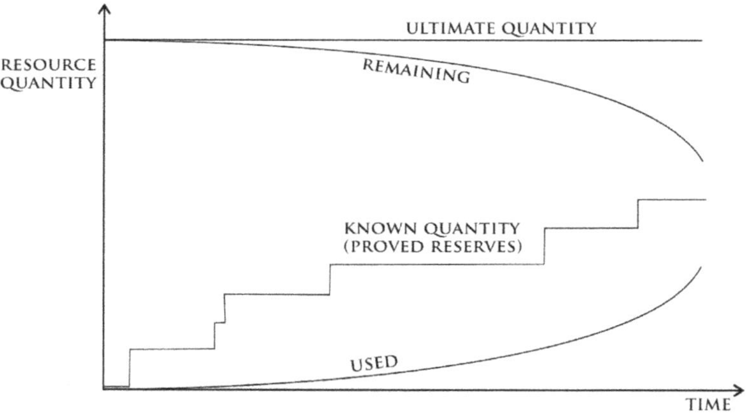

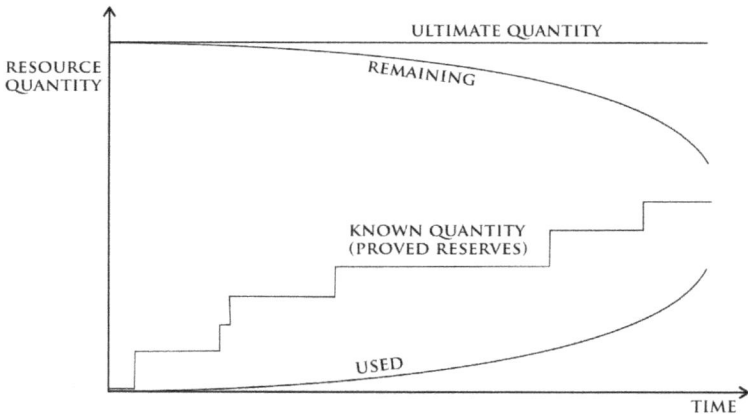

Fig. 4: Size of total resources and known resources as a function of time.

The key question is therefore not where we find ourselves today in relation to the known resources, as in Figure 3, but to the total resources in Figure 4.

These considerations can be reduced two competing scientific resource theories: the static theory and the dynamic theory. The static theory assumes that, at any given moment, we have a fixed, known amount of resources and certain possibilities of obtaining them, and we should not optimistically assume that this amount will ever increase. We cannot be certain that we will ever find new resources. Since resources are limited and we use them up, they will undoubtedly run out one day. For example, if we consistently consume 5 percent of the known reserves of a given resource every year, we will deplete them completely after 20 years. Our experience to date provides strong support for static theory. In many locations around the world that were once known for the exploitation of certain resources, nothing or almost nothing remains today. In 1896, gold-bearing sand was found in Bonanza Creek, a tributary of the Klondike River flowing through what is now Yukon Territory in Canada. This marked the beginning a period called the Klondike Gold Rush. Two years later, 30,000 prospectors were working in the town of Dawson and scouring the waters around it. By 1903, the gold had run out and the gold rush became just another page in the history books.

Another interesting example is Nauru, a tiny island in the Western Pacific. In 1900, the world's richest phosphate deposits were discovered on the island, and their intensive exploitation throughout the 20th century brought huge revenues to the island's ever-changing owners. In the 1980s, the leaders of the newly independent island country realized that the day when the last phosphate deposits would be exhausted was fast approaching and took several steps to change the income structure of the island's inhabitants. This was quite successful: today the phosphorites have almost completely run out, while their exploitation comprises less than 10 percent of the income of the island's inhabitants.[569]

The dynamic resource theory, on the other hand, assumes that it is completely unrealistic to assume that we have already detected and located all the resources on Earth and will never find any more. All our experience to date shows that, as a species, we make discoveries constantly. After all, progress is a question of work and effort, human knowledge, and in-depth research.

Not only do we then use more and more resources over time, but also accumulate knowledge about those resources. In the graph above, the line showing proved reserves does not run horizontally; instead, it rises incrementally. As our analysis above shows, we are not able to determine the exact volume of the resources available on Earth, so it is impossible to pinpoint the peak of this line. In the next chart, I will visualize the relationship between cumulative global oil consumption (counted from when organized oil production began in the world) and oil reserves known these days. The dashed line in Figure 5 shows the hypothetical increase in oil consumption and a hypothetical increase in known reserves over the next 30 years.

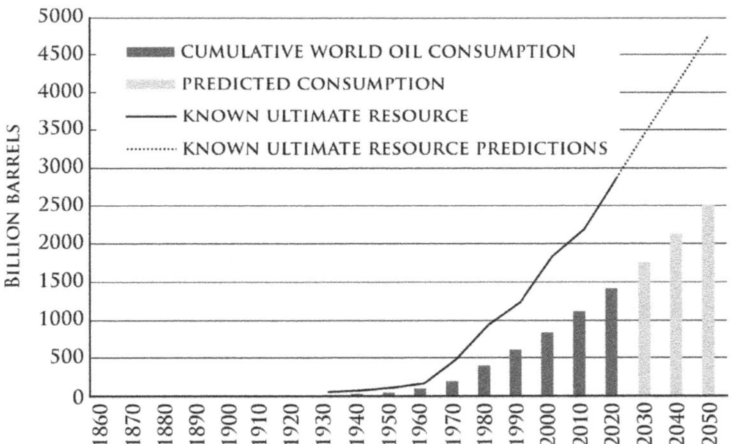

Fig. 5: Cumulative consumption and total oil reserves worldwide.[570]

Which of the theories above is a better reflection of reality – static or dynamic? Is it the one that assumes we have already discovered everything there was to discover on Earth, or the one whose core tenet is that every new exploration or strand of research will boost our chances of finding something new? There is a well-known saying among geologists: where there are geologists, there are deposits. In other words, if we send a geologist into the area and have them examine it, then sooner or later they will find something there. The geologist might not find exactly what they were looking for and the find may not immediately yield a bountiful motherlode, but they will certainly not come back empty-handed. And since millions of square miles of the Earth's surface remain untouched by geologists' hands, the chances of new discoveries are still high.

What areas are most promising in this regard? First and foremost, the ocean floor. Only a narrow strip in the immediate vicinity of continental masses called the continental shelf remains well studied, while our knowledge of most of the ocean floor proper – more than 70 percent, in fact – is very limited. As some argue in the context of the political tug of war for the oil reserves that allegedly sit under the Arctic Ocean, "Overall, maps of Mars are about 250 times better than maps of Earth's ocean floor."[571] The second almost completely unexplored area is the Antarctic continent, a land mass nearly twice as big as Australia and almost 50 percent larger than the United States. We often forget just how enormous the frozen continent is because we regularly use maps that significantly distort the size of different land masses, and Antarctica is often either obscured or even omitted entirely. The vast expanse of the frigid Russian region of Siberia, though also larger than the United States, is very poorly explored, to the point where some have called it the mine of the future, precisely due to the immensity of its unexplored areas. Add to that the Canadian High North, large stretches of western Brazil, and the Sahara in Africa and we have a picture of the resource potential of the future.

So where does the truth lie? Probably somewhere in the middle. The static theory makes the completely unsustainable assumption that humankind will cease to discover new deposits, and the dynamic theory contends that we will find a lot more than we know of today, which can also be easily challenged. It is also misguided to rely on inductive reasoning, that is, inferring larger trends from details and past precedent. In our case, this would mean arguing that, since we have always found something to extract from the depths of the Earth, we will continue to find it. Why? This argument is akin to saying that I will never win the lottery because, although I have bought many lottery tickets so far, I have never won anything. The graph below, which shows the size of the oil discoveries by year, offers strong support for opponents of the dynamic theory, especially in the context of oil.

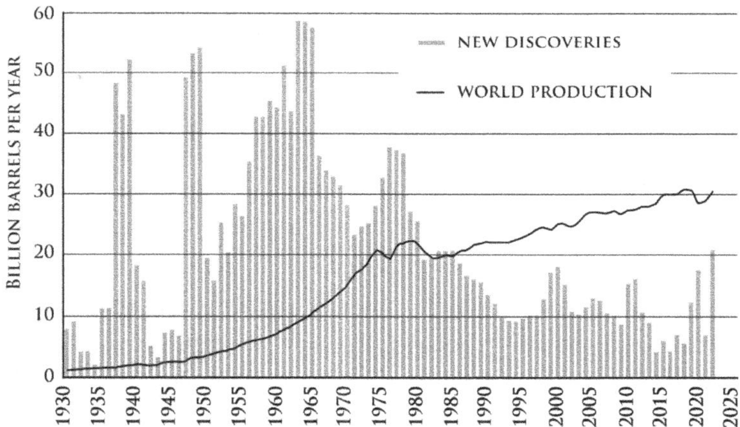

Fig. 6: Global oil production and new discoveries.[572]

As you can see, new discoveries reached their peak volume in the mid-1960s, while our annual oil production has exceeded the volume of new discoveries since the mid-1980s. We can also observe a clear downward trend in the volume of new discoveries, while the line that denotes oil consumption follows a slow but consistent upward trajectory. As a result, the amount of resources at our disposal in the future is perpetually decreasing. Does this mean that the pessimistic supporters of the static theory are closer to the truth than those who optimistically believe in the power of progress? Given the bank of available evidence, it is too early to pass judgment at this point, as we still have much analytical work to lay out in this chapter.

JUSTICE ABOVE ALL

The need to reformulate the basic assumptions of modern economics has been recognized since at least 1969, when UN Secretary General U Thant first warned about the imminent catastrophe awaiting humanity in a report presented to the UN General Assembly.[573] In the classical approach to economics, dating back to Adam Smith and David Ricardo, the environment was an inexhaustible fountain of resources that humanity could exploit with no checks or limitations. When it became clear that these theories were erroneous and resources could indeed be permanently depleted, the concept of sustainable development emerged. Sustainable development is an approach to managing nature's resources in such a way that meeting our current needs will not have a negative impact on the ability of our children, grandchildren, and the generations that follow them to meet their own needs. It is easy to imagine this concept using the example of a forest. Cutting it down slowly and gradually, starting from the oldest and tallest trees, gives the forest the opportunity to grow back revitalized. Smaller trees get more sunlight and grow, and when they are felled after some time, they give way to their successors, and the forest remains strong and vigorous. However, if we clear entire swathes of woodland, then it will need at least as many years to regenerate as the age of the oldest trees in the forest, which can sometimes mean several hundred years.

At first glance, the basic assumption of sustainable development cannot be challenged. After all, it is an undeniably rational and responsible approach not to bring a colossal calamity down on our children's generation just to meet the needs we have today. Safeguarding the welfare of others, and our children in particular, should be high on the list of core values for every decent person on Earth. In the context of oil exploitation, these assumptions should lead us to the conclusion that we should not extract too much.

However, two important questions arise. First, must the prosperity of future generations be based on oil, and is this dependence inevitable? Do people need oil as a raw material on a daily basis? Or can they make do with any fuel so long as it can power their chosen means of transportation? Do they need bottles or cups made of plastic derived from oil, or do they simply need bottles or cups to serve as receptacles for liquids, whereas the raw material those receptacles are made of is a secondary consideration from a user's perspective? Do they need plastic (oil-derived) shopping bags or just any kind of bags that can hold their groceries?

While embracing our collective role as stewards of the future, we often tacitly assume that our civilization cannot exist without oil. Perhaps this assumption is not entirely correct? Perhaps we can replace fuel derived from crude oil with new varieties? Whether this will be ethanol, electrical energy, hydropower, wind energy, solar power, or another source of fuel is something we will address shortly, but for now we are interested merely in the idea of replacing oil with other sources of energy. Indeed, we are already taking gradual steps in this direction today. We have long been able to replace plastic bottles and cups with their glass or metal counterparts, and we've supplemented them for some time now with vessels made of bamboo, wood (including nanocellulose derived from wood), industrial hemp, and wheat bran, and even mushrooms and seaweed![574] In many places, plastic shopping bags are being systematically replaced with reusable cotton bags. Literally every product created as a derivative from oil has its substitutes. Some of them have yet to become popular, others are still rather expensive to make, and others still are imperfect compared to their oil-based cousins – but all of this is changing fast. Why, then, do we assume that the welfare of future generations – our children and grandchildren – will inexorably be based on oil, and therefore we must preserve it to the extent possible? Once upon a time, our species got by well without oil. Today we are in the phase of widespread use, but there will come a time when oil will become history. Not because the wells will run dry, but because we will no longer need it. As the former Minister of Petroleum and Mineral Resources of Saudi Arabia, Sheikh Yamani so aptly put it, "Thirty years from now there will be a huge amount of oil – and no buyers. Oil will be left in the ground. The Stone Age came to an end, not because we had a lack of stones, and the oil age will come to an end not because we have a lack of oil."[575]

The second question, in the context of the need to extract oil at a reasonable pace, is a philosophical and mathematical one. How long should oil last us in order for us to view today's pace of extraction as appropriate, optimal, or not overly intensive? In our search for an answer, let us turn to Chuck Noland, the protagonist of Robert Zemeckis' famous film *Cast Away*, played by Tom Hanks. Chuck miraculously escapes with his life from a plane crash and finds himself marooned on a deserted island. Imagine something not part of the movie: He finds a container full of canned food in the flotsam drifting off the coast of his island. He drags it ashore and finds a thousand cans of food, each weighing a half a pound. If he wants to survive until he is rescued by the search team and knows he has to rely exclusively on the canned food to sustain himself, how many days will one can last him? Can he eat one a day? If he is rescued after no more than 1,000 days, then one can per day is a reasonable rate of consumption given Chuck's available food supply. A portion of half a pound of food a day is small – too small to provide him with proper nourishment – but it will allow him to survive. But what if the rescue mission does not arrive in time? Then Chuck will starve to death. What if it comes after a hundred days instead of a thousand? Then it will turn out that Chuck starved himself unnecessarily and could have eaten more every day. The problem is that Chuck doesn't know when help will arrive, so he must adopt the best possible strategy. The most sensible strategy seems to be to consume as little as possible of the current supply for as long as possible to just live to see the moment when the rescue teams appear on the horizon. But what exactly does minimal consumption mean in this case? One can a day? That would be enough for 1,000 days. Half a can? 2,000 days. Even less?

In the film, Chuck was rescued after four years, or about 1,500 days. He did not find a convenient container of canned goods, instead surviving on what he found on the island and in the waters around it.

Humanity and its consumption of oil has found itself in the same position as Chuck Noland and his crate of canned food. We have a certain amount of oil at our disposal. We can be confident in hypothesizing that there is much more oil under the surface, but we don't know how much. We want it to be enough for our children, for our grandchildren, and for long after they are gone. But therein lies the rub: for how long, exactly? Solving this problem will determine how fast we should extract oil today. Do we have enough for 50 years? Then our children and grandchildren are relatively safe. A hundred years? That puts us ahead by two more generations. Five hundred years? What we have here is one equation with three unknowns:

$$o = \frac{q}{t}$$

where "o" is the amount of oil we can extract per year according to the above assumptions, "q" is the total amount of oil we have on Earth, and "t" is the number of years that the available supply of oil will last us. How do we calculate "o" if "q" is unknown and "t" is debatable and ambiguous?

This exact discussion has been going on for years. Most of the parties involved are economists and conservationists. In broad terms, the debate revolves primarily around the optimal rate of economic growth in the context of the depletion of natural resources. Its genesis lies with Thomas Malthus's observations on the dilemmas of feeding a rapidly growing population in the face of constant or slowly growing food production, itself a result of the limited availability of land that is suitable for cultivation. (This is described in greater detail in Chapter 5.) Over time, this discussion has also grown to encompass other issues, including the availability of natural resources.[576] How, then, can we optimize our economic development to ensure the welfare of those living today while bequeathing a livable environment to future generations? From a mathematical point of view, tackling this problem is like attempting to square a circle: it is impossible to know with certainty how much we should consume and how much we should save to secure the highest level of prosperity for the planet, as Frank Ramsey argued in his classic work almost a hundred years ago.[577]

Harold Hotelling's work on this topic, which he described as the "cake-eating problem," is probably more familiar still to those who take a deeper interest in the availability of mineral resources specifically. Hotelling inquired how it might be possible to divide a cake that had a finite volume between consecutive periods in such a way that the same amount would be available in each period. He came to a rather obvious conclusion: that we can only make this calculation if we know how many periods there are. If their number is unknown, then the only way to ensure equal access across all periods is to reduce current consumption to zero. When consumption is greater than zero, there may come a time when we will run out of cake. In his conclusion, he argued that we must agree to limit future consumption to be able to use the resource at all in the present moment.[578]

It follows from these considerations that ensuring intergenerational equality and justice, understood as identical availability of a particular resource – for instance, oil – is both unnecessary (because at some point in the future no one will want to use oil) and mathematically impossible. Most importantly, the gradual depletion of oil does not spell impending doom or a sudden disaster. We started oil production more than a century and a half ago by tapping into the most accessible and richest deposits. Thanks to this, oil was cheap, and its exploitation yielded enormous profits thanks to the large volumes of oil flowing through the pipes every day. Nobody thought about searching for and extracting oil that was difficult to access and therefore expensive, because from an economic standpoint, that would be suicidal. Today, we extract oil that is more difficult to access and, as a result, more expensive. This is a slow, gradual transformation. Even if this trend holds, we will continue to move away from oil and turn our hopes and engineering finesse to other resources. Perhaps our standard of living will slowly decline if we do not find and introduce oil substitutes quickly enough. But in no circumstance will we one day awaken to the shocking discovery that all the oil in the world is gone. Oil is not an undersea volcano destined to suddenly erupt and drain the world of all its liquid potential.

It is also worth noting that the passage of time has always worked in the next generations' favor. Our lives today are much more comfortable and longer than those our parents lived when they were our age. Our parents had a better quality of life than our grandparents, who in turn could enjoy comforts and luxuries that their parents never experienced. Are the lives of our children worse than ours? And what kind of starting point can we envision for our grandchildren? My own grandfather on my father's side had eleven siblings. He used to say that each of the children would go to church at a different hour on Sunday because they only had one pair of shoes to share among themselves. They played with what they found in the yard, had no TV, and their parents could not afford to buy books for them. Four generations later, my three-year-old granddaughter has dozens of pairs of shoes in different colors for different occasions, her own room in her parents' house, lots of books, educational toys, and digital TV, where she watches cartoons in different languages to learn their melody as early as possible, which will help her get a head start in her adult life. Shouldn't the world accelerate boldly down the path of progress? Do the older generations really have to sacrifice everything (including oil) to leave enough for our children and our children's children?

THE BIRTH AND BUILDUP OF FEAR

Fear has been humanity's companion since time immemorial. Our ancestors dreaded hunger, war, wildlife, the cold, fire, the forest, thunderstorms, darkness, and even solar eclipses. The fear that scarcity of resources will lead us to the brink of death has also loomed over our species from since it emerged. The most necessary resource, without which no living creature can function, is food. Thus, it was precisely the potential shortage of food, induced by overpopulation, that evoked the anxiety of ancient thinkers, beginning with Confucius at the turn of the 6th and 5th centuries BC. On the grounds of these concerns, philosophers and demographers tried to persuade their contemporaries to limit their societies' rate of population growth. Although the oldest texts of written history do not reveal much about fears surrounding the depletion of resources, there are very clear signs of the fears that are common today in sources from the Middle Ages. In the 13th century, St. Thomas Aquinas, who called for humility and opposed wastefulness in his works, called for his contemporaries to make more efficient use of resources in order to minimize their consumption.[579] One can apply this reasoning exclusively to the exploitation of nature's goods as a whole, but it would also be reasonable to assume that the real prospect of non-renewable resources drying up was a direct impulse for contemporary thinkers who examined humanity's resource woes writ large.

We may of course argue that the thoughts of philosophers, theologians, journalists, and other thinkers are not a reliable source of information on the depletion of resources if those luminaries do not form part of a dedicated scientific community that deals professionally with issues related to the occurrence and exploitation of resources, or at least the economics of resource use. But how can we ignore the warnings of geologists who analyze these issues as their daily bread?

THE GEOLOGIST IS ALWAYS RIGHT

In 1865, English economist William Stanley Jevons published his famous book *The Coal Question*. The treatise resonated powerfully in the scientific community thanks to the bold and well-substantiated argument that an increase in the efficiency of energy-consuming devices will not lead to a decrease in energy consumption (as many of the author's contemporaries believed), but further growth. Today, this principle is called the Jevons paradox. However, the main thesis that the author defends in his book is completely different: he argues that Great Britain's supply of black coal will be exhausted in the relatively near future. Jevons viewed Britain's rapidly growing population as one of the main factors that would accelerate the end of coal.[580] Jevons' book is not about oil, but coal, as the latter was the most significant national product in the British Isles at the time. Coal was attributed great value and endless opportunities for use, while global oil production, largely concentrated in the

United States and Poland, was at an embryonic stage. However, *The Coal Question* is a solid starting point for reflections on the depletion of oil, as its author demonstrates through a precise and rigorous scientific approach that the resource considered to be most important for the national and global economy was facing impending exhaustion. Its output, as Jevons writes, would continue to grow until a certain point in its geometric progression, reach its peak, then collapse dramatically and dwindle to nothing. This would undoubtedly lead to a significant increase in coal prices and economic decline.

The UK reached the peak of its coal production in 1913, within the timeframe that Jevons predicted for the exhaustion of all coal deposits in the country, that is, less than a hundred years. The last black coal mine in the UK was shut down in December 2015, 140 years after the book was published. However, it was not closed because the UK had run out of coal reserves; a few years before the closure, these were estimated at 400 million tons.[581] Indeed, interestingly, rumors began circulating in 2019 of a possible return to coal extraction in the UK.[582] Much more importantly, however, the winding down of coal mining in the UK did not unleash an economic catastrophe, and today the country imports only one sixth of the amount of coal it used to produce and consume every year. Coal is no longer as necessary to the British people as it was a short time ago, and the country is still one of the world's largest global economic powers. Jevons was wrong.

The most important energy resource for both the UK and the world today is oil. The first forecast of the timeframe for the depletion of oil, prepared by the United States Geological Survey (USGS) and published in the *Titusville Herald* in 1909, concluded that all petroleum would run out by 1939.[583] In 1919, Van H. Manning, director of the United States Bureau of Mines, claimed that oil in the United States would last at most a dozen more years. A year later, USGS geologists announced that the United States, whose share in the world's oil production was a healthy 65 percent, had reached its maximum oil production capacity, and that oil would run out within ten years. At that time, the U.S. produced about one million barrels of oil a day, which is about twelve times less than today.[584] However, with the discovery of new deposits in California (the Huntington Beach Oil Field in the Los Angeles Basin) in 1920, it turned out that these fears stood on shaky foundations, and production continued to grow rapidly.[585]

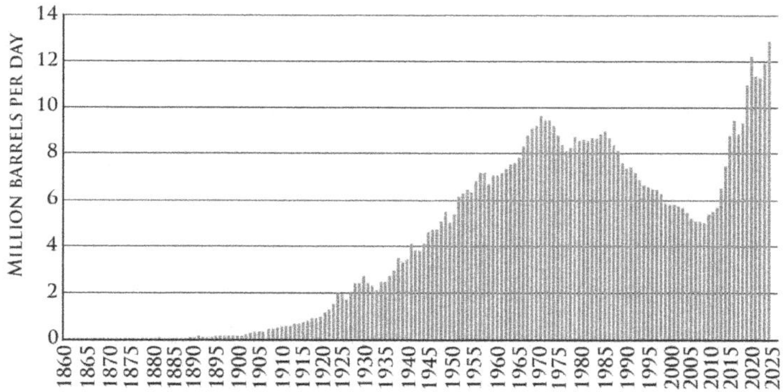

Fig. 7: Oil production in the USA between 1860 and 2023.[586]

Nevertheless, serious predictions of the impending petroleum collapse are still a dime a dozen. In 1937, the financial section of the *Brooklyn Daily Eagle* published a statement by H. A. Stuart, director of the U.S. Naval Petroleum Reserves, predicting that American oil fields would run out of oil within 15 years.[587] According to the *Oil and Gas Journal*, the United States reached the peak in oil production in 1943.[588]

However, a further increase in the volume of oil production has led to a certain level of optimism about future output. The much talked-about Mid-Century Conference on Resources for the Future, held in Washington, DC in 1953, brought together representatives from the worlds of science, industry, and other economic spheres to reflect on the future of the United States' resource supply. A detailed report summarizing these debates reveals widespread fear of the negative impact of the country's growing population and economic growth on the ability to meet its people's resource needs. However, a clear hopeful tone also shines through in the recorded statements regarding the positive effects of scientific research:

> "If we assume that the rate of technological development will continue if not increase with advancing scientific knowledge, our supply position, despite widespread depletion of many of the kinds of materials we use today, may be better than is at first apparent. At least it may be kept form serious deterioration as growing shortages cause us to turn to sources and methods that we are capable of developing and using, but which have not been used in the past because of the absence of economic incentive or compulsion."[589]

This last sentence shows that the participants clearly understood the impact of economic factors on the availability of resources. In the rest of the discussion, they agreed that market competition has a significant and positive impact on the optimization of oil production volumes.

Although the discussion quoted above did not go unnoticed, the readers of this book are much more likely to recognize a different debate that has garnered much appreciation in the scientific community. Its initiator was M. King Hubbert, an American geologist and geophysicist working for Shell Oil Company who presented a theory of changes in oil production in any given area at the American Petroleum Institute in 1956. The central concept assumes that total oil production from many wells grows rapidly in the initial phase of exploitation, reaches its maximum at approximately the moment when half of the resource has been extracted, and then rapidly drops to zero. This concept was represented in a well-known visualization in the form of a bell-shaped curve that was later dubbed the Hubbert curve. The peak volume of fossil fuel production, followed by an irreversible decline, is called peak oil. Hubbert assumed that the peak would arrive around 1965 or 1970, depending on the total volume of oil reserves in the United States, whereupon the country's production volume would start to fall at a rate similar to the increase that preceded it.[590]

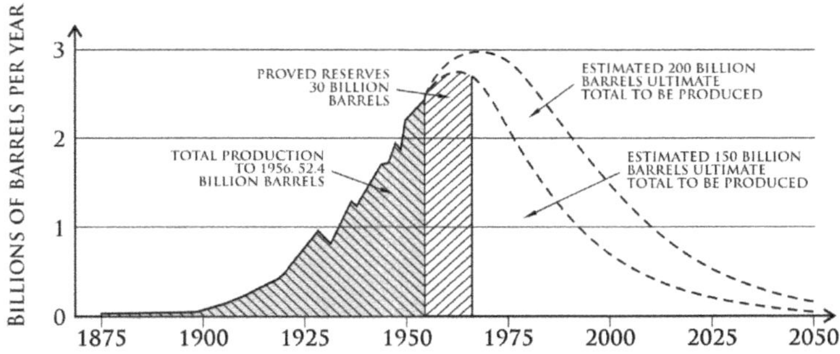

Fig. 8: The Hubbert curve.[591]

Hubbert's concept was initially discredited and ridiculed. However, when it turned out that oil production in the United States began to fall significantly after October 1970, Hubbert became a prophet almost overnight. He predicted a peak global oil production volume of 34 million barrels per day around the year 2000. Actual production that year reached 75 million barrels per day, so Hubbert made a significant miscalculation, but the seemingly perpetual increase in traditional oil extraction ended in 2005, only a few years later than Hubbert predicted nearly 50 years prior.[592] So, in the end, were the supporters of the concept of peak oil correct? As always, the devil is in the details. The critical detail in this case is the answer to the question of what we mean when we say "oil." We settle this issue shortly. For now, we can be confident in stating that there is likely no human in the history of our species who has contributed more than Hubbert to the fear of resource depletion, a prospect that additionally covers other resources such as natural gas and coal, both of which Hubbert also tackled in his writings.

After 1970 and the success of Hubbert's forecast for oil production in the United States, an avalanche of gloomy forecasts began. Many of them were excellent fodder for headlines, as the topic proved to grab readers' attention. In 1972, Richard Wilson, a professor of physics at Harvard University, predicted that American oil would run out in no more than 20 years, and that oil in the world as a whole would be gone within 40 to 50 years.[593] In 1977, the drafters of the Department of Energy Organization Act estimated that peak oil would arrive in the early 1990s and that the planet would run out of oil early in the 21st century.[594] In 1980, physicist Hans Bethe predicted that peak oil would occur before the year 2000 and that oil in the world would run out about 20 years later.[595] Another forecast, published in 2002 by an international group of experts, warned that peak oil would become a reality in 2010.[596] None of these forecasts proved correct – so, naturally, more and more began to appear.

Prophets of Impending Disaster

Hubbert's predictions were "verified" and reinforced in the early 1970s, fitting perfectly into the narrative of fear that began to dominate the world at the time. In 1968, Paul Ehrlich wrote his famous book *The Population Bomb*, in which he predicted that the world would be hit by a devastating famine as early as the 1970s. A year later, the aforementioned report by UN Secretary-General U Thant was published, indicating the absolute urgency of protecting the environment from destruction if we as a species wanted to avoid a massive disaster. In 1972, a group of scientists published *The Limits to Growth*, considered by many to be one of the most important books of the 20th century. In the context of the contemporary predictions of exponential population growth described in Chapter 5, the authors predicted a global collapse triggered by the scarcity of resources on Earth, including mineral resources. Assuming that the population and consumption trends observed so far would continue and the availability of oil would be limited to the resources known at the time, the authors calculated that the world would run out of oil within twenty years. If new fields were discovered, then the oil was to last for a maximum of fifty years.[597] As of now, petroleum continues to flow through pipelines worldwide. Even so, there has been practically no unequivocal public acknowledgment of the excessively pessimistic nature of the assessments made in *The Limits to Growth*.

When the global oil crisis broke out merely a year after the report was published, it was immediately interpreted as confirming the validity of the report – even though the actual causes of the crisis had nothing to do with the abundance of oil reserves, but instead derived from the attitude of the United States and its political allies toward the conflict between Israel and the Arab countries of the Middle East.

Although the authors of *The Limits to Growth* repeatedly emphasized that they were presenting the results of computer simulations rather than forecasts, that is exactly how these simulations were commonly read. Not only did the authors fail to protest this interpretation, but they also doubled down in 1992 by publishing another book in which they explained that humanity had already crossed many of the boundaries described in *The Limits to Growth*. Once again, our opportunities to enjoy a good, secure future of our species on our planet were diminishing because we had already exceeded the capacity of the Earth, and the problems stemming from resource depletion had not yet been addressed.[598]

All these publications consider the central cause of humankind's problems to be a population that is inflated in relation to the Earth's capacity. More people means a greater collective need for food and resources, and alarmist visions consider the improper management of these resources to be virtually a given. Mineral resources, including oil, have also received a lot of attention, largely concentrated on the near future.

Good forecasts draw on past experience. What experience do we have? Paul Ehrlich's projections of universal hunger in the 1970s did not come to pass. Oil did not dwindle to zero in the early 1990s, as predicted in the basic scenario presented in *The Limits to Growth*, and it failed to do so again early in the third decade of the 21st century, as forecast in the most optimistic scenario. If none of these visions came to fruition, what scenarios are we forming today? What kind of future do we expect?

Scientists are leading the way in building the wall of fear that towers over the possible end of oil. The number of scientific articles and books written on the subject is enormous. A simple Google search using the keywords "peak oil" and "article" yields 1,310,000 results. This excludes the possibility of analyzing all of them, so let's choose a few examples to illustrate the dominant approach to the depletion of oil.

One of the articles that paved the way for the peak oil fever was a 1998 paper by two retired geologists titled *The End of Cheap Oil*.[599] Although many papers on the subject had been published before, none of them reached similar levels of prominence and none of them echoed as loudly in the scientific world and beyond. Its authors, Colin Campbell and Jean Laherrère, warned of the consequences of the growing imbalance between the ever-increasing volume of oil production and the ever more meager new discoveries, which in the two decades preceding 1998 were smaller than current production every year. They argued that the oil industry's estimates of the volume of resources remaining in the ground were grossly overstated. Thus, known resources must have begun to shrink. According to the authors, this was to end in disaster in the near future. First, within no more than ten years, world oil production was to reach a maximum of 74 million barrels per day, then plummet irreversibly. Demand for oil was then to exceed supply, leading to economic earthquakes triggered by the rapid rise in oil prices. None of these forecasts came true. Why? Probably because the authors' analysis applied only to so-called conventional oil, the most typical variety, which has been extracted from the earth for a century and a half. They mention "unconventional" oil sources only in passing, as if not noticing that, from the market perspective, oil is oil.

In 2005, seven years after "The End of Cheap Oil," Pulitzer Prize-winning author Jared Diamond, one of the most respected intellectuals in the world[600], published a monumental work under the allegorical title *Collapse*. In the book, he juxtaposes modern human civilization with many earlier civilizations that collapsed because they did not see the symptoms of a catastrophe approaching in time. Diamond warns that, in principle, a decade or two is enough to transition from the moment a civilization reaches its maximum wealth to the moment when the situation begins to deteriorate rapidly, and the energy deficit and excessive consumption of resources are among the most important driving factors.[601] The popular science book was more likely to reach the average, moderately sophisticated reader and guide their reflections into narrow thought patterns that are then very difficult to get out of. The idea is that there is a catastrophe looming over us that will ultimately crush us because it has already done so many times. We are already familiar with this as a form of inductive thinking, whose logical fallacies and incorrect assumptions are easy to identify. But the fear remains.

But let us turn our attention back to more scientific publications. In 2012, the Club of Rome, which had commissioned

The Limits to Growth, released a subsequent report titled *Bankrupting Nature: Denying Our Planetary Boundaries*.[602] Already in the introduction, we learn that we are facing a crisis that will be exacerbated by mutually reinforcing factors: climate change, environmental deterioration, and shortages of mineral resources, especially oil. The authors' arguments include the steady decline of the EROEI (energy returned on energy investment) index, which is the ratio of the energy obtained from a given energy resource to the energy used to obtain it; extracting oil requires energy, after all. At the beginning of the 20th century, this index reached 100, but today it stands at around 20. Clearly, this implies that those who first extracted easily accessible oil were completely rational from an economic point of view. If they poured more capital into extracting oil from more challenging locations first, they would have been defeated on the market because their product would have been too expensive. In *Bankrupting Nature*, we also discover that "the era of cheap oil is over" (p. 61) and that "prices of $200 per barrel or more are expected soon" (p. 69). Twelve years have passed since this book was published, and the price of oil has fallen from $100-125 per barrel in 2011-2012 to $50 in 2015 and then $30 in early 2016, without even considering the impact of the COVID-19 pandemic, which saw prices cratering further to $20 in April 2020. Oil consumption in China, one of the fastest growing and largest oil markets in the world, was expected to reach 20 million barrels per day in 2020, while in reality the country consumed just over 14 million barrels in 2019. Consumption for the year 2020 was expected to be even lower, as all economic processes around the world were disrupted by the pandemic, but the authors' predictions fell short even if we treat 2020 as an outlier. The book also quotes many other works that expected peak oil to arrive between 2013 and 2020.

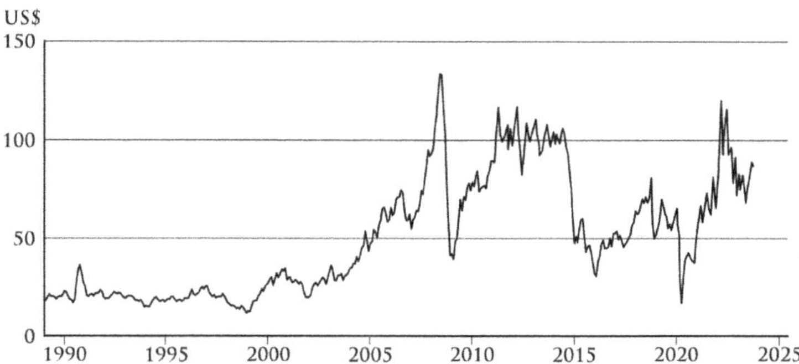

Fig. 9: Brent oil prices in the world, 1990-2023.[603]

Being a prophet is not an easy job, so from today's perspective it is not very charitable to discredit the authors for their erroneous predictions. Meteorologists can make mistakes even with very short-term weather forecasts, as we all know from our daily experience. Economists preparing medium-term forecasts make incorrect predictions about the inflation rate or the GDP growth rate. Geologists specializing in plate tectonics miss the mark with their estimates of the time and strength of volcanic eruptions and earthquakes. Futurologists and environmentalists dealing with the future of oil also have the right to be wrong. The point is that everyone – scientists in particular – should show a little more restraint and humility in offering their assessments of future events, rather than authoritatively stating that it will only get worse, as this kind of doomsday thinking is almost pure conformist opportunism, an attempt to fit into the dominant current of thinking about oil.

Some researchers are keen to point out that peak oil is already behind us and oil production will only decrease from now. Thinking back to 2005, Werner Zittel, a founding member of the European Business Council for a Sustainable Energy Future, wrote in 2013: "Peak oil has been long passed and no technology . . . is able to reverse this fact."[604] We have already seen a graph showing oil production in the world (Fig. 6), where it is clear that there was no peak in oil production in 2005 or any other year thereafter. So, what did the author have in mind? What he meant was that, in 2005, there was a peak in the volume of conventional oil production, while subsequent increases are mainly due to unconventional oil sources and the extraction of resources similar to oil, even if they are not the same thing in terms of their chemical composition. Examples of such resources include liquefied gas – which should be classified under production of gas rather than oil – as well as ethanol and processing gains. These increase the final amount of oil available for use, which, strictly speaking, does not count as new oil production. The author believes that none of these should be included in the calculation because they are not new oil. New sources of oil, including tar sands in Venezuela and Canada, will not have a significant impact on the global oil market, as obtaining oil from them is too expensive and takes too long, according to Zittel. Yet the global financial market treats all the substances mentioned above as oil, as it is possible to use them in exactly the same way as conventional oil is used in the chemical industry and in transport. To what extent is the driver of a car interested in whether the gasoline his vehicle uses comes from the production of the standard light oil, heavy oil, shale oil, liquefied gas, or processing gains? He is primarily interested in the price of whatever fuel he uses and making sure it is safe for his car's engine. From the point of view of the end user – the market – everything that can be used to produce gasoline is oil. Let's be honest: when we pull up to a gas station, the origin and type of oil from which our fuel was made is not something we deeply care about.

The well-known American geochemist John C. Ayers is much more subdued in his statements. In his 2017 book on sustainability, he correctly points out that the problem lies not in when the oil will eventually run out, but in when the peak will occur, as it is from that moment on that production volumes will start to fall irreversibly against our needs and expectations, exacerbating market turbulence.[605] Analyzing global changes in many elements of the environment, he notes that, for example, despite the pessimistic forecasts regarding global wild fish catch resulting from overfishing, the volume of fish capture has not fallen, as aquaculture is growing rapidly as a substitute for fishing. However, although the author sees many limitations to the usefulness and value of peak oil forecasts – including, among other things, our lack of knowledge about the actual volume of resources and future output, the changing influence of economic and political factors, innovations and inventions that do not exist yet, and even natural disasters – he still ventures a prediction that peak oil will arrive between 2020 and 2030.

One of the latest papers on peak oil is a kind of summary of the last few decades of discussions. Ugo Bardi notes the declining interest in the concept of peak oil in the world, but tries to explain it by attributing it to other factors and not the flaws of the concept itself. He focuses largely on analyzing Campbell and Laherrère's article as well as several works published by the Association for the Study of Peak Oil and Gas (ASPO), which was founded by Campbell in 2001. Bardi summarizes these works by identifying four main theses: "[1] The world's oil production should follow a bell-shaped curve. [2] The global production peak of conventional oil should occur not later than 2010 at a level of the order of 70-75 million barrels per day (Mb/day). [3] The discoveries of new crude oil resources should remain well below consumption. [4] Oil prices should rise sharply."[606]

Bardi's perspective on the accuracy of these forecasts is debatable. Regarding the bell-shaped curve, he writes: "In the case of the world's oil production, the bell curve is not clearly detectable today, but it could also be argued that peaking and declining are going to occur in the near future. Therefore, we can say that the result of this prediction is correct." So oddly, the bell curve is not visible, but the peak will occur anyway. His negative assessment of ASPO's second thesis is correct, as today's production is much higher than what was predicted. Bardi also deems the third thesis to be correct but immediately notes that discoveries of unconventional oil should not be taken into account because "non-conventional resources, such as shale oil, do not normally need to be discovered, their existence and location is known." The idea that we know everything there is to know about shale oil is bold, if not brazen. In Poland, American oil companies began drilling exploratory wells in 2010, expecting to find up to 7 trillion cubic yards of natural gas in the country's abundant oil shale. After two years, their estimates were lowered by a factor of more than 15. The last foreign company withdrew from Poland in 2017, seeing no further opportunities for economically justifiable shale gas production in the country.[607] Does this instill confidence in us that we know all there is to know about shale gas? Finally, in his 2019 assessment, Bardi also took on the fourth thesis – sharply rising prices, which he evaluates as accurate. To gauge whether this is correct, we need only take another look at Fig. 9.

Let's try to summarize all of the above forecasts. Most of them paint a bleak picture of the future. Even those authors who see deficits and errors in previous forecasts try to explain them in many ways so as to finally reach the conclusion that peak oil is inevitably approaching – or even that it has already arrived.

THE CRUDE PURSUITS OF OIL COMPANIES

Of course, we cannot ignore the outlook of the parties that are perhaps most interested in the prospect of resource depletion: oil companies and the countries that produce and export oil.

Let us start with a simple question: is it in the interest

of oil producers to show that there is little oil left and the day of reckoning is on the horizon, or do they stand to benefit more from the narrative that there is still an ocean of oil under humanity's feet? This question has no simple and satisfying answer. We can begin by making the obvious assumption that the operational goal of a company's activity in a market economy is to generate profit, while the shareholders long-term goal is to increase the value of the company. What would happen to the shares of oil companies if it turned out that the resource that forms the bedrock of their activities has been depleted and will soon no longer be processed? Their stock prices would fall, so they would be rather reluctant to admit that the long-term prospects for their continued existence are dim. On the other hand, a company's profits today depend on the price it can get for the product it sells. The price of oil on the market is a derivative of one of the most basic relations in the market economy – demand and supply. If supply is high in relation to demand, then the price is low: everyone wants to sell, and there are few people willing to buy. If the commodity is scarce and a lot of people are willing to buy, then the price is high. If we know that the commodity is running out, then its price has a chance to reach a higher level than in a situation where we know there are enormous volumes of the resource that are simply waiting to be extracted. As we can see, companies' long-term and short-term goals are at odds with each other. In the long run, companies should declare, in their own interest, that they have copious amounts of oil, and in the short run, that it will soon run out.

However, there are circumstances in which it is somewhat easier to assess the credibility of the declarations of oil companies and states by situating them in their economic context. For more than half a century, the largest player on the oil market has been the Organization of Petroleum Exporting Countries (OPEC). Founded in 1960, the organization initially brought together five countries for which oil exports were the most important source of income: Saudi Arabia, Iran, Iraq, Kuwait, and Venezuela. Over time, the number of OPEC members has grown. Today, there are thirteen member states, five of which are in the Persian Gulf, seven in Africa, and one in South America. The total oil production in these countries has remained stable at about 45 percent of world production for years. OPEC is characterized by high flexibility in its production volumes, largely due to the size of oil resources in the member countries, which are estimated to account for nearly 80 percent of the world's resources,[608] as well as the very high efficiency of their oil wells. It is capable of both reducing and significantly increasing production from one day to the next. This is even more important as the flexibility of production volumes among other oil producers is low. Moreover, unlike OPEC, other producers do not coordinate their activities, so it is difficult for them to react quickly and effectively in a situation where OPEC countries take coordinated action, for example, by reducing production volumes.

What is the purpose of OPEC? According to its statute, the mission of OPEC "is to coordinate and unify the petroleum policies of its Member Countries and ensure the stabilization of oil markets in order to secure an efficient, economic and regular supply of petroleum to consumers, a steady income to producers and a fair return on capital for those investing in the petroleum industry."[609] It would be excellent if OPEC truly cared about consumers, producers, and investors alike. However, it is impossible to satisfy the conflicting needs of these three groups simultaneously. Consumers benefit from oil that is widely available and cheap to purchase. Producer states benefit from expensive oil, and investors benefit from oil that is expensive but also has low production costs.

In a sense, consumers are passive players on the oil market. If we ignore the fluctuations caused by global and catastrophic events like the COVID-19 pandemic, demand for oil is relatively stable. By contrast, oil producers are the active players shaping the price of oil through changes in production volumes. Increasing production means lowering the price of a barrel of oil, and decreasing it means increasing that price. This is where they find themselves having to square the circle. To earn more, they have to either extract and sell more – but then the unit price of a barrel decreases – or extract less, but then sell it for a higher price per unit. For example, to earn $1,000 from a sale, you can either sell 20 barrels at $50 each or 10 barrels at $100 each. Given the more or less fixed costs of oil extraction for producers, the latter option is more advantageous because it allows them to make much more money while not disposing of their own resources at too fast a rate. The problem is that a single producer limiting their own production does not entail an increase in the price of oil on the market because the demand will be met instantly by another producer. As a result, a producer who reduces production on his own is shooting himself in the foot and depriving himself of part of his income. Therefore, from the perspective of each individual producer, it would be best to extract and sell as much as possible, and simultaneously persuade all the others to limit production. The issue is that this is exactly how every player in the game thinks, and as a result, everyone holds one another in check.

This is why OPEC is such an important player on the oil market. It provides an effective platform for a dozen or so important oil producers to develop a common stance and implement a common policy. They increase or reduce output together, and this translates into changes in oil prices on the market. But that leaves us with another question: how should OPEC divide the volume of oil production that its members jointly agreed to achieve? After all, each of the member states follows the mechanism described above to a tee: they want to produce as much oil as possible while demanding that others reduce their production. Within OPEC, the member states adopted a solution according to which each individual member's share in OPEC's total output is proportional to the volume of oil remaining in those states' possession. What, then, should a member state do to carve out a larger share of this cake? Declare that it has large resources, of course.

For these reasons, OPEC member states' declarations regarding their remaining oil reserves may be higher than those they have located. Here we do not mean their total resource; as we have already determined, these are not known and never will be. Instead, we are talking about reserves known at the time the declaration is made.

In this landscape of uncertainty, which sources of information on available oil reserves are reliable? In practice, there are no such sources. Proved reserves are those whose volume we have estimated and those we are able to extract given the current state of our technical knowledge and economic conditions. This brings the reliability of our estimates into question, especially since the resources that are produced can turn out to be slightly smaller or several hundred percent larger than the initial estimates. We also haven't firmly established whether only conventional oil should be considered when disclosing the size of one's resources or whether shale oil, oil from tar sands, and from natural gas should also be included. Meanwhile, our level of technical knowledge is increasing and our economic conditions, and the price of oil in particular, are in flux. If resource volume is derived from three elements, among which the one is based on questionable, low-quality information and the other two are sensitive to change, how can we claim to know how much oil we have?

Treat any estimate of oil reserves with skepticism. According to OPEC's annual report, in 2019, the world had 1.551 trillion barrels of oil in total.[610] The U.S. Energy Information Administration (EIA) estimates reserves at 1.659 trillion barrels,[611] while British Petroleum (BP) posits 1.734 trillion barrels.[612] The difference between the high and low estimates is considerable, at 11.8 percent. However, it is also worth taking a closer look at the national-level data that sums up to the global total. Although estimates from different sources are similar or even identical for most countries, the differences that do emerge are sometimes enormous. According to OPEC, Canada's resources stand at 5.3 billion barrels, while the EIA claims a figure of 167 billion and BP's estimate is 169.7 billion. Canada therefore has either the twenty-second largest oil reserves in the world, accounting for 0.3 percent of the global total, or the third largest reserves at nearly 11 percent of all the oil in the world! Similarly, the United States has either 52.6, 47.0, or 68.9 billion barrels, the United Kingdom has 2.6, 2.1, or 2.7 billion, and so on. In a nutshell: we do not know very well what oil reserves we have in the world or in individual countries.

How do we know all this: The role of the media

The widespread public fear of the imminent depletion of oil does not stem from the average person's regular study of scientific publications or reports prepared by OPEC and other oil industry players. The primary sources of information on this subject are the Internet, television, radio, and the press. Not the specialized press, scientific journals, or industry publications, but popular media.

All information channels are connected by a common goal: they keep the lights on by reaching as large a group of recipients as possible. The topics they cover must be punchy and catchy, the information should be packaged attractively, and the message should be easy to understand. How engaging would it be to report on the fact that we still have plenty of oil and that risk that we will ever run out is small, compared to coverage on the idea that if we divide the United States' estimated reserves of oil by the volume of its annual production, then the country only has enough oil for the next decade? The media are quite naturally inclined to amplify fears and tensions rather than to ease them.

There are numerous examples of messaging in the media that unilaterally promotes the peak oil hypothesis and sometimes even directly foretells the end of oil. First, let us look at the most accessible sources that consistently focus on communicating information about peak oil, that is, dedicated websites. A graph on the website peakoil.com shows that conventional oil reached its maximum production in 2005 and all types of oil put together followed suit in 2008.[613] Another website, peakoilbarrel.com, attempts to head off possible objections, arguing that those who doubt the peak oil theory are seriously exaggerating when they herald the death of the peak oil concept.[614] The list of websites that flood us with such gloomy speculation from all sides is probably endless.

In addition, many serious online economic affairs websites, including online versions of well-regarded newspapers, buy into the panic surrounding the end of oil or consciously co-create and amplify it. In 2008, when oil prices surpassed all previously known peaks, the respected Polish financial news and analysis website bankier.pl reported that "The world as we know it will soon cease to exist. This is not another prediction of a global catastrophe, but a fact that future generations will have to face."[615] In 2010, the Polish edition of *Newsweek* published an article titled "The End of Oil," which begins with the following statement: "The world's oil reserves will run dry much sooner than we expected. In a few years' time, the foundations of our civilization will be trembling." This was followed by a vision of exorbitant prices for plane tickets, bans on driving at speeds exceeding 80 kph, and a 250 percent increase in oil prices.[616] In the initial phase of the COVID-19 pandemic, when oil prices tanked, the British political magazine *New Statesman* published an article whose main thesis was that the problem of peak oil, while temporarily obscured due to falling demand for oil, would return very shortly unless we took the opportunity to switch the gears of the world economy and choose renewable energy.[617]

Films are a separate category of media messaging. Two popular films devote their running time to the bogeyman of oil depletion. In its very first frames, *World Without Oil - What If All the Oil Ran Out?* tells us that, "if it all suddenly disappeared," we would have an ever-deepening crisis on our hands, marked by widespread hunger in the United States and people fleeing the country. The creators describe this exercise in emotional manipulation as a "documentary." The film has racked up more than 300,000 views – a testament to the effectiveness of this strategy for reeling in the viewer.[618] Another "docu-horror" with the lengthy title *The End of the Oil Age, How Much Is Left and What Will Happen When We Run Out* envisions a world reminiscent of the *Mad Max* films, which the authors also directly reference.[619]

"We have lots of oil and there is no reason to worry" is a message that has no chance of breaking through the uproar triggered by the creators of media that dramatizes the depletion of resources. Their personal views on the subject are therefore of little importance. If they wish to make a splash, they must serve up an account of the approaching petroapocalypse.

Once these creators have managed to instill a sense of danger in the recipient, all that remains is to dole out prescriptions and recommendations on how we can protect ourselves from an inglorious fate. We should look for alternatives to fossil fuels and switch from cars to public transport or bicycles, or at least to less fuel-guzzling vehicles. We should reduce long-distance trips, travel less by plane, and buy products manufactured locally to reduce fuel consumption for long-distance transport of goods. In general, we should give up excessive consumerism and the pursuit of having lots of essentially unnecessary items, live more modestly and more slowly, and manage the resources given to us more economically.

All of these recommendations have a chance to contribute to making oil reserves last longer and improve the state of the environment that surrounds us. But we must ask ourselves on question: does the promotion of these behaviors in a global society require prior emotional manipulation and the deliberate triggering of fear that our oil will run dry? As a society, are we truly so ignorant that we need to be frightened into submission through one of the strongest emotional cues that rule our species so that we can be steered onto the "right" track? Would it not be more sensible and simply fairer to say, "We have a lot of oil, we are not threatened by its depletion, but it is wiser to look now for ways to replace it with more environmentally friendly sources of energy?"

Let us encourage sensible actions and proper behavior by highlighting facts and appealing to reason instead of bending reality to one's own visions, manipulating it, and tugging at the strings of the emotions elicited by these manipulations.

THE STATE

One glance at the political map of the world is enough to show is that nearly the entire land surface of Earth belongs to and falls within the borders of a country. There are few politically dependent areas that do not constitute separate states but are managed by other entities. In practice, what this means is that states have a crucial role to play in shaping social consciousness regarding oil, and above all, have the means to do so. Let us take a look at how they leverage these means.

WHY THE STATE SCARES US: THE AFFECT EFFECT

In modern democratic states, the coercive power of state structures is conferred to the state by its citizens, who in turn agree to submit to it. After all, it is the citizens who choose the authority that then governs them and forces them to abide by the rules it has put in place. The extent of the state's power and the severity of the apparatus of coercion therefore stem, to some degree, from citizens' expectations. Citizens usually want a state that will allow them a great deal of freedom, but at the same time limit the freedom of others whose behavior could threaten us. If we assume that citizens are equal in the eyes of the law, this is not possible – we either restrict the freedoms of everyone or no one at all. This is why, in democratic states as well, people relinquish part of their sovereignty and accept the transfer of many powers to state structures in the hope that the state will protect them from a threat, real or imaginary – including threats from their fellow citizens. Equipped with these powers, the state directs, manages, and coerces us. In our own best interest, of course.

The machinery of state power is not amorphous or impersonal. It comprises the people who have gained power over others through dynamics such as democratic elections, professional advancement, family connections, or even pure strokes of luck. Some of these people wish to remain in their positions and be re-elected. We can assume that this group comprises a significant proportion of the whole, because if someone wants to resign from the structures of power, they can usually do so – and we do not observe such overt resignations and complete withdrawals from politics too often. Power is like a drug – tempting, seductive, and addictive, and difficult to relinquish. It gives those who hold it a sense of clout and authority, it is deeply fulfilling, and it often allows them to set themselves up well in life. Many people in power pass through different positions, but all of them link back to the possession of authority. These are all well-known truths. But staying in power is an art form. How to accomplish it?

The affect effect theory gives us a succinct answer. It states that, since fear is one of the most fundamental emotions that guide human decisions, it can easily be used as a tool to gain more power. All it takes is to personalize the threat – to draw voters' attention to a particular person, political power, movement, or phenomenon – and then, in response to the fear of that threat, to offer them hope in the form of one's own person and solutions. This is how politicians gain support: the more frightening the calamities from which they will protect us, the more effective their messaging, per their own statements. Convinced by these narratives, we hand more and more of our freedoms over to the state, often under the mistaken impression that this will increase our level of security, while the state gains more and more control over us at our own request.[620] As Erich Fromm wrote in his classic book *Escape from Freedom*, sometimes we even fear freedom and choose to limit it so that someone else can take responsibility for the choices we make, relieving us from the burden of making decisions.[621] Societies accept, to a greater or lesser extent, the expansion of state powers, believing this process to be a prerequisite for security, as well as for culture, science, and prosperity to flourish. Many cannot or do not want to live in a high-risk environment. We have become accustomed to peace, to a comfortable life, to a range of benefits offered by the state, and we pay for each successive restriction and limitation with our freedom. And since security is one of human beings' most basic needs, we do so willingly and frequently.[622]

So what should people in power do to stay in power? They must manufacture or dramatize the enemy, use the enemy effectively to frighten their society, and then anoint and promote themselves as messiahs offering silver-bullet solutions. After all, people are obedient to those they fear.[623]

How do states and the structures of power they are built on behave when it comes to the depletion of resources? How to effectively strike fear into the public with the prospect of the exhaustion of oil? Easy as pie. All it takes is to constantly drive or fan the narrative of resource depletion, reserving a special place for oil. One also has to point out that these resources must be managed intelligently, as otherwise the wells will run dry. And when that happens, our comfortable life will end, the economy will be in shambles, and the foundations of our civilization will be destroyed. Who would like to live in a world shattered by such an apocalypse?

Over time, "green" parties advocating a reduction of fossil fuels have become increasingly popular in many countries. European Green Party, a coalition of "green" parties from all over Europe, stood for election in the European Parliament for the first time in 1979, winning over 2.5 percent of EU voters and not a single seat, while in 2019, they won an admirable 52 seats – 7.4 percent of the total.[624] This example illustrates that voters are increasingly concerned about environmental protection. Without in-depth research on the subject, it is impossible distill the role of the fear of peak oil among green voters' motivations at the voting booth. However, one may suspect that the mechanisms guiding voters are similar to the classical division of the political scene into the right and left wing. Right-wing parties throughout the European Union threaten their voters with the consequences of, among other things, an uncontrolled influx of refugees, which will supposedly occur if the left takes power; left-wing parties threaten a return to the dominance of nationalism in Europe, which will supposedly occur if the right takes power. What fear factor do the green parties use? Among other things, the coming end of oil.

ENVIRONMENTAL PROTECTION IS PARAMOUNT

Attempting to combat the school-bred conviction that we live in an era of vanishing resources is not only next to impossible, but also dangerous. The effects of such a struggle may be dangerous for the environment and for those who try to make others aware of how mistaken it is to drive this overly pessimistic narrative.

Dismantling or even undermining an established worldview built on the premise that we need to preserve the planet's resources can increase the consumption of those resources – from water and electricity to plastic products, gasoline, and other derivatives of oil. It will make it much more difficult to persuade such people to manage their resources wisely, which is obviously a rational action. However, it is an action that should not be induced by the threat of apocalyptic resource depletion, but from the need to use what we have in a reasonable way. We can compare this with the balance one has in their bank account; even if a wealthy person has a considerable amount of money, this doesn't mean they should splurge on everything they can.

It is easy to dismiss skeptics who argue the notion of total resource depletion is overblown, and it is easy to stigmatize them as slightly out of their mind given that their approach runs counter to that of the majority. After all, every bite of cheesecake brings us closer to the moment when the cheesecake will run out. Those who do not understand this and claim otherwise must be off their rocker, right? Who among us is persistent enough to dig through the arsenal of arguments challenging the idea that the cheesecake is a scare resource? Few of us can muster the wherewithal, and only this small group has a chance to change their own biases on this subject, as long as they are open enough to arguments that may undermine beliefs deeply rooted in their own minds.

While the direct risks of supporting and promoting the idea that we are not running out of resources are limited to a narrow group of people, environmental risks concern virtually all of humanity. Modern, highly developed countries – aware of the dangers of overexploiting environmental resources by logging, overfishing, or treating rivers as free sewage dumps – are creating various regulations aimed at inducing people to take actions that will allow us to keep the environment undisturbed. When it comes to mineral resources (particularly energy resources), states intervene through regulation aimed at changing the cost of producing energy from specific sources. In this way, some energy sources that are supported by these regulations gain a stronger position, while others that gradually become more expensive lose their status. In the European Union, in 2013-2018 alone, the burden on entities forced to buy emission allowances under the EU Emissions Trading Scheme increased from 4 to 14 billion euros, and the common-budget expenditure to fulfill climate objectives in the 2014-2020 period increased from around 16 to almost 35 billion euros, representing 13.7 percent and 21.0 percent of the EU budget, respectively.[625] The increase in the price of carbon emissions from the burning of coal, oil, and natural gas, which are purchased by the state and by companies producing electricity, heat, or substances such as cement, is invariably passed on to consumers. Thus, the cost of every product that is manufactured using fossil energy will increase.

To stay in the market and remain competitive with others, individual energy producers are gradually changing the way they obtain energy. Supported by governmental and EU subsidies, the so-called alternative energy sources, including wind, solar, and biomass energy in all its forms, are slowly gaining market share, while fossil-based sources are losing it. Oil-based fuels are increasingly enriched with fuel derived from plant processing. Corn or sugar beet can be used to produce alcohol that is added to gasoline; rapeseed can be used to produce oil that is added to diesel. In this way, larger and larger areas of arable land are allocated to the cultivation of plants for energy purposes, which alters the dynamics of the cultivated plants market, that is, the market of plants that are grown for their produce and, ultimately, human consumption. The costs of agricultural land are rising, so the costs of food plants follow suit. The high price of oil supports these changes, encouraging farmers to switch to growing crops that will eventually be converted to fuel. And so the wheel keeps turning.

What would happen if we planted a seed of awareness of the fact that we have enough oil and that the rapid depletion of resources is really not a looming threat? If the state wiped out one of the most important arguments in favor of abandoning oil itself, the effects on the natural environment could be truly miserable. Perhaps it is better to play it safe and avoid proclaiming far and wide how abundant our resources are. Perhaps it is better to continue supporting the development of alternative technologies, such as electric cars. The latter can be so uncomfortable for supporters of electrifying road transportation that they are rarely spoken of. Let's take a brief look at them.

First, the electric current used to charge electric cars comes from the sources we use to produce it. For example, 75 percent of the Netherlands' electricity is produced from fossil fuels, so for three out of every four kilometers driven, an electric car charging its battery at a Dutch charging station is relying on the burning of fossil fuels. Looking ahead, 62 percent of the potentially largest electric car market in the world – China – is powered by fossil fuels.[626] The use of electric cars therefore reduces the consumption of fossil fuels, but not to zero.

Secondly, a significant part of the energy used to charge the batteries does not really feed the batteries themselves but is converted into heat and heats the atmosphere. Energy loss occurs in the charging process through a device called the converter, which converts the alternating current from the mains into the direct current used in the car. Depending on the make and model of the car, these losses range from 9.9 to 24.9 percent. Currently, the icon of the electric vehicle market – the Tesla Model 3 LR – has the worst performance in this category.[627]

Thirdly, the production and disposal of the powerful batteries used in these cars has a huge impact on the environment, which is usually completely disregarded. As we all know, the small batteries we use to power alarm clocks belong not in the general waste garbage can, but in special containers. Why? Because they are also a threat to the environment. How great a threat do we face from car batteries that weigh about half a ton each?[628]

What is the cost-benefit analysis of electric cars in comparison with combustion engines? It is certainly beneficial to transfer the emission of pollutants from the production of energy used by electric cars outside the areas of heightened energy consumption, that is, to power plants outside large cities. This will make cities cleaner, and one large power plant can more easily control gas and particulate matter emissions than hundreds of thousands of cars in a city can. This is certainly attractive for countries producing clean electricity. It certainly contributes to reducing oil consumption. However, it is not as clean and ecological as we would like to believe.

What do these considerations mean in the context of peak oil and the depletion of resources? For one thing, they clearly indicate the direction in which the automotive industry, one of the largest consumers of oil, is heading. In Norway, in the first quarter of 2020, 51 percent of cars purchased in showrooms were electric vehicles, up from only 5.5 percent in 2013.[629] Norway is the world leader in this field, but the electric vehicle industry is growing almost everywhere. The oil giants have already noticed this and are increasingly declaring their desire to diversify their portfolios by moving toward emission-free energy production.

What drives them? Not the fear of their oil supply vanishing. On the contrary: it is the fear of such a large drop in demand for oil that much of it will remain in the ground and there will be no customers left to buy it. Therefore, in order to avoid losing the energy market and missing the moment they will be forced to introduce fundamental changes in their operating structures, companies like Shell and BP will restructure themselves.[630] Otherwise, they risk falling out of the race like Nokia when it failed to see the future in smartphones, like Eastman Kodak when it missed the train of digital photography, and like many other giants who disappeared into the void. It turns out that, instead of being faced with peak oil supply (the moment we reach our maximum capacity to extract oil from the ground due to the depletion of good deposits) oil suppliers may soon be threatened by peak oil demand (the moment after which they will extract and sell less and less oil due to the lack of potential buyers). This should trigger us to seriously re-evaluate our outlooks, right?

Despite all this, we are still subjected to fearmongering. The state, with its well-greased mechanisms of information transfer that provide us with selected visions of impending disaster, is successfully supported by ecological organizations, which sometimes take over its role. They mobilize communities and societies, attempting to influence states and bring about the changes they seek from the bottom up. These organizations are urging us to stop oil production because of the negative environmental impact of burning oil and products derived from it.[631] This convergence of goals makes environmental organizations unwitting allies of the purveyors of peak oil, and we, as the targets of media campaigns designed by both groups, are persuaded that we should move away from oil as soon as possible. Even if such a transformation would be beneficial to the environment – an argument I do not dispute, but one that lies outside the scope of this book – that does not justify presenting a skewed view of our planet's oil supply.

Conquering our fear

The time has come to bring order to our knowledge about how much oil there is on our planet, at what rate we are consuming it, and how much more time we have before the wells run dry.

Reserves vs. resources: What lies beneath?

Is everyone who talks about oil resources and reserves talking about the same thing? Definitely not. There are many terms that add specificity to each of the words "oil," "resources," and "reserves," and depending on what adjective we use to accompany them, we will give them different meanings. Moreover, there are far more than 160 different classifications that imbue these terms with different meanings and describe the same set of conditions using different terms, so the level of ambiguity is enormous.[632]

Resources can be defined as the total amount of a given substance calculated on a planetary level, regardless of how much of it could be extracted in the future. Geological research conducted to date has also allowed us to distinguish between identified (sometimes called industrial), hypothetical, and speculative resources. *Identified resources* are resources for the existence of which we have some degree of evidence. Some of these are called *measured resources*: we know their exact location, volume, and quality. Others are called *indicated* or *inferred resources*, both of which describe lower degrees of confidence about those three characteristics. The second category, *hypothetical resources*, are those we expect to find based on our general geological knowledge. For example, if we know that oil is extracted from sandstone or limestone, and we have found these rocks somewhere, we can assume that, somewhere in this area, there is some quantity of oil. The third group comprises *speculative resources*, which arise globally as a result of the known structure of the Earth as a planet, as presented in the initial part of this chapter. Most of these resources will probably never be within our reach.[633]

The second most important term is *reserves*. Reserves are resources that are already identified, measured, documented, deemed to be of sufficient quality, and possible to extract given the current level of technical knowledge and the current relationship between the costs of extraction and the chances of finding buyers on the market. In other words, they can be extracted for profit.[634]

One of the most popular alternative classifications divides all the above into reserves (which can be proved, probable, or possible), contingent resources, and prospective resources, with the chances of future commercialization as the key criterion.[635] Proved reserves are recoverable as long as a price above the cost of extraction can be obtained in the market. Probable and possible reserves correspond to indicated and inferred resources in the first typology. Contingent and prospective resources are so elusive and unpredictable that they are not considered in analyses of the timeframe for the depletion of oil.

According to the first of the above typologies, resources may also be reserves, but don't have to be. They may become reserves in the future, but we do not know if and when this will happen. Indicated and inferred resources may move to a higher category when they are better documented and meet a set of technical conditions, but they do not always do so. This may sound confusing enough but the lesson from all this is quite simple: when we talk about oil reserves and oil resources, we are talking about two different things. And when we talk about resources, we should ask ourselves what resources we are talking about.

In practice, when we talk about the exhaustion of oil, what we usually have in mind is identified resources (and specifically measured resources) if we follow the first typology or proved reserves if we follow the second one. Only in this slice of the two classifications can we make a credible estimate of how much oil we have – and even that estimate would be an approximation. We are not able to determine exactly how much oil is in a given location or keep the uncertainty level in the low single digits; in fact, that level sometimes reaches over 50 percent.[636] The amount of oil in all the other resource groups outlined above remains unknown; we can only forecast it. Only after we survey and conduct in-depth volumetric tests in a particular location we can really determine whether we are dealing with reserves or just identified resources that may or may not be recoverable. Further in this chapter, I will use the term "proved reserves," which is intuitively understandable in the context of the alleged depletion of oil.

HOW MUCH OIL DO WE HAVE? THE SHIFTING SANDS OF PEAK OIL

Proved reserves are not fixed, in line with the definition provided above. A given place on the world map becomes a proved reserve when we find oil there and make the requisite measurements. And because the search for new oil continues uninterrupted, these proved reserves grow, even with the constant, daily production of enormous amounts of oil. Let us take another look at Figure 5, which shows, among other things, changes in the size of proved crude oil reserves in the world over nearly 60 years, since the formation of OPEC. In 1960, there were 291 billion barrels of proved reserves, while in 2019 there were 1.551 trillion barrels, which denotes a more than fivefold increase.

There are also intriguing fluctuations in the estimates of the total amount of oil we will ever manage to obtain. In 1956, total reserves were estimated at 1.25 trillion barrels. By the year 2000, we had produced about 1 trillion barrels of oil on Earth, and the total amount of reserves that had yet to be extracted was estimated at 1.3 trillion barrels, even more than after half a century of oil production.[637]

Now let's come back to documented reserves. According to data from the Canadian government, taking into account Canada's rich deposits of oil sands, at the end of 2018, the world's proved reserves were visibly greater than in the year 2000, at 1.672 trillion barrels.[638] OPEC's estimates do not include Canada's oil sands, as they constitute unconventional reserves. This term usually refers to all reserves in which oil was found in any form other than the most typical one, which has dominated the scene since the first boreholes were drilled in Texas. Oil from tar sands, shale oil, and heavy oil all fall under unconventional reserves. Even oil that arises under similar geological conditions to those of Texas, but in the polar regions or under the seabed at considerable depths (that is, oil that is more difficult to access) is often described as unconventional oil. If we follow this approach, then only crude or conventional oil that is readily available, relatively light, and found on land or on the continental shelf near the coast can truly be called oil in the classical sense.[639]

The question we should ask here is: is oil derived from unconventional sources still oil? This is a rhetorical question. We have reached a point where we keep finding new sources from which we can obtain substances that retain all the properties of oil. The fact that we were once unable to obtain oil from these sources because we could not get there or extract it from a given type of rock does not mean that we will never be able to do so. Today, much of what used to be impossible has been shown to be possible. Thus, we muddy the waters of reality when we write that if it wasn't for the shale revolution in the United States, there would be no more oil,[640] or when we draw charts showing that if it wasn't for oil from beneath the seabed of the Gulf of Mexico or Alaska, the total production of oil in the world today would be falling. Instead, we are finding more and more oil. Perhaps in the future we will be able to classify more locations and greater volumes of what can certainly be called oil as proved reserves. Technological progress is the most important factor accounting for the perpetual shift of peak oil to more remote points in the future besides the discovery of new reserves. And even if the EROEI index (which, as we may recall, tells us how many units of energy can be obtained by investing a single unit of energy) for new reserves is lower than for those previously exploited, as long as it clearly exceeds 1, that is, more energy is obtained than invested, we are still in good shape. Oil rigs in Texas and Pennsylvania 150 years ago could use pressure to force oil to the surface in dramatic geysers and the EROEI was as high as 100 but this is nothing more than a story about the past. Today, the index only reaches a value of around 3-5 for shale oil 15 for conventional oil,[641] but this does not mean that we cannot use shale oil. Instead, it means that shale oil will probably be more expensive than conventional oil – nothing more, nothing less.

Oil market strategists from Saudi Arabia, Iran and Iraq made assumptions about the high cost of shale oil, assessing that there was no economic justification for its exploitation. Yet despite the significant political conflicts between these countries, in 2015, they attempted to jointly destroy American shale oil with low oil prices on the world market. This did not succeed: today, the United States produces an increasing volume of oil from shale and again is by far the largest oil producer in the world. This significantly changes our outlook for the future. To quote a consultant interviewed for the 2018 documentary *The Crude Poker Game*, "This is a new approach, completely different from the one we are used to. We have to realize that we have too much oil – not too little – and that humanity has to impose limits on itself . . . for the sake of the climate, the environment, and future generations."[642]

The exact point at which peak oil occurs and the point at which we run out of oil depends not only on whether we find it in the future, how much of it we find, or when we find it. It also depends on how much oil we will end up using. Supply and demand jointly determine whether and when we will begin to face serious problems.

A WORD ABOUT SUPPLY, OR WHERE ELSE WE CAN FIND OIL

The two factors mentioned above are far from the only ones that cause proved reserves to increase and peak oil to slowly but surely move farther away. Sixty years ago, American geologist and geochemist John Adams pointed out five main factors affecting the future availability of mineral resources. These included the creation of synthetic minerals, the development of substitutes, increasing demand for certain substances, the development of techniques for obtaining resources from poor-quality reserves, and the discovery of new reserves. In the context of oil, all of them remain valid today. Let us take a closer look at them.[643]

For several decades running, new discoveries have been the most important factor determining the size of oil reserves. Although, as we already know, identified reserves reached their peak in the 1960s, there are still vast unexplored or poorly researched areas where we can expect to find oil. Previously unknown or inadequately documented resources are discovered or explored regularly, then added to what we consider proved resources. Case in point: the reserves on Brazil's Atlantic shelf (Santos and Campos Basins); the reserves in the lower part of the Orinoco basin (Bolivar Coastal Fields), thanks to which Venezuela climbed to first place among oil-rich countries, displacing Saudi Arabia; or the deposits in the Caspian Sea (Kashagan Field), discovered only in 2000 and exploited since 2013.[644]

We can also assume that, in the poorly explored or completely unexplored areas of Antarctica, Siberia, or the Saharan part of Africa, there are still undiscovered provable reserves that await us, in time allowing us to reassess them as proved reserves.

Perhaps all the motivation we need to help make this a reality lies in the promise of future profits from finding new reserves, which becomes ever more enticing as the price of the resource in question increases, invariably accompanied by the depletion of the existing supply. The U.S. Atomic Energy Commission in the 1950s provided a very illustrative example. Due to the need to guarantee uranium supplies to its customers, the Commission promised to purchase all the uranium that anyone in the country would ever find at guaranteed, favorable prices. Just a few years later, it had to backpedal on this promise, as people had joined the search in droves and the availability of uranium on the market had risen sharply. Of course, many people then stopped looking for more uranium, which does not mean that there is no more uranium, only that the enthusiasm for exploiting it had died down.[645]

The second most important reason for the increase in proved reserves is that new technologies have enabled us to recover oil from ever greater depths below the water's surface. When we began to drill for oil on land more than 150 years ago, nobody dreamed of the possibility that we might effectively extract oil from the bottom of the sea. The first barges allowed us to reach oil located in basins no deeper than 50 meters. As recently as ten years ago, the most modern semi-submersible rigs reached a maximum depth of 2,200 meters. Today we have drill ships that allow us to unearth the riches beneath the ocean floor at a depth of more than two miles.[646] In this way, step by step, larger and larger areas of the ocean are emerging into sharper focus and more active exploitation. Thanks to advances in visualization and information processing technology (including 3D visualizations of the drilling process and its outcomes, which seem trivial today), we learned that there was oil in areas we had previously studied in the "analog era," finding no trace of oil. Finally, thanks to technological progress, we can now start exploiting less abundant reserves and obtain a final product of much higher purity, concentration, and quality in the refining process.

The third way to increase the supply of oil is to produce synthetic equivalents of substances that exist in nature, with the same functional properties as those substances. We have known for many decades that we can produce identical end products from the same substrates processed by completely different chemical processes; similarly, the same end product can be made from completely different substrates.[647] Synthetic crude oil can be obtained from biomass, natural gas, and even coal, through a technique called the Fischer-Tropsch process. This process has been known since the beginning of the 20th century, and the first plant producing liquid fuels using it was established in Germany in the 1930s. Although the scale of this production was small, the method found widespread use in South Africa after World War II. The country, banned from purchasing oil by an international embargo but very rich in coal, successfully managed to sustain itself in diplomatic and resource isolation for several decades thanks to the oil production from coal.

Producing one barrel of oil requires about one ton of coal to be processed through a very specific set of chemical conditions.[648] This means that even if we run out of oil before demand for it drops to zero, we can turn to coal, which we possess in abundance. Apart from the resources exploited today, which can last us anywhere between several dozen and several hundred years (depending on the country), coal mines are a logical fallback option. While most of them are closed in highly developed EU countries due to their economic unprofitability, we can always come back to them. As an example, according to data from the Polish Geological Institute, Poland has 64.3 billion tons of proved reserves of black coal, which means that the country possesses Europe's richest coal deposits. With an annual output of 64.1 million tons, the coal should last more than a thousand years.[649]

The fourth way to postpone the arrival of peak oil is to produce and use existing substances or invent new ones that are functional substitutes for oil. Our ability to find such substitutes depends on which of the many products of the oil refining process we are talking about. For example, we can use natural gas to replace liquefied petroleum gas (LPG), which is produced by refining petroleum. Gasoline can be replaced with ethanol, diesel with vegetable oils, asphalt for road construction with concrete. Some plastics can be replaced with glass (for bottles), wood (for window frames and floor coverings), wheat bran (for drinking cups or food trays), and cotton (for shopping bags), while others (such as disposable plastic food bags) we could finally give up completely.

Replacing different kinds of fuel is undoubtedly the greatest challenge we face. This includes gasoline, diesel, and heavy fuel oil (HFO), which is commonly used as fuel for commercial ships. It is possible to replace gasoline with ethanol, a high-grade alcohol, by implementing minor tweaks in a car engine. In Brazil, cars running on alcohol, primarily obtained locally from sugar cane, have been in use for several dozen years, and in the last two decades, several global automotive concerns have launched cars with engines designed in such a way that the driver can fill them with gasoline, alcohol, or a mixture of the two as they see fit, in completely arbitrary proportions. The first vehicle of this kind was rolled out in 2003.[650] In this way, Brazil is gradually divorcing itself from its dependency on oil while developing its automotive market. In a similar way, diesel engines can be modified to use rapeseed or sunflower oil through a process called esterification. For many years now, the European Union and many individual countries have been using the B5 biodiesel blend, in which 5 percent of the fuel is biodiesel and the rest is hydrocarbon-based fuel.

We can also take a more creative approach to the issue of substitutes for fuels derived from oil. After all, water can also be a substitute for gasoline or diesel. This does not mean we will devise highly efficient vehicle engines that run on water – which is little more than a pipe dream today – but electric motors charged with energy generated in hydroelectric power plants. Using the same framing, wind can be a substitute for heavy fuel oil, at least to some extent. Although we have long since relegated wind-powered ships to museums and replaced them in freight transport with vessels that rely on more predictable fuel, the pressure to cut costs and reduce emissions has resulted in solutions that have cleverly combined the combustion engines of huge commercial vessels with sails resembling a giant paraglider. Installing such a sail already saves up to 20 percent of the fuel burned, and we can expect this rate to increase with time and technological progress.[651]

The fifth factor that is kicking the specter of peak oil down the road is, paradoxically, the increase in demand for oil and the very fact that oil reserves are decreasing. As early as 1932, British economist John Hicks wrote that "as demand for energy increases and the supply of natural resources to produce energy diminishes, the price of energy will increase. These price signals will encourage investment in energy-efficient technological advancements."[652] When oil prices rise as a result of growing demand that is increasingly difficult to balance with supply, we will seek more energy-efficient solutions – which, according to the Jevons paradox described in this chapter, may lead to an increase in oil consumption rather than a decrease. But above all, we will intensify our efforts to pursue one of the four possibilities described above: new reserves, new methods of exploitation, synthetic equivalents, or substitutes for oil.

This is a concept known as induced innovation. Building on reflections presented in Chapter 5 of this book on the alleged overpopulation of the Earth, it corresponds to Esther Boserup's point that "necessity is the mother of invention." Those who undervalue and deride the spirit of progress by framing innovations as magical silver bullets promoted by starry-eyed optimists probably ignore one simple regularity. Most of the inventions that we have woven into the fabric of our daily lives were unforeseen and arguably unforeseeable. Leonardo da Vinci's famous helicopter is the exception rather than the rule.[653] With regard to the subject of this chapter, the extraction of oil from tar sands and shale is precisely this kind of innovation: while it was the stuff of dreams and fantasies not too long ago, today it is not only a reality, but is also radically altering the oil market and influencing the geopolitical landscape of the world. The United States, which for decades was not just the world's largest oil consumer, but also dependent on large exporters such as OPEC, is becoming less and less dependent on them today, satisfying more and more of its demand with its own production. Will there come a time when the United States will become completely independent of imports? Fatalists and doomsday prophets should look to the changes on the natural gas market before passing judgment. Today, the United States, which for years was one of the largest gas importers in the world, is able to export gas because it has effectively harnessed and scaled the production of gas from shale formations. Yet as recently as 2012, the authors of a book that fits perfectly into the fear-mongering narratives described in this chapter wrote the following about shale gas: "a combination of geological realities (...) and environmental concerns (...) will mean that the impact of shale gas on the US energy balance will be marginal."[654]

HAVE WE REACHED PEAK DEVELOPMENT?

It is flabbergasting how strongly we believe that if something does not exist today and we cannot imagine how it could be invented, then it most likely will never come into existence. In the past, organizing a meeting with ten friends or colleagues required written invitations or direct personal contact. Can you imagine how tedious it must have been to nail down a date for a meeting between ten different people living in ten different cities in the mid-19th century? Several decades later, this task theoretically would have gotten much easier because every potential guest would have had a telephone at home. But as recently 1988, Poland, then a member of the Eastern Bloc and now a member of the European Union, still had fewer than eight landline phones per 100 inhabitants on average, and only 2.2 per 100 in rural areas.[655] Since a single household counted 3.5 people on average, only one in four Polish families (and one in thirteen rural families) had a telephone. Thus, at the end of the 20th century, arranging a meeting was still no easy feat. Fast-forward to the present day: we organize meetings by email, social media, and similar tools. We are constantly inventing something new. Perhaps this is worth remembering in the context of oil as well.

Doubt and misgivings are part of the human condition. However, one should choose one's doubts wisely. In 2017, was it reasonable to fear whether, in the event of catastrophic oil depletion, the energy density in the batteries of electric cars would be sufficient to allow us to travel comfortably in passenger cars without having to charge them constantly?[656] The record holder at that time, Tesla's flagship Model S 100D, was able to travel 335 miles, or 539 kilometers, on a single charge. Not only is this comparable to the range achieved by cars with internal combustion engines, but it is also growing rapidly: according to the U.S. Department of Energy, the average range of an electric car increased by 56 percent in the six years prior to 2017.[657]

In the last five years alone, the number of patent applications submitted from around the world to the European Patent Office has increased by more than 13 percent, exceeding 181,000 per year.[658] That means nearly 500 applications per day! Pessimists will note that the bulk of this surge comprises applications from China and South Korea, and that the number of applications would be falling if it weren't for innovators from these two countries. But these innovators exist! This is what the volatility of the modern world is all about. What once did not exist or was beyond the reach of our technical capabilities and even our imagination now exists, and we use it abundantly, from cell phones to the internet. The idea that competition is getting fiercer and fiercer and it is getting more difficult to come up with the next breakthrough shows how oblivious we can be to the fact that history does not end today. The Earth and human civilization will continue to develop. We are not running the risk of stalling on the path of innovation. Progress depends on us. Because we are the ones who decide how much to invest in education, what conditions businesses will face in our country, and how much funding innovative research will receive. Large research expenditures do not guarantee success or technological progress, but their absence guarantees that no progress will be made.[659]

The myth lives on

It's a scared world after all

The myth of resource depletion, especially as it pertains to oil, is doing perfectly fine today. The reason for this can be traced back to ancient times. Thousands of years ago, our ancestors, unable to understand the many bewildering natural phenomena taking place in the world around them, created myths explaining the unexplainable, seeking the meaning of life in the religious systems they created. They invented the gods responsible for specific elements of their natural environment and created canons of ways to entreat these gods to ensure their safety. Living in the first century B.C., the Roman poet Statius is credited with saying that it was "fear first made gods in the world."[660]

Although many natural phenomena that were incomprehensible to the ancients are thoroughly understood today, we still find new reasons for concern. Every day we are assaulted by advertisements built on negative emotions: if we don't buy a specific drug or supplement, we will suffer the consequences, and we need insurance packages, weight loss medicine, cycling helmets, and many other items to reduce our fear and anxiety about the world. The prosperous societies of highly developed Western countries are most susceptible to campaigns that aim to build a civilization of fear. We who are so wealthy and well-fed are the ones with the most to lose. We can lose the capital we have accumulated, our stability and sense of security. At the same time, we are the ones who have uninterrupted access to the media, who live by feeding us what we welcome the most – fear. And thus, the circle closes.[661] This narrative of fear finds fertile ground in the notion that our wells will run dry, shaking the foundations of our civilization, taking away a large part of what we have achieved, and forcing us to give up our comfortable life. This fear is not a concern for people who do not yet know whether they will have anything to eat this afternoon.

The diffusion of knowledge: Do we ever change our minds?

Deep-rooted convictions are akin to knowledge. When learned at school (oil is running out), deemed intuitively correct, and above all confirmed by life experience (the cheesecake you eat at Aunt Bessie's birthday party disappears), they become unbreakable. Is it possible to change human attitudes and, above all, the level of awareness and information about resource depletion in modern societies? In Gould's classic approach, the spread and adoption of innovation is represented in the so-called logistic curve, a line showing how slowly the number of people aware of a certain change grows in the incipient stage. Over time, this awareness or knowledge begins to spread faster and faster, only to slow down significantly again in the final stage.[662] It must therefore take a very long time to convince everyone but perhaps it would be enough to convince the majority. If so, how?

Gould believes that ideas and innovations are most often hierarchically distributed. Knowledge is first acquired by those who occupy the highest positions in some hierarchy, and only then does this knowledge pass down to those on the lower rungs. In our case, scientists are undoubtedly at the top of the hierarchy. Paradoxically, this top rung does not just consist of geologists. To understand the idea of resources that do not get depleted, it is also necessary to grasp the basics of economics, history, engineering, and even a smattering of psychology. Only a holistic look at this issue allows us to break out of the cookie-cutter thinking patterns the world around us has forced us to follow. Only a clear message from scientists would have a chance to translate into changes in the content of school curricula and textbooks, which are often written by scientists with a penchant for pedagogy. With time, successive waves of students will begin to convey a slightly different vision of the future to their children when tackling the issue of oil and other mineral resources. We may have to wait for a new generation of teachers and students to see the results.

American economist Julian Simon tried to convince the skeptics in the early 1980s. He used a well-known law that describes the impact of the supply and demand for a given commodity on the price of that commodity. As you may recall, high supply and low demand guarantees a low price, while low supply and high demand translate into a high price. Simon concluded that with relatively constant demand, a change in the price of a commodity can be interpreted as a signal as to whether there is more or less of the commodity. The high market price of a product therefore signals its shortage on the market. Simon made some additional calculations, corrected the price changes for inflation and consumers' purchasing power (earnings) and concluded that, over the past two centuries, the prices of the vast majority of resources have decreased.[663]. Thus, the availability of resources is increasing.

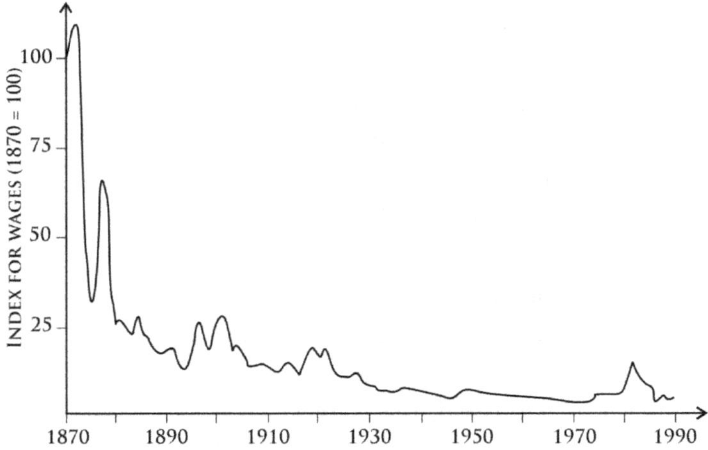

Fig. 10. The price of oil relative to wages in the United States, 1870-1990.[664]

In 1980, even before the book was published, Simon garnered attention through a wager. In a scientific journal, he challenged Paul Ehrlich (*The Population Bomb*), who had nearly attained the status of a prophet by then, to a bet based on the relationship described above. If the prices of the five selected resources rose over the following ten years, this would prove that they are becoming scarcer, and Simon would lose and pay. If the prices fell, Ehrlich would pay. Simon generously allowed Ehrlich to choose the resources that would be part of the wager, and he eagerly indicated copper, tin, chromium, nickel, and tungsten. Within ten years, the price of all five had fallen by an average of 57 percent. Ehrlich fulfilled his obligation and paid Simon several hundred dollars.[665]

This anecdote shows that Simon was probably right and that the availability of mineral resources in the world is increasing and not decreasing. However, it also proves that we as a species are extremely resistant to knowledge that does not fit into pre-established canons or the laws of nature we learn about and internalize. We instinctively view Ehrlich's position as based on common sense, as the narrative of peak oil is well grounded in us, ubiquitous in our social space, and evokes fear, which we fetishize and enjoy. Fear ends up dominating, and few people today know about Simon and Ehrlich's wager or the conclusions that societies should draw from it.

Simon also argued that our fears of resource depletion stem from a profound misunderstanding of what a resource is. There is no chance that we will go berserk and raze all the forests to cover the energy needs of the steel mills, as we are able to power them with coal. Yet as recently as the 19th century, such concerns were commonplace in places like the northeastern United States. There is also zero chance that we will cut down all the trees in the world to build ships, which was a popular fear beginning in the Age of Exploration at the latest, simply because today's shipbuilding industry uses steel. What this tells us is that the resource we are talking about is not wood, but an idea, which we warp and adorn as we see fit using the skills we learned.

In our common understanding, oil is a resource. That is a misconception. Oil is only one specific form that energy can take. We need energy, not oil. And this energy was once obtained from the sun, water, wood, coal, oil, and gas, and we have been using the energy released in nuclear decay for more than half a century. Wood, once the most basic fuel, today remains the dominant form of heating and source of thermal energy in certain less developed countries. In time, oil will also be replaced by other resources. We cannot predict whether this will happen before oil prices start to rise or whether cheap and efficient substitutes for oil will arise to unlock new possibilities and uses. However, we can be confident in defending the thesis that oil as such will never run dry.

Those who prefer to envision impending doom have one more argument up their sleeve. In every successive decade we discover less and less oil, but we consume more and more. As we already know, new discoveries reached their apex in the 1940s in the United States and two decades later globally. Around the mid-1980s, oil consumption reached the same levels as the volume of newly discovered reserves (see Fig. 6), which meant that the resources at our disposal began to shrink.

This would be a winning argument were it not for the fact that the new discoveries shown in the graph only encompass conventional oil. As we know, we are finding increasing volumes of unconventional oil, and a broad understanding of oil "resources," in line with Simon's view, allows us to conclude that there are still many discoveries to be made. Let us remember that certain energy resources are inexhaustible and will always be available, including the energy provided by the Sun, the wind, and the movement of rivers and seawater. It is only a matter of time before we are able to harness these energy sources to provide us with high-density energy wherever and whenever we see fit. The vast majority of our history as a species in the world does not involve the use of oil as a source of energy. And we will certainly stop using it one day. But when that day arrives, it will not be because we will have run out of oil, but because we will no longer need it.

STORYBOARDS FOR OUR PLANET'S DEVELOPMENT

How do we see the future in the context of all this? What can we expect? Jørgen Randers still believes that we are following one of the development trajectories indicated in *The Limits to Growth*, which he co-authored. However, this time, the global catastrophe will supposedly hit not before the year 2000, as that year fortunately came and went without major perturbations, but in the middle of the 21st century. This time, the apocalypse will be known as the *grocline*, which we can decipher as a combination of growth and decline. We will continue to grow, but this development will get slower and slower, forcing especially the wealthy countries of the Global North to reduce their current consumption, while the Global South will continue to struggle with poverty and social inequality.[666] Alas, postponing Armageddon and selecting a new date for it is characteristic of all prophets who failed to predict the previous date accurately. We saw this in the chapter about the end of the world, did we not?

It is safer to predict the future as one of many possible scenarios, as that gives us a better chance of getting it right. Polish nuclear physicist Marcin Popkiewicz draws three such scenarios in his impressive book about the need for a global energy revolution. In the first scenario, we do not have enough time to invent substitutes for oil, the output stops at a certain level and dovetails with the constantly growing demand for oil, suffocating the world economy leading to the end of the world as we know it. In the second scenario, we manage to obtain new oil resources, which we are able to produce thanks to progress, and thus the world develops according to the economic rules we follow today, taking a shorter path toward a climate crisis triggered by the explosive consumption of energy. In the third scenario, transportation is electrified, which results in a drop in oil production and yields a solution to two problems at the same time – the oil crisis and the upcoming climate crisis.[667] Popkiewicz correctly points to the last scenario as one we should strive for. We would not want to experience a large-scale economic crisis or dramatic climate change. But it is still a pity that Popkiewicz's narrative consistently relies on prodding our fear of resource depletion instead of pointing out that we have long been on the right path to solving our problems.

We can easily identify telltale signs that we are on this path by looking at the streets of medium or large cities in highly developed countries. In countries such as Germany, the Netherlands, Denmark, or Sweden, the bicycle has been a common means of transport for years. A few years ago, the idea of ride-sharing, which reduces the demand for new vehicles and limits oil consumption due to the widespread use of cars with economical hybrid engines, hit the European markets. Even in Poland, which is no leader in the realm of ecological transformation, more than two hundred cities enable their inhabitants to use this mode of transportation, and the number is growing every month.[668] The youngest member of this family is the electric scooter, which has taken entire countries and cities by storm. Let's take a closer look at this phenomenon.

The average scooter can cover a distance of about 15 miles on one charge. The 280 Wh battery can be fully charged using a 71 W charger in about four hours. To recharge, we use about 0.31 kWh, so slightly over 0.28 kWh, factoring in energy losses totaling about 10-15 percent in the converter/charger. Obviously, the cost of recharging depends on the price of electricity and pricing we use; in my case, the cheap evening rate is about 0.10 PLN, or 0.03 USD. That's right: riding a scooter about 15 miles costs three cents! A small passenger car consumes about two liters (around half a gallon) of gasoline over the same distance.

But we shouldn't jump the gun with our excessive optimism toward electric scooters. Taxes form a certain portion of the price of electricity and gasoline. This means that the governments that impose them can steer our choices by skillfully wielding them as an instrument. The higher the taxes on fuels such as gasoline, and the lower the taxes on electricity, the greater the advantages of using scooters and electric cars. But what happens if, in light of the fast-growing share of electric cars in the automobile industry, governments dramatically increase taxes on electricity, seeking new ways to address their own fiscal and budgetary woes? Moreover, the high efficiency of an electric motor in a scooter is one thing; the efficiency of a power plant that produces electricity for subsequent use is another. Coal-fired power plants have an efficiency of only 35-45 percent. Therefore, how we produce electricity is also important. If our sources are the sun, wind, or water, that is commendable. But if we burn oil, for instance, then practically all we are doing is moving the process of burning fuel from where it traditionally occurs (cars) to another, more centralized location (power plants). This immediately brings the environmental performance of scooters and electric cars into question. What good is it if we refrain from using fossil fuels at the point of consumption if we use them at an earlier stage in the chain of processes required to produce electricity?

A few decades ago, highly developed countries began to undergo a process called suburbanization. We move outside the city to enjoy the benefits of rural life, while working and shopping in the city, commuting almost daily. This is possible because we invented cars with combustion engines and learned to refine oil. Today, passenger cars are widely available goods and most of us can easily fit the costs of fueling into our home budget. Should we surrender all this in the name of preventing an oil disaster? Go back to the cities, live as close to the workplace as possible, give the car a pass? Perhaps, instead of trying to go backward in the development of civilization to an era before the popularization of passenger cars, we should move forward. The solution – the electric car – is already there, and it is developing rapidly.

In this way, we have a chance to add another chapter to the history of transformations that began with the invention of the horse-drawn carriage. This early mechanized vehicle, the longtime dream of all those who moved around only on foot, later became a symbol of the upcoming disaster. At the end of the 19th century, the number of horses in the big cities of Western Europe and North America was growing rapidly as more and more people could afford to move around in horse-drawn carriages – but there were no more people willing to work on removing the rapidly accumulating piles of horse dung they left in their wake. In 1898, the first international urban planning conference in New York was dominated by the coming apocalypse. According to completely serious forecasts, horse manure was to reach the second floors of houses in Manhattan by 1930, and London would be engulfed in excrement by 1950.[669] As we know now, this apocalypse never struck because motorized vehicles emerged and the problem solved itself. With time, the issue of increasing emissions and the harmful substances they contained replaced prior concerns. These concerns were also greatly reduced with the introduction of catalytic converters and particulate filters. Our exhaust pipes are no longer black from soot because it is stopped in the filters.

Today it is time to face the issue of the alleged exhaustion of our oil supply, which we are solving by gradually switching to cars with electric motors. Whether they will ultimately store their energy in batteries that use electricity drawn power plants, which is the direction we are observing today, or from their own hydrogen-powered fuel cells is something we cannot yet know. We do know, however, that the consumption of oil per capita in many highly developed countries, which are responsible for the majority of the world's oil consumption, has been slowly decreasing for several decades.[670] The American Oldsmobile of the 1960s, known from classic TV shows like *The Wonders Years*, uses up to 20 liters of fuel per 100 kilometers of mileage in the city (over 8 gallons for every 100 miles), making the Oldsmobile a thing of the past. With time, the cars that rule the streets of today's cities will also become a thing of the past. Even far back as the turn of the 6th and 5th century BC, philosophers like Heraclitus knew that the world's only constant feature is change. We should therefore strive to rid ourselves of the certainty that bad news is only a harbinger of worse news. That the time of great inventions is over. That oil will run dry, the good life we know will vanish, and the dawn of a *Mad Max* universe will arrive.

The future is unpredictable. Who could have predicted that on April 21, 2020, the price of a barrel of oil in futures contracts would crash through the floor to negative 37 USD? For a while, oil sales had to be subsidized – such was the scale of the shortages in our oil storage capacity in relation to the amount of oil on the market. Even if we assume that COVID-19 was the main culprit here, in spite of the prophets of doom and the gospel they preach, the price of oil in recent years has consistently stood at $40-60, a far cry from the $200 that some of the darker scenarios expected. So why do we persist in painting such bleak visions of the future? A quarter of a century ago, Julian Simon wrote that "Our supplies of natural resources are not finite in any economic sense. Nor does past experience give reason to expect natural resources to become scarce. Rather, if history is any guide, natural resources will progressively become less costly, hence less scarce, and will constitute a smaller proportion of our expenses in future years."[671]

The data says there is no peak oil, but we know better, because it is always the other side that is mistaken. This patronizing tone can be used as a cudgel wherever and whenever we wish to use it. But if the data spells out the opposite conclusion, we must examine it in detail before we continue to sow fear about the impending depletion of oil. In life, we have many reasons to be worried and to be afraid. Peak oil should not be one of them, as not all our fears turn out to be justified. With time, some of them – in fact the vast majority – end up in the dustbin of history.

SEVEN
ONE FEAR TO RULE THEM ALL: THE (UN)CERTAINTY OF TOMORROW

Jan Rydzak

The most amorphous of all human fears is the fear of the unknown – the fear of tomorrow. The uncertainty of survival likely underpinned fear as a defensive response among our ancestors, making it a likely candidate for one of the earliest human emotions. Early humans faced countless threats in a perpetually hostile environment: frostbite, wild animals, starvation, fire, and fellow hominins with a penchant for violence. The actions they undertook under the influence of fear were necessary for survival. The neural circuitry of the modern human brain has preserved many of these features and reproduces them in our behavior, nudged by experienced purveyors of fear. Political figures and many media outlets operate in fear-inducing feedback loops, exploiting our cognitive biases in pursuit of power or advertising revenue to cast others as enemies and rare events as existential threats. Religion has played its two-pronged role in the evolution of fear, offering punishment and salvation in equal measure – although there are signs of its power waning. Whoever is stoking the fire at any given moment, we consistently envision a worse tomorrow for our fellow humans despite decades of staggering improvement on nearly every socioeconomic and technological front.

The Invisible Threat

In early 2020, the coronavirus pandemic threw a wrench into the world's gears that sent them screeching to a halt. Economists and pundits who had spent years celebrating favorable growth rates found themselves making room for considerable declines in every socioeconomic metric – declines that represented the world plummeting into the void of socioeconomic despair. By June, the World Bank was projecting a 5.2 percent contraction in global GDP, per capita income was dropping in the largest percentage of countries since 1870,[672] and global remittances were set to take a nosedive, cutting off a lifeline for hundreds of millions of people living in poverty.[673] Buried under these grim numbers were countless individual stories of human suffering.

The pandemic threatened to blow up all of the pillars of human survival in the 21st century at once: economic stability, regular income streams, public health systems, and social trust. In the United States, COVID-19 triggered deep uncertainty about whether those pillars would survive. There was good reason for concern: in 2019, surveys showed that approximately three-quarters of Americans lived paycheck-to-paycheck[674], three in ten adults had no emergency savings whatsoever[675], and four in ten were either uninsured or had inadequate insurance.[676] On a global level, the World Bank's goal of ending extreme poverty by 2030 began to look like a pipe dream: extreme poverty was expected to rise for the first time in two decades, setting the world back by at least three years and thrusting up to 115 million more people into the stark reality of receiving less than $1.90 for a day's labor, which the World Bank has recognized since 2015 as the international poverty threshold.[677] Gig workers in countries with faltering social protection systems quickly became the new precariat – an army of poor urban workers with no place to go.

The scale of the emergency revealed not just how vulnerable the foundations of human societies can be in a moment of crisis but also how our interconnectedness can magnify that vulnerability. Tomorrow became a clear and present danger, and public apprehension about the next morning's headlines skyrocketed.

The fear of tomorrow – and the future writ large – is one of the earliest and most primal human emotions. It is all-encompassing, adaptable to individual circumstances, and potent at both the micro and macro scale. At the individual level, humans experience it as a threat to the bottom two rungs of Maslow's hierarchy of needs: the physiological requirements for our survival and the need for safety and order. Both are especially tenuous in times of crisis. At the societal level, it reveals itself in recurring questions that revolve around preserving an established order. Where is "our civilization" heading? What new and unfamiliar values will sudden or incremental "civilizational change" bring? We believe we are unable to predict the future before the future throws another curveball. This breeds a void of uncertainty that we fill with looming threats, framed as hazardous to our very existence. And because the source of these threats is always changing within and between human communities, the fear of tomorrow has become an evergreen feature of modern societies.

Take a moment to consider the overall state of the world. Overall, is it improving, declining, or neither? Now, hold onto your decision or write it down on the margins of this page. Whatever your assessment, if we zoom out on the global panorama, the evidence that the world is on an arc toward a better future is overwhelming. In 1820, 90 percent of the billion people that populated the world lived in abject poverty; today, extreme poverty rates have fallen off a cliff. Fewer people today live on less than $1.90 a day than there were humans alive 200 years ago, despite an eightfold increase in world population.[678] Child mortality in less- and least-developed countries has halved in the last 20 years and fallen in all but two of 195 sovereign countries.[679] As recently as the year 2000, the number of people with no education whatsoever was twice as high as the global population of college-goers; today, the latter outnumber the former by 100 million.[680] These trends have hardly ever wavered from their steep decline in the last 50 years.

Yet what is most striking about these findings is that we persistently refuse to accept them. If you responded above that the world is getting worse, you are not alone. Our species is imbued with a powerful pessimistic streak – and it only gets stronger in moments of chaos. Those living in high-income societies with a long history of industrialization appear to be most susceptible to gloomy visions of tomorrow.[681] A 2016 survey conducted in 17 countries found that more than six in ten respondents believed the world was getting worse, while only one in ten stated that it was improving.[682] This community of optimists was clustered in a single country – China, where four out of ten people expressed optimism about the future while most others wallowed in fatalism. Even when asked specific questions about poverty or child mortality, we routinely see reality as grimmer than it is. This is the "paradox of progress."[683]

The gap between reality and our perceptions of it is a critical ingredient of our fear of tomorrow. It is also practically ubiquitous, and once we become aware of it, we are likely to see it emerge across most aspects of our lives. Our disillusionment with reality seems to go hand in hand with our detachment from it. But existential dread is elusive: We don't know where it came from, why we feel it, and what passing threat our brains will latch onto next like barnacles to a wrecked ship. This chapter will sketch out some of the origins of our fear of tomorrow, some of its enablers, and some of the societal forces that can work to erode it. The keyword, you will have noticed, is "some." Unlike groaning iron locomotives and decomposed organic matter, tomorrow is not tangible; we cannot destroy it without destroying ourselves, and we have certainly not learned to cope with it.

The tale of our fear of tomorrow is, therefore, inevitably incomplete. But it begins eons ago, among the bones strewn across the grasslands in the cradle of humanity.

Predators and Primal Panic

A million and a half years ago, in what is now the outskirts of Johannesburg, a juvenile ancestor of the modern human met an untimely but mercifully quick fate. Two clean puncture wounds in the skull of the young *Paranthropus*, dealt with by what was thought to be a pointed weapon, spelled the end for the heavy-jawed hominin. Defeated in battle by a stronger contemporary, the primate breathed its last, and its lifeless form slipped down into an opening in the Earth's surface now known as Swartkrans Cave, the final resting place of many of its relatives.

For many years after scientists unearthed the skull fragment in 1949, the specimen was held up as an illustration of the killer ape hypothesis – the idea that human evolution unfolded as it did because a particular penchant for violence set us apart from other great apes. Violence and bloodlust, it claimed, were deeply anchored in human psychology, passed down through the eons as coexisting species butchered each other with primitive tools to survive and outpace the competition. Colorful descriptions painted *Australopithecus* as "carnivorous creatures, that seized living quarries by violence, battered them to death, tore apart their broken bodies, dismembered them limb from limb, slaking their ravenous thirst with the hot blood of victims and greedily devouring livid writhing flesh."[684] But this fantastical painting of a primate-eat-primate world was marred when further excavations found that the hapless hominin had not died in combat with one of its cousins. In reality, its skull was perforated by the jaws of a leopard that likely dragged its prey into the branches of a tree and cast the remains of its meal into the pit where it was found.[685]

For our ancestors, fear of the future and fear of death were synonymous. Long before they became the hunters, they were the hunted. Large carnivores were more diverse and much more abundant than they are today, and our ill-equipped progenitors, who were scarce and scattered over large areas, served as a fixture on the menus of leopards, saber-toothed cats, hyenas, and the occasional eagle.[686] Discoveries such as the Swartkrans skull cap were instrumental in reversing the assumption that early hominins were the dominant predators of their time. Even as *Australopithecus* butchered its first animal using stone tools some 3.4 million years ago[687], hominins lived in perpetual terror as prey rather than predator. Dusk brought dread: with poor night vision and a plethora of nocturnal predators, *Australopithecus* spent its nights in utter uncertainty about its prospects for surviving until dawn.

But fear triggered growth. In all likelihood, exposure, and vulnerability to predation were precisely the catalysts that our ancestors needed to reach the next rung of the evolutionary ladder. Descending from the trees and transitioning to a terrestrial life made sleep a scarce resource, as constant threats intertwined with new opportunities for social interaction. Some researchers believe that this pushed our predecessors to conclude that long sleep is for the weak. Newly terrestrial in a hostile environment, they were forced to adapt their behavior to the need for constant vigilance. This meant longer periods of wakefulness to acquire and share information, and less (but deeper) sleep to consolidate it.[688]

Today's humans may be the beneficiaries of this evolutionary adaptation: our sleep patterns are shorter than those of other primates, and we spend significantly more time deep in REM sleep, which takes the scattered pieces of the day's memories and glues them together into consolidated blocks.[689] What gains the most from a good night's sleep? Motor skills and cognitive abilities that do not require us to consciously think about them once thoroughly practiced. This is what gives us the power to avoid thinking about every rotation of the pedals on a bicycle, every stroke in freestyle swimming – or, as the theory goes, every fire starting strike of flint on flint.

Conquering fear was an essential step on our road to controlling fire, and vice versa. For our prehistoric predecessors, until approximately a million years ago, a burning forest meant the same thing as it did for most other species: death and destruction. Since both were imminent, there was no tomorrow, and they fled the flames in disarray, with fear as their fuel.

But to grasp the benefits of fire, early hominins first had to observe them. Much like today's natural disasters bring on the impulse to adapt and build more resilient structures that will withstand the next shockwave, early hominins likely realized that what they could salvage from the smoldering embers – bird eggs, lizards, rodents – was not only edible but also more digestible when accidentally cooked.[690] Naturally occurring fires likely exposed such delectable resources often enough to produce a eureka moment in the neural pathways of hominins: their great fear could be a great asset. Indeed, they were probably not unique in their opportunistic use of fire; many of today's birds of prey congregate at the margins of wildfires to scoop up terrified prey flushed out by the blaze and even carry burning tufts of grass to fuel the flames.[691]

For hominins, the cognitive implications of fire foraging were most likely immense. Whether rapidly or gradually, our ancestors began to live and move in larger groups bound together by the shared purpose of survival. Safety in numbers countered fear of death but also offered long-term benefits. Foraging escapades required planning; planning required a basic understanding of the future, and the future was safer if scattered individuals faced their fears together.[692] It is virtually certain that human cognitive abilities improved with rapidly expanding brain size – possibly because we faced intense pressure to manage increasingly complex social systems.[693] The first enlightenment was close; ignition was only a step away.

The power to kindle fire distinguished its likely inventor (*Homo erectus*) from the opportunistic scavengers and arsonists that came before it. The reorganization of life around the source of warmth and protection shaped us into social animals. The increased opportunities to communicate, coordinate, and plan for the future released a steady flow of collaborative innovation. By half a million years ago, another of our possible predecessors achieved further milestones in the conquest of basic fears, mastering the use of fire-hardened spears as thrusting weapons and projectiles, regularly hunting large game, and raising the wooden palisades of the first shelter.[694] Fire, one of the great prehistoric fears, had been weaponized and transformed into a source of comfort while serving to ward off other fears. The hunted had definitively become the hunter.

What do the trials and tribulations of our primate predecessors have to do with the present day? After all, thousands of years have passed since our species became the world's 'super predator,' and today's apex predators behave like prey when confronted with human presence.[695] Why, then, has our fear of the unknown endured over millions of years of evolution? The most fundamental aspiration of modern humans is unchanged from what it was for our distant evolutionary relatives: survival. Survival and development in a world where primates were among the more anatomically impaired mammals were possible only through the nexus of three processes that we ultimately inherited: fear, learning, and memory.

But let's hold on a minute. What is fear? A subjective state? A cocktail of hormones? A universal circuitry pre-installed in every animal? The question sparks vigorous debates among neuroscientists and evolutionary psychologists, and no one vision ever gains sway for long.[696] What we do know is that fear is associated with a rich buffet of processes in a range of regions in the brain. One scans for threats and automatically raises red flags for the body to respond; another activates our fight-or-flight response; another instructs the adrenal glands to flood our system with hormones; and yet another reads the situation and compares it to past experiences.[697] Little is known about how this fear machine works to nourish our vague existential anxieties about the state of the world. Still, scientists broadly agree that we inherited at least some of it in the evolutionary software package installed in our minds.[698] Online personality tests with four-letter outcomes have dubious scientific backing. Yet our oversensitivity to uncertain future events, known in psychology and neuroscience as "intolerance of uncertainty," seems to be linked to a specific cluster of neurons.[699]

Perfectly healthy humans often see fear as nothing but a motivator and have trouble understanding how crippling the threat of an unknown enemy can be. Others reveal just how the deep imprint of fear can turn into a liability rather than an evolutionary advantage. Many mental disorders are linked to the brain's inability to control fear, which lingers even if their root causes no longer exist.[700] Studies on sufferers of post-traumatic stress disorder have consistently shown that those mentally traumatized by past experiences are especially vulnerable to fear, even in safe conditions.[701] Over time, bombarding the brain with what it disproportionately transcribes as trauma can lead to a kind of learned helplessness, where the depths of despair are so great that we lose all hope of things ever getting better.[702]

From these pits of despair comes one of the thorniest questions in psychology: can fear ever truly be controlled? Although the jury is still out on this, part of the secret might lie in fear's ability to trigger our learning processes and permanently lodge their lessons in our minds. Only the most foolish *Homo erectus* would approach a sleeping saber-toothed cat unarmed; if he got out alive somehow, he certainly wouldn't make the same mistake again, or evolution would have him for dinner. Uncertainty commanded attention and almost certainly forced early hominins to learn because letting their guard down almost always meant death. Today, terrifying memories still haunt our minds like few others, and evidence suggests that we encode information much more effectively when tangible threats force us to.[703] Thus, even though the future is not something we can wrestle to the ground in the jungle, there is a chance that we are able to mitigate our fear of it by learning about what fuels it, or who.

Fuelers of the Fear of the Future

The ultimate enabler of our fear of tomorrow is our brain; every external force that supports it only rides on the possibilities that our human frailties provide. The mechanics of how our brains make us fearful may have been a mystery to the dominant classes of ancient civilizations, but the existence of fear itself was not. If the prehistoric neurobiological processes are at least partly responsible for infusing us with fear of the unknown, then human institutions naturally cropped up to take advantage of them. One trinity of purveyors can boast notable contributions to this field in recent history: political figures and formations, media and biased framing, and institutionalized religion. All of them have relied on one primary strategy of control: the perpetuation of uncertainty. We will explore some illustrations in this section. All of these are vignettes of fear used as a weapon. These vignettes are not exhaustive; thousands of additional forces are involved in weaving uncertainty and fear into our existence.

These institutions have also had an undeniable role to play as the building blocks of today's societies. This is more of a paradox than a contradiction: at the dawn of modern civilizations and throughout their history, governance through fear and enforcement of wrath was not simply an option but a legitimate necessity to maintain some semblance of social order. But as we will see, times have changed. The precariousness that gripped the world when these institutions emerged is being shattered across the world. Today, we can openly challenge their foundations – and the foundations of our fear of what is to come. We begin with the source of control that is perhaps most deeply embedded in the human psyche, as it has been our companion since humans abandoned isolation and formed into bands.

PUNITIVE PIETY

The underworld of Maya mythology is Xibalba – the "Place of Fear." Six deadly houses await visitors who descend into its bowels, each filled with dangers that often claim their lives: jaguars, blades, bats, frost, fire, and darkness. But the twelve gods of death did not send the souls of the dead to their grisly doom to purify them or punish them for their sins; by all accounts, they did it to keep themselves entertained.[704] Life led to death, but death led to reincarnation or a range of more obscure fates, the record of which has been partly lost to time. Eternal damnation in Xibalba, however, was not one of them.

The endless cycle of human existence, according to the Maya, was interrupted when a new deity came into the picture – Hunab Ku, the One God. The Spanish conquest depleted the already thinned-out ranks of indigenous communities and fused their pre-existing supernatural forces into one syncretic Creator. More importantly, it turned Xibalba into not simply the Place of Fear but also a place of punishment. From now on, an individual's fate was tethered to their behavior. Xibalba became eternal damnation, but the Maya peoples of Mesoamerica could avoid it by remaining obedient to Hunab Ku, who channeled his divine will through the King or Queen of Spain. If the remaining Maya communities refused, they would not simply pass into the Place of Fear, they would be dragged there by their local Franciscan friar.[705]

Monotheism gave civilizations around the world something to strive for and something they could aspire to escape – a sliver of agency in a deterministic world. It also provided human communities with a powerful sense of purpose, which the doctrinaires of faith used diligently to build a common identity. Polytheistic and animist societies were relatively easy to harness once physically conquered, and their history was quickly usurped and distorted.[706] Forced conversion was a critical tool because the whip and sword were primed for those who refused it. But the divine singularity also offered a simpler, more attractive, and often more codified moral compass than the myths and legends of old, and the risk of eternal hellfire was a bonus incentive to abandon the old gods. Simplifying the world into two extremes required common enemies, too, and none were better suited for that role than other monotheistic religions that sought to further their reach.

Religion was vital to the evolution of human cooperation. In particular, human cooperation became the name of the social game through the threat of supernatural punishment.[707] Thousands of years ago, our nascent cultures faced a significant problem to which today's economists dedicate their entire lives. Resources were scarce, and to survive, bands of humans with weak genetic bonds had to work together. But the temptation to scrape a few more strips of meat from the mammoth's bone threatened everyone at the barbecue. For every meaty reward, there had to be a method of controlling ravenous appetites.

Furthermore, this method had to persuade free riders who were unwilling to join the hunt but always first at the dinner table. Selfish behaviors, therefore, had to be discouraged and punished. But entrusting fellow hominins with the task of punishing every minor infraction was impossible when death lurked in the shadows. The punishers could eventually betray the cause and side with the troublemakers, or slaughter everyone involved. And coming up with a code of conduct is challenging without the power of writing or a superhuman enforcement mechanism. For many, fear was the only path forward.

The supernatural punishment hypothesis states that the fear of an uncertain but grisly future cooked up by otherworldly forces is the key to the secret of human cooperation. Selfishness is ingrained in us; God is the Panopticon that keeps us from utter dog-eat-dog anarchy.[708]

The gears of risk assessment embedded in our primate brains were firmly tuned to this idea. We naturally avoid more costly errors. If a *Homo erectus* mistook the shadow of a tree trunk for the shadow of a leopard, they would at most face the mocking grunts of their brethren; if they mistook a leopard for a tree trunk, they would face a bloody death. The uncertainty this created meant that excessive optimism was a game of Russian roulette. Or consider our hard-won control of fire. Every civilization of the ancient world was fascinated by the flickering flames. Religions over the eons have used fire prolifically as a symbol of the double-edged sword of divine grace and wrath, from the fire gods of Mesoamerican mythologies to the rain of brimstone that destroyed the Biblical cities of Sodom and Gomorrah. Fire itself has the natural power to both reward and extinguish human communities. Reaching into an element so key to the emergence of our species made it an optimal vehicle for divine will.

Whichever illustration we choose, death, hell, spoiled meat, and ruined crops were all severe enough prospects to persuade us to choose collaboration over isolation. Supernatural punishment was also a simple and digestible concept that early humans might even have been predisposed to accept by default.[709] After all, if our fellow band members were able to inflict severe punishment on a transgressor, we can imagine the kind of pain that may rain down from the almighty supernatural police force.

This pairing of carrot and stick incentives may have given us an evolutionary advantage. In an era where natural phenomena and the causes of disasters remained shrouded in mystery, interpreting them as the wrath of the gods was not just convenient but helpful in building societies. Supernatural surveillance does not even require a single omnipotent punisher god. Reincarnation and the concept of karma in all its varieties are built around balancing great rewards with severe punishment, whether through the forces of many deities (as in Hinduism) or the natural order of the universe (as in Buddhism).[710] In Austronesian cultures, vague notions of supernatural punishment were enough to kickstart politically complex societies without the need for moralizing high gods to cast thunderbolts and shake the Earth.[711] Although cultures have varied enormously in how they approach supernatural punishment, the concept is everywhere.

Perhaps more than in any other circumstance, the correlation between fear and beliefs comes into high relief in times of crisis. When things go awry, our minds follow a simple feedback loop: we seek shelter from danger in religious faith, and the shelter we feel we receive mitigates our fear.[712] This association of "death anxiety" with increasing religious fervor (especially among those who are uncertain to begin with) is a well-known psychological phenomenon that has been studied and validated extensively, at least in the "Global North." It interacts with a complex set of undercurrents, as faith comes with built-in rituals and communities that amplify the notion that we have sailed into a safe harbor. When the World Health Organization declared COVID-19 a pandemic in March 2020, the number of Google searches for "prayer" surged to the highest levels ever recorded, outperforming annual religious celebrations by a significant margin and rising in all but the least religious countries.[713] In more than a dozen countries, most prominently the United States whose levels of religiosity are unusually high compared to that of other highly developed countries, more people stated that the pandemic had strengthened their faith than considered it weakened by the disaster.[714] For many, the insecurity of the pandemic felt permanent, offering a microcosm of the precariousness that historically made active participation in religion the only available option.

Humanity's most recent brush with mass mortality is hardly unique in its ability to reinforce religious beliefs. One influential recent study showed a persistent link between the occurrence of earthquakes and rising levels of religiosity in the same areas in their aftermath.[715] When an unforeseeable disaster strikes, the fear it generates may unleash a two-pronged effect. One is religious coping – a cognitive response to stress and trauma in which humans seek spirituality as a defense mechanism. The other is mutual insurance, the rational choice to build or reinforce a set of risk-sharing structures or actions anchored in a pre-existing religious community. Faith, in a way, is a competitor to the welfare state, as it offers an alternate, more personal, and potentially more controllable framework for dealing with adverse life events, free from the shackles of political squabbles.

What's more, once such structures are assembled, or once

religious coping becomes part of the social bloodstream, their impact tends to endure. The same earthquake study found that children of immigrants from the affected areas are uniquely inclined to follow the faith of their parents, echoing similar findings on other natural calamities. Fear of the unknown and everything it entails may thus be passed down from generation to generation.

Still, while fear and uncertainty have been crucial tools of control both within and outside the context of crisis, some of the positive ripple effects of this process can be seen to this day. Psychological research consistently finds a link between religiosity and pro-social behavior.[716] In fact, the punitive hand of the gods may be a significant driver of altruism as long as we are not experiencing extreme levels of personal insecurity.[717] But in an era of unshackled humanism and unprecedented progress, declining religiosity does not mean that our altruism will disappear with the gods. The path that led humanity to its prime is not destined to be the same as the path our species will take.

Nevertheless, even if the outward signs of religiosity continue to decline in the coming decades, our fears may simply find another outlet. Accurate or not, deities are authorities, supernatural expressions of forces we cannot control. Unexpected financial ruin, a stock market collapse, and bureaucratic quagmires are all modern manifestations of those forces, especially when we know that there is no safety net to catch us. Thus, the uncertainty that drives the fear of tomorrow may not recede; instead, it may secularize.

VOTING FOR THE BOGEYMAN

Governments of all stripes have developed a penchant for perpetuating mass fear. Virtually all authoritarian governments in history (and many allegedly democratic regimes) have experimented with state terror, mass incarceration, extreme brutality by security forces, intimidation, kidnapping, and murder. Nighttime raids on the dwellings of anonymous partisans and opposition figures alike are only the culmination of complex information control schemes. Some recruit and train networks of professional and civilian informants. Others deploy sophisticated surveillance software developed by private companies.[718] Others still have relied on a Panopticon of watchful senior citizens reporting on suspicious movements in their neighborhood. Long-standing dictatorships have occasionally managed to so thoroughly inject fear through terror into the people they govern that public dissent is unfathomable.[719]

But directly terrorizing citizens is only one of many pathways to spreading the seeds of fear. A more universal approach is to link fears to roughly identifiable threats and let a distorted version of patriotism – one that crosses the thin line that divides it from nationalism – run through the social bloodstream. Real and imagined threats to borders, national culture, public safety, and national security are perfect for this, to the point where people accept state violence as a natural reaction to a cruel world that is out to destroy us.[720] The connective tissue of these strategies is that they all take advantage of information asymmetries to keep the populace loyal (and political opponents preferably in the dark). Just as the government of Myanmar has portrayed all Rohingya refugees as "Bengali terrorists," so did the George W. Bush administration count on the nation it governed to accept the claim that Saddam Hussein's Iraq possessed weapons of mass destruction. In both cases, even tepid supporters of the government experienced a surge in fear-induced enthusiasm for the state that committed violence in their name. The subject and object differ; the specter of danger and death is the same.

Whatever the strategy, the underlying idea has always been the same: information is power. Controlling the channels through which it flows is critical to maintaining an atmosphere of uncertainty in which only those in power can provide security. History provides plenty of examples. The *Gazette de France* served as the French monarchy's propaganda mouthpiece and a single source of truth as early as the 1600s; no other outlet was allowed wide circulation lest the Crown lose its iron grip on the narrative.[721] When the French Revolution transformed and diversified the landscape of the media, the very idea of circulating information in Europe shifted from state control toward popular control. As printing presses churned out millions of books and newspapers per year, many regimes gave up on the idea of simply controlling the narrative.

Instead, they resorted to extinguishing it. Hundreds of newspapers that had flourished after the French Revolution were shut down in the years following the Reign of Terror, leaving Paris with only four heavily censored papers in 1811.[722] A century and a half later, the leaders of the Iranian Revolution shut down dozens of outlets opposed to theocratic rule, branding them as "corrupt elements."[723] Every time a purge of inconvenient media and opposition voices occurs, the goal is to minimize uncertainty for the government and maximize it for everybody else.

Today, one of the most striking modern illustrations of how governments weaponize uncertainty is the global explosion of network shutdowns – deliberate blackouts of digital communication channels that disrupt cell phone service, social media, and other communication tools, or even the entire Internet. During the Arab Spring, protesters, and organizers strategically used social media to mobilize friends and family to step out into the streets in an expression of collective outrage against despotic rulers and economic calamity.[724] Though optimism about the liberating potential of new communication technologies proved premature,[725] aspiring despots and those already in power seized the opportunity to bend them to their will. The simplest way to do this, they discovered, was by shutting them down completely. Governments in more than 50 countries have imposed massive disruptions to internet access, social media, and the entire digital communication system hundreds of times since the Arab Spring.[726] When protests are vigorous, or elections are approaching, these blackouts can blanket entire countries and turn into digital sieges that squeeze their citizens for weeks or months.[727] Worse, digital repression is contagious: once a routine phenomenon primarily in authoritarian countries, internet blackouts are now part of the fabric of life in democracies. India – the most populous democracy of all – is also by far the greatest purveyor of this tactic, indiscriminately extinguishing access to communication hundreds of times under the pretense of quashing unrest.[728]

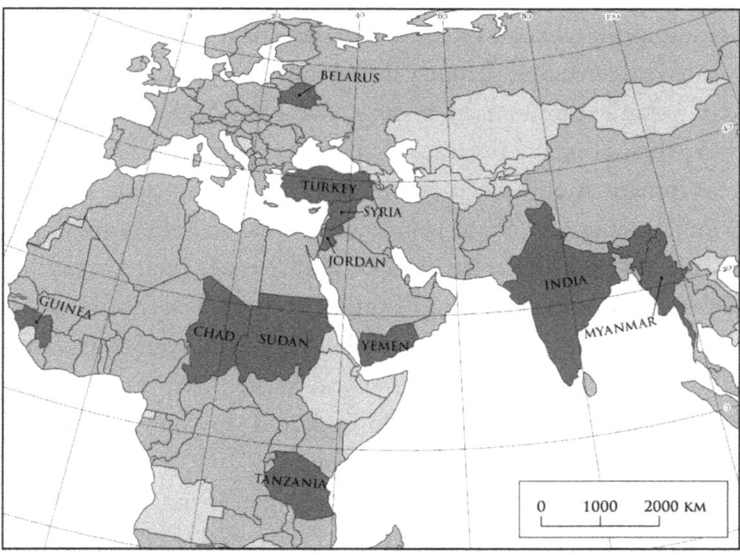

Fig. 1. Countries that imposed network shutdowns in response to protest, unrest, and other circumstances in 2020, based on a sample of 12 telecommunications companies operating in 125 countries worldwide. Lighter shades of grey indicate countries of operation that did not experience network shutdowns.[729]

Regimes virtually always offer the same reasoning whenever they impose a shutdown: protecting public safety, preserving stability, and safeguarding national security. The actual underlying motive also tends to be the same: instilling fear and discouraging dissent. Depriving their citizens of a critical channel of communication means severing their ties not only with the media but often with their friends and family as well, primarily as connectivity skyrockets and low-income people rely on low-cost tools such as WhatsApp.[730] In principle, cutting off communication completely should intimidate both those of us whose outrage is fueled by images and videos on social media and those who decide to join street protests because someone we know and trust is already there.[731]

The disappearance of these channels places the world behind a digital smokescreen. Imagine for a moment how you would react to being abruptly thrust into an information vacuum at a volatile moment in history. All your devices have gone dark, the sound of firecrackers reaches your window, and the government mouthpiece on the only active television channel is announcing that chaos is unfolding outside: bullets are flying, rioters are pilfering store shelves, and masked men are pelting pedestrians with stones and bottles. In your heart, you oppose the shriveled strongman who has held power in your country for 20 years. You face a choice: either you muster the courage to step out into the streets, or you hold back and stay home with your family and the government mouthpiece.

The government's gamble is simple: in an environment of uncertainty, most people will be frightened into staying put. Human beings have a natural aversion to ambiguity: we are not rigged to make choices with uncertain outcomes.[732] Like a villain in a horror film, the government cuts the phone line to strengthen its advantage, shatter morale, and divide the victims. Just as importantly, it does not matter whether the landscape of mayhem presented by the government mouthpiece has anything to do with reality. What matters is that we no longer have any notion of our chances of being shot in the head as soon as we walk out the door.

Conversely, we can be reasonably confident that nobody will break down our door and bundle us into a van full of masked paramilitaries. We roughly understand the risks of the safe choice; we know nothing about the risks of what is out there. Our survival instincts dictate that we should fill the vacuum with dark scenarios, and those dark scenarios compel us to remain where we are.

Yet research has consistently shown that even extreme forms of digital repression as network shutdowns backfire spectacularly, whether by compelling protesters to regroup into neighborhood clusters that are smaller and harder to control, by convincing previously passive individuals to join the peaceful resistance, or by encouraging demonstrators to switch tactics.[733] Dictatorial regimes in Egypt, the Gambia, Algeria, and Sudan, all of which tried to stem the tide of outrage by disconnecting digital networks, collapsed shortly after that; those that survived have enjoyed a dubious track record of success at containing public protest. Governments routinely overestimate the organizing potential of technology and underestimate that of innovative human beings. Precisely for this reason, their attempts to generate uncertainty and isolation among the people who stand against them have a penchant for failure.

Stoking the fear of impending change is a time-honored tradition, even in consolidated democratic societies. Most of us are familiar with the mechanics of this process because it mirrors a persuasion strategy that is widespread in the commercial world: the fear appeal.[734] Marketing strategies and fear-inducing political messaging often stem from the same root and follow similar persuasion tactics, most notably dividing, reconsolidating, and conquering. Today's social media managers work for both corporations and politicians, often blending the worlds of commercial and political communication. Yet technology has only provided a new environment for methods of persuasion that have long been used in both settings, building on the bedrock of familiar thought patterns.

Listerine, first sold in the 1880s as a surgical antiseptic, struggled to reach a market beyond enthusiastic American surgeons and the occasional dentist, even after the brand began to explore its potential as mouthwash in 1914. But in the Roaring Twenties, Listerine changed its tactics. "Halitosis makes you unpopular," read one ad from 1928, featuring a lone woman forsaken by a dance partner for her bad breath. "Often a bridesmaid, never a bride," read another. "Are you unpopular with your own children?" read a third. Capitalizing on young people's fears of losing their social status, Listerine saw its revenue multiply by 40 in six years.[735]

Listerine tapped into a widespread pattern of thinking. First, is the threat severe? Indeed, the prospect of being exiled from a thriving and increasingly wealthy social circle constitutes a life-changing hazard. Second, am I vulnerable to the threat that is being presented? Halitosis is not something most of us are aware of if we suffer from it ourselves. Estimates of its prevalence vary widely today and were virtually non-existent in the 1920s.[736] Finally, do I possess the competence and willpower to take action, and will the action I take mitigate the impact of the problem? Why, all I have to do is purchase a bottle of Listerine – the first and most potent mouthwash on the market, recommended by dental hygienists everywhere.

The sequence above is a simplified version of a well-known psychological model of behavioral change – one of many to incorporate the fear factor.[737] Crucially, if the target audience does not find the threat severe or themselves especially susceptible to it, they will take no action. When they recognize the threat but see themselves as helpless in the face of it, they will turn inward and try to control their fear instead of making an external choice. Similar models carry over smoothly into the fertile ground of politics.

In increasingly polarized two-party political systems like the United States, half of the groundwork is already there.[738] The structure of the American electoral system favors an endless cycle of two-party battles that survives even the collapse and resurrection of political parties.[739] This boils most electoral choices down to a zero-sum game in which third parties virtually never prevail. Over time, the accumulation of either-or choices can encourage increasingly extreme portrayals of the opposite side's policies, especially when blended with no-holds-barred free speech norms.

Attack ads are a vivid expression of this and one that is ubiquitous in American political culture. In 1964, as the world stood on the precipice of a nuclear calamity, Lyndon B. Johnson's presidential campaign launched the "Daisy" ad, which presented Americans with a simple choice: John F. Kennedy's vice-president or atomic holocaust.[740] A little girl plucks petals off a daisy, counting down as she goes. As she picks the final petal, a booming voice drowns out her countdown. Five, four, three, two, one... then the blinding whiteness of a nuclear blast, and in its wake, a mushroom cloud climbing up to the sky. The prospect, however contrived, of children turned to ashes by a catastrophic nuclear attack was too much for American voters to bear. LBJ defeated his opponent in a landslide. Since "Daisy," similar ads have populated US elections at every level, often invoking parents' fear of crime or fear for their children's safety – two of the American public's most potent anxieties.[741] Populists around the globe are the most enthusiastic purveyors of fear in their ads, and at least some of the emotions that political ads conjure survive in us for weeks, thanks in part to the media frenzies they generate.[742] If your pen has ever trembled at the voting booth, it is precisely that moment that such campaigns live for – all it takes is a small dose of uncertainty to bring you over the line.

But many of us today live in politically, demographically, and economically splintered societies. What makes for a better captive audience for the political fear stream? If most of our friends are on the same side of the political fence as us, would shrewd political operatives bombard us with the same threats their counterparts use on the other side?

Of course, all sides of the political spectrum are vulnerable to manipulation, and those who self-sort to the left side of the ideological divide have their fears and prejudices that tend to engulf them.[743]

THE FUNHOUSE MIRROR OF THE MEDIA

On an overcast morning in May 1994, listeners across Rwanda tuned into Radio Télévision Libre des Mille Collines, a major radio station with state backing whose programs were broadcast throughout the country. The host, popularly known as Kantano, was reading a letter from a young schoolgirl. "The remaining cockroaches should accept negotiations before we finish them off. Our soldiers are hunting them in order to kill them all." The author of the letter then asked for the host to greet her classmate Françoise. Shortly afterward, Kantano wished the adolescent girl "resilience on this rainy morning" and rolled the tapes on a music program "so that our army continues to dance – to dance and defeat those daredevils."[744]

In the aftermath of the Rwandan Genocide, Radio Mille Collines became the gruesome portrait of how mass media could incite fear and fuel the fires of hate. By dehumanizing the Tutsi minority, goading the Hutu majority into mass murder, and encouraging its listeners to target specific victims, the station baked genocide into its audience's daily routine. The mechanism was familiar, common, and deceptively simple: take a pot of simmering ethnopolitical tension, add a dash of real and manufactured chaos, select a broad out-group to demonize, and wait for the spark that starts the fire. In Rwanda, the spark was the assassination of Rwanda's Hutu president, Juvénal Habyarimana, in April 1994, which Radio Mille Collines weaponized to call for a "final war" that would exterminate all Tutsi.[745] Researchers estimate that the broadcasts incited more than 50,000 genocidaires to slaughter their compatriots, including many who took them as a signal to recruit others before spilling out into the killing fields.[746]

Kigali's hate radio leveraged havoc and uncertainty to weaponize the fear and anger of some 6 million Hutu and direct it toward the most convenient victims. It achieved infamy as the most extreme modern manifestation of the media's ability to exploit and inflame divisions. But the transcripts from its transmissions also reveal something else: the banality of fear and its normalization.

As you read these words, the idea of sending warm wishes to your Françoise while calling for the extermination of an ethnic group will seem surreal. But these stories are simply the boiling point of a long process of building simple narratives, choosing tangible enemies, and framing chaos as the new normal. Between letters, phone-ins, and pop songs, Kantano not only appealed to the masses but also ultimately convinced them that if they did not come after the bogeyman, the bogeyman would come after them. Juxtaposing everyday life with death and music with murder only served to make the underlying message more digestible.

If politicians strategically encourage instability to shift the tide in their favor, then mass media gives their message the opportunity to ride its waves. The power of media outlets' ability to stoke fear comes through, especially clearly when they blend heavy political influence with a transparent ethnoreligious foundation.[747] Listeners and viewers come to expect a view of the world that positions their in-group as the sole Spartan regiment in the battle against social and moral decay. Radio Mille Collines is the most egregious example of the consequences of this approach, but outlets that do not directly call for violence are tinderboxes of the same. Fear of the unknown led our prehistoric kin to cooperate because ten primates can forage more berries and fight off more leopards than one. But mass media (and yellow journalism before it) unchained that fear from its physical confines. Angry pundits relieve us of having to see the spears of our enemies to believe they exist and mean us harm, and we don't have to see our band of primates to believe they're just like us.

Traditional media outlets, long a powerful opinion-shaping force, have faced additional incentives to drive narratives of fear in the last decade. The vanishing of local news has been one of them. Changes in readership and viewership have thrust smaller outlets into a perpetual fight for survival – particularly the meteoric rise of online media consumption, combined with smaller publishers' inability to catch the wave of advertising revenue it brought in. Between 2005 and 2018, Great Britain lost 245 local newspapers, placing most of the country outside the reach of a regional outlet and indirectly compelling consumers to commit their loyalties to the media conglomerate that most effectively aligned with their biases. Cited in *The Guardian*, media executive Mark Thompson pointed out that "[a] society which fails to provide its different communities and groups with the means to listen and come to understand each other's pasts and presents shouldn't be surprised if mutual incomprehension and division are the consequence."[748] A study from 2016 indicated that the monopolization of local news led to a "democratic deficit," marked by reduced community engagement and increased distrust of public institutions. The hollowing-out of local news has taken on even more dramatic overtones in the United States where it has left more than 65 million Americans in news deserts – areas with only one local newspaper or none at all.[749]

What's more, every mass disappearance of local news creates an opening for larger outlets to shore up their audience. In Poland, state capture of public television and radio outlets has transformed them from relatively neutral conveyor belts of information to "national media" whose stated purpose is to represent unabashed "patriotism," fully aligned with the ideology of the dominant political party. Public television, in particular, maintains a captive audience that it bombards with fear appeals, persuading them that their value system and the stability of the country (inextricably linked to the stability of the party) is in jeopardy. In 2020 alone, evening news broadcasts featured headlines such as "Leftist fascism is destroying Poland," "Children for sale to homosexuals," and when millions of demonstrators took to the streets to oppose a near-total abortion ban implemented by a party-aligned judiciary in the midst of the pandemic, "Harvesters of death among the protesters."[750] Priming society's concerns about health, morality, and systemic stability with no burden of proof and weak accountability mechanisms both magnifies the loyalty of a fearful audience and perpetuates the spiral of fear.

At the same time, in countries with robust political currents that undermine democratic norms, even relative media plurality creates fertile ground for the erosion of truth. Under the presidency of Donald J. Trump, traditional right-wing outlets produced increasingly alarmist material in an attempt to secure a solid user base and outbid one another in their loyalty to the personality in power. The normalization of narratives that sowed doubt about the foundations of democratic institutions found its maximum expression in "alt-right" news channels such as Newsmax and One America News Network (OANN), both of which fueled unfounded distrust of the outcome of the November 2020 elections, ultimately helping to inspire the violent insurrection at the U.S. Capitol in January 2021.[751] Such a media landscape, which has been replicated in other countries, rewards polarization consolidation into media empires but also the splintering of news into mainstream outlets and fringe media with no editorial standards and real potential to attract a sizable audience.

Still, media outlets need not be partisan to channel dread. Violence and the prospect of violence are the greatest triggers of fear channeled through mass media, and mass media is the most effective conduit of that fear. Anyone who has ever flipped through a television channel knows the mechanics: blood sells. Both partisan and moderate news channels maintain a morbid appetite for bloodshed, activating all of our primal anxieties at once. Crime reporting is by far the most notorious and deeply studied example of this. Rare crimes, unusual crimes, random crimes, violent crimes, friendly-next-door-neighbor crimes – all of them generate vastly more coverage than their mundane non-violent counterparts, with few exceptions across societies.[752] In fact, the more media we consume, the more likely it is that we will see this distorted picture as the truth.[753] The result? In 18 of 22 surveys conducted by Gallup in the United States over 25 years, 60 percent or more respondents believed crime was increasing, even though the opposite was overwhelmingly true.[754] Simply put, most of us are inept at diagnosing our country's performance on crime because reality does not match the violent delights served to us through our screens.

Terrorist violence and mass shootings also embody the tensions and contradictions of this system. All terror attacks have two simple goals: to generate fear and uncertainty and to provoke a media reaction with minimal resources. Most of the time, they achieve both. In 2015 and 2016, wall-to-wall coverage of attacks by the "Islamic State" thrust residents of Paris and

Ankara alike into fear of what mortal danger may lurk behind the next pillar in the concrete jungle. Extensive media coverage of such terror attacks is fraught with dilemmas. On the one hand, it provides extremist groups with a platform and indirectly encourages copycat attacks[755]; on the other, it may give the public the information it needs not only to remain safe but also to help law enforcement apprehend attackers.[756]

But the critical downstream effect of mass violence is that it deepens the cleavages that already exist in society through complex patterns of fear. Partisan media frame attacks in diverging ways and displace all other topics with the one that taps into our fear of death. Mass shootings occur every 12.5 days in the United States; as they ramped up in the 2000s and early 2010s, media outlets worked like clockwork to publicize the perpetrators' images, manifestos, life stories, and body counts.[757] Every time, future shooters observed that their predecessors' aims were fulfilled. Random mass murders have almost single-handedly made gun violence the single most polarizing issue in American politics – mainly when they targeted children.[758]

Reporting on terrorism involves the same dynamics: planting a kernel of fear for the safety of those around us who make up our extended tribe.[759] That kernel feeds our existing doubt about just how equipped our government is to deal with future attacks, uprooting support for those in power when we decide they are ill-prepared.[760] Our imperfect perceptions are supremely sensitive to shock, and terrorist attacks can easily hijack our cognitive functions and general opinions about the world. Remember the survey that revealed most people are convinced the world is getting worse? France and Australia were at the very bottom of the ranking; only 3 percent of respondents in each country expressed optimism about the future. When the study was conducted, Paris had just suffered the worst terror attack in its history; Sydney had experienced a deadly hostage situation at the Lindt Cafe the previous year. Both attacks had dominated the news cycle for months. Social trust unravels in democratic societies precisely because of the fear of future attacks, with active consumers of media leading to the deterioration.[761] The silos where we forage for news only tell us whom to fear.

Reporting, even in the most prestigious outlets, is plagued by an interlocking set of biases that skews our perception of the severity of threats, almost all of which end up feeding our fears. Carnage implicitly takes on new layers of importance when its perpetrators strike targets in the "Global North." The Islamic State's terror attacks in Paris and later Nice (2016) triggered coverage that focused on shock, disbelief, and the stories of the victims, generating an outpouring of empathy from around the world. But Dhaka and Baghdad had both suffered devastating attacks two weeks prior, with a death toll of 22 in the capital of Bangladesh as gunmen raided a popular cafe and at least 341 in its Iraqi counterpart as a suicide truck bomb tore through a crowd in the middle of Ramadan. Both, however, quickly fell out of the news cycle. Headlines on brutal events that occur in remote places tend to focus on cold facts: death tolls, locations, and helpful descriptors such as "Hezbollah stronghold" that help Western audiences situate the violence.[762] But evening news programs and breaking news desks are unlikely to focus on the emotional toll of such tragedies on faraway communities or remember individual victims. Paris is familiar; Dhaka requires a caption.[763]

In the same way, news outlets magnify the prominence of violent events that form a small slice of humanity's lead causes of death. Cardiovascular disease (typically followed by cancer) is our species' number one killer in the vast majority of countries around the world, whatever their level of development. But in 2016, despite ending the lives of nearly a third of all Americans who died that year, it commanded little more than 2 percent of the coverage in both *The New York Times* and *The Guardian*.[764] Violence flips this table: brutal deaths commanded an enormous share of all reporting on death in both papers – 70 percent – with terrorism alone claiming a third of the news cycle. Yet, taken together, the three categories were responsible for less than 3 percent of all deaths. To an extent, this is reflected in our fascination with bloodshed: Google searches also disproportionately focused on the morbid, but the scale of the skew did not reach anywhere near that of the major news outlets, strong editorial standard notwithstanding. As individuals and newsrooms, we are drawn to the rare and the unusual. Still, the perpetual focus on dramatic breaking news erects a barrier to our awareness of long-term solutions for humanity's most pressing problems, however mundane they may seem.

Unbreaking the Circle

Thus, and as the previous chapters have shown, natural biases plague humans, and the inflated fear of tomorrow is their paramount expression. Every turning point described in the previous pages – from the rise of the railroad to the vision of doomsday – triggered fear of the unknown. In every case, the expansion of knowledge ultimately repelled obscurantism or continues to erode its bases today. Grasping the mechanics of the steam engine or why the Earth didn't plunge into the Maya underworld of Xibalba in 2012 provides us with snapshots of how information and experience enabled us to conquer a single manifestation of fear.

But like a rapidly evolving apex predator, our brain generates new existential fears to take the place of the old. Therefore, the first step toward dethroning our fears is to look inside our minds and understand the relationship between economic growth, the decline of poverty, and education.

KNOWLEDGE PUNCHES THROUGH

There is a significant cognitive bias that underpins the fear of tomorrow. In every era of human history, new problems emerge that did not exist in our collective consciousness in the era before it. Many of these are new iterations of old dilemmas. For instance, the trolley problem of the 20th century – the moral conundrum between killing five human beings through inaction or one through action when no other choice is available – has been carried over to the world of autonomous vehicles today. However, we still design the algorithms that power them. Just as many of today's pressing concerns have existed for millennia but were perceived as an integral part of the fabric of reality. In the sunbaked towns of the western frontier in the United States of the Civil War era, few would bat an eye at a human being lying motionless in the middle of a dirt road. Medieval Edinburgh was a putrid clump of humanity where festering human waste lined the streets, and corpses disappeared into the open sewer at the base of the hill on which the city stood. Human rights untethered from religious, moral authority were an inconceivable concept for centuries on end.

Because these problems were universal, they were seen as a shared burden. And like most shared burdens in times of slow progress, they were rationalized and normalized. The status quo reigned supreme, with little hope of change, let alone from the grassroots. But when the sands begin to shift, and the underlying issues become rarer, our senses sharpen up, and we become more perceptive of them. Recent scientific advances have revealed our tendency to detect both tangible visual signals and intangible problems in sharper contours when they become less common.[765] Our fear of tomorrow follows the same pathway: not only are we more acutely aware of social problems as they become rarer, but we also feel the rapid pace of change and dread the prospect of society hurtling in a direction we disagree with. A single murder in a sleepy neighborhood will do more to affect public perception of crime than the fifth one this week in a neighborhood immersed in permanent turmoil.

There is a second layer to this, however. We have already seen that the gap between reality and our perceptions of it is often colossal. But we also have an innate optimism bias – it's just that we apply it to ourselves.[766] Surveys consistently find that people are generally either optimistic about their future or expect their lives to be unchanged, while few express pessimism.[767] Meanwhile, our expectations of the future for our economies and societies are not only gloomier but also more erratic. One explanation is that we are more ignorant of big-picture trends. For the average human, statistics are complicated and don't spark much joy. Today, in particular, we are used to living in the moment, and the moment tends to be captured by major events amplified by the media. But at the same time, our optimism may be linked to our feeling of control over what we do and *can* do in our own lives.[768] When we widen the scope of society, we begin to feel like powerless cogs in a machine, and the only outlet we find for our lack of control is resignation and pessimism about the state of our reality.

Dozens of big-picture trends are helping societies overcome the fear of the unknown. Still, most of them flow from the enabling power of three interlocking forces: economic growth, the decline of poverty, and rising education. While only our brains can fight our intolerance of uncertainty, it is critical to remind ourselves of these external forces if we want to go beyond starry-eyed optimism.

About 108 billion people have ever lived on Earth.[769] At the dawn of the 19th century, one billion of them milled around the world. Ninety percent of them lived in extreme poverty; ninety percent of them were illiterate.[770] Those born under such precarious conditions had virtually no hope of social mobility, held in place by scarce education, rock-solid class systems, and religious currents that largely favored the status quo. In a zero-sum world where millions of humans were still enslaved, everyone played zero-sum games, which meant that personal progress typically came at the cost of others.[771]

The aftermath of World War II was a game-changer. As recently as 1950, two-thirds of the world lived in extreme poverty. In the late 1960s, for the first time in human history, postwar progress allowed those who did not to catapult ahead in sheer numbers. In fact, the chasm between the number of those who lived in abject poverty and those who did not continued to widen. Even as the planet's population began to surge, the odds of being born into a situation of extreme deprivation in 1970 were already lower than those of being born outside of the zone of despair. The world hit another milestone in the mid-1980s when the absolute number of people living in extreme poverty dropped for the first time in recorded history after slowly creeping upward for centuries. As it turned out, this decline was prophetic. After 1999, humanity embarked on an unbroken 20-year streak. The raw number of the abjectly poor dropped like a stone, falling below 1 billion in 2011 and below 10 percent of the global population in 2015. Globally, the number of people below most other commonly accepted poverty lines has followed the same patterns.[772] Only the coronavirus pandemic halted this trend – and although its fallout will continue to echo for years, there is no reason to believe its effects will be permanent.

Of all significant metrics, the struggle to reduce poverty is where our perceptions sit in perhaps the starkest contrast with reality. The global market research firm IPSOS found that, despite experiencing the most dramatic fall in absolute poverty in its history over the last 20 years, most of the world still believes the exact opposite and only about a fifth get it right.[773] Although pessimists outnumber optimists everywhere but in China, the study found the most knowledgeable respondents in developing countries that had recently seen the impact of vigorous growth with their own eyes, such as Kenya, India, and Indonesia. These same countries overwhelmingly expect positive trends to continue in the future. Our knowledge about poverty is also continuing to grow as satellite technology, and other innovations enable us to conduct poverty assessments in places they have never been conducted before.[774] Although much of the world still lives in relative deprivation, we are better equipped to make interventions more targeted, and the eradication of extreme poverty has appeared on the horizon.

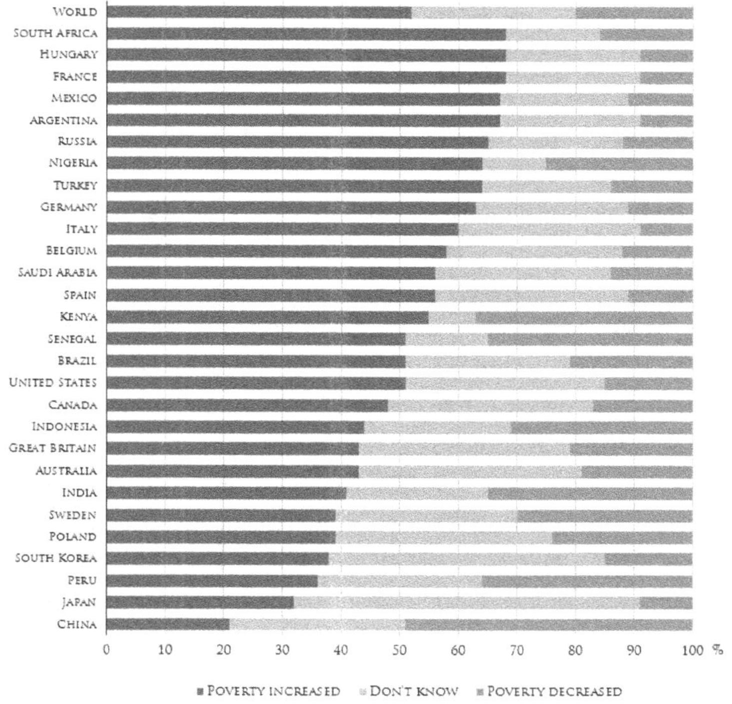

Fig. 2. Perceptions of change in global extreme poverty levels across 28 countries. The survey asked, "In the last 20 years, the proportion of the world population living in extreme poverty has...?"[775]

The eradication of poverty will not single-handedly chase away humanity's existential fears or increase our collective resilience. Education, however, may. Research has revealed a powerful link not just between schooling and individual income but also national economic growth and stronger social capital – the collective value of our social networks and their willingness to embrace standard norms through reciprocity and trust, especially when educational attainment is surging.[776] The world today is more educated than ever before, owing to a staggering pace of progress that has gone hand in hand with poverty reduction. Global literacy has performed a 180-degree turn from the early 19th century, approaching 90 percent in 2020.[777] The poorest countries are leading the surge in primary school enrollment after decades of stagnation, most of them improving by double digits since the year 2000. Societies are mercilessly whittling down gender gaps in education as well. In the mid-1930s, women in Asia-Pacific could expect to spend a quarter of the time in school that their male friends spent. Today, that gap is almost closed.[778] By 2100, projections suggest that only about 83 million people in the world will have no formal education – fewer than live today in West Bengal, India's fourth most populous state.[779]

Of course, more schooling by itself is not a silver bullet. There is no straight line between education and enlightenment, and the quality and substance of what is taught, as well as the educational structures in which young generations are embedded, are likely to weigh heavily on our success in mitigating or eradicating fear, as other chapters in this book persuasively demonstrate. In the United States, where educational attainment reaches new peaks every year, the government consumer protection and fraud watchdog received nearly 500,000 reports of online and offline impostor scams in 2020, which cost its victims upward of $1.2 billion, over three and a half times more than they did in 2017.[780] Even advance-fee scams (popularly but inaccurately known as "Nigerian prince scams") cost Americans nearly a million dollars a year and continue to achieve success in other countries despite having long since become the subject of scornful humor and a mark of extreme naïveté.[781] As our technology evolves, so do the vectors of attack of those who prey on the gullible: emails give way to Facebook messages, while dollar transfers via Western Union cede to cryptocurrency transactions.

Global calamities instill in us an additional feeling of urgency mixed with desperation, rendering us not only more susceptible to fraud and less inclined to use reason but also possibly more likely to fall back on superstition. While there are no credible cross-national data on revenue streams among clairvoyants, astrologers, and numerologists, isolated reports from India and other countries suggest that the perpetual lockdown and the financial woes of the COVID-19 pandemic were a boon for the industry, which thrives on purporting to bring order to uncertainty.[782] Palm readers, too, adapted to social isolation by studying detailed photographs of clients' hands instead of inspecting them in person.

All these examples are iterations of the same tendencies that have structured our patterns of thinking for millennia. After all, superstition and fear are old bedfellows. However, while this may seem immune to change, the smokescreen of a prolonged crisis should not overshadow long-term trends. Besides its association with better economic outcomes, education is an independent force that reduces religiosity, religious acts, and superstitious beliefs in one fell swoop, according to recent research.[783] It exerts the same effect on anti-immigration attitudes, implicitly reducing our fear of the unknown stranger.[784]

But what about war and peace? What about the forward march of democracy? Famed psychologist Steven Pinker has argued that the "better angels of our nature" have come to dominate in the new millennium. We are now immersed in the "Long Peace," where violence has simmered down, and regimes have drifted toward democracy.[785] The vast majority of humanity today lives under some form of a democratic regime, while the population living under the yoke of totalitarianism is overwhelmingly concentrated in China.[786] At the same time, the spread of democracy is a very recent phenomenon. In 1900, 112 autocracies existed in the world, compared to a single, lone democracy in the form of the United States, and democratic systems only gained a numerical advantage in the 21st century.[787] When coupled with functional mechanisms to enforce the rule of law, democratic governance instills confidence in us that our political convictions will not lead us to the hangman's noose and that, however haltingly, the rights of various minorities will be protected or at least acknowledged, and indeed to a greater degree than in regimes that steamroll them.

But the relative freshness of democracy is precisely why it is too early to herald the "end of history" and embrace the thought that peaceful liberal democracy is here to stay. Democracies might not always be the ones to provide the balm against the fear of tomorrow. At the same time, variations in violence are extremely sensitive to the fickleness of human decision-making. In the 21st century, bloodshed may be readily replaced by more crippling hostile tactics, including technological dominance. Authoritarian practices have increased even in democratic regimes, and constitutional challenges are not always an effective breakwater. In 2020 alone, the world's most populous democracy shut down the Internet more than 70 times, anticipating or reacting to turmoil, and the president of the world's first modern democracy refused to state that he would peacefully concede in a democratic contest.

In these circumstances, how certain can we be that democracy is here to stay and thrive? Pasquale Cirillo and Nassim Taleb believe it is impossible to figure out the risk of violence or the ultimate triumph of democracy. All it takes is a single "black swan" – an unpredictable event with extreme consequences – to blow apart the entire structure and turn the "Long Peace" into a statistical blip.[788] The flagship *Freedom in the World* report published by the US-based NGO Freedom House has consistently warned of the erosion of civil and political liberties, its growing urgency encapsulated in increasingly alarming titles: *Democracy in Crisis* (2018), *Democracy in Retreat* (2019), and *A Leaderless Struggle for Democracy* (2020).[789] Every year since 2006, countries with net declines in the freedoms measured in the organization's report have outnumbered those with net improvements. However, recent iterations have shown that these declines are concentrated at the top and bottom of the scale.[790] In particular, regimes led by strongmen with a penchant for defying democratic norms even when those same norms elevated them to office tend to crack down on everyday criminality with an iron fist, replacing violence on the streets with violence by security forces, as illustrated in the Philippines by the brutal harvest of President Rodrigo Duterte's war on drugs, which saw thousands of indiscriminate murders committed by police forces.

Winston Churchill's famous quip that "democracy is the worst form of government, except for all those other forms" fittingly describes the dual-edged relationship between democracy and uncertainty. Democratic processes allow us to make our voices heard, but under the right circumstances, they lead us to elect leaders who are anathema to those processes. Acknowledging that democracy brings innumerable benefits to society while recognizing its tenuous and fragile nature is a critical element of taming our fear of tomorrow because it reminds us that positive change must be cultivated to take root. There is a difference between the prevalence of democracy and peace on the one hand and the eradication of poverty and rising education on the other. For the former, we are not able to confidently assess risk. For the latter, the chances of a long-term reversal of fortune are minimal. Literacy and education rates have been improving for at least two hundred years – sometimes at a trot, sometimes at a gallop, through world wars and unforgiving pandemics. In combination with our renewed understanding of our minds' weaknesses, the long-term certainty of these trends is one of our most promising weapons in the struggle against uncertainty.

(Fear of) Tomorrow Never Dies

Flipping the Script in Our Darkest Hour

This chapter opened with an invisible specter of doom – the first global airborne pandemic with a death toll of more than one million in most people's living memory. Its social and economic impact will continue to ripple through the world for years to come.

But even at the height of the crisis, rays of hope emerged. Fears of a social recession, characterized by an extreme and widespread feeling of isolation-induced loneliness, were shown to be potentially conquerable.[791] Our networks of mutual support sprang into action once we crowded into our improvised bunkers and shut the door behind us. In some places, loneliness spiked in the early stages of the lockdown, but as the crisis dragged on, the feeling of abandonment not only returned to baseline levels but, in some cases, even improved.[792]

As COVID-19 ravaged the world, the social fabric that binds us pushed us to reconnect with long-lost friends, strengthen our bonds with our families, check up on elderly neighbors, join support groups, and explore new ways of doing old things. Obsessive hoarding of essential goods gave way to online and offline community building.[793] Thriving new spaces emerged to provide critical services remotely.[794] Unforeseen optimism about the prospects for more inclusive work environments surged in the wake of the pandemic.[795] Zooming into the household, surveys revealed that working from home improved fathers' relationships with their children.[796] The spread of the virus drove a growing sentiment of national unity in some countries, albeit with notable exceptions like the United States, where it drove the stake of polarization further into the ground.[797] Around the world, people parried the blow of physical isolation by intensifying their virtual connections, turning a shared existential fear into a shared existential burden.

These explosions of empathy and solidarity in the fallout of a crisis are nearly universal. Cataclysmic events "dra[g] us into emergencies that require we act, and act altruistically, bravely, and with initiative in order to survive or save our neighbors, no matter how we vote or what we do for a living."[798] And accounts of self-sacrifice are not just exceptions in a sea of selfishness; in fact, the darkest hour brings out our greatest qualities. Hundreds of field studies have shown that the dominance of collective panic and antisocial behavior during disasters is a false myth that has filtered into public consciousness through the media.[799] In Katrina-swept New Orleans, organized, pro-social behavior by loosely knit groups of people dwarfed the looting that the newscasts claimed reigned supreme.[800] The minutes following the 2001 World Trade Center attack were full of altruism toward strangers on the stairwells, and subsequent surveys showed increases in kindness, spirituality, and teamwork among Americans.[801] And lest we think that altruistic impulses are limited to adults in wealthy, democratic societies of the Global North, the 2008 Sichuan earthquake in China – one of the deadliest in recorded history – spurred massive civic engagement against a backdrop of authoritarianism, including among children.[802] Emerging research suggests that the same personality traits that give us a stronger shot at survival during a disaster also make us more inclined to lend a helping hand.[803] Fearfulness is not among them.

Positive precedents like these do not mean that we should embrace crises with naive optimism. They do not negate the high death toll of the coronavirus pandemic or the disproportionate and often hidden impact of the pandemic on the poor.[804] On the contrary, they set forth a challenge to infuse post-pandemic life with knowledge gained during the crisis. One final look a hundred years into the past gives us grounds to remain hopeful in that regard. The devastating harvest of the 1918 Spanish flu awakened public awareness of human health, kindled the first plans for universal healthcare in countries like Germany and Russia, and unlocked vast troves of funding for vaccine research that led to the development of the first vaccines for tuberculosis, diphtheria, scarlet fever, and whooping cough in the first ten years after the pandemic swept over the world.[805] The "mother of all pandemics" also gave birth to the tools to defeat them.

What innovations and long-term progress will germinate from the coronavirus pandemic and the one that follows it? Today, we have a better scientific and statistical foundation than ever before to play Nostradamus – but we also have to embrace uncertainty. What we resist tends to persist. It is critical to understand the external forces that should help deactivate our fears as well as our own brain's tendency to inflate them. But we must also come to terms with never being fully in control; otherwise, our intolerance of uncertainty will continue shattering the roof of our minds, reaching new heights, and leaving us more miserable even as the world continues to improve. In the words of Margaret Heffernan, "Anyone who tries to tell us they know the future is simply trying to own it."[806]

A CONSTANT COMPANION

Of all the fears discussed in this book, the fear of tomorrow is the most amorphous. Its distinguishing feature is adaptability: much like our Australopithecine ancestors adapted to danger through fear, our fear of what is to come has adapted to the updated expectations of modern times. As an intangible shapeshifter detached from any one target, it will survive as a spectral presence in our lives. Although we cannot eradicate it, we can mitigate it – not just by stepping away from old sources of prejudice and striving to fill our knowledge gaps, but most importantly, by acknowledging the flaws in our thinking.

At their core, the enablers of fear we have discussed in this volume are fragile – even the mightiest of them fall. Societies driven by progress over superstition are antifragile; disorder increases their long-term resilience as they overcome and learn from challenges.[807] While we should not welcome chaos, we must use every opportunity to extract knowledge from it. None of what you have read in these pages means that it's time to rest on our laurels. None of it means that we can switch to autopilot because the eradication of poverty and disease is set in stone (it is not). And none of it diminishes the importance of defending human rights from the encroachment of repression. If anything, the opposite is true. As the uncertainty of physical survival recedes for most of humanity, and self-expression values take the reins, it is critical to identify the areas in which we fall short and prevent ourselves from backsliding. But anchoring our pursuit of a new Enlightenment in the idea that the world is getting worse is a straight path to activist burnout.[808] It is futile to crave a simpler time before the dawn of the Internet, mass media, political personalities, and religion because it was also a time of smallpox, open sewers, public executions, and normalized desperation.

Instead, we should confront our modern fears with the understanding that we are contributing to the betterment of the world that is already happening. The modern-day gives us the opportunity to fight for rights that most of us could not fight for five decades ago and did not know we had a century ago. If we grasp that we are not chained by the mental darkness championed by institutions that stoke the fire, then surviving today's crises can help us not just counter the fear of tomorrow but come out stronger than before.

EIGHT
CLOSING FEAR(S): MINORITY REPORT

Wojciech Janicki

Fear is one of the oldest and strongest human emotions. There are countless reasons why we are afraid, with fear of the unknown occupying a prominent place among the most important.[809] Suppose the scarcity of knowledge that is the breeding ground of fear falls on the fertile ground of poverty and anxiety about tomorrow. In that case, we try to tame a significant part of our fears by placing ourselves in the care of supernatural forces. These forces, if we plead with them effectively enough, will allow us to survive and spare us from the cascade of misfortunes that we will undoubtedly experience if we do not obey them. Or, to go a step further, it is not the supernatural forces themselves that we must obey, but those who consider themselves to be the anointed messengers of heaven. And they share with us arcane knowledge about what heaven expects of us, how we should live, what is right and what is wrong, what is moral and according to God's will, and what God disapproves of.

We would fear much less if only religious systems of all persuasions demanded that we reject nefarious inventions like railroads and electricity. If they did, then liberating ourselves from the constraints of religious beliefs would be a gate to a path through a forest of rational explanations for the phenomena that surround us. Ultimately, this would mitigate all our fears. The development of civilization and progress of knowledge and science would guarantee that, instead of fearing the unknown, we would intensify our efforts to learn about it. Those who are not bound to any religion – and who in their lives are guided not by faith but by reason (and morality) – would guarantee that the myths that generate many of our fears would gradually be consigned to the dustbin of history.

Unfortunately, our fear and dread of the unknown thrive not only on the grounds of religion. Every day, we sail into ever-wider waters of knowledge, we understand more, more of us can read and write, and the percentage of people with university degrees is growing. Yet fear is still ubiquitous. Granted, we mythologize fewer and fewer phenomena. We are less inclined than ever to use faith and religion to explain the causes of previously incomprehensible phenomena, and science has already explained much of what we did not know. Yet it is still doubtful whether we can distinguish better than our ancestors between what is desirable, safe, and beneficial from what is undesirable, dangerous, and threatening.

The mind-killer: What we know we shouldn't fear but do

In the last 150 years or so, we have learned that electricity is useful and that trains are not an instrument of Satan whose temptation will lead us straight to the gates of hell but rather a convenient, fast, and safe means of transportation. Today, nearly all of us understand this. Far fewer of us, even in countries with a high level of education and near-zero illiteracy rates, are aware that the so-called end of the world, as prophesied by holy scriptures and self-proclaimed prophets and understood in biblical terms, will not happen during our lifetime or even in the foreseeable future. Many of us join the ranks of the opponents of nuclear energy, completely ignoring the fact that every indicator that assesses the safety of different types of power plants speaks against coal-based energy, and nuclear power plants are safe. In the last half-century, humanity has lived through at least 29 ends of the world, as predicted by various soothsayers, and the world continues to spin. Exactly 50 years ago, when the world's population was almost 3.9 billion, Donella Meadows' team issued the famous report *The Limits to Growth*,[810] which predicted a global catastrophe around the year 2000 caused by a growing population that we would not be able to feed, and depleting mineral resources without which the world economy would collapse. Today, the Earth is home to twice as many people as it was then – 8 billion – and the number of those who are malnourished and hungry continues to decline.

Meanwhile, we have also lived through at least 19 dates for which serious institutions predicted the arrival of peak oil,[811] yet world oil production continues to rise. The standard of living of people around the world has been steadily improving for at least two hundred years, but we stubbornly refuse to see it and overwhelmingly believe that things are bad and will get worse. The unknown is perhaps what we fear most – and tomorrow is the epitome of the unknown.

How do we explain these surprising regularities? Why is it that societies in highly developed countries, which in principle are most empowered to use knowledge shaped by the educational system to interpret the reality that surrounds them, are so often afraid of things that should not be feared at all? Do we really not see that we are acting akin to our 19th-century ancestors, driven by panicked fear of electricity or trains, when we talk about our fears today?

Perhaps the widespread fear of many phenomena stems from the fact that literacy and a school or even university diploma are not at all enough to broaden our horizons sufficiently. The educational systems of most modern countries have their roots in European thought, which, on the invisible assembly line of the late colonial era, transmitted its ideas about teaching to almost the entire world. The Prussian school, which was the first to make education compulsory for all, occupies a prominent place in this. Created nearly 200 years ago, the conceptual basis of this school, whose task was to prepare throngs of devoted and obedient state subjects equipped with the same competencies and knowledge as if they were all molded from a giant matrix, has not been significantly modified to this day. The school is still a production line where top-down curricula, sets of readings, textbooks approved by state commissions, and the rhythmic cadence of class-break-class-break shape more or less successful copies of the Citizen. At the end of the conveyor belt is a state hungry for officials thinking in schemes according to predesigned guidelines, not deviating too much from the expected pattern. It teaches encyclopedic knowledge, verifies it with final state exams, and disallows interpretations different from those provided in the answer key for the high school exam by teachers who are a generation older than today's high school graduates – teachers who themselves were shaped according to the same pattern.

How can a person who, for years, was taught to reproduce what was required of them at school obediently have a mind that is open to novelty? How are they supposed to question the standard way of thinking about the reality around them, and how are they supposed to go beyond the framework into which they have been forced? Of course, many of us are doing just that – eschewing the system. How many of us are there? What portion of society are those who look critically at reality, able to step out of the shoes sewn by the educational system and take a bird's eye view of everything to adopt a different perspective and be able to see more? It really doesn't matter whether we use the standard distribution curve, the modified Pareto principle, or yet another distribution to find the answer. Some of us will never question certain truths – and it is only by questioning truths and stepping outside the box that we can move forward.

We can also try to explain everything on the basis of evolutionary biology. One of the attributes we inherited from our ancestors is the so-called reptilian brain, which triggers automatic reactions in a threatening situation. This is the mechanism that is responsible for our instinctive reflexes, the one that spares us from having to think about whether to run when it's clearly time to run, which saves us precious seconds and may even save our lives. The activity of this brain blocks the work of the logical brain; when we are afraid, we do not reason. The question is, are we really unable to separate these momentary emotions of fear in a situation of sudden danger from the instilled and manufactured fear that we have cultivated within ourselves? We should be able to; after all, we are different from our cave-dwelling ancestors.

CHANGE, CHANGE, CHANGE

It is puzzling that many of us are unable to understand not only the need to step outside the box but also to learn from what we see and experience, often for many years. Progress is one of our most common everyday experiences. It will soon be 150 years since the first telephone rang for the first time in the history of the world. Its physical appearance had so little in common with today's telephone that only a select few would be able to correctly identify it upon encountering it at the museum. Over time, the telephone evolved, a speaker and microphone were integrated into a single handset, and the switchboard operator who manually connected conversations between two people using a panel with holes, each corresponding to one end user, was replaced by a spinning dial. Today's young people no longer remember this type of telephone, often struggling to retrieve from the depths of their memories even the landline phone – a device with small, square buttons attached to the wall by a wire. Today, we have cell phones. In fact, we have portable computers because placing calls is just one of the several hundred functions of a smartphone. On top of that, we have satellite phones, which allow voice communication and digital data transfers between any location on the globe.

We know all this, don't we? And each of us could probably give at least a dozen examples of other inventions whose emergence and subsequent evolution are perfectly mundane, obvious proof that the world is changing continuously. That tomorrow will not be the same as today, and yesterday was still different.

Today, we can grow a human ear on the back of a rat or grow it under the skin on a person's forearm and then transplant it to where it belongs.[812] We are able to build and program a tractor that will independently plow a field, saving the farmer the trouble – essentially a more sophisticated version of the robotic home vacuum cleaner, which has already become a component of our everyday life. We are able to produce light despite a lack of access to the power grid, batteries, or a generator: all we need is an old plastic bottle, some water, and a few drops of chlorine to capture sunlight during the day and enjoy several hours of light at night.[813] Our most modern trains levitate on a magnetic cushion over the track and run at 430 kph, and we are testing even faster ones.[814] A trip across the United States on board such a train, from New York to San Francisco, would not take several weeks, as it did by stagecoach in the mid-19th century, nor even seven days, as the first trains on this route did – but less than twelve hours. The fact that we are able to launch a rocket into the sky at a speed enabling it to be permanently placed into orbit around the Earth, that is, exceeding 7.9 kilometers per second, does not impress anyone anymore – even though such a speed achieved in horizontal motion would carry passengers on our cross-country American route in less than ten minutes! Similarly, splitting an atomic nucleus – a body with a diameter about a billion (!) times smaller than the diameter of a human hair – has also settled into our everyday reality. Today, we treat it as normal.

How is it possible that we consider normal and obvious inventions that the average person is unable to grasp with their mind and explain how they work, but at the same time, we are not ready to admit that progress as such is taking place? And that, since it has happened in the past and is happening before our very eyes, the probability that we will suddenly stop progressing is virtually zero.

Brakemen are among us

Well, there are those among us who wish to stop development at all costs. Whenever a new invention comes along, the lead brakemen are almost always representatives of religious movements. This is hardly surprising, as it is in the nature of religion to have fixed beliefs and behaviors. Many of us subconsciously transfer our moral conservatism to our attitude toward technical inventions, automatically looking for nefarious or even Satanic undertones in how they operate – despite the fact that one has absolutely nothing to do with the other. However, it was in this spirit that bishops in the 19th century called for the abandonment of electricity, claiming it would lead to the destruction of the world. Some refuse to use this invention even today and, for similar reasons, derived their unconventional lifestyle from moral principles. For some Mennonite communities, the light of oil and gas lamps is moral, but the light of an electric bulb is against the will of the Almighty and should not be used. Incidentally, girls in these communities attend school only until the age of 12, as they don't need more – the primary skill they need to master is how to run their future husband's household and how to clean, wash, and cook. In case they do not know something that their peers will learn in school in the later stages of education, they can always ask the pastor.[815]

Luminaries from the world of science and literature can also be a brake on development and progress. These are people from whom one would expect openness to change, progressiveness, and the ability to apply the scientific method to learning about the world rather than placing one's feelings and emotions above experience and knowledge. Unfortunately, trains were universally feared by doctors, writers, philosophers, and intellectuals of all stripes. This is problematic, as seeing the fanatical resistance of religious circles to change, one would be inclined to seek support for the idea of progress on the hallowed grounds of knowledge and science – but all too often, this community also positions itself as part of the canon of resistance to change. Moreover, it is on this ground that the virus of fear of what awaits us in the future grows exceptionally well. Scientists are the ones who have long been convincing us that there are too many of us on Earth, that mass starvation is just around the corner, and that natural resources (and especially oil) will soon run out and a global calamity will occur. The fact that none of these catastrophic predictions, which have been pouring out of the scientific literature for many decades, has ever come true somehow does not seem to bother anyone. In particular, it does not bother the authors of these forecasts. Immediately after their predicted catastrophe fails to materialize, they set out to prove that they did not mean it, or that it was only one of many variants of how the situation might develop, and that one of the remaining variants will most likely come true any minute now. Alternatively, they move on and get busy preparing another forecast. They formulate it using the same tools, which have produced incorrect results more than once, but they remain undeterred without drawing any lessons from their failure.

A third group of those who oppose the introduction of technological innovations are those who stand to lose from them because they compete with emerging inventions. Thus, the owners of stagecoaches and navigable canals blocked the development of railroads in every possible way, and Thomas Edison argued that the alternating current produced by his competitors, which today runs through every outlet on Earth, was terrible, and that only the direct current offered by his company was good. In all likelihood, he was fully aware that he was lying. But what wouldn't one do to beat the competition in a market game? This has happened in the past, and the cycle will continue. An excellent contemporary example is poultry meat produced from stem cells without raising or killing animals, which is called clean meat by the company producing it. This lab-grown meat was created in response to the ever-increasing demand for meat and in the face of increasingly vocal opposition to animal farming and slaughter, whether for humanitarian reasons or due to concerns about the impact of animal farming on global climate change. On the one hand, in 2020, a product of this kind was approved for sale in Singapore; on the other, a few years earlier in the United States, American cattle breeders asked the authorities to ban the use of the name "clean meat," claiming that it is not meat – even though that is exactly what it is. Here, the fear of competition is evident.[816]

Finally, there is a fourth group of brakers. They form a rather distinctive collective, as they do not have to be convinced that progress and development are a threat to us. They can only spread and exploit the widespread fear of the unknown for their purposes. Politicians are the primary messengers through whom we receive news and views of the world by way of media outlets, only too willing to give them a platform. Those who select the information that will find its way into the daily news service know a truth as old as the world: blood sells. Especially if it is blood that is spilled in our neighborhood and in places generally considered safe. In highly developed countries, the institution of the state promises us safety, so it is here that any event that disrupts this sense provides excellent material to broadcast or publish.[817] Inducing and sustaining a sense of danger guarantees viewership. As we showed in Chapter 7, the media's gigantic overrepresentation of terrorism and murder as causes of death triggers panic about the people whom viewers identify as terrorists, and no amount of statistics will convince them that cardiovascular disease is our most prolific killer. Every one of us could reduce the level of danger to ourselves by taking better care of our own diet or physical activity. Still, we are not afraid of these things, as the television has not provided us with information about them.[818] Thus, the media, as a transmission belt for information, certainly contributes to increasing our level of fear of anything it considers to be a suitable scarecrow. New inventions usually lend themselves to this purpose quite well.

Whether out of ill will, narrow-mindedness, lack of knowledge, religious fanaticism, or fear of increasing competition, many end up bearing the banners of fear of change, and they use them to persuade their fellow human beings successfully. As a result, our societies fear what is new, reject change, and live in constant fear of tomorrow. Fortunately, they sometimes reflect on the mistakes of the past, but those reflections often take a long time to emerge. And when they do, we express them with a bitter smile on our faces – as when Pope John Paul II, recapitulating the long-standing resistance of the Catholic clergy to the railroad, spoke of "momentary misunderstandings."[819]

RARE BLACK BIRDS AND THE PERILS OF FORECASTING

In every era, humanity faces a multitude of problems. We face both their objective reality and our fears about whether the coping methods we have adopted will be successful and produce the desired results. And we are afraid of failing. We scare ourselves by focusing on the problem as such and getting high on our predictions of impending disaster. We also scare others to win them over to our idea and to make the rest of us realize how deeply wrong they are if they are not afraid.

But perhaps it would be better not to focus on rehashing what the future might have in store for us according to one of our numerous scenarios because our ability to predict the future is unbelievably poor. Perhaps our fears, whatever they pertain to, will not come true, just as our fears about electricity or railroads have not come true, just as our fears about nuclear energy are unfounded in light of publicly available data, and just as we are unnecessarily afraid of the depletion of resources or overpopulation. After all, none of these phenomena, despite numerous analyses and forecasts, have occurred.

Why do we make forecasting mistakes and fail to learn from them? Well, forecasting itself is inherently difficult. The world is much more complex and complicated than we think. At the same time, to describe this complexity in our models, we only include what is predictable, repeatable, measurable, and what we have come to think of in the first place. Meanwhile, events that were not predicted by anyone happen so often and have such an overwhelming impact on our reality that all our predictions go haywire. Who predicted, in the second half of the 1980s, that the Soviet Union would cease to exist in five years? Who predicted that, in 2014, Crimea (and later Donetsk and Lugansk) would be invaded by a battalion of "green men" and Ukraine would *de facto* lose part of its territory? Who predicted the suicide attacks on the World Trade Center towers and the Pentagon in September 2001? Nobody. If anyone had predicted even this last event, it would never have happened. And the changes that each of these events precipitated on the global geopolitical chessboard were enormous.

Shock events are not the only ones that radically alter our reality. Gradual changes, which slowly creep into our world, also have this quality. Who thought that the *Electronic Numerical Integrator and Computer* (ENIAC), constructed in 1943-1945 – a behemoth that occupied 1600 square feet and helped the military carry out complex mathematical calculations – would transform a few decades later into a handheld, portable computer we could use to read, write, calculate, watch movies, listen to music, and make a video call to an aunt living on the other side of the world in near-real time? Who in the mid-20th century foresaw the rise of the Internet – a universally accessible network for the exchange of data and information that would change the way the entire world works as radically as possible? Neither the first computers nor the original form of today's Internet were foreseen, planned, or appreciated at first.

In our forecasts of future events and developments, we find no room for what we do not yet know. How can we make room for what we don't know if we don't know it? That is exactly the problem. We do not know how to take into account the occurrence of rare, unknown events in the future – events that we are not able to deduce from the experience of our past. Nassim Nicholas Taleb, an American economist, philosopher, and trader, calls such events black swans. Their occurrence is so rare and so unlikely as to make them essentially impossible – and yet they happen. As in Taleb's example, a turkey can be fed for a thousand days by humans, whom the turkey comes to trust, thinking them to be such friendly creatures since they give it food every day. And then comes a cold day at the end of November, called Thanksgiving by these friendly beings. All of the turkey's assessments, extrapolations of past experiences into the future, and growing trust in these beings turn out to be worthless. Its prediction of a good life until a peaceful, natural death has failed.[820]

Black swans may or may not be beneficial to us. Something may happen that makes our lives very difficult: another large meteorite hitting the Earth, for instance, not in the Siberian outback, but in the densely populated Netherlands, killing many people, destroying many buildings and roads, and upsetting the stability of the markets. Or something may come along that makes our lives easier, and one of the problems that has been keeping us up at night will disappear from the headlines because it will no longer be a problem. What can serve as an example? That is much harder to predict. We can easily predict the repetition of a bad scenario that is known to us from the past. On the other hand, to predict an event that is beneficial to us or a technology that will solve our problems and does not exist today requires magical clairvoyance, which we do not possess. At most, we can provide examples from the past where we have successfully solved a problem thanks to progress – as in Chapter 6, where we described the solution to the fear that New York City would be flooded with horse dung up to the second floor of Manhattan houses before 1930 due to of a glut of horse-drawn carriages in the Big Apple.

Doomed to die? From Melancholia to Waterworld

We are at the threshold of the third decade of the 21st century. We have solved, for better or worse, many of the problems our grandparents suffered from half a century ago. We are slowly and laboriously confronting other problems, and new ones are emerging every day. One of those, which we increasingly perceive as the greatest threat to ourselves and the generations to come, are the changes to the Earth's natural environment caused by ever-increasing human pressure. With more and more people and ever-increasing levels of consumption, the Earth's fragile ecosystem is facing increasingly difficult challenges.

According to many, the biggest of the problems in this category is climate change. Fears about the rising temperature of the Earth and all its effects are becoming more common. We are afraid that the melting ice caps of Antarctica and Greenland and the vanishing mountain glaciers and ice covering the Arctic Ocean will raise the water level in seas and oceans so much that densely inhabited coastal areas will be partially flooded. We fear an increase in the frequency and intensity of extreme weather events like thunderstorms and tornadoes. We fear murderous heat waves, droughts resulting in forest fires, dried-up rivers in the summer, and floods in the winter. We fear the desertification of agricultural and other hardly habitable lands, which will undoubtedly trigger local food disasters and increased migratory processes, with all the consequences they bring. We are afraid of losing jobs in agriculture, forestry, tourism, and the energy industry. We fear for the disappearing species of plants and animals, whose adaptation to rapidly changing living conditions is often impossible.[821]

Just to be clear, before anyone labels us denialists, we are not disputing the fact that rapid climate change on Earth is occurring. Nor are we discussing whether and to what extent human activity is responsible for the process and its consequences. Tens of thousands of scientific texts have been devoted to this issue, and most of them, including every single report of the Intergovernmental Panel on Climate Change (IPCC) established in 1988, indicate a probability close to one hundred percent that humans have caused these changes.[822]

For the sake of completeness, however, it should be noted that there are scientific works that demonstrate that the climate on Earth is a volatile force and has been changing since the beginning of our planet's existence; it was changing in violent and radical ways even when nobody in the Universe had heard of *Homo sapiens* and its activities yet. However, this is not a discussion we want to contribute to here. We accept that human activity is responsible for climate change. Our question is: should we fear it? Do the fears we verbalize make sense? Will it not turn out, sometime from now, that the efforts we are making today in the field of modern technology will lead – perhaps quite accidentally – to the appearance of a black swan? An unforeseen and unpredictable thing, as the very nature of black swans implies, that will solve our problem? Or it may be that our many models indicating the future negative impact of the rise in Earth's temperature levels have missed some important factor – one that will affect the situation so dramatically that our problems will be solved precisely because of it.

Adopting a wait-and-see attitude and doing nothing makes sense in the case of a future collision between the Earth and another celestial body half the size of the Moon. We have nowhere to run anyway, so it's not even worth trying to, as beautifully depicted by Lars von Trier in his multi-layered and ambiguous film *Melancholia*. Therefore, we do not call for readers to give in to passive inertia but to reflect on two issues.

First and foremost, let's reflect on whether we are certain that the changes looming on the horizon will be a disaster for humanity. This is worth pondering, as perhaps the common denominator of all our fears about what the climate of particular places on Earth will look like is the fear of change itself and the fear of tomorrow. An excellent, sober analysis of the situation will lead us to the conclusion that, according to our scenarios, the world will look different than it does today, but this does not automatically entail a catastrophe, whether for *Homo sapiens* as a species or individual humans.

According to the IPCC's Fifth Assessment Report of

2014, the combined impact of all the factors that are causing ocean levels to rise is less than 3 millimeters per year. Even if the predictions of sea level rise of a few dozen centimeters by the end of this century prove true, we should draw a line on hypsometric maps showing the new coastline to see which artifacts of humanity will really be flooded.[823] Among other things, this exercise will show us that the tiny islands scattered across the Pacific, whose future inundation we hear about regularly, are home to only 3.5 million people (slightly more than the population of Athens) and are primarily mountainous, which means they are absolutely safe. The most populous country in this part of the world, Fiji, with a population of nearly one million, is located on several hundred islands with elevations of more than 4,000 feet above sea level. The rise in sea level by several dozen centimeters in the lifetime of three generations means that the next generations will build their houses a little higher than before, rather than on the seashore. This is not a dramatic outcome: people have permanently moved and changed their place of residence, and the process of construction and gradual degradation of the substance used for their buildings has been in place since time immemorial. The scale of this displacement forced by climate change will be much greater in southern Vietnam, Bangladesh, and some parts of the coasts of China and Thailand, among others, because many more people live in these places. Still, here, too, we can envision people who will only be born in several decades building new houses in higher locations than before.

Sea level rise is just one of the many consequences of climate change on Earth, but it is perhaps the most obvious. All of them are worth examining individually in a similar way. Perhaps it will turn out that we are afraid of the change as such, while in a few generations, people facing new circumstances will cope no worse than we do now.

Second, let's reflect on whether the changes we are forecasting today are certain to occur. Back in the 1970s, scientists confidently predicted a coming ice age. This event was to run a similar course as the Little Ice Age known from the Middle Ages, which lasted from the 16th century to the middle of the 19th century. We feared that the cooling would deplete our energy resources and lower our potential for food production and that these factors combined would lead to widespread hunger. Today, we fear rising temperatures, falling potential for food production, and, thus, widespread hunger. Is the current temperature distribution on Earth the only one that is safe for humanity and the only one we are able to accept? Is every change – any change – a catastrophic threat? Even today, some scientists continue to warn us of the imminent cooling of the Earth. Changes in the activity of the Sun would be the primary culprit, especially changes in our star's magnetic field, which, according to some researchers, will soon lead to a significant global drop in temperature.[824]

Which group of scientists is right? Does this problem not bring to mind the widespread fears of overpopulation that we dealt with in Chapter 5, which today are accompanied by the fear of mass aging and the impending depopulation of much of the world's countries? Many believe that world population decline will be one of the most important megatrends we will see in the 21st century. According to one of the latest forecasts published in the prestigious scientific journal *Lancet*, Poland, which today is home to 38 million people, will have a population of only 15 million in the year 2100![825]

On a similar note, can we confidently rule out the possibility that some time from now, an invention will emerge that will consign all our carbon problems to the dustbin of history? Perhaps it will be one of Elon Musk's teams,[826] or perhaps some other team, who will go down in history as the one that solved our problem, and a hundred years from now, someone will be writing about it the way we write about Stephenson's locomotive fears. As Taleb writes, to predict what will happen in the future is to predict technological innovation, which is fundamentally unpredictable. We do not know what we will invent. If we knew it now, we would invent it and start developing it today. In other words, we won't find out today what we don't know precisely because the future conceals it from us – all the more since most inventions occur by accident. We did not invent the wheel because we planned to invent the wheel. Nor did we "discover" America because we set out to.[827]

The longer the time frame in which we want to predict the future, the more sensitive our predictions are to changes in the input data. Suppose we predict that, in 80 years, the sea level will rise by, for example, 30, 50, or 80 centimeters. In that case, we can only do so on the assumption that the dynamics we know today will run in the same way as they do today and will react similarly to changes in the values of the input parameters that control the process. Incidentally, geologists follow a similar line of reasoning when interpreting past events. They assume that past processes were similar to present ones – the so-called principle of geological actualism. We are now reversing this principle, directing its blade towards the future and forecasting how things will be. However, we tend to forget about the butterfly effect, which humanity has long observed: a slight change in the input data can cause absolutely radical changes in the future state of affairs. And the further into the future we look, the more significant the differences between the scenarios we draw. In meteorology, where this regularity was discovered in the 1960s, this means that the fluttering of the wings of a butterfly in Malaysia that we tried to catch in a net can lead to a cyclone that will ravage the Caribbean two months later. And if we hadn't frightened it away, there wouldn't have been a cyclone. If this does not convince anyone, recall the fate of Ashton Kutcher in *The Butterfly Effect*.

In addition to those scientists who predict a future warming or cooling of the Earth, there are many others who, while not taking sides in this argument, turn to yet another set of climate considerations. The Earth is a complex natural system that responds and adapts to changing circumstances – that is a statement we would probably all agree with. As early as the 1970s, James Lovelock added an interesting, illustrative extension to this thesis, comparing the Earth to a complex living organism that not so much adapts to its environment as co-shapes it to tailor it to its needs. The various components of the system all have their roles to play. When the balance is disturbed, the Earth, Gaia, tries to restore it and has the tools to do so. Lovelock concludes that any effort to change the climate to warmer or cooler outcomes is pointless, as it will regulate itself in ways we cannot predict.[828] In his view, humans attribute far too much causal power to themselves.

Norwegian futurologist Jørgen Randers ties into the same current with his report from 2012.[829] Randers was one of the co-authors of 1972's famous *Limits to Growth*, where, as we know, he predicted an impending catastrophe, so he is clearly part of the group of those who see the future in bleak colors. He still believes that, since the 1980s, we have been living in a state of constant overshoot – that is, we have been consuming more resources than the environment can reproduce. However, his predictions about the effects of climate change are more surprising. His detailed analyses showed that the increase in carbon dioxide and other greenhouse gases in the atmosphere and the resulting warming will accelerate desertification in the Global South but encourage agricultural development in the Global North. The global food balance that these changes will create is inconclusive, which for Randers means that we should be promoting economic growth and fighting poverty so that people can afford to buy food rather than battle climate change, which is costly and rife with uncertain effects. In the meantime, however, most of us see in Randers only a vision of impending catastrophe and view his publication as support for the thesis that climate change on Earth must be stopped.

A decade earlier, Danish scientist Bjørn Lomborg came to similar conclusions despite following a completely different path. In his famous *The Skeptical Environmentalist*, he posits that there is no point in spending enormous amounts of money to fight greenhouse gas emissions. It is enough to allocate some of this money to find technical solutions that will allow us to find better sources of energy and ways of dealing with the problems we face. This would be much cheaper and more effective than trying to stop what, in any case, we cannot stop.[830]

You probably won't be surprised to hear that the works of Lovelock and Lomborg have been subjected to withering criticism by most of the climate science and futurology communities. It is interesting that, although the conclusions of their deliberations are somewhat similar to those of Randers' major recent work, the first two are widely criticized, and the third is celebrated.

With all this in mind, are you still confident that you know what lies ahead in a few decades?

THINKING THE UNTHINKABLE

What is in store for us? I do not know. But those who do not like the conclusions above do not know either. We are not even sure what the weather will be like tomorrow (maybe it will rain, maybe not), what the euro/dollar exchange rate will be like in a week (maybe, again, a few innocuous words from the Chairman of the Board of Governors of the Federal Reserve System will shake the world financial system), whether in a month a serious war will break out in the Far East (maybe a rocket launched by North Korea will hit Seoul after all), whether in a year we will be able to travel freely around the world, or whether a pandemic will re-emerge (either COVID-19 or another global menace that will force us to stay at home). And what will happen in 80 years to the Earth's climate? Do we really *know* that? Though writing in a slightly different context, Margaret Hefferan summed it up beautifully: "Anyone who tries to tell us they know the future is simply trying to own it."[831]

It is impossible to know the future accurately by analyzing the past; think of the life plans of the Thanksgiving turkey we mentioned a few pages above. Inductive reasoning has a way of leading us astray. The fact that we have always coped with problems and avoided catastrophes does not mean that we will do it again and that climate change will not finish us off. But it also doesn't mean that we won't cope.

Paradoxically, the less precisely we try to describe the future, the more accurate our forecast will be. The broader the spectrum of future events we allow for, the greater the chance that someone reading our predictions decades from now will conclude that we were actually right. It's a bit like predicting the end of the world in Chapter 3 or waiting for peak oil in Chapter 6: some believe it has already happened if only we correctly interpret predictions made years ago.

Does this mean it is not worth making predictions if the risk of the long-term forecast being incorrect is so high? On the contrary, it is worthwhile, even necessary. Before we start making projections of future changes to anything – the climate included – we should acknowledge the circumstances in which we make them. The world's complexity and its shallow level of predictability, and in particular, our experience of hundreds and thousands of unverified predictions from the past, dictate that a reasonable and honest forecaster should be very cautious in formulating complex theses. Why mention again the thousands of failed forecasts? Because forecasts that have failed no longer occupy our minds, they disappear into the darkness of the past, and they are hardly ever quoted. The authors of accurate forecasts are quoted more often than all others and are praised for their exceptional accuracy. The fact that the same people have been wrong many times before on the same or similar issues is forgotten, and we focus squarely on their success. The same is true for marathoners, sprinters, or swimmers. No one knows how many 100-meter sprints Usain Bolt lost or how many times Michael Phelps lost the 200-meter butterfly before he won his first medal at the Olympics. But every fan of those sports knows how many medals each of them has won.

On top of that, we are quite easily fooled by repeatable predictions. The fact that many authors make the same prediction in the mainstream does not mean that they are correct and that their prediction will come true.

Therefore, if a forecast is to be credible, it should take into account not only the course of various phenomena observed today but extrapolate them into the future. It should also consider one of the most important features that distinguishes humans from other living beings on Earth: the ability to use abstract thinking. It is precisely the fact that some of us can imagine the unimaginable that is changing this world much faster than we think. The uncertainty of tomorrow does not only pertain to the global political scene, where now and then, events arise that were impossible to imagine and predict a decade earlier, such as the Arab Spring and all its consequences or Great Britain's exit from the European Union.[832] We are also oblivious to what technical solutions will become our daily bread a few years from now. If you want to imagine the world 80 years from now – the default time frame for many of those who try to predict climate change – then think back to the world 80 years ago. In 1940, was anyone able to foresee a world with personal computers, cell phones, and the Internet? In fact, not even 80 but 20 years ago, no one could have imagined that in some countries today, more than half of the cars sold throughout the year would be purely electric. Norway in 2020 fulfilled that impossible reality.[833]

One more time for the people in the back: Education is the key

Human capital – the set of skills, knowledge, abilities, attitudes, and motivation thanks to which we are able not only to work efficiently but also to change the world – has been viewed as the most important of all the resources that a company can possess for several dozen years now. It is more important than physical capital (or, in lay terms, money) and environmental resources (e.g., raw materials). Consider that we are not particularly surprised that Iceland is a country where people enjoy a high standard of living. In contrast, in the Democratic Republic of the Congo, the quality of life of the average person is frighteningly low. However, if we were to take a moment to consider the potential of the environmental resources in both places, we would quickly conclude that it should be exactly the opposite. In Iceland, apart from heat from geothermal waters, there are no real resources, the climate is not conducive to farming (even in the summer, the temperature rarely exceeds 10°C), and there are no forests at all. Still, there are plenty of glaciers and volcanoes. In the Democratic Republic of the Congo, located in the central part of Africa, the entire periodic table lies under the feet of the population, heating is unnecessary, forests cover two-thirds of the country, and the land is capable of producing almost anything. Yet the resources of the environment, paradoxically, are much less important than the human potential, which stems from what we already know and the capacities we possess.

Yes, good education and learning are the keys to everything. If we start teaching today what we need most as a world community, then three generations from now, most human minds will be wired a little differently than they are today. This process will be arduous and lengthy because changing the consciousness of an entire generation of children requires changing the consciousness of the generation of teachers that educate them, whose consciousness was, in turn, shaped by the previous generation, and so on. In a sense, the parents' generation is the generation of brakemen. And this is why social change often occurs more slowly than technological change. It is for this reason that, to this day, there are significant differences in demographics, levels of entrepreneurship, and political choices between the eastern and western parts of Poland – even though the period of just over a hundred years when the country was partitioned between the three foreign powers, with the eastern part of today's Poland shaped by Russian influence and the western part shaped by German influence, closed with the end of World War I over a hundred years ago.

It would be good if, at the same time, we chose to start using the best educational models available instead of reinventing the wheel. Suppose we rebuilt the education system and abandoned the Prussian, Bismarckian drill in favor of the enormously successful Finnish school of modern education. If we started to teach foreign languages, as the Dutch do. Suppose we introduced compulsory teaching of economics in schools to no lesser an extent than we teach history. If we allowed our children's generation to free itself from the shackles of myths and fears in which we are stuck. To reap, we must first sow. In sowing a good education, we must be prepared to wait a long time – a generation – for the harvest. But someday, this process must begin.

We learn slowly, with difficulty, and we are very reluctant to change our views. We constantly and subconsciously search to confirm our own opinions, and when we find such confirmation, we become convinced that our thoughts are correct. This effect was described in the mid-20th century by American psychologist Bertram Forer.[834] If, on the other hand, we learn something that does not fit our vision of the world, we reject it as untrue. This is why the shaping of our children's minds should be entrusted with great care to those who will not format or mold them in the wrong way. Those who will leave their minds open to change and who will instill in them the ability to critically evaluate reality rather than merely implanting incontestably accurate interpretations of that reality that do not allow any deviation from the rules. Fundamentalism is always wrong because it closes minds.

Implementing this call to action is not easy. As parents, we rarely have a choice as to what our children are taught. Even today, it is the institutions of the state in which we live that define the canon of compulsory reading with which the youth is supposed to get acquainted – a model created in 19th-century Prussia! Fortunately, the era of banning books and burning them at the stake is over, so we can choose what we like as additional reading. This means that the problem lies in us and the choices we make. We choose fear and worry. Will we be able to change that? Yuval N. Harari is skeptical, writing that "if you dream of a society in which truth reigns supreme and myths are ignored, you have little to expect from Homo sapiens. Better try your luck with chimps."[835]

Or perhaps it is a good thing that the world is not perfect and presents us with challenges? If it were – if we were able to enjoy optimal conditions to thrive and live without obstacles and enemies – we might end up like the mice in the famous experiment by American behaviorist John B. Calhoun. Calhoun proved that the removal of all the natural obstacles that they face every day as individuals and as a community led to the collapse of social structures and the gradual death of all their members.[836]

Will better education keep us from being needlessly afraid and help us treat successive threats as challenges rather than catalysts of fear? Will we be able to inspire reflections among the youth of today that we once failed to engage? Will we more readily seek explanations for certain phenomena and events in the realm of science rather than unquestioningly believe omniscient prophets of all stripes? One can hope that this is what will happen. Over time, we are slowly but consistently moving the slider on the faith–knowledge axis to the right. And "faith" does not exclusively refer to religious belief. However, it is a fact that as the level of economic development rises, the percentage of people declaring themselves to be believers tends to drop, as can be observed in the empty churches of rich Western European countries. Even in many less developed countries, the process of moving away from religion has already become a noticeable trend.[837] It is also – and perhaps above all – the uncritical belief that those around us who are numerous and loud are always correct. To gain awareness, it is worthwhile always to verify what we hear with a critical eye. Belief and knowledge are two completely different things: when you know something, you no longer believe it because you already know.

Minority report

Perhaps the perspective we adopted in this book reflects the views of a small minority – indeed, that is very likely the case. But we can easily find common ground with nearly everyone by collectively casting doubt on the absolute validity of claims made by those who are numerous and vociferous, especially when they talk about unpredictable things like the future. We vastly overestimate our ability to predict it accurately, and we often cynically exploit the natural human tendency to fear the unknown to quickly gain a captive audience for our projections of the future.

All these doubts come from the firm belief that the only constant in the Universe is change and that progress has accompanied humanity since the dawn of time and will continue to do so. Those who ridicule it using the now classic expression "*that ridiculous spirit of innovation*" should stop using bicycles, telephones, photocopiers, and all other useful inventions. If only for a month. Let them feel for themselves what really exists and stop scaring everyone around them with the notion that the process of innovation will grind to a halt.

In any case, all our predictions will only be tested in the future. So perhaps it is worthwhile to embrace a degree of humility in drawing trajectories of future changes and trying to prove we are right. The more confidently we do it and the louder we shout, the greater the humiliation when the fate of humanity turns out to be different because the truth is not always on the side of the majority.

APPENDIX

Predicted ends of the world throughout history.[838]

634 BC	**Romans.** Rome was to be destroyed within 120 years. According to the myth about the founding of Rome, Romulus saw 12 birds, each of which represented ten years of the city's continued existence.
389 BC	**Romans.** The city was to be destroyed after 365 years. According to the legend of the founding of Rome, Romulus saw 12 birds, with a second interpretation claiming that the birds represented the number of days in the year.
1st c. AD	**Christians.** Christians believed that Jesus would return within a generation following his death, and with his return, the apocalypse would begin.
66–70	**Essenes.** The Jewish revolt against the Romans was to be the final battle of the end of the world.
365	**Hilary of Poitiers (bishop).** The end of the world was to occur in a year that corresponded to the number of days in the calendar.
375–400	**Martin of Tours (bishop).** He claimed that the Antichrist had been born and was already among men and that the end of the world would come once he reached his full strength (adulthood).

500	**Hippolytus of Rome (theologian), Irenaeus of Lyon (bishop), Sextus Julius Africanus (historian).** All three predicted that Jesus would return in a year associated with the dimensions of Noah's Ark. After this prediction failed, Sextus Julius Africanus set a new date for the end of the world: the year 800.
Apr 6, 793	**Beatus of Liébana (monk, geographer).** The first precise date is known to modern scholars. After this failed, the monk set a new date for the year 800.
799–806	**Gregory of Tours (bishop, historian).** He calculated, with a relatively large margin of error, that the end of the world would occur in those years.
847	**Thiota (first female doomsday prophet).** After her prophecy failed to come true, she confessed to having fabricated it.
922–995	**Christians.** Within three years of the coincidence of Good Friday and the Annunciation, the Antichrist was to appear on Earth and usher in the end of the world.
Dec 31, 999 / Jan 1, 1000	**Sylvester II (Pope) and others.** The end of the world was to come with the dawn of the new millennium. This widespread fear stemmed from the fact that the calendar year was henceforth to be marked by four digits, not three, as before.
1033	**Christians.** Christians expected the end of the world to come 1,000 years after Jesus's death.
1186	**John of Toledo (astronomer).** The alignment of the planets was supposed to herald the beginning of the end of the world, accompanied by storms and earthquakes.
1260	**Joachim of Fiore (mystic).** Based on Joachim's vision, the end was to occur between 1200 and 1260. After the prophecy failed, his followers moved the end of the world to 1290, then to 1335, and finally to 1378.

1284	**Innocent III (Pope).** The world was to end 666 years after the birth of Islam.
1346–1351	**Europeans.** The plague that raged in Europe was interpreted as a sign of the End Times.
1504	**Sandro Botticelli (painter).** Greatly impressed by a series of sermons on the end of the world by the monk Savonarola, Botticelli painted The Mystical Nativity and included an inscription in which he claimed that the world had arrived at a point described in the 11th chapter of the Book of Revelation. The Devil had been set free for three and a half years.
Feb 1, 1524	**Astrologers.** Some astrologers' calculations indicated that the end of the world would begin with a great flood in London. Subsequent analyses led to a postponement of the date by 100 years. Another prediction involved a mighty wind that was to occur in 1683.
Feb 20, 1524	**Johannes Stöffler (astronomer).** An unusual alignment of the planets presaged the coming end of the world. After this proved false, Stöffler postponed doomsday to 1528.
1533	**Melchior Hofmann (Anabaptist).** The coming of Jesus was to take place in Strasbourg, where only 144,000 people would be saved; the rest were to die in the flames. Another Anabaptist leader, Jan Matthys (a baker), set the date of Judgment Day for April 5, 1534, and only the city of Münster was to be spared.
Oct 19, 1533	**Michael Stifel (monk, mathematician).** Based on his calculations, the end of the world was to begin at 8 a.m. that day.

1555	**Pierre d'Ailly (cardinal, astrologer).** D'Ailly reasoned that 6,845 years of human history had already passed and humanity would only survive until 7,000. Another prediction involved the world ending in 1789.
1600	**Martin Luther (theologian, reformer).** The Apocalypse was to occur no later than 1600.
1603	**Tomasso Campanella (monk, philosopher).** The end of the world was supposed to occur with the Sun colliding with the Earth, which would burn away humanity's sins and allow Jesus to return. To confirm his supposition, Campanella sought assistance with his calculations from Galileo Galilei, who ultimately rebuked him.
1648	**Sabbatai Zevi (rabbi).** Zevi's apocalypse was based on kabbalah (a mystical-philosophical school of thought). After it failed, he set a second date in 1666.
1656	**Christopher Columbus (explorer).** This date is mentioned in Columbus' *Book of Prophecies.* Another estimate places the apocalypse at the beginning of 1658. The world was to end after 7,000 years of existence, with Year Zero excluded from the calculation.
1655–1657	**Fifth Monarchists.** This extreme Puritan sect claimed the end of the world would come in a final war. Subsequent apocalypses were scheduled for 1666, 1673, and 1700.
1666	**Christians.** The number 666 was associated with Satan, and events like the return of the plague to London and a great fire in the city fueled renewed fears of End Times.
1688	**John Napier (mathematician, physicist).** Napier based his estimate on the Apocalypse of St. John. After his prediction failed, he set a new date in 1700.

1694 **Johann Jacob Zimmermann (theologian).** Based on astrology and the Book of Revelation, he predicted that the main events of the end of the world were to take place at the edge of the wilderness, i.e., in Pennsylvania, and that a group of people affiliated with "The Society of the Woman in the Wilderness" were to await the second coming of Jesus.

Apr 5, 1719 **Jacob Bernoulli (mathematician).** Bernoulli expected that a comet would slam into the Earth, destroying it.

Oct 16, 1736 **William Whiston (mathematician).** Whiston also predicted that a comet would hit the Earth.

1780 **People of New England, United States.** Dark skies were supposed to portend the end of the world; only later were they recognized as a natural phenomenon created by a combination of forest fires, low-hanging clouds, and dense fog.

1805 **Christopher Love (preacher).** A great earthquake was supposed to trigger the end of the world.

1806 **Residents of Leeds, England.** A hen purportedly started laying eggs bearing the words "*Christ is coming*." It turned out that its owner, Mary Bateman (an English criminal), was writing these words on the eggs and then pushing them back into the hen's oviduct.

1836 **John Wesley (founder of the Methodist Church).** Wesley interpreted chapter 12 of the Book of Revelation and selected 1836 as the year of the final collapse.

1843–1844 **William Miller (farmer).** Based on a literal interpretation of the Bible, Jesus would come to Earth between the spring of 1843 and the spring of 1844. He and his followers pointed to April 28 and December 31, 1843, as well as March 21 and October 22, 1844, as potential dates for doomsday.

1853–1856	**Many voices.** The Crimean War was considered by many to be the war of the end of the world.
1862	**John Cumming (clergyman).** The world was to end 6,000 years after its creation.
1874	**Jehovah's Witnesses.** Their first prediction of the end of the world. Subsequent dates included 1878, 1881, 1908, and 1914 (the "end of a 30-year battle"), 1916 (with the ongoing war interpreted as a sign of the end of the world), 1918 (end of Christianity), 1920 (worldwide anarchy), 1925 (new order on Earth), 1941, 1975, 1984, and around the year 2000.
1891	**Joseph Smith (founder of the Mormon Church).** After a conversation with God in 1835, he announced that Jesus would return within 56 years.
1892–1911	**Charles Piazzi Smyth (astronomer).** Using the size of the Great Pyramid of Giza, Smyth chose these years as the timeframe for Jesus's Second Coming.
1901	**Catholic Apostolic Church.** Jesus was to return before the death of the last of the 12 founders.
1910	**Camille Flammarion (astronomer).** Halley's Comet and the toxic gas in its tail were to bring an end to life on Earth. Special "comet pills" were sold as a panacea.
1914–1918	**Many voices.** The Great War was expected to bring an end to human civilization.
Feb 13, 1925	**Margaret Rowen (founder of the Seventh-day Adventist Church).** Rowen stated that the Archangel Gabriel indicated this date to her in a vision.
1935	**Wilbur Glenn Voliva (evangelist).** The world was to explode and disappear.

1936	**Herbert Armstrong (founder of the Worldwide Church of God).** Jesus was to return to Earth in order to stop the self-destruction of humankind, and the members of the organization were to assist him as humanity's saviors. Hitler and Mussolini were associated with the Beast and False Prophet, respectively. Armstrong later made similar predictions for 1943, 1972, and 1975.
1947	**John Ballou Newbrough (dentist).** Newbrough claimed to be a clairvoyant and predicted the end of the world was to bring anarchy and the destruction of all nations.
Dec 21, 1954	**Dorothy Martin (housewife, president of the Brotherhood of the Seven Rays).** Martin claimed to have received a message from the planet Clarion, according to which the end of the world would come as a result of a great flood. The surviving believers would escape in a spaceship.
Feb 4, 1962	**Jeane Dixon (astrologer), Hindu astrologers.** A great catastrophe was to occur due to a rare alignment of the planets. Dixon made another doomsday prediction for 2020, which was to mark the beginning of the final battle between good and evil, lasting until 2037.
1967	**Jim Jones (preacher, founder of Peoples Temple).** Based on a vision, Jones predicted that the world would end through nuclear war.
Aug 20, 1967	**George Van Tassel (ufologist).** A nuclear attack on the coast of the United States, initiated by the Soviet Union, was expected to occur as a sign of the apocalypse. Van Tassel received this information from an alien named Ashtar.

1969	**Charles Manson (criminal, founder of The Family).** Based on an interpretation of one of The Beatles' albums, Manson predicted that an apocalyptic race war would precipitate the end of the world.
January 1974	**David Berg (founder of Teens for Christ).** Berg viewed the Comet Kohoutek as a sign. Another prophecy pointed to 1989 and 1993 as the years of Jesus's Second Coming.
1980	**Leland Jensen (reformer).** A nuclear catastrophe would be followed by 20 years of conflict, culminating with the founding of the Kingdom of God. Jensen also predicted that, in 1986, Halley's Comet would trapped in Earth's orbit, wreaking great destruction on Earth.
1980–1990	**Hal Lindsey (preacher).** The end of the world could occur through a communist takeover or Soviet nuclear attacks, among other things. Another prophecy involved Jesus returning to Earth in 1988, within a generation of the creation of the state of Israel, assuming a generation lasts 40 years.
Mar 10, 1982	**John Gribbin (astrophysicist), Stephen Plagemann.** Gravitational disturbances and natural disasters caused by the alignment of planets—the so-called Jupiter effect.
Apr 23, 1990	**Elizabeth Clare Prophet (spiritual teacher).** A nuclear would break out, leading to the end of the world 12 years later.
1991	**Louis Farrakhan (religious leader).** The Gulf War was to be humanity's final war.
May 2, 1994	**Neal Chase (cult leader).** An atomic bomb would be dropped on New York City, and the final battle of Armageddon would take place 40 days later.

Sep 6, 1994	**Harold Camping (writer, radio broadcaster).** They calculated a date for the end of the world using information from the Bible and calendar cycles. Subsequent predictions included September 29 and October 2, 1994, March 31, 1995, and May 21 and October 21, 2011.
Dec 17, 1996	**Sheldan Nidle (psychologist).** Sixteen million spaceships and angels would arrive, triggering the end of the world.
March 1997	**Monte Judah (rabbi).** Based on numerology and the psalms, the rabbi claimed that the end of the world was to begin with chaos in March 1997.
Mar 26, 1997	**Marshall Applewhite (founder of Heaven's Gate).** The end of the world was to arrive with the passage of Comet Hale-Bopp. The only way to escape was to commit suicide and board the spacecraft that accompanied the comet.
Oct 23, 1997	**James Ussher (Archbishop).** The end of the world would occur 6,000 years after its creation.
Mar 31, 1998	**Hon-Ming Chen (leader of the True Way Cult).** God was supposed to come to Earth in a flying saucer, and a nuclear holocaust was to begin in 1999.
1999	**Nostradamus (astrologer, mystic).** The date is estimated based on calculations from the Book of Revelation. Another date, which concludes his series of predictions and is believed to correspond with the end of the world, is the year 3797.
2000	**Many voices.** The "Y2K problem" was expected to destroy many computers and cause worldwide chaos, through which Satan would achieve total power.
2000	**Isaac Newton (physicist).** The alleged beginning of Christ's Millennium. An alternative date based on the Bible is 2060.

2000	**Ruth Montgomery (journalist).** The Earth's axis would shift, and the Antichrist would be revealed.
May 27, 2003	**Nancy Lieder (founder of the website ZetaTalk).** A message relayed to Lieder by aliens suggested that Nibiru (Planet X) would pass through the solar system and cause the Earth's poles to switch places.
Oct 30 – Nov 29, 2003	**Aum Shinrikyō.** Nuclear war would prompt the end of the world.
Sep 12, 2006	**House of Yahweh.** Nuclear war would break out.
Sep 10, 2008 – Mar 30, 2010	**Many voices.** The launch of the Large Hadron Collider was expected to produce Earth-consuming micro black holes.
Dec 21, 2008 – Dec 21, 2015	**Herbert Stollorz (engineer).** Apocalyptic years were identified based on studying the Bible and applying methods from advanced technical devices.
July–October 2011	**Multiple voices.** Comet Elenin was expected to collide with the Earth or cause a disruption in the Earth's crust, causing massive earthquakes and waves.
Jun 30, 2012	**José Luis de Jesús (religious leader).** Governments and economies would founder and collapse. The chosen would transform and gain the ability to fly and penetrate walls.
Dec 21, 2012	**Many voices.** The end of the Maya calendar was supposed to herald the end of the world through an alien invasion, a supernova explosion, destruction by an asteroid or other object, a shift in the Earth's poles, eruptions on the Sun, and more.
Sep 23, 2013	**Grigori Rasputin (mystic).** A storm would destroy life on Earth, and the survivors would find comfort in Jesus.
2014–2015	**John Hagee, Mark Biltz (evangelists).** Four blood moons visible in the sky in 2014 and 2015 were deemed to portend the end of the world.

Sep 23, 2017	**David Meade (writer).** The Earth would collide with the planet Nibiru (Planet X). After this failed, Meade postponed the apocalypse to October, then March, then finally, April 23, 2018.
2018–2028	**F. Kenton Beshore (pastor).** Jesus will return to Earth within one generation of the creation of Israel, assuming an age of 70-80 years.
2020	**Stephen Hawking (astrophysicist).** Hawking concluded that the date predicted by the Maya contained miscalculations (double-counting holidays) and that the actual end of the world would occur eight years later. Another theory involved the Earth turning into a massive fireball by the year 2600.
2020–2030	**Bill Joy (programmer).** Modern technologies such as robotics, genetic engineering, and nanotechnology will bring about the end of humanity.
Jun 21, 2020	**Paolo Tagaloguin (scientist).** The date is estimated based on the Maya calendar, taking into account the changes resulting from the transition from the Julian calendar to the Gregorian calendar.
2026	**Messiah Foundation International.** The end of the world will occur when an asteroid smashes into the Earth.
Nov 13, 2026	**Heinz von Foerste (physicist) et al.** Humanity will no longer be able to feed itself, and this will be compounded by high temperatures caused by greenhouse gas emissions.
2031–2051	**Malcolm Light (scientist).** Humanity will die from the release of methane into the atmosphere due to climate change.
2129	**It was said Nursî (theologian)** – prediction based on calculations from the hadiths.

2239–3239	**Jews.** The Messiah will come 6,000 years after the creation of Adam, and the end of the world may take place 1,000 years later.
2280	**Rashad Khalifa (biochemist).** Purportedly deciphered code found in the Qur'an.
5079	**Baba Wang (mystic, medicine woman).** Humankind is expected to transcend the Universe and leave it. Other predicted apocalyptic events include the emergence of a new disease that will cause humans to age rapidly (2088), a great drought (2170), an explosion in the Sun, falling satellites and space stations, and changing gravitational fields (2296), a great famine (2371), and the disappearance of life on Earth (3797).
100 million years	**Stephen A. Nelson (scientist).** Catastrophic impacts might be unleashed if an asteroid more than 10 km in diameter hits the Earth, which happens once every 100 million years.
1 billion years	**Scientists.** Life on Earth is expected to become impossible due to high temperatures and evaporating oceans.
1.6 billion years	**Scientists.** The scarcity of carbon dioxide is expected to cause the extinction of eukaryotic life.
5 billion years	**Scientists.** The Earth will be engulfed or burned by the Sun, which will turn into a red giant.
22 billion years	**Scientists.** The Universe will end as a result of the Big Rip. Since the universe is expanding faster and faster, it will eventually tear apart all matter, including galaxies, stars, planets, and even atoms.
10^{100} years	**Scientists.** In the "heat death of the Universe," all the Universe's parameters will become constant. The Universe will be incapable of sustaining motion or life.

ABOUT THE AUTHORS

Most members of the author team hold positions at the Institute of Socio-economic Geography and Spatial Management (Institute) of the University of Maria Curie-Sklodowska (UMCS) in Lublin, Poland.

WOJCIECH JANICKI, PhD, is a professor and director of the Institute. Educated in Poland and United States, his research focuses on political geography, migration, regional development, global issues, and conflict areas. He is the author or editor of nine books and more than sixty articles. He has taught in Poland, Germany, Czech Republic, Finland, Sweden and Ireland. He actively popularizes science, having given over 150 radio and TV interviews and public lectures.

KAROL KOWALCZYK, PhD, is a transportation geographer. A graduate of UMCS, he also studied at the University of Oulu, Finland. He is currently an assistant professor at the Institute and specializes in the geographic aspects of railroads – today and in the past. He is also interested in railroad cartography and the influence of this branch of transport on the socio-cultural sphere. Privately, he is a railroad enthusiast and a fan of traveling on rails.

DOROTA I. DYMEK, PhD, is a research and teaching associate at the Institute. She was educated at the University of Life Sciences in Lublin, the University of Agriculture in Cracow and UMCS. She focuses on issues of sustainable development, spatial management and revitalization. She is the author of several scientific articles.

JOLANTA JÓŹWIK, PhD, is a research and teaching associate working at the Institute. She is a graduate of the University of Life Sciences in Lublin, the Agricultural University in Cracow and UMCS. In her scientific work, she deals with issues related to settlement, urban planning, and socio-economic development. She is the author of several scientific articles.

GRZEGORZ IWANICKI, PhD, is an assistant professor in the Institute. He is a member of Light Pollution Think Tank. A graduate of UMCS and Jagiellonian University in Cracow, he focuses on sustainable development issues. He is the author or editor of one book and more than twenty articles.

JOLANTA RODZOŚ, PhD, is a socio-economic geographer and academic teacher in the Institute. Her research interests include a wide range of issues related to human activities in their living environment and education. She is the author of textbooks for children and adults introducing various fields of geographical knowledge. She actively popularizes scientific knowledge.

JAN RYDZAK, PhD, is a graduate of language studies at UMCS. He defended his doctoral thesis in Government and Public Policy at the University of Arizona in Tucson and was associate director of the Global Digital Policy Incubator program at Stanford University. He works as an analyst and, since 2021, as a manager at Ranking Digital Rights. He works with many public and private entities acting on tech companies' transparency regarding freedom of expression and privacy issues. The author of more than a dozen academic articles, he speaks five languages fluently.

ENDNOTES

INTRODUCTION

1 Y.N. Harari 2014. Sapiens. A Brief History of Humankind. Harvill Secker, London.

2 E.L. Gettier 1963. Is Justified True Belief Knowledge? Analysis, Vol. 23, 121-23.

3 G. Mandler 1985. Cognitive psychology: An essay in cognitive science. Hillsdale, Lawrence Erlbaum Associates; K.M. Wiig 1993. Knowledge Management Foundations: Thinking About Thinking – How People and Organizations Create, Represent, and Use Knowledge. Schema Press, Arlington; I. Nonaka 2005. A dynamic theory of organizational knowledge creation. In: I. Nonaka I. (ed.), Knowledge management: critical perspectives on business and management, Routledge, New York, 153–156; W. G. Stock, M. Stock 2013. Handbook of Information Science. De Gruyter Saur.

4 B. Malinowski 1948. Magic, Science and Religion and Other Essays. The Free Press, Glencoe; C. Lévi-Strauss 1958. Anthropologie structurale. Plon, Paris; G. Dumézil 1973. Mythe et épopée Gallimard; M. Eliade 2002. Aspects du mythe. Gallimard, Paris; M. Klik 2016. Teorie mitu. Współczesne literaturoznawstwo francuskie (1969–2010). Wydawnictwa Uniwersytetu Warszawskiego, Warszawa.

5 R. Barthes 1957. Mythologies. Editions du Seuil, Paris; M. Midgley 2003, The myths we live by. Routledge, London and New York.

6 P.R. Gould 1969. Spatial Diffusion. Resource Paper no. 4, A.A.G.: Commission on College Geography, Washington D.C.

7 E.R. Fox 1987. Fear of the unknown. Western Journal of Medicine, 7(3): 22–25; B. Gallagher 2008. Fear of the unknown. Safer Communities, Vol. 7(3): 22–25.

8 F. Furedi 2007. Politics of fear. Beyond left and right. Continuum.

9 W. James 1884. What is an emotion? Mind 9(34): 188–205; S. Schachter, J. Singer 1962. Cognitive, social, and physiological determinants of emotional state. Psychological Review 69(5): 379–399; R.S. Lazarus, S. Folkman 1984. S. Stress, appraisal, and coping. Springer Publishing Company; D.G. Myers 2004. Theories of Emotion. In: Psychology: Seventh Edition. Worth Publishers.

10 J.A. Gray 1987. The Psychology of Fear and Stress (2nd ed.). Cambridge University Press, Cambridge, England; R. Misslin 2003. The defense system of fear: Behavior and neurocircuitry. Clinical Neurophysiology. 33(2): 55–66.

11 N.N. Taleb 2007. The Black Swan: Second Edition: The Impact of the Highly Improbable. Random House.

12 A. Tversky, D. Kahneman 1974. Judgment under Uncertainty: Heuristics and Biases. Science 27(185), 1124–1131; D. Kahneman, A. Tversky 1979. Prospect Theory: An Analysis of Decision under Risk. Econometrica 47(2): 263–291.

13 F.R., rolnik nadwiślański 1900. Kanalizacya miasta Warszawy jako narzędzie judaizmu i szarlatanerii w celu zniszczenia rolnictwa polskiego oraz wytępienia ludności słowiańskiej nad Wisłą. G. Gebethner i spółka, Kraków.

14 R. Bregman 2018. Utopia for Realists and How We Can Get There. Bloomsbury Publishing PLC.

15 J. Wanniski 1978. Taxes, Revenues, and the 'Laffer Curve.' The Public Interest, Winter; A. Laffer 2004. The Laffer Curve: Past, Present, and Future. The Heritage Foundation. https://web.archive.org/web/20071201225944/http://www.heritage.org/Research/Taxes/bg1765.cfm (accessed: 5.12.2019).

16 S. Huntington 2004. Who Are We? The Challenges to America's National Identity. Simon & Schuster.

17 M. Zaremba 2006. Den polske rörmokaren och andra berättelser från Sverige. Stockholm, Norstedts.

18 M. Heller, 2013. Bóg i nauka. Moje dwie drogi do jednego celu. Michał Heller w rozmowie z Giulio Brottim. Copernicus Center Press, Kraków, p. 177-178. Translated from Polish.

19 Y.N. Harari 2014, *op cit.*

20 T. Phillips 2018. Humans: A Brief History of How We Fucked It All Up. Wildfire.

21 A. Giddens 1998. The Third Way: The Renewal of Social Democracy. Polity Press, Cambridge; G. Esping-Andersen, D. Gallie, A. Hemerijck, J. Myles 2002. Why We Need a New Welfare State. Oxford University Press, Oxford; G. Esping-Andersen 2009. Incomplete Revolution: Adapting Welfare States to Women's New Roles, Cambridge; A. Luci-Greulich, O. Thévenon 2013. The Impact of Family Policies on Fertility Trends in Developed Countries. European Journal of Population, Vol. 29, No. 4, p. 387–416; European Child Health Services and Systems: Lessons without Borders, 2013, (ed.) Wolfe I., McKee M. Open University Press, New York.

22 As recently as 2020, the Polish government claimed that the first of three main goals of the *Family 500+* program was to increase the number of births in the country and underscored that "the fertility rate grew from 1.29 in 2015 to 1.45 in 2017." The subsequent decrease in this rate to 1.44 and then to 1.42 went largely unreported since doing so would undermine the legitimacy of introducing this costly program and its alleged impact on the number of children born in Poland, as would the fall in fertility rates to the same levels recorded before the program was launched. See https://www.gov.pl/web/rodzina/rodzina-500-plus (accessed 17.05.2020). A. Gromada 2018. Czemu służy program Rodzina 500 Plus? Analiza celów polityki publicznej i polityki partyjnej. Ruch Prawniczy, Ekonomiczny i Socjologiczny, Rok LXXX, vol. 3, p. 231-244.

23 F. Furedi 2007, *op. cit.*.

24 L. Kołakowski 2009. Czy Pan Bóg jest szczęśliwy i inne pytania. Kraków, Wyd. Znak, p. 149. Translated from Polish.

Chapter One: Off the Rails

25 Ch. Wolmar 2007. Fire and Steam: How the Railways Transformed Britain. Atlantic Books, London; J. Holland, D. Spaven 2013. Mapping the Railways,

Harper Collins, Glasgow.

26 N. Faith 1990. The World the Railways Made, Pimlico, London; D. Hayes 2017. The First Railways: Atlas of Early Railways, Times Books, Glasgow.

27 D. Hayes 2010. Historical Atlas of the North American Railroad. University of California Press, Berkeley; D. Hayes 2017, *op. cit.*

28 J. Matejko 1885. Dzieje Cywilizacji Ludzkości - Wynalazek kolei żelaznej. Drawing, height: 28 cm, width: 41 cm, object number: MNK IX-898, photographed by Anna Olchawska. Courtesy of the National Museum in Krakow (Muzeum Narodowe w Krakowie).
29 D. Hayes 2017, *op. cit.*
30 F. Trevithick 1872. Life of Richard Trevithick: With an Account of His Inventions. E. & F. N. Spon, London and New York.
31 N. Faith 1990, *op. cit.*; Ch. Wolmar 2009. Blood, Iron, and Gold: How the Railways Transformed the World. Atlantic Books, London.
32 Harper's New Monthly Magazine. 1874, August, 49(291): 377. Source of the digital version: The Cornell University Library. Making of America Collection. Public domain. Available at: https://babel.hathitrust.org/cgi/pt?id=coo.31924079637587&seq=387 (accessed: 29.12.2023).
33 D. Hayes 2010, *op. cit.*
34 High-Speed Rail Atlas, 2022, International Union of Railways, Paris.
35 Own elaboration based on: E. Cheysson 1889. Album de Statistique Graphique de 1888. Ministere des Travaux Publics, Paris; E. Cheysson 1906. Album de Statistique Graphique de 1900. Ministere des Travaux Publics, Paris; R. W. Huenemann 1984. The Dragon and the Iron Horse: The Economics of Railroads in China, 1876-1937. Council on East Asian Studies, Harvard University, Cambridge (Mass.).
36 Eisenbahn-Karte von Europa zu Hendschel's Telegraph [Map]. Ravensteins Geographische Verlagsanstalt und Druckerei, Frankfurt (Main). Source of the digital version: POLONA - Digital Collections of the National Library of Poland, object number: ZZK 1 239. Public domain. Available at: https://polona.pl/item-view/3cf4e8c0-e586-4b0c-ae1e-3077a1c3c471?page=0 (accessed: 29.12.2023).
37 R. Koselleck proposed to divide the history of the world into three major eras: pre-horse, horse, and post-horse; R. Koselleck 2004. Der Aufbruch in die Moderne oder das Ende des Pferdezeitalter. In: B. Tillmann (ed.). Historikerpreis der Stadt Münster: die Preisträger und Laudatoren von 1981 bis 2003. LIT-Verlag, Münster.
38 Fliegende Blätter. 1854, 19(451): 148. Source of the digital version: Universitätsbibliothek Heidelberg. Heidelberg historic literature – digitized. Public domain. Available at: https://doi.org/10.11588/diglit.2119#0148 (accessed: 29.12.2023).
39 Quoted in: E. Lea 1916. Observations of an Operating Officer. In: S. Thompson (ed.). The Railway Library 1915: A Collection of Addresses and Papers on Railway Subjects, Mostly Delivered or Published During the Year Named, Also Statistics for 1915. Stromberg, Allen & Co., Chicago: 229.
40 Part of a transcribed speech quoted in: S. Holbrook 1947. The Story of American Railroads. Crown Publishers, New York: 41.
41 D. Brandon, A. Brooke 2019. Railway Haters: Opposition to Railways from the 19th to 21st centuries. Pen & Sword, Yorkshire and Philadelphia.
42 Quoted in: W. Tomlinson 1914. The North Eastern Railway: Its Rise and Development. Andrew Reid & Company, Newcastle-upon-Tyne: 373.
43 The Stirling Observer and Midland Counties Advertiser. 1865, December 21, 29(1507): 6.
44 P. Negri 1968. Gregorio XVI e le ferrovie in alcuni documenti dell'Archivio di Stato di Roma e dell'Archivio di Stato di Bologna. Rassegna degli Archivi di Stato, 28: 103–126.
45 P. M. Kalla-Bishop 1971. Italian Railways. David & Charles, Newton Abbot.
46 G. Hanser, M. Fillmore 1856. Post- und Eisenbahn-Reisekarte: Deutschland, Holland, die Schweiz, Italien bis Neapel, der grösste Theil von Frankreich, Ungarn, Polen etc.: mit besonderer Rücksicht auf Eisenbahnen u. Seedampfschiffahrt [Map]. Serz & Cie, Nürnberg. Available at: https://www.loc.gov/resource/g6031p.fi000185r (accessed: 20.12.2023). Papal States appear on the map as "Kirchen Staat". Railroads are marked with a dashed line.

47 P. Negri 1968, *op. cit.*
48 J. F. Pollard 2005. Money and the Rise of the Modern Papacy: Financing the Vatican, 1850-1950. Cambridge University Press, Cambridge.
49 One view, expressed by an American representative of the Congregational Church, is presented in: H. Bushnell 1846. A Letter to His Holiness Pope Gregory XVI. Ward and Co., London.
50 G. Moroni 1854. Dizionario di erudizione storico-ecclesiastica da S. Pietro sino ai nostri giorni. Volume 70. Tipografia Emiliana, Venice: 159.
51 W. Pol 1847. Z wycieczki. Biblioteka Naukowego Zakładu imienia Ossolińskich, 2(5): 555. Translated from Polish.
52 *Ibidem*: 546. Translated from Polish.
53 Ph. Drozdov 1884. Ph. Drozdov 1884. Pis'ma mitropolity Moskovskogo Filareta k namestniku Sviato-Troitskiia Sergievy lavry arkhimandritu Antoniiu 1831–1867. Volume 1, Moscow: 324. Translated from Russian.
54 Translated in: J. N. Westwood 1964. A History of Russian Railways. Allen and Unwin, London: 45; Original text found in: A. I. Del'vig 1913. Moi vospominaniia. Volume 3, Imperatorskii Moskovskii i Rumiantsevskii Muzei, Moscow: 29.
55 A. I. Del'vig 1913, *op. cit.*
56 G. Voinov 1888. Vospominaniia o vysokopreosviashchennom mitropolite Moskovskom Filarete. Universitetskaia tipografiia, Moscow: 23. Translated from Russian.
57 The excerpt comes from an unsent draft (Geneva, April 9, 1857) of a letter that was later sent to Turgenev but has not survived. Translated in: R. F. Christian (ed.) 1978. Tolstoy's Letters: Volume I 1828-1879. Selected, edited and translated by R. F. Christian. Charles Scribner's Sons, New York: 97.
58 L. Tolstoy 1890, The Kreutzer Sonata. Benjamin R. Tucker, Boston (Massachusetts): 122.
59 P. Birukoff 1911. The Life of Tolstoy. Cassell and Company, London, New York, Toronto and Melbourne.
60 Ch. Wolmar 2014. The Iron Road. An Illustrated History of the Railroad. DK Publishing, New York.
61 T. Knox 1886. The Boy Travellers in South America. Harper & Brothers, New York: 39.
62 H. Finch-Hatton 1886. Advance Australia!: An Account of Eight Years' Work, Wandering, and Amusement in Queensland, New South Wales, and Victoria. W. H. Allen & Co., London.
63 Sydney Punch. 1881, August 20: 75. Cartoon available at: http://nla.gov.au/nla.news-page28017240 (accessed: 15.06.2020).
64 T. De Quincey 1849. The English Mail-Coach, or the Glory of Motion. Blackwood's Edinburgh Magazine, 66(408): 485-500.
65 G. Goy 1911, Hommes et choses du P. L. M.. Devambez, Paris.
66 A. Philip, L. Philip 2000. Histoire des faits économiques et sociaux de 1800 à 1945. Dalloz, Paris: 66. Translated from French.
67 P. Ch. Laurent de Villedeuil 1907. Bibliographie des chemins de fer: préface, index chronologique (1771-1846). Librairie Générale, Paris: 46–47. Translated from French.
68 Translated in: Railroad Gazette. A Journal of Transportation, Engineering and Railroad News. 1889, August 30, 21: 575; German text quoted in: W. Pöls (ed.) 1976. Deutsche Sozialgeschichte - Dokumente und Skizzen. Band 1: 1815-1870, C. H. Beck, Munich: 371; Researchers are divided on the actual authorship of these words, as the original document has not survived in the archives. See: B. Joerges 1994. Expertise Lost: An Early Case of Technology Assessment. Social Studies of Science, 24(1): 96-104.
69 Der Adler. Die erste Dampflok in Deutschland. 2021. Archived at: https://web.archive.org/web/20210414115251/https://www.dbmuseum.de/museum_de/ausstellungen_fahrzeuge/fahrzeuge/fahrzeughalle_I/adler-2602454 (accessed: 14.04.2021).

70 C. Wiessner 1835. Die Ludwigs-Eisenbahn zwischen Nürnberg und Fürth. Available at: https://artsandculture.google.com/asset/nuremberg-fuerth-railway-wiesner-maker/nQGm0lhua17p0g (accessed: 21.12.2023).
71 The Mechanics' Magazine, Museum, Register, Journal, and Gazette. 1836, August 13, 25(679): 326-327.
72 S. K. Baker 2013. Rail Atlas Great Britain and Ireland. 13th Edition. Oxford Publishing Co., Ian Allan Publishing, Hersham, Surrey.
73 R. Harrington 1998. The Neuroses of the Railway: Trains, Travel and Trauma in Britain, c.1850-c.1900. University of Oxford (PhD Thesis).
74 The Influence of Railway Travelling on Public Health (from "the Lancet"). 1862, London: 44.
75 *Ibidem*: 53.
76 *Ibidem*: 54.
77 J. R. Reynolds 1883. Travelling: Its Influence on Health. In: M. Morris (ed.). The Book of Health. Cassell & Company, London, Paris and New York: 579-584.
78 *Ibidem*: 581.
79 R. D. Blumenfeld 1930. R. D. B.'s Diary, 1887-1914 William Heinemann Ltd, London: 6-7.
80 J. Johnson 1837. The Railroad Steamer. The Medico-Chirurgical Review, and Journal of Practical Medicine, 27(54): 591.
81 Harper's Weekly. 1865, September 23, 9(456): 600. Available at: https://babel.hathitrust.org/cgi/pt?id=iau.31858029244336&seq=206 (accessed 27.12.2023).
82 *Ibidem*: 593-594.
83 H. R. Wilson 1925. Railway Accidents. Legislation and Statistics 1825-1924. The Raynar Wilson Company, London.
84 The Influence of Railway Travelling..., *op. cit.*: 23.
85 Canals and Rail-Roads, 1825. The Quarterly Review 31(62): 349-378.
86 For a sample of press coverage, see: The Manchester Courier and Lancashire General Advertiser. 1830, September 18, 6(299): 3.
87 The letter was written on May 24, 1842; Ackerknecht, Erwin, 1952: Villermé and Quetelet, *Bulletin of the History of Medicine*, 26(4): 327. Translated from French.
88 One example is a lithograph by an unknown author entitled: "8 mai 1842". It depicts the derailed train in fire and a multitude of casualties. Available at: https://gallica.bnf.fr/ark:/12148/btv1b8414950k/f1.item.zoom (accessed: 28.12.2023).
89 L. Armand (ed.) 1963. Histoire des chemins de fer en France. Les Presses modernes, Paris.
90 W. Schivelbusch 2014. The Railway Journey: The Industrialization of Time and Space in the Nineteenth Century. University of California Press, Oakland (California).
91 The Influence of Railway Travelling..., *op. cit.*: 8; When interpreting accident data, we must bear in mind the possibility of underestimating some values, particularly the number of deaths. Smaller-scale incidents may not have been reported in the summary statistics. One can notice discrepancies when juxtaposing different sources. Mark Aldrich, in his study on the United States, included comparative data for Great Britain. They show that, in the period between 1857 and 1860, counting only passengers, 172 people (not 111) died in accidents. *Cf.* M. Aldrich 2006. Death Rode the Rails: American Railroad Accidents and Safety, 1828-1965. Johns Hopkins University, Baltimore.
92 The Influence of Railway Travelling..., *op. cit.*: 9.
93 Ch. Dickens 1866. No. 1 Branch Line. The Signal-Man. In: Ch. Dickens (ed.). Mugby Junction: The Extra Christmas Number of All the Year Round. Chapman & Hall, London: 20-25; M. Pope 2001. Dickens's"The Signalman" and Information Problems in the Railway Age. Technology and Culture, 42(3): 436-461.

94 Ch. Dickens (ed.) 1866, *op. cit.*: 50; A. L. Bowley 1905. The Statistics of Wages in the United Kingdom During the Last Hundred Years. (Part XI.) Engineering and Shipbuilding. Journal of the Royal Statistical Society, 68(2): 373-391; Life insurance. 2020. Available at: https://www.comparethemarket.com/life-insurance/ (accessed: 18.11.2020); Annual Survey of Hours and Earnings time series of selected estimates. 2020. Available at: https://www.ons.gov.uk/employmentandlabourmarket/peopleinwork/earningsandworkinghours/datasets/ashe1997to2015selectedestimates (accessed: 11.12.2020).

95 M. Foley 2013. Britain's Railway Disasters. Fatal Accidents from the 1830s to the Present Day. Pen & Sword, Barnsley; P. Fyfe 2013. Illustrating the Accident: Railways and the Catastrophic Picturesque in The Illustrated London News, Victorian Periodicals Review, 46: 61-91; G. Strachan 2015. Forgotten tale of Tay Bridge Disaster engine. Available at: https://www.thecourier.co.uk/news/scotland/263915/forgotten-tale-of-tay-bridge-disaster-engine (accessed: 16.11.2020).

96 Christian Herald and Signs of Our Times. 1880, London edition, January 7, 14(1). Title page available at: https://www.leisureandculturedundee.com/virtual-gallery-lamb-collection (accessed: 29.12.2023); Christian Herald and Signs of Our Times. 1880, New York edition, January 29, 14(5): 65. Available at: https://archive.org/details/christianheralds1312unse/page/n728/mode/1up (accessed: 29.12.2023).

97 Quoted in: The Dundee Courier & Argus. 1880, January 9, 8258: 5.

98 Truth. 1880, January 8, 7(158): 39.

99 P. R. Lewis, C. Gagg 2004. "Aesthetics versus function: the fall of the Dee bridge, 1847". *Interdisciplinary Science Reviews*, 29(2): 177-191; W. Taylor 2013. "Iron, Engineering and Architectural History in Crisis: Following the Case of the River Dee Bridge Disaster, 1847". *Architectural Histories*, 1(1): Art. 23.

100 *The Builder*. 1847, June 26, 5(229): 298.

101 P. R. Lewis, C. Gagg 2004, op. cit.

102 W. Schivelbusch 2014, *op. cit.*

103 D. Brandon, A. Brooke 2019, *op. cit.*

104 Punch, or The London Charivari. 1853, 25: 161.

105 Punch, or The London Charivari. 1850, 18: 4. Cartoon available at: https://doi.org/10.11588/diglit.16605#0012 (accessed: 29.12.2023)

106 R. Barrow 2015. Rape on the Railway: Women, Safety, and Moral Panic in Victorian Newspapers. Journal of Victorian Culture, 20(3): 341-356.

107 The Times. 1864, July 12: 11. Quoted in: *Ibidem*: 344.

108 W. Schivelbusch 2014, *op. cit.*; R. Barrow 2015, *op. cit.*; R. Ruddell, S. Decker 2017. Train Robbery: A Retrospective Look at an Obsolete Crime. Criminal Justice Review, 42(4): 333-348.

109 The Quarterly Review. 1825, March, 31(62): 361.

110 The Staffordshire Advertiser. 1828. February 9, 34: 3.

111 Ch. Wolmar 2007, *op. cit.*; A. Dawson 2018. The Rainhill Trials. Amberley Publishing, Stroud.

112 W. H. Brown 1874. The History of the First Locomotives in America. D. Appleton and Company, New York: fold-out sheet behind page 144. Available at: https://babel.hathitrust.org/cgi/pt?id=coo1.ark:/13960/t6n01q158&seq=161 (accessed: 29.12.2023).

113 Ch. Wolmar 2009, *op. cit.*; D. Hayes 2010, *op. cit.*

114 W. H. Brown 1874, *op. cit.* : fold-out sheet behind page 122. Available at: https://babel.hathitrust.org/cgi/pt?id=coo1.ark:/13960/t6n01q158&seq=135 (accessed: 29.12.2023).

115 H. H. Gerlach 1986. Atlas zur Eisenbahn-Geschichte: Deutschland, Österreich, Schweiz. Orell Füssli, Zürich and Wiesbaden.

116 T. Wolff 1909. Vom Ochsenwagen zum Automobil: Geschichte der Wagenfahrzeuge und des Fahrwesens von ältester bis zu neuester Zeit. Wissen und Können 10, Johann Ambrosius Barth Verlag, Leipzig: 128. Translated from German.

117 J. Francis 1851. A History of the English Railway; Its Social Relations and Revelations: 1820–1845. Volume I, Longman, Brown, Green and Longmans, London; N. Faith 1990, *op. cit.*; Ch. Wolmar 2007, *op. cit.*; D. Brandon, A. Brooke 2019, *op. cit.*
118 D. Hayes 2010, *op. cit.*
119 Text on poster as reproduced in: K. C. Kelly 2000. Anti-Railroad Propaganda Poster: The Growth of Regionalism, 1800-1860. National Archives and Records Administration, Washington, D.C. : 9.
120 J. Hepp 2015. Railroad Stations. Available at: https://philadelphiaencyclopedia.org/essays/railroad-stations (accessed: 07.12.2020).
121 S. Orth, A. Blinda 2012. Sorry, wir haben uns verfahren: Kurioses aus der Bahn. Ullstein, Berlin. Translated from German.
122 H. H. Gerlach 1986, *op. cit.*
123 Ch. Wordsworth 1851. Memoirs of William Wordsworth. Volume 2, Edward Moxon, London; I. Whyte 2000. William Wordsworth's "Guide to the Lakes" and the Geographical Tradition. Area, 32(1): 101-106; S. Yoshikawa 2020. William Wordsworth and Modern Travel: Railways, Motorcars and the Lake District, 1830-1940. Liverpool University Press, Liverpool.
124 S. O'Brien, D. Paterson (eds.) 2013. Train Songs: Poetry of the Railway. Faber & Faber, London: 42.
125 S. Yoshikawa 2020, *op. cit.*
126 W. Wordsworth 1845; Kendal and Windermere Railway: two letters re-printed from the Morning Post. R. Branthwaite and Son, Kendal: 6; The letters were sent to the newspaper in 1844 and were published with the sonnet in one pamphlet.
127 *Ibidem*: 12.
128 *Ibidem*: 16.
129 *Ibidem*: 17, 19.
130 *Ibidem*: 21.
131 J. Otley 1849. The District of the Lakes [Map]. In: J. Otley. A Descriptive Guide to the English Lakes and Adjacent Mountains: With Notices of the Botany, Mineralogy, and Geology of the District. 8th Edition, Keswick: fold-out sheet before the title page. Available at: https://babel.hathitrust.org/cgi/pt?id=coo1.ark:/13960/t2z32hp1g&seq=6 (accessed: 30.12.2023)
132 S. Yoshikawa 2020, *op. cit.*
133 The slogans were compiled from a Google image search using the keywords "Lake District railway poster."
134 W. F. Bailey 1906. The Story of the First Trans-Continental Railroad: Its Projectors, Construction and History. Pittsburgh Printing Co., Pittsburgh; Ch. Wolmar 2009, *op. cit.*; D. Hayes 2010, *op. cit.*
135 D. Hayes 2010, *op. cit.*; J. P. Rodrigue 2020. Mail Delivery Times between New York and San Francisco, 1840-2000 (in days). Available at: https://transportgeography.org/contents/chapter1/transportation-and-space/time-mail-delivery-new-york-san-francisco (accessed: 17.12.2020).
136 P. Crush 1999. Woosung Road: The Story of China's First Railway. The Railway Tavern, Hong Kong; H-Ch. Wang 2015. Merchants, Mandarins, and the Railway: Institutional Failure and the Wusong Railway, 1874-1877. International Journal of Asian Studies, 12(1): 31-53.
137 P. Crush 1999, *op. cit.*; H-Ch. Wang 2015, *op. cit.*
138 Punch, or The London Charivari. 1853, 25: 98-99. Source of the digital version: Universitätsbibliothek Heidelberg. Heidelberg historic literature – digitized. Public domain. Available at: https://doi.org/10.11588/diglit.16612#0110 (accessed: 30.12.2023).
139 D. Brandon, A. Brooke 2019, *op. cit.*
140 P. M. Kalla-Bishop 1971, *op. cit.*; B. Prusak 2004. The Church Unfinished: Ecclesiology Through the Centuries. Paulist Press, Mahwah (New Jersey).
141 A. Bruers 1953. La Chiesa e le Ferrovie. L'Osservatore Romano, 26–27 Dicembro, 300: 3.

142 M. Panconesi 2005. Le ferrovie di Pio IX. Nascita, sviluppo e tramonto delle strade ferrate dello Stato Pontificio (1846-1870). Calosci, Cortona; The wagons have survived to the present day and can be viewed in Rome's Centrale Montemartini museum; Room of the Train of Pius IX (formerly Boiler Room no. 2). 2020. available at: http://centralemontemartini.org/en/collezioni/percorsi_per_sale/sala_del_treno_di_pio_ix_gia_sala_caldaie_n_22 (accessed: 14.09.2020).

143 M. Dantesi 1863. Pio IX affacciato dal treno papale alla stazione di Velletri [Photograph]. Museo di Roma, object number: AF 689. Available at: https://passatoprossimo.museodiroma.it/pio-ix-affacciato-dal-treno-papale-alla-stazione-di-velletri (accessed: 30.12.2023).

144 John Paul II 1980. Visita pastorale a Velletri. Discorso di Giovanni Paolo II alla stazione ferroviaria. Available at: http://www.vatican.va/content/john-paul-ii/it/speeches/1980/september/documents/hf_jp-ii_spe_19800907_velletri.html (accessed: 29.08.2020).

145 John Paul II 1979. XXI Giornata Del Ferroviere. Omelia di Sua Santità Giovanni Paolo II. Available at: https://www.vatican.va/content/john-paul-ii/it/homilies/1979/documents/hf_jp-ii_hom_19791108_giornata-ferroviere.html(accessed: 29.08.2020). Translated from Italian.

146 La Ferrovia dello Stato della Città del Vaticano. 2001. Available at: http://www.vatican.va/news_services/press/documentazione/documents/sp_ss_scv/ferrovia/ferrovia_it.html (accessed: 29.08.2020).

147 B. Prusak 2004, *op. cit.*

148 Khramy na kolyosakh. 2015. In: Atlas Zheleznykh Dorog Rossii. Feoriya, Institut Ekonomiki i Razvitiya Transporta, Moscow: 224-225.

149 Own elaboration based on: Aldrich 2006, *op. cit.*; Statistical data set: Rail accidents and safety (RAI05). 2020. Available at: https://www.gov.uk/government/statistical-data-sets/rai05-rail-accidents-and-safety (accessed: 24.11.2020); Office of Rail and Road data portal. Passenger rail usage: Table 1220 - Passenger journeys. 2020. Available at: dataportal.orr.gov.uk/statistics/usage/passenger-rail-usage/table-1220-passenger-journeys (accessed: 24.11.2020).

150 Ch. Wolmar 2014, *op. cit.*

151 Own elaboration based on: O. S. Nock 1978. World Atlas of Railways, Intercontinental Book Productions, London.; A. Huurdeman 2003. The Worldwide History of Telecommunications. John Wiley & Sons, Hoboken (New Jersey); W. Schivelbusch 2014, op. *cit.;* Ch. Wolmar 2014, *op. cit.*

152 A. Huurdeman 2003, *op. cit.*; Ch. Wolmar 2014, *op. cit.*

153 Ch. Wolmar 2014, *op. cit.*

154 Shanghai Maglev Official Website. 2020. available at: http://www.smtdc.com/en/index.html (accessed: 29.12.2020).

155 In modern Greek, rail transportation described with the word *sidirodromos* (σιδηρόδρομος).

156 J. Rigler 1879. Ueber die Folgen der Verletzungen auf Eisenbahnen insbesondere der Verletzungen des Rückenmarks: mit Hinblick auf das Haftpflichtgesetz dargestellt. G. Reimer, Berlin; D. Subba 2014. Philosophy of Fearism: Life Is Conducted, Directed and Controlled by the Fear, Xlibris.

157 The Medical Times and Gazette. 1879, 1(1504): 462.

158 P. A. Jones 2017. The Cabinet of Linguistic Curiosities: A Yearbook of Forgotten Words. The University of Chicago Press, Chicago; L. Fritscher 2019. Coping With Siderodromophobia, or the Fear of Trains. Available at: https://www.verywellmind.com/siderodromophobia-2671877 (accessed: 10.12.2020).

159 P. Cozens, R. Neale, D. Hillier 2004. Tackling Crime and Fear of Crime While Waiting at Britain's Railway Stations. Journal of Public Transportation, 7(3): 23-41.

160 List of terrorist incidents involving railway systems. 2020. Available at: https://en.wikipedia.org/wiki/List_of_terrorist_incidents_involving_railway_systems (accessed: 12.12.2020).

161 Arctic Corridor: Growth through Arctic resources. 2020. Available at: https://arcticcorridor.fi (accessed: 15.12.2020).
162 Protest slogans compiled from Google image search results, using the keywords "Arctic Railway Saami" (accessed: 16.12.2020).
163 T. Nilsen 2020. The dream of an Arctic railway fades as Sami herders signal 'veto'. Available at: https://www.arctictoday.com/the-dream-of-an-arctic-railway-fades-as-sami-herders-signal-veto (accessed: 15.12.2020).
164 High Speed 1. 2020. Available at: https://highspeed1.co.uk (accessed: 16.12.2020); High Speed 2. 2020. Available at: https://www.hs2.org.uk (accessed: 16.12.2020).
165 Protest slogans compiled from Google image search results, using the keywords "Stop HS2" (accessed: 16.12.2020).
166 High Speed 2. 2020, *op. cit.* (accessed: 16.12.2020).

Chapter Two: Currents of Fear

167 A. Beltran, P. Carré 2016. La vie électrique. Histoire et imaginaire (XVIIIe-XXIe siècle). Belin, Paris.
168 J. Priestley 2013. The History and Present State of Electricity: With Original Experiments. Cambridge University Press, Cambridge. https://doi.org/10.1017/CBO9781139866309.010
169 M. W. Jernegan 1928. Benjamin Franklin's "Electrical Kite" and Lightning Rod. The New England Quarterly, 1(2): 189. P. 180–196
170 G. K. H. Zupanc, T.H. Bullock 2005. From Electrogenesis to Electroreception: An Overview. In T. H. Bullock, C. D. Hopkins, A. N. Popper, R. R. Fay (Eds.) Electroreception. Springer Handbook of Auditory Research, 21. Springer, New York, 6. https://doi.org/10.1007/0-387-28275-0_2.
171 M. Piccolino 1998. Animal electricity and the birth of electrophysiology: the legacy of Luigi Galvani. Brain Research Bulletin, 46(5): 381-407. https://doi.org/10.1016/s0361-9230(98)00026-4.
172 E. Redliński 1979. Konopielka. Ludowa Spółdzielnia Wydawnicza, Warsaw, 19.
173 C. Marvin 1988. When Old Technologies Were New: Thinking About Electric Communication in the Late Nineteenth Century. Oxford University Press, New York.
174 S. Di Grazia 2020. Quello che non conosciamo ci fa paura. Available at: http://www.medbunker.it/2020/01/quello-che-non-conosciamo-ci-fa-paura.html (accessed: 10.03.2020).
175 G. Moore 2016. The Last Days of Night: A Novel. Random House, New York, 15.
176 S. King 2014. Revival. Gallery Books - Simon & Schuster, New York, 18.
177 F. R. Upton 1880. Edison's Electric Light. Scribner's Monthly, An Illustrated Magazine For the People., 19: 544.
178 N. Tesla 1939. A Story of Youth Told by Age Dedicated to Miss Pola Fotitch by its Author Nikola Tesla. Hotel New Yorker. Letter. New York.
179 Editorial Paragraphs 1886. The Electrical World (June 5), 7(23): 257.
180 S. Volkering 2020. Just send them all to Mullumbimby. Available at: https://www.exponentialinvestor.com/energy/just-send-them-all-to-mullumbimby/ (accessed: 07.08.2020).
181 Electrical Review 1888, August 18. 4.
182 Rural Electrification Administration, U. S. Department of Agriculture 1954. Web Alison's CATROONS Spark Rural Power Story. Rural Lines, 1(1): 13.

183 L. Simon 2004. Dark Light: Electricity and Anxiety from the Telegraph to the X-ray. Harcourt, INC., Orlando, Austin, New York, San Diego, Toronto and London, 145.
184 M. Bartusiak 2013. 'The Age of Edison: Electric Light and the Invention of Modern America' by Ernest Freeberg. Available at: https://www.washingtonpost.com/opinions/the-age-of-edison-electric-light-and-the-invention-of-modern-america-by-ernest-freeberg/2013/03/01/257a76c4-6f04-11e2-8b8d-e0b59a1b8e2a_story.html (accessed: 01.09.2020).
185 New York Sun 1878, September 16. EDISON'S NEWEST MARVEL, 3.
186 E. Freeberg 2014. The Age of Edison: Electric Light and the Invention of Modern America. The Penguin Books, New York.
187 The Aberdare Times 1879, August 30. Electricity as a motive power, 3.
188 K. De Decker 2009. Electrical generators from the 1880s. Available at: https://www.lowtechmagazine.com/dynamos-electric.html (accessed: 24.09.2020).
189 G. Gooday 2016. Domesticating Electricity: Technology, Uncertainty and Gender, 1880-1914. University of Pittsburgh Press, Pittsburgh.
190 Editorial Paragraphs 1886, June 05. The Electrical World, 7(23): 257.
191 G. Gooday 2016, op. cit.
192 D. W. Denno 1994. Is Electrocution an Unconstitutional Method of Execution? The Engineering of Death over the Century. William & Mary Law Review, 35.
193 Edison Electric Light Company 1887. A warning from the Edison Electric Light Co. The Company, New York, 46.
194 H. P. Brown 1888. Letter to the Editor of the Evening Post. The Evening Post, July 05, 7.
195 Footage available at: https://www.youtube.com/watch?v=Gr6xBz-h99U (accessed: 07.06.2020).
196 Electrical Eingineer 1888. Mr. Brown's Rejoinder. Elecrical Dog Killing, 7: 369.
197 J. Jonnes 2003. Empires of Light: Edison, Tesla, Westinghouse, and the Race to Electrify the World. Random House, New York.
198 M. Winchell 2019. The Electric War: Edison, Tesla, Westinghouse, and the Race to Light the World. Henry Holt and Company, New York, 142.
199 P. J. Kocin 1983. An Analysis of the "Blizzard of '88". Bulletin American Meteorological Society, 64(11), 1258-1272. https://doi.org/10.1175/1520-0477(1983)064<1258:AAOTO>2.0.CO;2.
200 T. A. Edison 1889. The Dangers of Electric Lighting. The North American Review, 149(396): 629. 625–634
201 The Indianapolis Journal 1889, October 14. Electric-Light Perils, 5.
202 D. L. Wuebben 2019. Power-Lined: Electricity, Landscape, and the American Mind. University of Nebraska-Lincoln, Lincoln.
203 C. Juma 2016. Innovation and Its Enemies: Why People Resist New Technologies. Oxford University Press, New York. https://doi.org/10.1093/acprof:oso/9780190467036.001.0001 .
204 M. Essig 2005. Edison and the Electric Chair: A Story of Light and Death. Walker & Company, New York.
205 New York Times 1889, December 29.
206 'The Electric Light and its Friends' 1881. Journal of Gas Lighting, Water Supply and Sanitary Improvement, 38 .
207 T. A. Edison 1889, *op. cit.*, 632.
208 C. Brandon 1999. The Electric Chair: An Unnatural American History. McFarland & Company, Jefferson, 8.
209 M. Essig 2005, *op. cit.* , 231.
210 M. Essig 2005, *op. cit.*
211 T. S. Reynolds, T. Bernstein 1989. "Edison and 'the chair' [legal electrocution, history]". IEEE Technology and Society Magazine, 8(1): 19-28. https://doi.org/10.1109/44.17683.
212 C. Brandon 1999, op. cit. 125.
213 Los Angeles Herald 1890, August 07. How Kemmler Died, 1.

214 New York Times 1890, August 07, Far Worse Than Hanging, 1.
215 H. P. Brown 1889. The New Instrument of Execution. The North American Review, 149(396), 593. .
216 Death Penalty Information Center 2020. Description of Each Execution Method. Available at: https://deathpenaltyinfo.org/executions/methods-of-execution/description-of-each-method?fbclid=IwAR3Rijikc1IviU4px1J1TCsrwMZkTXN_Wd3oEBqQBpz4At_D9tgWm75Io5k (accessed: 25.09.2020).
217 Death Penalty Information Center 2020. Methods of Execution. Available at: https://deathpenaltyinfo.org/executions/methods-of-execution?fbclid=IwAR0ttvNWw1qiKu7k0Fg89k53Beok46Kpt08wVWBMKb14DQCxSapSTJpNO8U (accessed: 25.09.2020).
218 Little Falls Weekly Transcript 1897, September 10. It Impairs Sight, 5.
219 Iron County Register 1898, January 06. Electric Light Blindness, 7.
220 Oakland Tribune 1879. Oakland, California, Friday, February 7, 1879, 1.
221 Salt Lake Daily Herald 1881, December 4. The Illumination of Cities, 12.
222 The Rock Island Argus 1908, November 20. Electric Ophthalmia, 17.
223 G. Moore 2016, *op. cit.*
224 C. Juma 2016, *op. cit.* , 148.
225 J. Marseille 1998. L'electricité: Une peur française. Available at: http://archives.lesechos.fr/archives/1998/Enjeux/00140-072-ENJ.htm (accessed: 19.08.2020).
226 G. Gooday 2016, *op. cit.*
227 P. Fitzgerald 1894. The Savoy Opera and the Savoyards. Chatto & Windus, London, 97.
228 K. Sporzyński 1904. Dziwy elektryczności. Nakład Gebethnera i Wolffa, Warsaw, 14.
229 R. R. Daniels 1915. The Hygienist. Hygienist Pub. Co., Denver, Colorado, 5: 14.
230 N. N. Vladimirova 2016. Превращение электричества из диковинки в новинку. Подходы к изучению культурной истории электрификации. Общество. Среда. Развитие (Terra Humana), 4(41): 48–55.
231 G. Gooday 2007. Illuminating the Expert-Consumer Relationship in Domestic Electricity. In A. Fyfe, B. Lightman (Eds.) Science in the Marketplace: Nineteenth-Century Sites and Experiences. University of Chicago Press, Chicago: 237.
232 Musée d'Art Moderne de Paris 2020. La Fée Electricité. Available at: https://www.mam.paris.fr/fr/oeuvre/la-fee-electricite (accessed 14.07.2020).
233 The Aberdare Times 1884, September 6. The Electric Light in Mines, 2.
234 The Aberdare Times 1893, October 7. Electricity will cure you, 4.
235 Electrified Portsmouth, NH Bright Idea In 1900? 1900. Available at: http://www.seacoastnh.com/electricity-sparks-fears-in-1900/?showall=1 (accessed: 16.08.2020).
236 E. Hawks 1939. Książka o elektryczności. Gebethner i Wolff. Zakład Narodowy im. Ossolińskich, Warsaw, 66.
237 Magazyn Radia TOK FM, K. Głowacka, T. Zasuń, B. Derski 2019. „Wiek energetyków", czyli elektryzująca historia elektryfikacji Polski, audycja radiowa. Available at: https://audycje.tokfm.pl/podcast/74587,-Wiek-energetykow-czyli-elektryzujaca-historia-elektryfikacji-Polski (accessed: 02.09.2020).
238 V. C. Lagendijk 2008. Electrifying Europe: the power of Europe in the construction of electricity networks. Aksant, Amsterdam.
239 The Indianapolis Times 1988, August 12. Text of Roosevelt's Address at Barnesville, Ga, 6.
240 W. Hausman, P. Hertner, M. Wilkins 2008. Global electrification: Multinational enterprise and international finance in the history of light and power, 1878-2007. Cambridge University Press, Cambridge. https://doi.org/10.1017/CBO9780511512131.
241 *Ibidem*, 3.
242 R. Tadeusiewicz 2019. Od bursztynu do prądnicy – czyli początki przygody ludzkości z elektrycznością. Napędy i sterowanie, 7/8: 121.

243 M. Krupiński 2019. Jak elektryczność zmieniła nasze życie? Available at: https://nafalinauki.pl/jak-elektrycznosc-zmienila-nasze-zycie/ (accessed: 10.09.2020).

Chapter Three: Apocalypse Now?

244 F. Kermode 2000. The Sense of an Ending. Studies on the Theory of Fiction with a New Epilogue. Oxford University Press, p. 44-45.
245 A.T. Beck 1963. Thinking and Depression. Archives of General Psychiatry, 9(4): 324-333. DOI: 10.1001/archpsyc.1963.01720160014002; A.T. Beck, A.J. Rush, B. Shaw, G. Emery 1979. Cognitive therapy of depression. The Guilford Press, New York. M. Słodka, D. Skrzypińska 2016. Perfekcjonizm i myślenie dychotomiczne w paradygmacie poznawczo-behawioralnym – przejawy oraz techniki terapeutyczne. Psychiatria i Psychoterapia, 12(2): 20–41.
246 G. Alexander 1973. The Four Horsemen of the Apocalypse. Ambassador College Press, Pasadena, California. T. Pippin 1999. Apocalyptic Bodies: The Biblical End of the World in Text and Image. Routledge, London and New York.
247 M.H. Khan 1982. The physics of the Day of Judgment. Available at: http://www.endphysics.com/ (accessed: 20.07.2020).
248 C.C. Combs, M. Slann 2007. Encyclopedia of Terrorism: revised edition. Facts on File, New York: xiii.
249 A.J. Atchison, K.M. Heide 2010. Charles Manson and the Family: The Application of Sociological Theories to Multiple Murder. International Journal of Offender Therapy and Comparative Criminology, 55(5): 771-798. DOI: 10.1177/0306624X10371794
250 M. Staniul 2014. Samobójstwo Świątyni Ludu. Wyznawcy wielebnego Jima Jonesa zabili własne dzieci. Available at: https://opinie.wp.pl/samobojstwo-swiatyni-ludu-wyznawcy-wielebnego-jima-jonesa-zabili-wlasne-dzieci-6126018012849793a (accessed: 19.08.2020). Translated from Polish.
251 M. Kilduff, P. Tracy 1977 (August 1). New West, p. 30-38.
252 M. Maaga 1998. Hearing the Voices of Jonestown: Putting a Human Face on an American Tragedy. Syracuse University Press, Syracuse, New York. C. Lys 2005. The Violence of Jim Jones: A Biopsychosocial Explanation. Cultic Studies Review, 4(3): 268-294.
253 J.F. Mayer 1999. Les Chevaliers de L'apocalypse: L'ordre de Temple Solaire et ses adeptes. In F. Champion, M. Cohen (eds.), Sectes et Démocratie. Editions du Seuil, Paris: 220. Translated from French.
254 B. Beit-Hallahmi 2003. Apocalyptic Dreams and Religious Ideologies. The Psychoanalytic Review, 90(4): 403-439. DOI: 10.1521/prev.90.4.403.23912
255 R. Janik 1999-2000-2001. Aum Shinkrikyo - Najwyższa Prawda. Prace Naukowe, Pedagogika, 8-9-10: 85–89.
256 W. Davis 2000. Heaven's Gate: A Study of Religious Obedience. Nova Religio: The Journal of Alternative and Emergent Religions, 3(2), 241-267. DOI: 10.1525/nr.2000.3.2.241.
257 Glnody 1997. Earth Exit Statement. Available at: http://www.heavensgate.com/misc/exitgln.htm (accessed: 18.08.2020).
258 E. Croddy, C. Perez-Armendariz, J. Hart 2002. Chemical and Biological Warfare: A Comprehensive Survey for the Concerned Citizen. New York, Springer.
259 R. Kopeć 2014. Zastosowanie broni biologicznej w konfliktach zbrojnych i atakach terrorystycznych. Annales Universitatis Paedagogicae Cracoviensis, Studia de Securitate et Educatione Civili, 4(166): 49–71.
260 Planetary and Space Science Centre University of New Brunswick Fredericton 2020. Available at: http://www.passc.net/EarthImpactDatabase/New%20website_05-2018/Index.html (accessed: 30.08.2020).

261 L.W. Alvarez, W. Alvarez, F. Asaro, H.V. Michel 1980. Extraterrestrial Cause for the Cretaceous-Tertiary Extinction. Science, 208(4448): 1095-1108. DOI: 10.1126/science.208.4448.1095; P. Schulte, L. Alegret, I. Arenillas, J. Arz, P. Barton, P. Bown, P. S. Willumsen 2010. The Chicxulub asteroid impact and mass extinction at the Cretaceous-Paleogene boundary. Science, 327(5970): 1214-1218. DOI: 10.1126/science.1177265; G.S. Collins, N. Patel, T.M. Davison, A.S.P. Rae, J.V. Morgan, S.P.S. Gulick, IODP-ICDP Expedition 364 Science Party, Third-Party Scientists 2020. A steeply-inclined trajectory for the Chicxulub impact. Nature Communications, 11(1480):1-10. DOI: 10.1038/s41467-020-15269-x

262 ZetaTalk: Communications, 1995. Available at: http://www.zetatalk.com/transfor/t18.htm (accessed: 28.08.2020).

263 How the World Ends, episode 4, 2016. Canada.

264 E. Siegel 2017. The Four Ways the Earth Will Actually End. Available at: https://www.forbes.com/sites/startswithabang/2017/09/27/the-four-ways-the-earth-will-actually-end/#77820a1d4f0f (accessed: 05.09.2020).

265 J. Hogue 2013. Nostradamus 2012: The End of End Times. HogueProphecy Publishing, Langley, WA.

266 M. de Nostredame 2018. Nostradamus: The Complete Prophecies in English and French. Zem Books, p. 11. C1Q35.

267 S. Gerson 2012. Nostradamus: How an Obscure Renaissance Astrologer Became the Modern Prophet of Doom. St. Martin's Press, New York.

268 M. de Nostredame 2018, *op. cit.*, p. 265, C10Q72.

269 J. Hogue 2013, *op. cit.*

270 M. Rathford 2006. The Nostradamus Code: World War III. Truth Revealed Publishing, Massapequa Park, NY; J. Hogue 2014. The Essential Nostradamus. HogueProphecy Publishing.

271 E. Neila, M. Neila 2020. Wszystko co wiemy o UFO. Prószyński I S-ka, Warszawa, p. 21. Translated from Polish.

272 J. Fiebag, Fiebag P. 1992. Himmelszeichen. Eingriffe Gottes oder Manifestationen einer fremden Intelligenz? Goldmann Verlag, München.

273 United Nations Development Programme, 2019. Human Development Report 2019. Beyond income, beyond averages, beyond today: Inequalities in human development in the 21st century, New York.

274 A.F. Aveni 2016. Apocalyptic Anxiety: Religion, Science, and America's Obsession with the End of the World. University Press of Colorado, Boulder, Colorado, p. 215.

275 B. Pascal 1671. Pensées de M. Pascal: sur la religion, et sur quelques autres sujets. Paris. Available at: http://samizdat.qc.ca/arts/lit/Pascal/Pensees_1671_mod.pdf (accessed: 22.11.2020).

276 S. Czerwiński 1938. Koniec świata: 15 września 1936 roku. Druk. Br. Chazanczuk, Równe, p. 2. Translated from Polish.

277 T. Pippin 1999, *op. cit.*

278 W.S. Carus, 2001. Bioterrorism and Biocrimes: The Illicit Use of Biological Agents Since 1900. Center for Counterproliferation Research, National Defense university, Washington, D.C.

279 V. Courtillot 1999. Evolutionary Catastrophes: The Science of Mass Extinction. Cambridge University Press, Cambridge.

280 National Aeronautics and Space Administration 2012. Beyond 2012: Why the World Didn't End. Available at: https://www.nasa.gov/topics/earth/features/2012.html (accessed: 05.09.2020).

281 Y.N. Harari 2019. 21 Lessons for the 21st Century. Penguin Books.

282 National Aeronautics and Space Administration 2019. Planetary Defense Coordination Office. Available at: https://www.nasa.gov/planetarydefense/overview (accessed: 05.09.2020).

283 National Aeronautics and Space Administration 2019. Near-Earth Object Observations Program. Available at: https://www.nasa.gov/planetarydefense/neoo (accessed: 05.09.2020).

284 Center for Near Earth Object Studies 2020. Available at: https://cneos.jpl.nasa.gov/stats/totals.html (accessed: 24.09.2020).
285 Horoscopes: Pisces, 2020. Available at: https://www.horoscope.com/us/horoscopes/general/horoscope-archive.aspx?sign=4&laDate=20200823 (accessed: 23.08.2020).
286 B.R. Forer 1949. The fallacy of personal validation: A classroom demonstration of gullibility. Journal of Abnormal and Social Psychology, 44: 118-123.
287 D. Wooding 2001. Nostradamus' prophecies debunked in book, video set for Oct. release. Available at: https://www.baptistpress.com/resource-library/news/nostradamus-prophecies-debunked-in-book-video-set-for-oct-release/ (accessed: 20.08.2020).
288 S. Gerson 2012, *op. cit.*
289 P. Lorie 2002. Nostradamus 2003-2025: A History of the Future. Pocket Books, New York, p. 4-5.
290 K. Tomecki 2018. Papieska Lista Malachiasza. Renesansowa wizja Kościoła II tysiąclecia. Available at: https://www.academia.edu/37887100/Papieska_Lista_Malachiasza_Renesansowa_wizja_Ko%C5%9Bcio%C5%82a_II_tysi%C4%85clecia (accessed: 21.08.2020).
291 C.A. Ward 2007. Oracles of Nostradamus. Cosimo Classics, New York, NY, p. 33.
292 J. Randi 1993. The Mask of Nostradamus: The Prophecies of the World's Most Famous Seer. Prometheus Books, Amherst, NY.
293 C.A. Pickover 1998. The Science of Aliens. Basic Book, New York, NY, p. 177.
294 S.A. Clancy 2005. Abducted: How people come to believe they were kidnapped by aliens. Harvard University Press, Cambridge.
295 National Public Radio, M. Brand, S.A. Clancy 2005. 'Abducted': The Myth of Alien Kidnappings. Available at: https://www.npr.org/templates/story/story.php?storyId=5005775 (accessed: 30.08.2020)
296 A. de Saint-Exupéry 2018 The Little Prince. Rupa Publications India, New Delhi, p. 77.
297 Billionaire bunkers: How the 1% are preparing for the apocalypse 2019. Available at: http://edition.cnn.com/style/article/doomsday-luxury-bunkers/index.html (accessed: 30.08.2020).
298 Doomsday Preppers, season 1, episode 8, 2012. Sharp Entertainment, NGC Studios, United States.
299 D. Duray 2012. The NASA Scientist Who Answers Your 2012 Apocalypse Emails. Available at: https://www.theawl.com/2012/09/the-nasa-scientist-who-answers-your-2012-apocalypse-emails/ (accessed: 30.08.2020)
300 National Public Radio, N. Conan, D. Morrison 2012. Ask A NASA Astrobiologist About Dec. 21 'Doomsday'. Available at: https://www.npr.org/transcripts/165928588 (accessed: 30.08.2020)
301 P. Geryl, 2015. How to survive 2012. Adventures Unlimited Press, Kempton; C. Goffard 2011. Harold Camping is at the heart of a mediapocalypse. Available at: https://www.latimes.com/archives/la-xpm-2011-may-21-la-me-rapture-20110521-story.html (accessed: 20.08.2020); How to survive 2012. Available at: http://web.archive.org/web/20120423112240/http://www.howtosurvive2012.com/htm_night/survival_01.htm (accessed: 25.08.2020).
302 Data source: Bulletin of the Atomic Scientists 2024. Timeline. Available at: https://thebulletin.org/doomsday-clock/past-statements/ (accessed: 07.03.2024).
303 Data source: https://trends.google.com/trends/explore?date=all&q=world%20end (accessed: 31.08.2020).
304 F.D. Roosevelt 2008. Inaugural Address of Franklin Delano Roosevelt: Given in Washington, D.C. March 4th, 1933. Project Gutenberg.

Chapter Four: Never Trust an Atom

305 K. Jay 1961. Nuclear Power, Today and Tomorrow. Methuen & Co. Ltd., London.

306 UNSCEAR 2011. Sources, effects and risks of ionizing radiation. UNSCEAR 2008 Report to the General Assembly, Vol. II, Scientific Annex D. UN, New York. UNSCEAR 2014. Sources, effects and risks of ionizing radiation. UNSCEAR 2013 Report to the General Assembly, Vol. I, Scientific Annex A. UN, New York.

307 J. Conca 2012. How Deadly Is Your Kilowatt? We Rank The Killer Energy Sources. Forbes. Available at: https://www.forbes.com/sites/jamesconca/2012/06/10/energys-deathprint-a-price-always-paid/?sh=249a9998709b (accessed 18.12.2020).

308 B.S. Dhillon 2018. Safety, Reliability, Human Factors, and Human Error in Nuclear Power Plants. CRC Press, Boca Raton.

309 J.W. Mansfield 1984. The Nuclear Power Debate. A Guide to the Literature. Garland Publishing Inc., New York and London: 2.

310 S.R. Weart 1988. Nuclear Fear: A History of Images. Harvard University Press, Cambridge and London. S.R. Weart 2012. The rise of nuclear Fear. Harvard University Press, Cambridge and London.

311 A. Blowers 2017. The Legacy of nuclear power. Routledge, Abingdon and New York.

312 F. Pearce 2018. Fallout: Disasters, Lies, and the Legacy of the Nuclear Age. Beacon Press.

313 IAEA 2020. Nuclear power reactors in the world. Reference data series no 2. IAEA, Vienna.

314 Road traffic injuries 2020. World Health Organisation. Available at: https://www.who.int/news-room/fact-sheets/detail/road-traffic-injuries (accessed 20.12.2020).

315 Atom Energy Hope is Spiked by Einstein: Efforts at Loosing Vast Force Is Called Fruitless 1934. Pittsburgh Post-Gazette, 29 December.

316 Atom-Powered World Absurd, Scientists Told 1933. New York Herald Tribune, September 12: 1.

317 R. Millikan 1928. Speech to Chemists' Club, in: C.R. Richmond 1988. Population Exposure from the Fuel Cycle: Review and Future Direction. Report Prepared by the Oak Ridge National Laboratory: 6.

318 F. Soddy 1912. The Interpretation of Radium. Murray, London: 251.

319 I.F. Clarke 1979. The Pattern of Expectation 1644-2001. Basic Books, New York.

320 G. Le Bon 1903. New York World. William Hammer Collection, National Museum of American History, Smithsonian Institution, Washington, D.C.

321 T.J.C. Martyn 1929. In Science Lies the Challenge to War. New York Times Magazine, 30 June: 4-5.

322 Museum 1903. Salem Massachusetts Newspaper, 29 September, reprinted from N.Y. Sun, Hammer Collection.

323 G. Le Bon 1909, L'Evolution de la Matiere. Flammarion: 57.

324 R. Brecher, E. Brecher 1969. The Rays: A History of Radiology in the United States and Canada. Williams and Wilkins, Baltimore.

325 The Phantom Empire 1935. Mascot Pictures.

326 J.B. Priestley 1938. The Doomsday Men: An Adventure. Heinemann, London.

327 S.R. Weart 1979. Scientists in Power. Harvard University Press, Cambridge.

328 A. Troller 1939. Les Transmutations de l'uranium. La Nature 67(2): 197-201. B. Bliven 1941. The World-Shaking Promise of Atomic Research. Reader's Digest, July: 103-106.

329 New York Times 1939. 5 March, section 2. Page 9, in S.R. Weart 1988, *op. cit.*

330 V-3? 1944. Time 44.27: 88.

331 L. Giovannitti, F. Freed 1963. The Decission to drop the bomb. Coward McCann, New York: 197.
332 H.S. Truman 1955. Memoirs, Volume I: Year of Decisions. Garden City. Doubleday & Company, New York.
333 H.V. Kaltenborn 1945. NBC radio, August 6, in S.R. Weart 1988, *op. cit.*: 104-105.
334 Atoms... broken loose 1946. Reuters, 4 February.
335 E.A. Shils 1956. The Torment of Secrecy: The Background and Consequences of American Security Policies. Free Press, Glencoe.
336 J.R. Oppenheimer 1955. The Open Mind. Simon & Schuster, New York.
337 U.S. National Archives, Record Group 77, Records of the Chief of Engineers, Manhattan Engineer District, Harrison-Bundy File, folder #76.
338 R.K. Kennedy 1969. Thirteen Days. W.W. Norton, New York: 180.
339 H.G. Nicholas 1981. Washington Despatches, 1941-1945: Weekly Political Reports from the British Embassy. University of Chicago Press, Chicago.
340 W. Kaempfert 1947. New York Times, January 28: 16.
341 R.G. Hewlett, J.M. Holl, Jack 1989. Atoms for Peace and War, 1953-1961: Eisenhower and the Atomic Energy Commission. University of California Press.
342 C. Cerf, V. Navasky 1984. The Experts Speak: The Definitive Compendium of Authoritative Misinformation. Pantheon Books.
343 E. Teller 1953. Reactor Hazards Predictable. Nucleonics, 11(11): 80.
344 New York Times 1955. 11 August: 11.
345 A.P. Armagnac 1956. How Safe Are Our A-Power Plants. Popular Science, 169: 134.
346 J.S. Walker 2004. Three Mile Island: A Nuclear Crisis in Historical Perspective. University of California Press, Berkeley.
347 R.F. Pocock 1977. Nuclear Power: Its Development in the United Kingdom. Unwin, Surrey.
348 J. Urquhart, M. Palmer, J. Cutler 1984. Cancer in Cumbria: the Windscale connection. United Kingdom. Lancet, 28(1): 217-18.
349 M.C. Hatch, S. Wallenstein, J. Beyea, J.W. Nieves, M. Susser 1991. Cancer rates after the Three Mile Island nuclear accident and proximity of residence to the plant. American Journal of Public Health. 81(6): 719–724.
350 UNSCEAR 2011, *op. cit.*
351 T. Parfitt, Tom 2006. Opinion remains divided over Chernobyl's true toll. The Lancet, 367 (9519): 1305-1306.
352 The Chernobyl Catastrophe. Consequences on Human Health 2006. Greenpeace, Amsterdam.
353 UNSCEAR 2011, *op. cit.*
354 Chernobyl's Legacy: Health, Environmental and Socio-Economic Impacts. The Chernobyl Forum: 2003-2005. Available at: http://chernobyl.info/Portals/0/Docs/en/pdf_en/chernobyl_digest_report_EN.pdf (20.12.2020).
355 D. Trichopoulos, X. Zavitsanos, C. Koutis, P. Drogari 1987. The victims Chernobyl in Greece: induced abortions after the accident. British Medical Journal, 295: 1100. L.B. Knudsen 1991. Legally-induced abortions in Denmark after Chernobyl. Biomedicine & Pharmacotherapy, 45(6): 229-231.
356 Demonstration on Chernobyl Day near WHO in Geneva to ask for the amendment of the WHO-IAEA agreement. Pictures of liquidators 2011. Available at: https://commons.wikimedia.org/wiki/File:20110426-IWHO-22.jpg (accessed 12.09.2020).
357 I. Eckerman 2005. The Bhopal Saga-Causes and Consequences of the World's Largest Industrial Disaster. India Universities Press.
358 R. Greenslade 2011. How the papers are covering Japan's catastrophe. The Guardian, 16 March.
359 UNSCEAR 2014, *op. cit.*: 10.

360 Japan confirms first Fukushima worker death from radiation 2018. BBC News. Available at: https://www.bbc.com/news/world-asia-45423575 (accessed 20.12.2020).
361 S. Sekine 2020. Nine years later, 32 more deaths in Fukushima tied to disaster. The Asahi Shimbun. Available at: http://www.asahi.com/ajw/articles/13199954 (accessed 20.12.2020).
362 J. Meese, J. Frith, R. Wilken 2020. COVID-19, 5G conspiracies and infrastructural futures. Media International Australia, 177(1): 30-46.
363 L. Kołakowski 2009, *op. cit.*
364 F. Soddy 1935. Foreword to The Frustration of Science, in: G.B. Kaufmann (ed.) 1986. Frederick Soddy (1877-1956). Early pioneer in radiochemistry. D. Riedel Publishing Company, Dordrecht: 24.
365 R.W. Rydell 1985. The Fan Dance of Science: American World's Fairs in the Great Depression. Isis, 76: 525-542.
366 W.E. Williams 2018. Can we trust experts? Arkansas Democrat-Gazette, July 26.
367 J. Goodman, F. Carmichael 2020. Coronavirus: Bill Gates 'microchip' conspiracy theory and other vaccine claims fact-checked. BBC News. Available at: https://www.bbc.com/news/52847648 (accessed 10.09.2020).
368 M. Howorth 1958, Pioneer Research on the Atom: ... The Life Story of Frederick Soddy. New World, London: 274.
369 A. Brzozowski 2012. *Kalendarium życia Marii Skłodowskiej-Curie*. Mówią Wieki. Magazyn Historyczny, 3: 6-7.
370 A. Wattenberg 1982. December 2, 1942 BAS 38(10): 2232.
371 MUC-AC-89, 16 February 1943 MUC files.
372 Our Friend the Atom 1956. Walt Disney.
373 President Toasts Milk with Milk Fall-Out Surveillance 1962. New York Times, 24 January.
374 B.D. Melber et al. 1977. Nuclear Power and the Public: Analysis of collected survey research. Report PNL-2430, in: S.R. Weart 1988, *op. cit.*: 366.
375 A. Dylikowa, D. Makowska, J. Makowski, T. Olszewski 1997. Ziemia i człowiek. Handbook of geography for secondary school. WSiP, Warsaw: 267.
376 K. Chyla 1985. Fizyka dla IV klasy technikum i liceum zawodowego. WSiP, Warsaw.
377 M. Fiałkowska 2012. Świat fizyki. Podręcznik dla szkół ponadgimnazjalnych, zakresu podstawowy. ZamKor, Kraków.
378 E. Rutherford 1905. Harper's Magazine, in: C.R. Richmond 1988, *op. cit.*: 9.
379 C.R. Richmond 1988, *op. cit.*.
380 A.O. Gettler, C. Norris 1933. Poisoning from Drinking Radium Water. Journal of the American Medical Association, 100: 400-402.
381 D. Normile 2018. Bucking global trends, Japan again embraces coal power. Science. 360(6388): 476–77.
382 Nuclear reactor restarts in Japan displacing LNG imports in 2019. EIA. Available at: https://www.eia.gov/todayinenergy/detail.php?id=38533 (accessed 21.12.2020).
383 Germany shuts down atomic plant as nuclear phase-out enters final stretch 2011. DW. Available at: https://www.dw.com/en/germany-shuts-down-atomic-plant-as-nuclear-phase-out-enters-final-stretch/a-51845616 (accessed 15.12.2020).
384 Italy nuclear: Berlusconi accepts referendum blow 2011. BBC News. 14 June.
385 L. Strauss 1956. AEC Folder 1955-56 (4): 4, in: S.R. Weart 1988, *op. cit.*
386 W. Rudig 1990. Anti-nuclear Movements: A World Survey of Opposition to Nuclear Energy. Longman.
387 L.D. Smith 1972. Evolution of Opposition to the Peaceful uses of Nuclear Energy. Nuclear Engineering International, 17: 461-468.
388 A.B. Lovins 1976. Energy Strategy: The road not taken? Forreign Affairs (55): 93.

389 R. Jungk 1979. The New TYranny: How Nuclear Power Enslaves Us. Grosset and Dunlap, New York.
390 B.D. Melber, W.L. Rankin, 1983. Public Opinion and Nuclear Energy. D.C. Heath, Lexington.
391 M. Hvistendahl 2007. Coal Ash Is More Radioactive Than Nuclear Waste. Scientific American. Available at: https://www.scientificamerican.com/article/coal-ash-is-more-radioactive-than-nuclear-waste/ (accessed 22.12.2020).
392 Mississauga Miracle: Remembering the disaster that forced 240,000 people to flee 2019. CBC News. Available at: https://www.cbc.ca/news/canada/toronto/mississauga-miracle-remembering-the-disaster-that-forced-240-000-people-to-flee-1.5354329 (accessed 21.12.2020).
393 Typhoon Nina-Banqiao dam failure 2020. Encyclopaedia Britannica. Available at: https://www.britannica.com/event/Typhoon-Nina-Banqiao-dam-failure (accessed 18.12.2020).
394 N. Gee 2020. Case Study: Machhu Dam II (Gujarat, India, 1979). Available at: https://damfailures.org/case-study/machhu-dam-ii-gujarat-india-1979/ (accessed 18.12.2020).
395 P. Ball 2014. J. Lovelock reflects on Gaia's legacy. Nature. Available at: https://www.nature.com/news/james-lovelock-reflects-on-gaia-s-legacy-1.15017 (accessed 15.09.2020).
396 J. Lovelock 2014. A rough ride to the future. Harry N. Abrams Press: chapter 8.
397 M. Lamp 2011. Colorado Radiation Levels Are High, And That's Normal. CPR. Available at: https://www.cpr.org/2011/03/22/colorado-radiation-levels-are-high-and-thats-normal/ (accessed 10.09.2020).
398 International Commission on Radiological Protection 1984. Principles for Limiting Exposure of the Public to Natural Sources of Radiation, ICRP Publication, 39.
399 National Radiological Protection Board 1986. Living with Radiation, Great Britain.
400 C.R. Richmond 1988, *op. cit.:* 20.
401 P.A. Kharecha, J.E. Hansen 2013. Prevented Mortality and Greenhouse Gas Emissions from Historical and Projected Nuclear Power, Environmental Science & Technology, 47 (9): 4889-95.
402 Polish academics urge end to Germany's nuclear phaseout 2019. World Nuclear News. Available at: https://world-nuclear-news.org/Articles/Polish-academics-urge-end-to-Germany-s-nuclear-pha (accessed 20.09.2020).
403 I. Kantor-Pietraga, R. Machowski (Eds) 2012. Przemiany przestrzenne oraz społeczne Bytomia i jego centrum. Studia i materiały. Uniwersytet Śląski, Wydział Nauk o Ziemi. Sosnowiec.
404 R.R.K. Nair, R. Balakrishnan; A. Suminori, P. Jayalekshmi, M.K. Nair, P. Gangadharan, K. Taeko, H. Morishima, S. Nakamura, T. Sugahara 2009. Background Radiation and Cancer Incidence in Kerala, India-Karanagappally Cohort Study. Health Physics. 96 (1): 55–66.
405 Death rates from energy production per TWh 2020. Our world in data. Available at: https://ourworldindata.org/grapher/death-rates-from-energy-production-per-twh (accessed 17.12.2020).
406 Radioactive Waste Management 2020. World Nuclear Association. Available at: https://www.world-nuclear.org/information-library/nuclear-fuel-cycle/nuclear-wastes/radioactive-waste-management.aspx (accessed 15.19.2020).
407 Data source: Our World in Data 2020. Available at: https://ourworldindata.org/grapher/death-rates-from-energy-production-per-twh (accessed 17.12.2020).
408 Picture available at: https://www.green-news.pl/1222-nie-atom-nie-oze-tylko-wegiel-zwiazkowcy-protest-PGE (accessed 10.12.2020).
409 C-N. Martin 1956. The Atom, master of the world. Centurion, Paris: 194.
410 First HTR-PM vessel head in place 2018. World Nuclear News. Available at: https://www.world-nuclear-news.org/NN-First-HTR-PM-vessel-head-in-place-0401185.html (accessed 19.09.2020).

411 G. Locatelli, M. Mancini, N. Todeschini, 2013. Generation IV nuclear reactors: Current status and future prospects. Energy Policy. 61: 1503–1520.
412 A. Hoffman 2016. How Leonardo DiCaprio Got People to Care About Climate Change. Time. Available at: https://time.com/4441219/leonardo-dicaprio-oscars-climate-change/ (accessed 17.12.2020).
413 A. France 1909. Penguin Island. Dodd, Mead, New York.
414 Kurzgesagt - In a Nutshell 2015. Three reasons why Nuclear Energy is terrible! Youtube. Available at: https://www.youtube.com/watch?v=HEYbgyL5n1g (accessed 22.12.2020).
415 Verge Science 2018. 88,000 tons of radioactive waste - and nowhere to put it, 28. Youtube. Available at: https://www.youtube.com/watch?v=YgVyPwhkoJs (accessed 22.12.2020).
416 H. Caldicott 2011. After Fukushima: Enough Is Enough, New York Times, 2 December. Available at: https://www.nytimes.com/2011/12/02/opinion/magazine-global-agenda-enough-is-enough.html (accessed 15.09.2020).
417 TIME Magazine Cover 1979. Three Mile Island. Time, April 9. Available at: http://content.time.com/time/covers/0,16641,19790409,00.html (accessed 17.09.2020).
418 F. Furedi 2007. The only thing we have to fear is the 'culture of fear' itself NEW ESSAY: How human thought and action are being stifled by a regime of uncertainty, Spiked, 4 April. Available at: https://www.spiked-online.com/2007/04/04/the-only-thing-we-have-to-fear-is-the-culture-of-fear-itself/ (accessed 20.11.2021).

Chapter Five: Is the Earth Big Enough for Us All?

419 A. Ehrlich, 1985. The Human Population: Size and Dynamics. American Zoologist, 25: 395-406.
420 R. Nielsen 2017. Economic Growth and the Growth of Human Population in the Past 2,000,000 Years. Journal of Economics Bibliography 4 (2): 128-149.
421 D. Pimentel, M. Pimentel 2008. Food, Energy and Society. Third Edition. CRC Press, Boca Raton, London, New York.
422 J. Tanton 1994. End of the Migration Epoch? Time For a New Paradigm. The Social Contract Journal 4(3): 162-173. United States Census Bureau. Historical Estimates of World Population. Available at: https://www.census.gov/data/tables/time-series/demo/international-programs/historical-est-worldpop.html (Accessed: 21.08.2020).
423 *Ibidem.*
424 United Nations 2019. World Population Prospects. Average annual rate of population change by region, subregion and country, 1950-2100 (percentage). UN Population Division, Department of Economic and Social Affairs. Online Edition. Rev. 1. Available at: https://population.un.org/wpp/Download/Standard/Population/ (accessed: 01.12.2020).
425 Genesis 1:28.
426 M. H. Levin 1992 Religion, Sex and Holiness. Bioethics Forum 8 (3): 31-35.
427 K. Mishra, A. Dubey, 2014. Indian Women's Perspectives on Reproduction and Childlessness: Narrative Analysis. International Journal of Humanities and Social Science Vol. 4, No. 6 (1): 157-164.
428 B. A. Lemu, F. Heeren 2003. Woman in Islam. Kano: The Islamic Foundation, Nigeria.
429 O. Nydahl 2012. Buddha and Love. Timeless Wisdom for Modern Relationships. Brio Books, Australia.

430 V. Skirbekk M. Stonawski, S. Fukuda T. Spoorenberg, C. Hackett, R. Muttarak, 2015. Is Buddhism the low fertility religion of Asia? Demographic Research 32 (1): 1-28.
431 F. Festini, M. de Martino 2004. Twenty five years of the one child family policy in China. Journal of Epidemiology & Community Health, 58(5): 358-360.
432 B. Stark 2005. International family law: an introduction. Ashgate Publishing Limited, Aldershot.
433 P. Neurath 1994 (2015 edition). From Malthus to the Club of Rome and Back. Problem of Limits to Growth, Population Control and Migrations. Routledge, Taylor &Francis Group, London and New York.
434 Z. Pavlik 2016 Thomas Robert Malthus (1766-1834). Demography 58 (4): 338–348.
435 M. Liebig 2016. Statecraft and Intelligence Analysis in the KauäilÏya-ArthaàÈstra. In: P. K. Gautam, S. Mishra, A. Gupta (eds). Indigenous Historical Knowledge: Kautilya and His Vocabulary. Pentagon Press, New Delhi: 33-62.
436 R. H. Feen 1996. Keeping the Balance: Ancient Greek Philosophical Concerns with Population and Environment. Population and Environment 17(6): 447-458.
437 N. Keyfitz 1991. Population and Development Within the Ecosphere: One View of the Literature. Population Index 57(1): 5-22.
438 M.I. Hassan 2020. Population Geography: A Systematic Exposition. Routledge, London & New York.
439 E. S. Brezis, W. Young 2014. Population and economic growth: Ancient and modern. European Journal History of Economic Thought 23(2): 246-271.
440 M.I. Hassan 2020, op. cit.
441 Y. Charbit 2002. The Political Failure of an Economic Theory: Physiocracy. Population (English edition) 57(6): 855-883; D. Gleicher 1982. The Historical Bases of Physiocracy: An Analysis of the "Tableau Economique". Science & Society, 46 (3): 328-360.
442 J. J. Spengler 1970. Adam Smith on Population. Population Studies 24 (3): 377-388.
443 Ch. Siegel 2011. Classical liberalism, Preservation Institute, Berkeley.
444 R. Raico 2012. Classical liberalism and the Austrian School. Ludiwg von Mises Intitute, Auburn.
445 Z. Pavlik 2016, op. cit.
446 T.R. Malthus 1798. An Essay on the Principle of Population, as it Affects the Future Improvement of Society with Remarks on the Speculations of Mr. Godwin, M. Condorcet, and Other Writers. J. Johnson, London. (Electronic Scholarly Publishing Project, 1998) Available at: https://rescuingbiomedicalresearch.org/wp-content/uploads/2015/04/Malthus-1798.pdf (accessed 16.08.2020)
447 R. Bailey 2015. The End of Doom: Environmental Renewal in the Twenty-first Century. Saint Mark Press, New York, p. 9.
448 K. Levitan 2008. Redundancy, the Surplus Woman Problem, and the British Census, 1851-1861. Women's History Review 17(3): 359-376.
449 P. Atkins, I. Bowler 2001. Food in society: economy, culture, geography Arnold, London.
450 B. Ward 1966. Spaceship Earth. Columbia University Press, New York, p. 15.
451 P. Ehrlich 1968. The population bomb. Ballantine Books, New York.
452 J. Conrad, 2010. Resource Economics, second edition. Cambridge University Press, New York.
453 P. Ehrlich 1968, op. cit. , p. xi.
454 Population of Kolkata 2020. https://indiapopulation2020.in/population-of-kolkata-2020.html (accessed: 6.01.2021).
455 P. Ehrlich, A. Ehrlich 1990 The Population Explosion. Simon & Shuster. New York.
456 R. A. Bulatao, E. Bos, P. W. Stephens, M. T. Vu 1989. World Population Projections. 1989-90 Edition. Short- and Long-Term Estimates. The Johns Hopkins University Press, Baltimore & London.

457 D. H. Meadows, D. L. Meadows, J. Randers, W. W. Behrens 1972. The Limits to Growth. University Books, New York.
458 G.K. Heilig 1996. World Population Prospects: Analyzing the 1996 UN Population Projections. Laxenburg, Austria (IIASA Electronic Document and Working Paper). Available at: http://pure.iiasa.ac.at/id/eprint/4882/1/WP-96-146.pdf (Accesed: 21.10.2020).
459 The State of Food Security and Nutrition in the World 2020. Transforming food systems for affordable healthy diets. Rome, FAO. Available at: https://docs.wfp.org/api/documents/WFP-0000117811/download/ (accessed: 09.12.2020).
460 D. H. Meadows, D. L. Meadows, J. Randers, W. W. Behren 1972, op. cit.
461 D. H. Meadows, D. L. Meadows, J. Randers 1992. Beyond the Limits: Confronting Global Collapse, Envisioning a Sustainable Future. Chelsea Green Publishing Co, Vermont.
462 D. H. Meadows, D. L. Meadows, J. Randers 2004. Limits to Growth. The 30-year Update. Chelsea Green Publishing Co, Vermont.
463 G.O. Barney (Ed.) 1980. Global 2000 Report to the President. Vol. 1: Entering the Twenty-first Century. U.S. Government Printing Office, Washington.
464 United Nations 1958. The Future Growth of World Population. Population Studies 28. Department of Economic and Social Affairs UN, New York.
465 Population: The Numbers. Popualtion Matters. https://populationmatters.org/the-facts/the-numbers (accessed: 23.09.2020).
466 United Nations 2019, op. cit.
467 P. Ehrlich 1968, op. cit.
468 R. Brown, G. Gardner, B. Halweil 1999. Beyond Malthus: Nineteen Dimensions of the Population Challenge. W.W. Norton & Company, New York London.
469 D. Lam 2005. How the World Survived the Population Bomb: An Economic Perspective. In: S. Asefa (Ed). The Economics of Sustainable Development. W.E. Upjohn Institute for Employment Research, Kalamazoo, Michigan: 99-132.
470 M. L. Tupy 2018. Julian Simon Was Right. A Half-Century of Population Growth, Increasing Prosperity, and Falling Commodity Prices. Economic Development Bulletin 29:1-12, p. 8.
471 C. Marquette 1997. Turning But Not Toppling Malthus: Boserupian Theory on Population and the Environment Relationships. Chr. Michelsen Institute, Development Studies and Human Rights. Working Paper 16. Available at: http://hdl.handle.net/11250/2435923 (accessed: 23.08.2020).
472 E. Boserup 1965. The Conditions of Agricultural Growth: The Economics of Agrarian Change Under Population Pressure. G. Allen and Unwin, London. E. Boserup, 1981. Population and Technological Change. University of Chicago Press, Chicago.
473 C. Bloom, D. Canning, J. Sevilla 2003. The demographic dividend: A new Perspective on the Economic Consequences of Population Change. Rand, Santa Monica.
474 C. Marquette 1997, op. cit.
475 E. Boserup 1965, op. cit.
476 S. Kuznets 1967. Population and Economic Growth, in Population Problems. Proceedings of the American Philosophical Society 3, 170-93.
477 P. D. Aligica 2009. Julian Simon and the "Limits to Growth" Neo-Malthusianism. The Electronic Journal of Sustainable Development. 1(3): 73-84.
478 J. Simon 1981. The Ultimate Resource. Princeton University Press, Princeton, New York.
479 J. Simon 1999. Hoodwinking the Nation. Transaction, New Brunswick, New York.
480 *Ibidem*, p. 35-36
481 C. Bloom, D. Canning, J. Sevilla 2003, op. cit.
482 P. Neurath 1994, op. cit.

483 B. Mirkin 2005. Evolution of National Population policies since the Untated Nations 1954 World Population Coneference. Genus 61(3-4). Trends And Problems Of The World Population In The XXI Century, 50 years since Rome 1954: 297-328.
484 J. Olszynko-Gryn, C. Rusterholz 2019. Reproductive Politics in Twentieth-Century France and Britain. Medical History 63(2): 117-133.
485 G. Heilig, T. Buttner, W. Lutz 1990. Germany's Population: Turbulent Past, Uncertain Future. IIASA Research Report (Reprint). IIASA, Laxenburg, Austria: RR-91-010. Reprinted from Population Bulletin, 45(4):1-46. Available at: http://pure.iiasa.ac.at/id/eprint/3363/ (accessed: 28.10.2020).
486 K.L. Brashler 2015. Mothers for Germany: a look at the ideal woman in Nazi propaganda. Graduate Theses and Dissertations 14354. Iowa State University. Available at: https://lib.dr.iastate.edu/etd/14354 (Accessed 23.10.2010).
487 E. Oinonen 2008. Families in Converging Europe: A Comparison of Forms, Structures and Ideals, Palgrave Macmillan, Hounfmills, Basingstoke, Hampshire.
488 M. Livi-Bacci 2007. A concise History of World Population (4th ed.). Blackwell, Malden MA.
489 R.H. Feen 1996, op. cit.
490 W. Huang 2017. How does the one child policy impact social and economic outcomes? IZA World of Labor 387. Available at: https://wol.iza.org/uploads/articles/387/pdfs/how-does-the-one-child-policy-impact-social-and-economic-outcomes.pdf (accessed: 18.10.2020).
491 W. Feng, Y. Cai, B. Gu 2012. Population, Policy, and Politics: How Will History Judge China's One-Child Policy? Population and Development Review 38 (Supplement): 115-129.
492 M. Frey 2011. Neo-Malthusianism and development: shifting interpretations of a contested paradigm. Journal of Global History 6: 75-97.
493 T. Schultz 1980. Nobel Lecture: The Economics of Being Poor, Journal of Political Economy, 88 (4): 639-51, p. 640.
494 M. Frey 2011, op. cit.
495 J.F. May 2012. World Polulation Policies: Their Origin, Evolution and Impact, Springer, New York.
496 M. Connelly 2006. Population Control in India: Prologue to the Emergency Period. Population and Development Review 32(4): 629-667.
497 J. Peron 1995. Exploding Population Myths. Fraser Forum. Critical Issues Bulletin: a supplement to the monthly publication from The Fraser Institute. The Fraser Institute, Vancouver, B.C. Canada.
498 G. Hardin 1968. The tragedy of the commons. Science, 162 (3859): 1243-1248, p. 1248.
499 S. Greenhalgh 2005. Missile Science, Population Science: The Origins of China's One-Child Policy. The China Quarterly, 182: 253-276.
500 W. Feng, Y. Cai, B. Gu 2012, op. cit.
501 A.Y. Ebenstein, E.J. Sharygin 2009. The Consequences of the "Missing Girls" of China. World Bank Economy Review, 23(3): 399-425.
502 W. Feng, Y. Cai, B. Gu 2012, op. cit.
503 M. T. Yap 2003. Fertility and Population Policy: the Singapore Experience. Journal of Population and Social Security (Population), Supplement to Volume 1: 643-658.
504 T. Wong, B. Jeoh 2003. Fertility and the Family: An Overview of Pro-natalist Population Policies in Singapore. Asian MetaCentre Research Paper Series 12. Asian MetaCentre For Population and Sustainable Development Analysis, Singapore.
505 G. Heilig, T. Buttner, W. Lutz 1990, op. cit.
506 M. Connelly 2006, op. cit.
507 United Nations 2019 p. cit.

508 F. L. Cooke 2017. The two-child policy in China: a blessing or a curse for the employment of female university graduates? In Making Work More Equal. Ed. D. Grimshaw, C. Fagan, G. Hebson, I. Tavora. 227-245. Manchester University Press. Manchester UK.
509 M. T. Yap 2003, op. cit.
510 M. Lee, Y-H Lin 2016. Transition from Anti-natalist to Pro-natalist Policies in Taiwan. In: R. Rindfuss, M. Choe (eds). Low Fertility, Institutions, and their Policies, 259-281. Springer, Cham.
511 J. Peron 1995, op. cit.
512 D. L. Poston, E. Conde, B. De Salvo 2011. China's unbalanced sex ratio at birth, millions of excess bachelors and societal implications. Vulnerable Children and Youth Studies 6 (4): 314-320.
513 R.H. Feen 1996, op. cit.
514 P. Atkins, I. Bowler 2001. Food in society: economy, culture, geography. Arnold, London.
515 J. Cohen 1995. Population Growth and Earth's Human Carrying Capacity. Science 269 (5222): 341-346.
516 T. Frejka 1981. World population projections: A concise history. Center for Policy Studies Working Papers. The Population Council, New York. Availabe at: https://pdf.usaid.gov/pdf_docs/PNAAR555.pdf (accessed 23.09.2020).
517 Gianmaria Ortes on The Limits Of Population Growth. Population and Development. Review 2019, 44: 833-838, p. 835.
518 P. Ehrlich 1968, op. cit.
519 D. Willey 2000. An optimum world population. Medicine, Conflict and Survival 16 (1): 72-94.
520 J.P. Holdren 1991. Population and the energy problem. Population and Environment 12: 231-255.
521 J. Cohen 1995. How many people can the Erth support? W.W. Norton & Company, New York.
522 C. Clark 1967. Population and food, in Population Growth and Land Use. Macmillan, London, UK.
523 G.K. Heilig 1996, op. cit.
524 J. C. J. M. Van Den Bergh, P. Rietveld 2004. Reconsidering the Limits to World Population: Meta-analysis and Meta-prediction. BioScience 54(3): 195-204.
525 L.R. Taylor 1970 (ed.). The Optimum population for Britain: Proceedings of a symposium held at the Royal Geographical Society, London, on 25 and 26 September, 1969. Academic Press, London, New York.
526 P. Whelpton 1947. Forecasts of the Population of the United States 1945-1975. United States Government Printing Office, Washington. Available at: https://apps.dtic.mil/sti/pdfs/ADA366309.pdf (accessed: 10.10.2020).
527 L. H. Day, A. T. Day 1964. Too Many Americans. Houghton Mifflin, Boston.
528 T. Schultz 1980, op. cit.
529 J. Peron 1995, op. cit.
530 Irving 1985, cited in J. Peron 1995, op. cit, p. 27.
531 D. H. Meadows, D. L. Meadows, J. Randers, W. W. Behrens 1972, op. cit.
532 P. Harrison 1983. Land and People, the Growing Pressure. Earthwatch 13: 1-8.
533 L. R. Brown 1996. Tough choices: facing the challenge of food scarcity. W.W. Norton & Company. New York.
534 World Grain Production, Area, and Yield, 1950-2012. Earth Policy Institute. Available at: http://www.earth-policy.org/?/data_center/C24/ (accessed: 10.10.2020).
535 A. de Waal 2018. Mass Starvation: The History and Future of Famine, Polity Press, Cambridge.
536 J. Hasell, M. Roser 2013. Famines. Available at: https://ourworldindata.org/famines (accessed: 10.10.2020).
537 R. Pankurst 1992. Resettlement and famine in Ethiopia. The villagers' experience. Manchester University Press Manchester. J. Peron 1995, op. cit.

538 A. de Waal 2018, op. cit.
539 F. M. Lappe, J. Collins, P. Rosset, L. Esparza 1998. World Hunger: 12 Myths. Grove Press, New York.
540 M. Roser, H. Ritchie 2013. Hunger and Undernourishment. Published online at OurWorldInData.org. Available at: https://ourworldindata.org/hunger-and-undernourishment (accessed: 13.10. 2020).
541 World Bank. GDP (current US$). All countries and economies. Available at: https://data.worldbank.org/indicator/NY.GDP.MKTP.CD (accessed 08.10.2023)
542 Countries in the world by population 2020. Worldometer. Available at: https://www.worldometers.info/world-population/population-by-country/ (accessed: 14.10.2020).
543 M. Roser, E. Ortiz-Ospina 2013 (revision 2019). Global Extreme Poverty. Available at: https://ourworldindata.org/extreme-poverty (accessed: 29.11.2020).
544 N. Birdsall 1988. Economic Approaches to Population Growth and Development. In H. B. Chenery & T. N. Srinivasan (ed.). Handbook of Development Economics 1: 477-542. Amsterdam, Elsevier.
545 N. Birdsall, A. C. Kelley, & S. W. Sinding (eds) 2001. Population Matters: Demographic Change, Economic Growth, and Poverty in the Developing World. Oxford University Press, Oxford.
546 World Bank. Poverty headcount ratio at $1.90 a day (2011 PPP) (percent of population) - China. Available at: https://data.worldbank.org/indicator/SI.POV.DDAY?locations=CN (accessed: 14.10.2020).
547 F. Furuoka, Q. Munir 2011. Population growth and standard of living: A threshold regression approach. Economics Bulletin 31(1): 844-859.
548 F. Götmark, M. Andersson 2020. Human fertility in relation to education, economy, religion, contraception, and family planning programs. BMC Public Health 20(1): 1-17. E. Bbaale 2014. Female Education, Labour Force Participation and Fertility: Evidence from Uganda. The African Economic Research Consortium, Nairobi. Available at: https://media.africaportal.org/documents/RP282.pdf (accessed: 16.10.2020).
549 G. R. Taylor 1970. The Doomsday Book: Can the World Survive? Thames & Hudson Ltd. London.
550 United Nations, Department of Economic and Social Affairs, Population Division 2018. World Urbanization Prospects: The 2018 Revision, Online Edition. Available at: https://population.un.org/wup/Download/ (accessed: 20.10.2020).
551 Z. Liu, Ch. He, Y. Zhou, J. Wu 2014. How much of the world's land has been urbanized, really? A hierarchical framework for avoiding confusion. Landscape Ecology 29: 763-771.
552 J. Peron 1995, op. cit.
553 D. Tilman, C. Balzer, J. Hill, B. L. Befort 2011. Global food demand and the sustainable intensification of agriculture. Proceedings of the National Academy of Sciences of USA. Available at: https://www.pnas.org/content/108/50/20260 (accessed: 30.10.2020).
554 J.A. Foley, N. Ramankutty, K.A. Brauman, E.C. Cassidy, J.S. Gerber, M. Johnston, N.D. Mueller, C. O'Connell, D.K. Ray, P.C. West, Ch. Balzer, E. M. Bennett, S. R. Carpenter, J. Hil, Ch. Monfreda, S. Polasky, J. Rockstro, J. Sheehan, S. Siebert, D. Tilman, D. P. M. Zaks 2011. Solutions for a cultivated planet. Nature 478: 337-342.
555 H. Ritchie, M. Roser 2017. Crop Yields. Our World in Data. Available at: https://ourworldindata.org/crop-yields (accessed: 30.10.2020).
556 K. L. Steenwerth, A.K. Hodson, A. J. Bloom, M.R. Carter, A. Cattaneo, C.J. Chartres, J.L. Hatfield, K. Henry, J.W. Hopmans, W.R. Howarth, B.M. Jenkins, E. Kebreab, R. Leemans, L. Lipper, M.N. Lubell, S. Msangi, R. Prabhu, M.P. Reynolds, S.S. Solis, W.M. Sischo, M. Springborn, P. Tittonell, S.M. Wheeler, S.J. Vermeulen, E.K. Wollenberg, L.S. Jarvis, L.E.l. Jackson 2014. Climate-smart agriculture global research agenda: scientific basis for action. Agriculture & Food Security 3(11).

557 The State of Food and Agriculture 2019. Moving forward on food loss and waste reduction. FAO Rome. Available at: http://www.fao.org/policy-support/tools-and-publications/resources-details/en/c/1242090/ (accessed: 1.11.2020).
558 J. Birkby 2016. Vertical Farming. The World's Largest Indoor Vertical Farm Is Coming to New Jersey. ATTRA Sustain. Agric. 2016, 1–12.
559 I. H. El-Ghonaimy, N. Javed 2018. Concomitant of Global Warming and Land Reclamation: Designing a new interface between human kind and sea. Proceedings of the International Conference on Industrial Engineering and Operations Management. Pretoria / Johannesburg, South Africa, October 29 - November 1, 2018.

Chapter Six: Down to the last barrel

560 P. Byrne 2007. The Many Worlds of Hugh Everett. Scientific American, December 2007; M. Heller 2008. The ultimate explanation of the universe. Universitas, Kraków.
561 T. Gold 1992. The deep, hot biosphere. Proceedings of the National Academy of Sciences of the United States of America, 89(13): 6045-6049. G.P. Glasby 2006. Abiogenic origin of hydrocarbons: a historical overview. Resource Geology, 56 (1): 85-98.
562 M. Midgley 2003, The myths we live by. Routledge, London and New York.
563 *Ibidem.*
564 Kopalnia KW na Lubelszczyźnie ma ruszyć za 11 lat, kosztem 3,7 mld zł, 2013. Available at: https://www.money.pl/gospodarka/wiadomosci/artykul/kopalnia;kw;na;lubelszczyznie;ma;ruszyc;za;11;lat;kosztem;3;7;mld;zl,47,0,1255727.html (accessed: 8.01.2021).
565 Projekt Polityki Surowcowej Państwa (wersja z 25 stycznia 2019 r.). Polityka surowcowa państwa 2019(4): 26. Available at: https://www.pgi.gov.pl/dokumenty-pig-pib-all/psp/7163-6-polityka-surowcowa/file.html (accessed: 6.08.2020).
566 H. Ritchie, M. Roser 2017. CO_2 and Greenhouse Gas Emissions. Available at: https://ourworldindata.org/co2-and-other-greenhouse-gas-emissions (accessed: 30.07.2020).
567 Own calculation based on https://ourworldindata.org/fossil-fuels (accessed: 30.07.2020).
568 Data sources: H. Ritchie, M. Roser 2015. Energy. Available at: https://ourworldindata.org/energy (accessed: 13.09.2020). H. Ritchie, M. Roser 2017. CO_2 and Greenhouse Gas Emissions. Available at: https://ourworldindata.org/co2-and-other-greenhouse-gas-emissions (accessed: 13.09.2020).
569 N.J. Pollock 2014. Nauru Phosphate History and the Resource Curse Narrative. Journal de la Société des Océanistes, 107-120, https://doi.org/10.4000/jso.7055; A. Davies, B. Doherty 2018. Corruption, incompetence and a musical: Nauru's cursed history. Available at: https://www.theguardian.com/world/2018/sep/04/corruption-incompetence-and-a-musical-naurus-riches-to-rags-tale (accessed 4.08.2020).
570 Data sources: Annual Statistical Bulletin 2020. OPEC. https://asb.opec.org/ASB_Charts.html?chapter=10; World Oil Reserves 1920-1995, 1995. Energy Exploration & Exploitation, World Energy Review Issue, 13 (1), 55-64. https://doi.org/10.1177/014459879501300105. H. Ritchie, M. Roser 2015. Energy. Available at: https://ourworldindata.org/energy. R. Bousso 2015. BP sees technology nearly doubling world energy resources by 2050. Reuters. Available at: https://www.reuters.com/article/energy-tech-bp/bp-sees-technology-nearly-doubling-world-energy-resources-by-2050-idUSL8N12X2HT20151102 (accessed: 13.09.2020).

571 R.L. Hotz 2007. U.S. Draws Map of Rich Arctic Floor Ahead of Big Melt. Science Journal, Wall Street Journal, 31.08.2007, B1. Available at: https://www.wsj.com/articles/SB118848493718613526 (accessed: 31.07.2020). See also: W. Janicki 2012. Why Do They Need the Arctic? The First Partition of the Sea. Arctic, 65(1): 87-97. Calgary, Arctic Institute of North America.

572 Data sources: https://www.rystadenergy.com/newsevents/news/press-releases/global-oil-and-gas-discoveries-reach-four-year-high-in-2019/ ; https://www.statista.com/statistics/1088739/global-oil-discovery-volume/; https://yearbook.enerdata.net/crude-oil/world-production-statistics.html; https://ourworldindata.org/ (accessed: 13.09.2020).

573 U'Thant 1969. The problems of human environment. United Nations, Economic and Social Council, E/4667, May 26, 4-6, New York. https://doi.org/10.1177/096701067000100112

574 R. Link 2018. Kombucha SCOBY: What It Is and How to Make One. Available at: https://www.healthline.com/nutrition/kombucha-scoby; Ooho Water, the edible bottle, 2019. Available at: http://www.oohowater.com/ (accessed 4.08.2020).

575 M. Fagan 2000. Sheikh Yamani predicts price crash as age of oil ends. Available at: www.telegraph.co.uk/news/uknews/1344832/Sheikh-Yamani-predicts-price-crash-as-age-of-oil-ends.html (accessed 4.08.2020).

576 P.C. Garg 1979. Optimal Economic Growth with Exhaustible Resources. Garland Publishing, Inc. New York & London.

577 F. P. Ramsey 1928. A Mathematical Theory of Saving. The Economic Journal, 38 (152): 543-559. Available at: https://www.jstor.org/stable/2224098 (accessed 4.08.2020).

578 H. Hotelling 1931. The Economics of Exhaustible Resources. Journal of Political Economy, 39 (2): 137-175. See also: T.J.C. Robinson 1989. Economic Theories of Exhaustible resources. Routledge Library Editions: Environmental and Natural Resource Economics, vol. 15, London-New York.

579 St. Thomas Aquinas, 1966. Treatise on Justice: Summa Theologica, vol. 18, (2-2, qu. 57-80). Veritas, London.

580 W. S. Jevons 1865. The Coal Question; An Inquiry Concerning the Progress of the Nation, and the Probable Exhaustion of Our Coal Mines. London & Cambridge: Macmillan & Co.

581 The Coal Authority. Annual Report & Accounts 2006-2007. Available at: https://assets.publishing.service.gov.uk/government/uploads/system/uploads/attachment_data/file/250565/0942.pdf (accessed 6.08.2020).

582 H. Pidd 2019. Government under fire for approval of new coalmine in Cumbria. Available at: https://www.theguardian.com/uk-news/2019/nov/03/government-under-fire-after-approval-of-new-coal-mine-in-cumbria (accessed 6.08.2020).

583 M. Novak 2020. Oil and Gas Will Eventually be Exhausted (1909). Available at: https://paleofuture.com/blog/2009/6/14/oil-and-gas-will-eventually-be-exhausted-1909.html (accessed 13.09.2020).

584 Oil Dependence and U.S. Foreign Policy 1850-2017. Available at: https://www.cfr.org/timeline/oil-dependence-and-us-foreign-policy (accessed 10.08.2020).

585 N. Nordhauser 1973. Origins of Federal Oil Regulation in the 1920's. The Business History Review, 47 (1): 53-71. doi: 10.2307/3113603

586 U.S. Energy Information Administration. Available at: https://www.eia.gov/dnav/pet/hist/LeafHandler.ashx?n=PET&s=MCRFPUS2&f=A (accessed 13.09.2020).

587 Available at: https://www.newspapers.com/image/53707879/ (accessed 13.09.2020).

588 Available at: https://www.newspapers.com/newspage/76700239/ (accessed 13.09.2020).

589 H. Jarrett (ed.) 1954. The Nation Looks at its Resources. Routledge Revivals 2017, p. 18.

590 M. King Hubbert 1956. Nuclear Energy and Fossil Fuels, Shell Development Company, Publication No. 95; T. Priest 2014. Hubbert's Peak: The Great Debate over the End of Oil. Historical Studies in the Natural Sciences 44 (1): 37-79. DOI: 10.1525/hsns.2014.44.1.37
591 T. Priest 2014, op. cit.
592 R. Rapier 2016. What Hubbert Got Really Wrong About Oil. Available at: https://www.forbes.com/sites/rrapier/2016/09/08/what-hubbert-got-really-wrong-about-oil/#3fb9a2492a3b (accessed 10.08.2020).
593 R. Wilson 1972. Power Policy - Plan or Panic? Science and Public Affairs. Bulletin of the Atomic Scientists. XXVIII (5).
594 Department of Energy Organization Act 1977. Hearings before a Subcommittee of a Committee on Government Operations. House of Representatives, Ninety-Fifth Congress, First Session on H.R. 4263. U.S. Government Printing Office, Washington.
595 Syracuse Post Standard, 1980. October 17. Available at: http://ezproxy.lapl.org/login?url=http://access.newspaperarchive.com/us/new-york/syracuse/syracuse-post-standard/1980/10-17/page-82 (accessed 13.09.2020).
596 Oil experts warn about decline in crude supplies, 2002. The Index-Journal from Greenwood, South Carolina, May 25, p. 7.
597 D.H. Meadows, D.L. Meadows, J. Randers, W.W. Behrens III 1972. The Limits to Growth; A Report for the Club of Rome's Project on the Predicament of Mankind. New York: Universe Books.
598 D.H. Meadows, D.L. Meadows, J. Randers 1992. Beyond the Limits. Chelsea Green Publishing.
599 C.J. Campbell, J.H. Laherrère 1998. The End of Cheap Oil. Scientific American 278(3): 78-83.
600 D. Herman 2005. Prospect/FP Top 100 Public Intellectuals Results. Available at: https://foreignpolicy.com/2005/10/15/prospectfp-top-100-public-intellectuals-results/ (accessed 11.08.2020).
601 J. Diamond 2005. Collapse: How Societies Choose to Fail or Succeed. Viking Press.
602 A. Wijkman, J. Rockström 2012. Bankrupting Nature. Denying our planetary boundaries . Routledge.
603 Data source: U.S. Energy Information Administration 2020. Available at: https://www.eia.gov/dnav/pet/hist/LeafHandler.ashx?n=PET&s=RWTC&f=M (accessed 29.09.2020).
604 W. Zittel 2013. The end of the black epoch, p.32. In: A. Exner, P. Fleissner, L. Kranzl, W. Zittel (Eds), Land and Resource Scarcity. Capitalism, struggle and well-being in a world without fossil fuels. Taylor & Francis Group, pp. 30-45.
605 J. C. Ayers 2017. Sustainability: An Environmental Science Perspective. CRC Press, Taylor & Francis Group.
606 U. Bardi 2019. Peak oil, 20 years later: Failed prediction or useful insight?, p. 258. Energy Research & Social Science 48, February: 257-261. https://doi.org/10.1016/j.erss.2018.09.022
607 I. Trusewicz 2018. Gaz łupkowy, czyli stracone złudzenia. Available at: https://www.rp.pl/100-lat-polskiej-gospodarki-ropa-naftowa-i-gaz/180419853-Gaz-lupkowy-czyli-stracone-zludzenia.html (accessed 13.08.2020).
608 Annual Statistical Bulletin 2020. OPEC. Available at: https://asb.opec.org/ASB_Charts.html?chapter=10 (accessed 16.08.2020).
609 OPEC Statute 2012. Available at: https://www.opec.org/opec_web/en/about_us/23.htm (accessed 9.09.2020).
610 Annual Statistical Bulletin 2020, op. cit.
611 U.S. Energy Information Administration 2020. Available at: https://www.eia.gov/international/data/world (accessed 16.08.2020).
612 Statistical Review of World Energy 2020. Available at: https://www.bp.com/content/dam/bp/business-sites/en/global/corporate/pdfs/energy-economics/statistical-review/bp-stats-review-2020-full-report.pdf (accessed 16.08.2020).

613 Exploring Hydrocarbon Depletion, 2020. Available at: https://peakoil.com/what-is-peak-oil (accessed 17.08.2020).
614 Peak Oil Barrel 2020. Available at: http://peakoilbarrel.com/ (accessed 17.08.2020).
615 J. Ryba 2008. Peak oil, czyli początek końca. Available at: https://www.bankier.pl/wiadomosc/Peak-oil-czyli-poczatek-konca-1689454.html (accessed 17.08.2020).
616 M. Rybarczyk, M. Rębała 2010. Koniec ropy. Newsweek Polska. Available at: https://www.newsweek.pl/swiat/koniec-ropy/jslvsn6 (accessed 17.08.2020).
617 T. Vettese 2020. Is this the end of the oil era? NewStatesman, 23.04.2020. Available at: https://www.newstatesman.com/world/north-america/2020/04/end-oil-era (accessed 17.08.2020).
618 R. E. Cathy, TV PG World Without Oil - What If All The Oil Ran Out? 2010. A Cream Productions Inc., Quiet Planet 2 Productions Inc. Available at: https://www.youtube.com/watch?v=WiNtrOS88rs (accessed 17.08.2020).
619 The End of the Oil Age, How Much Is Left and What Will Happen When We Run Out, The Vendor 101, 2015. Available at: https://www.youtube.com/watch?v=yGsPc3fptoY (accessed 17.08.2020).
620 G. E. Marcus, W. R. Neuman, M. MacKuen, A. N. Crigler (Eds) 2007. The affect effect: dynamics of emotion in political thinking and behavior. The University of Chicago Press.
621 E. Fromm 1941. Escape from Freedom. Farrar & Rinehart.
622 A. Maslow 1943. A Theory of Human Motivation. Psychological Review, July: 370–396.
623 J. Rokita 2017. Strach i polityka. In: B. Bodzioch-Bryła, L. Dorak-Wojakowska (Eds), Anatomia strachu. Strach, lęk i ich oblicza we współczesnej kulturze. Humanitas, Studia kulturoznawcze: 457-466.
624 European Parliament. Available at: https://www.europarl.europa.eu (accessed 19.08.2020).
625 Report from the Commission to the European Parliament and the Council. Preparing the ground for raising long-term ambition. EU Climate Action Progress Report 2019. COM(2019) 559 final, Brussels. Available at: https://ec.europa.eu/transparency/regdoc/rep/1/2019/EN/COM-2019-559-F1-EN-MAIN-PART-1.PDF (accessed: 23.08.2020).
626 WorldData.Info 2020. Available at: https://www.worlddata.info/ (accessed: 23.08.2020).
627 C. Ch. Jancke 2020. Schummelsoftware bei Elektroautos – ein Fall für die Deutsche Umwelthilfe? Available at: https://drehmomentblog.wordpress.com/2020/07/24/schummelsoftware-bei-elektroautos-ein-fall-fur-die-deutsche-umwelthilfe/?fbclid=IwAR3Qo6zuXkO0lIVbDqMxmckRE0xdA-PCCGgG-NqzU143Q095pPSWMzCJGJ8 (accessed: 23.08.2020).
628 Tesla Model S, 2020. Available at: http://www.roperld.com/science/TeslaModelS.htm (accessed: 23.08.2020).
629 T. Rawa 2020. Już co drugi nowy samochód sprzedawany w Norwegii jest elektryczny. Available at: https://wysokienapiecie.pl/28952-juz-co-drugi-nowy-samochod-sprzedawany-w-norwegii-jest-elektryczny/ (accessed: 23.08.2020).
630 Even the oil giants can now foresee the end of the gasoline age, 2020. Available at: https://www.theguardian.com/business/2020/jun/21/even-oil-giants-now-foresee-end-of-gasoline-age-shell-bp-profitability-pandemic (accessed: 23.08.2020).
631 Greenpeace 2020. Stopping Offshore Drilling. Available at: https://www.greenpeace.org/usa/arctic/stopping-offshore-drilling/ (accessed: 24.08.2020).
632 UNECE's pivotal role in developing a global framework classification for energy and mineral resources. 2004. UNECE Weekly No. 76.
633 J.R. Craig, D.J. Vaughan, B.J. Skinner 1988. Earth Resources and the Environment. Pearson Prentice Hall.
634 J. C. Ayers 2017, op. cit.

635 SPE Petroleum Resources Management System Guide for Non-Technical Users, 2007. Available at: https://www.spe.org/industry/docs/PRMS-Guide-for-Non-Technical-Users-2007.pdf (accessed: 24.08.2020). Key Changes from the Petroleum Resources Management System (PRMS 2007) to the PRMS 2018. Available at: https://www.spe.org/industry/docs/PRMS-2018-Key-Changes.pdf (accessed: 24.08.2020).
636 J. Cust, D. Mihalyi 2017. Evidence for a presource curse? oil discoveries, elevated expectations, and growth disappointments. Policy Research Working Paper, 8140, World Bank Group. Available at : http://documents.worldbank.org/curated/en/517431499697641884/Evidence-for-a-presource-curse-oil-discoveries-elevated-expectations-and-growth-disappointments (accessed: 24.08.2020); N. LePan 2019. Mapped: The World's Biggest Oil Discoveries Since 1868. Available at: https://www.visualcapitalist.com/map-worlds-biggest-oil-discoveries-since-1868/ (accessed: 24.08.2020).
637 R. Rapier 2016, op. cit.
638 Government of Canada 2020. Crude oil facts. Available at: https://www.nrcan.gc.ca/science-data/data-analysis/energy-data-analysis/energy-facts/crude-oil-facts/20064 (accessed: 24.08.2020).
639 U. Bardi 2019. Peak oil, 20 years later: Failed prediction or useful insight? Energy Research & Social Science 48, February: 257-261. https://doi.org/10.1016/j.erss.2018.09.022
640 M. Popkiewicz 2019. Rewolucja energetyczna? Ale po co? Wydawnictwo Sonia Draga, Katowice.
641 A. Wijkman, J. Rockström 2012, op. cit.
642 J. Crepu 2018. The Crude Poker Game. Antipode, ARTE, Radio Canada, NRK Norway, RTS.
643 J.A.S. Adams 1959. New Ways of Finding Minerals. In: Science & Resources, 75-92.
644 J. Cust, D. Mihalyi 2017, N. LePan 2019, op. cit.
645 J.A.S. Adams 1959, op. cit.
646 Subsea Oil and Gas Directory 2020. Drilling Rigs. Available at: https://www.subsea.org/drilling-rigs/ (accessed: 24.08.2020); W. Janicki 2012. Why Do They Need the Arctic? The First Partition of the Sea. Arctic, 65 (1): 87-97. Calgary, Arctic Institute of North America.
647 E.P. Stevenson 1959. Past Gains and Future Promise. In: Science & Resources, 115-129.
648 A. Wijkman, J. Rockström 2012, op. cit.; S. Novak, R. J. Madon, H. Suhl J. 1981. Models of hydrocarbon product distributions in Fischer-Tropsch synthesis. Chem. Phys. 74, 6083, https://doi.org/10.1063/1.441051
649 The balance of mineral resources deposits in Poland as of 31.12.2019. 2020. Państwowy Instytut Geologiczny, Państwowy Instytut Badawczy, Warsaw. Available at: http://geoportal.pgi.gov.pl/css/surowce/images/2019/pdf/bilans_2019.pdf (accessed 25.08.2020).
650 M. Curcio 2018. Carro flex chega aos 15 anos com 30,5 milhões de unidades. Available at: http://www.automotivebusiness.com.br/inovacao/56/carro-flex-chega-aos-15-anos-com-305-milhoes-de-unidades (accessed 26.08.2020).
651 Sky Sails Marine Performance 2020. Available at: https://www.skysails-mp.com/index.html (accessed 26.08.2020).
652 J. Hicks 1932. The Theory of Wages. Macmillan, London, p. 124-125.
653 J.M. Polimeni, K. Mayumi, M. Giampietro, B. Alcott 2009. The Myth of Resource Efficiency. The Jevons Paradox. Earthscan, UK-USA.
654 Wijkman, J. Rockström 2012 op. cit.
655 J. Okrągły 1999. Odpowiedź podsekretarza stanu w Ministerstwie Łączności - z upoważnienia ministra - na interpelację nr 2523 w sprawie przyspieszenia telefonizacji wsi. Available at: http://orka2.sejm.gov.pl/IZ3.nsf/main/7EB6C0D2 (accessed 10.08.2020).
656 J.C. Ayers 2017, op. cit.

657 PHOTO #1008, 2017: Median All-Electric Vehicle Range Grew from 73 Miles in Model Year 2011 to 114 Miles in Model Year 2017. Available at: https://www.energy.gov/eere/vehicles/articles/fotw-1008-december-18-2017-median-all-electric-vehicle-range-grew-73-miles (accessed 26.08.2020); Samochody elektryczne 2017 z największymi zasięgami na jednym ładowaniu [RANKING TOP 20], 2017. Available at: https://elektrowoz.pl/auta/samochody-elektryczne-2017-z-najwiekszymi-zasiegami-na-jednym-ladowaniu-ranking-top-20/ (accessed 26.08.2020).

658 Welcome to the Patent Index 2019. Available at: https://www.epo.org/about-us/annual-reports-statistics/statistics/2019.html (accessed 31.08.2020).

659 E.P. Stevenson 1959, op. cit.

660 B. Bodzioch-Bryła, L. Dorak-Wojakowska 2017. Anatomia strachu. Strach, lęk i ich oblicza we współczesnej kulturze. Humanitas, Studia kulturoznawcze.

661 A. Regiewicz 2017. Cywilizacja strachu, czyli Nowe Średniowiecze. W: B. Bodzioch-Bryła, L. Dorak-Wojakowska (ed.), Anatomia strachu. Strach, lęk i ich oblicza we współczesnej kulturze. Humanitas, Studia kulturoznawcze, pp. 467-484.

662 P. R. Gould 1969. Spatial diffusion. Association of American Geographers, Commission on College Geography, Washington D.C.

663 J. Simon 1981. The ultimate resource. Princeton University Press.

664 S. Codrington 2005. Planet Geography. Solid Star Press, Sydney, p. 50.

665 P. Sabin 2013. The Bet. Paul Ehrlich, Julian Simon, and Our Gamble over Earth's Future. New Haven, Yale University Press.

666 J. Randers 2012. 2052: A Global Forecast for the Next Forty Years. White River Junction, Chelsea Green Publishing.

667 M. Popkiewicz 2019, Op. cit.

668 Panek Car-Sharing 2020. Available at: https://panekcs.pl/gdzie-jestesmy (accessed 6.09.2020).

669 B. Johnson 2020. The Great Horse Manure Crisis of 1894. Historic UK. Available at: https://www.historic-uk.com/HistoryUK/HistoryofBritain/Great-Horse-Manure-Crisis-of-1894/ (accessed 6.09.2020).

670 M. Popkiewicz 2019, op. cit.

671 J. Simon 1996. The Ultimate Resource 2. Princeton University Press.

Chapter Seven: One Fear to Rule Them All

672 World Bank 2020a. Global economic prospects, June 2020. Washington, DC: World Bank. DOI: 10.1596/978-1-4648-1553-9. Available at: https://openknowledge.worldbank.org/bitstream/handle/10986/33748/9781464815539.pdf (accessed: 12.07.2020).

673 D. K. Ratha, S. De, E. J. Kim, S. Plaza, G. K. Seshan, N. D. Yameogo 2020. COVID-19 crisis through a migration lens. Migration and Development Brief no. 32. Washington, D.C.: World Bank Group. Available at: http://documents.worldbank.org/curated/en/989721587512418006/COVID-19-Crisis-Through-a-Migration-Lens (accessed: 12.07.2020).

674 PR Newswire 2019. Survey finds majority of Americans live paycheck to paycheck. Available at: https://www.prnewswire.com/news-releases/survey-finds-majority-of-americans-live-paycheck-to-paycheck-300915266.html (accessed: 12.07.2020).

675 S. R. Collins, H. K. Bhupal, M. M. Doty 2019. Health insurance coverage eight years after the ACA: Fewer uninsured Americans and shorter coverage gaps, but more underinsured. Commonwealth Fund Biennial Health Insurance Survey: Survey brief. Available at: https://www.commonwealthfund.org/sites/default/files/2019-08/Collins_hlt_ins_coverage_8_years_after_ACA_2018_biennial_survey_sb_v2.pdf (accessed: 12.07.2020).

676 A. Dixon 2019. A growing percentage of Americans have no emergency savings whatsoever. Bankrate. Available at: https://www.bankrate.com/banking/savings/financial-security-june-2019/ (accessed: 12.07.2020).
677 World Bank 2020b. Reversal of fortune: Poverty and shared prosperity 2020. World Bank Group. Available at: https://openknowledge.worldbank.org/bitstream/handle/10986/34496/9781464816024.pdf (accessed: 12.07.2020).
678 M. Roser 2019. The short history of global living conditions and why it matters that we know it. Our World in Data. Available at: https://ourworldindata.org/a-history-of-global-living-conditions-in-5-charts (accessed: 18.07.2020).
679 UN IGME [United Nations Inter-agency Group for Child Mortality Estimation] 2020. Levels & Trends in Child Mortality: Report 2020. United Nations Children's Fund. Available at: https://www.un.org/development/desa/pd/sites/www.un.org.development.desa.pd/files/unpd_2020_levels-and-trends-in-child-mortality-igme-.pdf (accessed: 16.07.2020).
680 W. Lutz, A. Goujon, S. Kc, M. Stonawski, N. Stilianakis, 2018. Demographic and human capital scenarios for the 21st century: 2018 assessment for 201 countries. Publications Office of the European Union. Available at: http://publications.jrc.ec.europa.eu/repository/bitstream/JRC111148/jrc_cepam_report_demographic_and_hc_scenarios_pdf.pdf (accessed: 14.08.2020).
681 M. Roser 2018. Most of us are wrong about how the world has changed (especially those who are pessimistic about the future). Our World in Data. Available at: https://ourworldindata.org/wrong-about-the-world (accessed: 17.07.2020).
682 YouGov 2016. YouGov survey results: Optimism - 12th-13th November, 2015. YouGov. Available at: https://d25d2506sfb94s.cloudfront.net/cumulus_uploads/document/z2knhgzguv/GB_Website.pdf (accessed: 17.07.2020).
683 IPSOS 2017. Global perceptions of development progress: 'Perils of perceptions' research. IPSOS. Available at: https://www.ipsos.com/en/global-perceptions-development-progress-perils-perceptions-research (accessed: 3.08.2020).
684 R. Dart, 1953. The predatory transition from ape to man. International Anthropological and Linguistic Review 1(4): 201-218.
685 J. Lee-Thorp, J. F. Thackeray, N. van der Merwe 2000. The hunters and the hunted revisited. Journal of Human Evolution, 39(6): 565-576.
686 L. R. Berger, R. J. Clarke 1995. Eagle involvement in accumulation of the Taung child fauna. Journal of Human Evolution, 29(3): 275-299.
687 S. P. McPherron, Z. Alemseged, C. W. Marean, J. G. Wynn, D. Reed, D. Geraads, H. A. Béarat 2010. Evidence for stone-tool-assisted consumption of animal tissues before 3.39 million years ago at Dikika, Ethiopia. Nature, 466(7308): 857-860. More conservative estimates place the first use of tools for carving flesh at around 2.6 million years ago. See M. Domínguez-Rodrigo, L. Alcalá 2016. 3.3-million-year-old stone tools and butchery traces? More evidence needed. PaleoAnthropology 2016, 46-53.
688 D. R. Samson, C. L. Nunn 2015. Sleep intensity and the evolution of human cognition. Evolutionary Anthropology: Issues, News, and Reviews, 24(6): 225-237.
689 S. Mednick, K. Nakayama, R. Stickgold 2003. Sleep-dependent learning: a nap is as good as a night. Nature neuroscience, 6(7): 697-698.
690 J. A. Gowlett 2016. The discovery of fire by humans: a long and convoluted process. Philosophical Transactions of the Royal Society B: Biological Sciences, 371(1696): 20150164.
691 M. Bonta, R. Gosford, D. Eussen, N. Ferguson, E. Loveless, M. Witwer 2017. Intentional fire-spreading by "Firehawk" raptors in Northern Australia. Journal of Ethnobiology, 37(4): 700-718.
692 T. Twomey 2013. The cognitive implications of controlled fire use by early humans. Cambridge Archaeological Journal, 23(1): 113.
693 R. I. Dunbar 1998. The social brain hypothesis. Evolutionary Anthropology: Issues, News, and Reviews: Issues, News, and Reviews, 6(5): 178-190.

694 Y. Sahle, W. K. Hutchings, D. R. Braun, J. C. Sealy, L. E. Morgan, A. Negash, B. Atnafu 2013. Earliest stone-tipped projectiles from the Ethiopian Rift date to> 279,000 years ago. PLoS one, 8(11), e78092; K. S. Brown, C. W. Marean, A. I. Herries, Z. Jacobs, C. Tribolo, D. Braun, J. Bernatchez, J. 2009. Fire as an engineering tool of early modern humans. Science, 325(5942): 859-862.

695 J. A. Smith, J. P. Suraci, M. Clinchy, A. Crawford, D. Roberts, L. Y. Zanette, C. C. Wilmers 2017. Fear of the human 'super predator' reduces feeding time in large carnivores. Proceedings of the Royal Society B: Biological Sciences, 284(1857): 20170433.

696 D. Mobbs, R. Adolphs, M. S. Fanselow, L. F. Barrett, J. E. LeDoux, K. Ressler, K. M. Tye 2019. On the nature of fear. Scientific American. Available at: https://www.scientificamerican.com/article/on-the-nature-of-fear/ (accessed: 19.08.2020); T. Steimer 2002. The biology of fear-and anxiety-related behaviors. Dialogues in clinical neuroscience, 4(3): 231-249.

697 *Ibidem.*

698 R. Adolphs 2013. The biology of fear. Current Biology, 23(2): R79-R93.

699 M. J. Kim, J. Shin, J. M. Taylor, A. M. Mattek, S. J. Chavez, P. J. Whalen 2017. Intolerance of uncertainty predicts increased striatal Vol. Emotion, 17(6): 895–899.

700 J. E. LeDoux 2002. Emotion, memory and the brain. Scientific American. Available at: http://people.brandeis.edu/~teuber/emotion.pdf (accessed: 31.07.2020).

701 T. Jovanovic, S. D. Norrholm, N. Q. Blanding, M. Davis, E. Duncan, B. Bradley, K. J. Ressler 2010. Impaired fear inhibition is a biomarker of PTSD but not depression. Depression and anxiety, 27(3): 244-251.

702 L. Y. Abramson, M. E. Seligman, J. D. Teasdale, J. D. 1978. Learned helplessness in humans: critique and reformulation. Journal of abnormal psychology, 87(1): 49-74.

703 J. S. Nairne, J. N. Pandeirada, S. R. Thompson 2008. Adaptive memory: The comparative value of survival processing. Psychological Science, 19(2): 176-180. Students should not take this as an encouragement to cram for an exam the night before.

704 D. Tedlock 2011. 2000 years of Mayan literature. University of California Press.

705 W. F. Hanks 2010. Converting words: Maya in the age of the cross. University of California Press.

706 One prominent example is the death of Hypatia, a Hellenistic astronomer, mathematician, and philosopher murdered and dismembered by a Christian mob in 415 AD and subsequently co-opted by Christian tradition as paragon of Christian virtue.

707 D. Johnson, O. Krüger 2010. The good of wrath: Supernatural punishment and the evolution of cooperation. Political theology, 5(2): 159-176.

708 D. Johnson 2016. God is watching you: How the fear of God makes us human. Oxford University Press.

709 C. H. Legare, E. M. Evans, K. S. Rosengren, P. L. Harris 2012. The coexistence of natural and supernatural explanations across cultures and development. Child Development, 83(3): 779-793.

710 D. Johnson 2016, *op. cit.*

711 J. Watts, S. J. Greenhill, Q. D. Atkinson, T. E. Currie, J. Bulbulia, R. D.Gray 2015. Broad supernatural punishment but not moralizing high gods precede the evolution of political complexity in Austronesia. Proceedings of the Royal Society B: Biological Sciences, 282(1804): 20142556.

712 J. Jong, R. Ross, T. Philip, S. H. Chang, N. Simons, J. Halberstadt 2018. The religious correlates of death anxiety: A systematic review and meta-analysis. Religion, Brain & Behavior, 8(1): 4-20.

713 J. Bentzen 2020. In crisis, we pray: Religiosity and the COVID-19 pandemic. Centre for Economic Policy Research.

714 Pew Research Center 2021. More Americans than people in other advanced economies say COVID-19 has strengthened religious faith. Pew Research Center. Available at: https://www.pewforum.org/2021/01/27/more-americans-than-people-in-other-advanced-economies-say-covid-19-has-strengthened-religious-faith/ (accessed: 24.02.2021); D. Meza 2020. In a pandemic are we more religious? Traditional practices of Catholics and the COVID-19 in Southwestern Colombia. International Journal of Latin American Religions, 4(2): 218-234.

715 J. Bentzen 2019. Acts of God? Religiosity and natural disasters across subnational world districts. The Economic Journal, 129(622): 2295-2321.; P. Ager, A. Ciccone 2018. Agricultural risk and the spread of religious communities. Journal of the European Economic Association, 16(4): 1021-1068.

716 V. Saroglou, I. Pichon, L. Trompette, M. Verschueren, R. Dernelle 2005. Prosocial behavior and religion: New evidence based on projective measures and peer ratings. Journal for the scientific study of religion, 44(3): 323-348.

717 B. G. Purzycki, C. Apicella, Q. D. Atkinson, E. Cohen, R. A. McNamara, A. K. Willard, J. Henrich, 2016. Moralistic gods, supernatural punishment and the expansion of human sociality. Nature, 530(7590): 327-330; R. A. McNamara, A. Norenzayan, J. Henrich 2016. Supernatural punishment, in-group biases, and material insecurity: experiments and ethnography from Yasawa, Fiji. Religion, Brain & Behavior, 6(1): 34-55.

718 B. Marczak, J. Scott-Railton, S. McKune, B. Abdul Razzak, R. Deibert 2018. Hide and Seek: Tracking NSO Group's Pegasus Spyware to operations in 45 countries. Citizen Lab Research Report No. 113, University of Toronto. Available at: https://tspace.library.utoronto.ca/handle/1807/95391 (accessed: 23.08.2020).

719 B. Demick 2010. Nothing to envy: Real lives in North Korea. Granta.

720 N. Megoran 2016. From Presidential Podiums to Pop Music: Everyday Discourses of Geopolitical Danger in Uzbekistan. In: R. Pain, S. Smith. Fear: Critical Geopolitics and Everyday Life: 43-54. Routledge.

721 N. Hassanpour 2016. Leading from the periphery and network collective action. Cambridge University Press.

722 L. Bergeron, R. A. Palmer 1981. France under Napoleon. Princeton University Press.

723 B. Moin 2015. Khomeini: Life of the Ayatollah. Macmillan.

724 Z. Tufekci, C. Wilson 2012. Social media and the decision to participate in political protest: Observations from Tahrir Square. Journal of communication, 62(2): 363-379.

725 L. Diamond 2010. Liberation technology. Journal of Democracy, 21(3): 69-83.

726 J. Rydzak 2018. Disconnected: A human rights-based approach to network disruptions. Global Network Initiative. Available at: https://globalnetworkinitiative.org/wp-content/uploads/2018/06/Disconnected-Report-Network-Disruptions.pdf (accessed: 16.08.2020); Access Now 2020. Targeted, cut off, and left in the dark: The #KeepItOn report on internet shutdowns in 2019. Access Now. Available at: https://www.accessnow.org/cms/assets/uploads/2020/02/KeepItOn-2019-report-1.pdf (accessed: 16.08.2020).

727 S. N. Ghosh, V. Kaul, M. Reshi, M. Shah 2020. Kashmir's internet siege: An ongoing assault on digital rights. Jammu Kashmir Coalition of Civil Society. Available at: https://jkccs.net/report-kashmirs-internet-siege/assets/Kashmirs-Internet-Siege-18MB.pdf (accessed: 25.08.2020).

728 J. Rydzak 2019. Of Blackouts and Bandhs: The Strategy and Structure of Disconnected Protest in India. Available at SSRN 3330413.

729 J. Rydzak, E. M. Renieris 2021. Context before code: Protecting human rights in an emergency. Ranking Digital Rights. Available at: https://rankingdigitalrights.org/index2020/spotlights/context-before-code (accessed: 26.02.2021).

730 *Ibidem.*

731 S. Lohmann 1994. The dynamics of informational cascades: The Monday demonstrations in Leipzig, East Germany, 1989-91. World Politics, 47(1): 42-101.

732 D. Ellsberg 2017. The doomsday machine: Confessions of a nuclear war planner. Bloomsbury.

733 J. Rydzak 2019, *op. cit.*; N. Hassanpour 2016, *op. cit.*; J. Rydzak, M. Karanja, N. Opiyo 2020. Dissent does not die in darkness: Network shutdowns and collective action in African countries. International Journal of Communication 14: 4264-2487.

734 M. B. Tannenbaum, J. Hepler, R. S. Zimmerman, L. Saul, S. Jacobs, K. Wilson, D. Albarracín 2015. Appealing to fear: A meta-analysis of fear appeal effectiveness and theories. Psychological bulletin, 141(6): 1178-1204.

735 T. Wu 2017. The attention merchants: The epic scramble to get inside our heads. Vintage.

736 U. Kapoor, G. Sharma, M. Juneja, A. Nagpal 2016. Halitosis: Current concepts on etiology, diagnosis and management. European journal of dentistry, 10(2): 292-300.

737 K. Witte 1992. Putting the fear back into fear appeals: The extended parallel process model. Communications Monographs, 59(4): 329-349.

738 Pew Research Center 2019. In a Politically Polarized Era, Sharp Divides in Both Partisan Coalitions. Pew Research Center. Available at: https://www.pewresearch.org/politics/2019/12/17/in-a-politically-polarized-era-sharp-divides-in-both-partisan-coalitions/ (accessed: 27.08.2020).

739 M. Duverger 1959. Political parties, their organization and activity in the modern state. Methuen.

740 Library of Congress 2016. "Daisy" Ad (1964): Preserved from 35mm in the Tony Schwartz Collection. Available at: https://www.youtube.com/watch?v=riDypP1KfOU (accessed: 2.09.2020).

741 N. Rader 2017. Fear of crime. In Oxford Research Encyclopedia of Criminology and Criminal Justice. Available at: https://oxfordre.com/criminology/view/10.1093/acrefore/9780190264079.001.0001/acrefore-9780190264079-e-10 (accessed: 9.10.2020); S. Klar 2013. The influence of competing identity primes on political preferences. Journal of Politics, 75(4): 1108-1124.

742 A. Nai 2018. Fear and loathing in populist campaigns? Comparing the communication style of populists and non-populists in elections worldwide. Journal of Political Marketing, 1-32; S. J. Hill, J. Lo, L. Vavreck, J. Zaller 2013. How quickly we forget: The duration of persuasion effects from mass communication. Political Communication, 30(4): 521-547.

743 J. G. Voelkel, M. J. Brandt, M. Colombo 2018. I know that I know nothing: Can puncturing the illusion of explanatory depth overcome the relationship between attitudinal dissimilarity and prejudice? Comprehensive Results in Social Psychology, 3(1): 56-78; C. D. Bader, J. O. Baker, L. E. Day, A. Gordon 2020, Fear Itself: The Causes and Consequences of Fear in America. NYU Press.

744 UNICTR [United Nations International Criminal Tribunal for Rwanda] 1995. Radio Télévision Libres des Mille Collines: Transcript (May 16-17, 1994). Available at: https://repositories.lib.utexas.edu/bitstream/handle/2152/7182/unictr_rtlm_0002_eng.pdf?sequence=2 (accessed: 23.08.2020).

745 J. F. Metzl 1997. Rwandan genocide and the international law of radio jamming. American Journal of International Law: 628-651.

746 D. Yanagizawa-Drott 2014. Propaganda and conflict: Evidence from the Rwandan genocide. The Quarterly Journal of Economics, 129(4) : 1947-1994.

747 K. Pędziwiatr 2016. Church and state relations in Poland, with special focus on the Radio Station Mary. In: G. Simons, D. Westerlund. Religion, Politics and Nation-Building in Post-Communist Countries. Routledge, 163-178.

748 T. Adams 2019. Final editions: Why no local news is bad. The Guardian. Available at: https://www.theguardian.com/media/2019/sep/29/local-newspapers-closing-down-communities-withering (accessed: 25.02.2021).

749 C. Hedrickson 2019. Local journalism in crisis: Why America must revive its local newsrooms. Brookings Institution. Available at: https://www.kcl.ac.uk/policy-institute/assets/cmcp/local-news.pdf (accessed: 25.02.2021).
750 B. Świderski 2021. Finał plebiscytu na najlepszy pasek „Wiadomości". To teraz hit polskiego Facebooka. NaTemat. Available at: https://natemat.pl/333529,final-plebiscytu-na-najlepszy-pasek-wiadomosci-to-hit-facebooka (accessed: 25.02.2021).
751 D. Folkenflik 2020. Newsmax rises On wave Of resentment toward media—especially Fox News. NPR. Available at: https://www.npr.org/2020/11/30/939030504/newsmax-rises-on-wave-of-resentment-toward-media-especially-fox-news (accessed: 25.02.2021).
752 C. D. Bader, J. O. Baker, L. E. Day, A. Gordon 2020, *op. cit.*
753 A. M. Nellis, J. Savage 2012. Does watching the news affect fear of terrorism? The importance of media exposure on terrorism fear. Crime & Delinquency, 58(5): 748-768.
754 J. Gramlich 2019. 5 facts about crime in the U.S. Pew Research Center. Available at: https://www.pewresearch.org/fact-tank/2019/10/17/facts-about-crime-in-the-u-s/ (accessed: 17.08.2020).
755 J. N. Meindl, J. W. Ivy 2017. Mass shootings: The role of the media in promoting generalized imitation. American journal of public health, 107(3): 368-370.
756 C. D. Bader, J. O. Baker, L. E. Day, A. Gordon 2020, *op. cit.*, 74.
757 J. N. Meindl, J. W. Ivy 2017, *op. cit.*
758 Pew Research Center 2019)., *op. cit.*
759 A. M. Nellis, J. Savage 2012, *op. cit.*
760 R. Van Der Does, J. Kantorowicz, S. Kuipers, M. Liem 2019. Does Terrorism Dominate Citizens' Hearts or Minds? The Relationship between Fear of Terrorism and Trust in Government. Terrorism and Political Violence: 1-19.
761 A. Godefroidt, A. Langer 2020. How fear drives us apart: explaining the relationship between terrorism and social trust. Terrorism and Political Violence, 32(7): 1482-1505; H. Williamson, S. Fay, S., T. Miles-Johnson 2019. Fear of terrorism: media exposure and subjective fear of attack. Global Crime, 20(1): 1-25.
762 N. Ajaka 2015. Paris, Beirut, and the language used to describe terrorism. The Atlantic. Available at: https://www.theatlantic.com/international/archive/2015/11/paris-beirut-media-coverage/416457/ (accessed 21.02.2021).
763 Other studies have shown that attacks committed in the U.S. by assailants who were Muslim generated orders of magnitude more media coverage, despite making up less than 13 prcent of all incidents. H. Ritchie, J. Hasell, C. Appel, M. Roser 2019. Terrorism. Our World in Data. Available at: https://ourworldindata.org/terrorism (accessed: 26.02.2021).
764 H. Ritchie 2019. Does the news reflect what we die from? Our World in Data. Available at: https://ourworldindata.org/does-the-news-reflect-what-we-die-from (accessed: 26.02.2021).
765 D. E. Levari, D. T. Gilbert, T. D. Wilson, B. Sievers, D. M. Amodio, T. Wheatley 2018. Prevalence-induced concept change in human judgment. Science, 360(6396): 1465-1467.
766 T. Sharot 2011. The optimism bias. Current Biology, 21(23): R941-R945.
767 M. Roser, M. Nagdy 2014. Optimism and pessimism. Our World in Data. Available at: https://ourworldindata.org/optimism-pessimism (accessed: 13.10.2020).
768 D. Mellor, Y. Hayashi, L. Firth, M. Stokes, S. Chambers, R. Cummins 2008. Volunteering and well-being: Do self-esteem, optimism, and perceived control mediate the relationship? Journal of Social Service Research, 34(4): 61-70.
769 T. Kaneda, C. Haub 2019. How many people have ever lived on Earth? Population Reference Bureau. Available at: https://www.prb.org/howmanypeoplehaveeverlivedonearth/ (accessed: 1.10.2020).

770 M. Ravallion 2016. The economics of poverty: History, measurement, and policy. Oxford University Press.
771 M. Roser, 2019, *op. cit.*
772 M. Roser 2017. No matter what extreme poverty line you choose, the share of people below that poverty line has declined globally. Our World in Data. Available at: https://ourworldindata.org/no-matter-what-global-poverty-line (accessed: 1.10.2020).
773 IPSOS 2017, *op. cit.*
774 World Bank, 2020c. Cutting-edge survey techniques power first poverty assessment in Somalia in decades. World Bank. Available at: https://www.worldbank.org/en/results/2020/01/24/cutting-edge-survey-techniques-power-first-poverty-assessment-somalia-decades (accessed: 10.10.2020).
775 IPSOS 2017, *op. cit.*
776 J. F. Helliwell, R. D. Putnam 1999. Education and social capital (No. w7121). National Bureau of Economic Research.
777 M. Roser, E. Ortiz-Ospina 2020. Global education. Our World in Data. Available at: https://ourworldindata.org/global-education (accessed: 14.10.2020).
778 J. W. Lee, H. Lee 2016. Human capital in the long run. Journal of Development Economics, 122: 147-169.
779 W. Lutz, A. Goujon, S. Kc, M. Stonawski, N. Stilianakis, 2018, *op. cit.*
780 M. Vaca 2021. The top frauds of 2021. United States Federal Trade Commission. Available at: https://www.consumer.ftc.gov/blog/2021/02/top-frauds-2020 (accessed: 26.02.2021); M. Vaca 2018. The top frauds of 2017. United States Federal Trade Commission. Available at: https://www.consumer.ftc.gov/blog/2018/03/top-frauds-2017 (accessed: 26.02.2021).
781 M. Leonhardt 2019. 'Nigerian prince' email scams still rake in over $700,000 a year—here's how to protect yourself. CNBC. Available at: https://www.cnbc.com/2019/04/18/nigerian-prince-scams-still-rake-in-over-700000-dollars-a-year.html (accessed: 25.02.2021).
782 A. Jaiswal, A. Singh 2020. Covid fears bring good fortune for astrologers. Times of India. Available at: https://timesofindia.indiatimes.com/city/lucknow/covid-fears-bring-good-fortune-for-astrologers/articleshow/75419977.cms (accessed: 25.02.2021).
783 N. Mocan, L. Pogorelova 2017. Compulsory schooling laws and formation of beliefs: Education, religion and superstition. Journal of Economic Behavior & Organization, 142: 509-539.
784 C. Cavaille, J. Marshall 2018. Education and anti-immigration attitudes: Evidence from compulsory schooling reforms across Western Europe. American Political Science Review, 113(1): 254-263.
785 S. Pinker 2012. The better angels of our nature: Why violence has declined. Penguin Group.
786 Roser 2019, *op. cit.*
787 M. Coppedge, J. Gerring, C. H. Knutsen, S. I. Lindberg, D. Ziblatt 2020. V-Dem [Country–Year/Country–Date] Dataset v10. Varieties of Democracy (V-Dem) Project. Available at: https://www.v-dem.net/en/data/data/v-dem-dataset/ (accessed: 10.10.2020).
788 P. Cirillo, N. N. Taleb 2016. On the statistical properties and tail risk of violent conflicts. Physica A: Statistical Mechanics and its Applications, 452: 29-45.
789 Freedom House 2021. Freedom in the world report hub. Freedom House. Available at: https://freedomhouse.org/report/freedom-world (accessed: 26.02.2021).
790 Freedom House 2020. Freedom in the world 2020: A leaderless struggle for democracy. Freedom House. Available at: https://freedomhouse.org/report/freedom-world/2020/leaderless-struggle-democracy (accessed: 26.02.2021).
791 V. H. Murthy, A. T. Chen 2020. The coronavirus could cause a social recession. The Atlantic. Available at: https://www.theatlantic.com/ideas/archive/2020/03/america-faces-social-recession/608548/ (accessed: 3.09.2020).

792 B. W. Nelson, A. Pettitt, J. E. Flannery, N. B. Allen 2020. Rapid assessment of psychological and epidemiological predictors of COVID-19. International Journal of Methods in Psychiatric Research, 21(3): 169-184; D. Folk, K. Okabe-Miyamoto, E. Dunn, S. Lyubomirsky 2020. Did social connection decline during the first wave of COVID-19?: The role of extraversion. Collabra: Psychology, 6(1), 37; M. Luchetti, J. H. Lee, D. Aschwanden, A. Sesker, J. E. Strickhouser, A. Terracciano, A. R. Sutin 2020. The trajectory of loneliness in response to COVID-19. American Psychologist.

793 M. Frankel 2020. Social media communities and reporting of the COVID-19 pandemic. Reuters Institute for the Study of Journalism, University of Oxford. Available at: https://reutersinstitute.politics.ox.ac.uk/social-media-communities-and-reporting-covid-19-pandemic (accessed: 3.09.2020).

794 S. Liu, L. Yang, C. Zhang, Y.T. Xiang, Z. Liu, S. Hu, B. Zhang 2020. Online mental health services in China during the COVID-19 outbreak. The Lancet Psychiatry, 7(4): e17-e18.

795 Catalyst 2020. The impact of Covid-19 on workplace inclusion: Survey. Catalyst. Available at: https://www.catalyst.org/research/workplace-inclusion-covid-19/ (accessed: 3.09.2020).

796 R. Weissbourd, M. Batanova, J. McIntyre, E. Torres 2020. How the pandemic is strengthening fathers' relationships with their children. Harvard Graduate School of Education. Available at: https://mcc.gse.harvard.edu/reports/how-the-pandemic-is-strengthening-fathers-relationships-with-their-children (accessed: 13.09.2020).

797 K. Devlin, A. Connaughton 2020. Most approve of national response to COVID-19 in 14 advanced economies. Pew Research Center. Available at: https://www.pewresearch.org/global/2020/08/27/most-approve-of-national-response-to-covid-19-in-14-advanced-economies/ (accessed: 3.09.2020).

798 R. Solnit 2009. A paradise built in hell: The extraordinary communities that arise in disaster. Penguin, p. 7.

799 E. L. Quarantelli 2008. Conventional beliefs and counterintuitive realities. Social Research: An International Quarterly, 75(3): 873-904.

800 H. Rodriguez, J. Trainor, E. L. Quarantelli 2006. Rising to the challenges of a catastrophe: The emergent and prosocial behavior following Hurricane Katrina. The annals of the American academy of political and social science, 604(1): 82-101.

801 C. Peterson, M. E. Seligman 2003. Character strengths before and after September 11. Psychological Science, 14(4): 381-384; P. A. Linley, S. Joseph, R. Cooper, S. Harris, C. Meyer 2003. Positive and negative changes following vicarious exposure to the September 11 terrorist attacks. Journal of Traumatic Stress, 16(5): 481-485.

802 B. Xu 2017. The politics of compassion: the Sichuan earthquake and civic engagement in China. Stanford University Press; Y. Li, H. Li, J. Decety, K. Lee 2013. Experiencing a natural disaster alters children's altruistic giving. Psychological science, 24(9): 1686-1695.

803 M. Sugiura, R. Nouchi, A. Honda, S. Sato, T. Abe, F. Imamura 2020. Survival-oriented personality factors are associated with various types of social support in an emergency disaster situation. PLoS one, 15(2), e0228875.

804 World Bank 2020b, *op. cit.*

805 L. Spinney 2017. Pale rider: The Spanish flu of 1918 and how it changed the world. PublicAffairs.

806 M. Heffernan 2020. Uncharted: How to navigate the future. Avid Reader Press/Simon & Schuster, p. 5.

807 N. N. Taleb 2012. Antifragile: Things that gain from disorder. Random House.

808 P. C. Gorski, C. Chen 2015. "Frayed all over:" The causes and consequences of activist burnout among social justice education activists. Educational Studies, 51(5): 385-405.

Chapter Eight: Closing Fear(s): Minority Report

809 H.P. Lovecraft 1973. Supernatural Horror in Literature, New York: Dover Publications.
810 D.H. Meadows, D.L. Meadows, J. Randers, W.W. Behrens 1972. The Limits to Growth. University Books, New York.
811 R.W. Bentley 2002 Oil Forecasts, Past and Present. Energy Exploration & Exploitation 20(6): 481-492.The author of this paper concludes that some of the forecasts were accurate and some were wrong. One of his most interesting conclusions is that most of the correct forecasts were made by serious institutions, while the wrong ones were made by less reputable institutions.
812 B. Spector 2018. How Did This Soldier 'Grow' an Ear on Her Forearm? Livescience. Available at: https://www.livescience.com/62532-how-to-grow-ear-on-forearm.html (accessed: 20.02.2021).
813 Liter of light 2021. Available at: https://literoflight.org (accessed: 20.02.2021).
814 Shanghai Maglev Official Website. 2020. available at: http://www.smtdc.com/en/index.html (accessed: 29.12.2020).
815 M. Wojciechowska 2017. Kobieta na krańcu świata, sezon 9, odcinek 4. TVN.
816 Good meat. The future of meat is here, 2021. Available at: https://goodmeat.co/ (accessed 20.01.2021).; Daily Sabah 2020. World's first lab-grown 'clean' meat goes on sale in Singapore. Available at: https://www.dailysabah.com/life/food/worlds-first-lab-grown-clean-meat-goes-on-sale-in-singapore (accessed 20.01.2021).
817 Y.N. Harari 2019, *op cit.*
818 H. Ritchie 2019. Does the news reflect what we die from? Available at: https://ourworldindata.org/does-the-news-reflect-what-we-die-from (accessed: 28.02.2021).
819 John Paul II 1980. Visita pastorale a Velletri. Discorso di Giovanni Paolo II alla stazione ferroviaria. Available at: http://www.vatican.va/content/john-paul-ii/it/speeches/1980/september/documents/hf_jp-ii_spe_19800907_velletri.html (accessed: 29.08.2020). Translated from Italian.
820 N.N. Taleb 2007. The Black Swan: Second Edition: The Impact of the Highly Improbable. Random House.
821 European Commission, Climate Action, Climate change consequences 2021. Available at: https://ec.europa.eu/clima/change/consequences_en (accessed: 21.02.2021).
822 Climate Change 2014. Synthesis Report. The Intergovernmental Panel on Climate Change. Available at: https://www.ipcc.ch/report/ar5/syr/ (accessed: 21.02.2021).
823 Such a map can be viewed here, among other places: https://coastal.climatecentral.org/ (accessed: 24.02.2021). It does not allow users to estimate sea level rise in centimeters, but it does allow them to adjust qualitatively defined inputs that affect the magnitude of sea level change, which gives us an idea of the situation.
824 See research conducted at the observatory of the Space Research Institute at the Russian Academy of Sciences, led by Habibull Abdusamatov, as well as the work of of Valentina Zharkova of Northumbria University in the UK.
825 S.E. Vollset, E.Goren, Ch.-W. Yuan, J. Cao, A.E. Smith, T. Hsiao, C. Bisignano, G.S. Azhar, E. Castro, J. Chalek, A.J. Dolgert, T. Frank, K. i Fukutaki, S.I. Hay, R. Lozano, A.H. Mokdad, V. Nandakumar, M. Pierce, M. Pletcher, T. Robalik, K.M. Steuben, H.Y. Yong Wunrow, B.S. Zlavog, C.J.L. Murray 2020. Fertility, mortality, migration, and population scenarios for 195 countries and territories from 2017 to 2100: a forecasting analysis for the Global Burden of Disease Study. The Lancet, 396(10258): 1285-1306, DOI:https://doi.org/10.1016/S0140-6736(20)30677-2.

826 When I started this book, Elon Musk was the 31st richest person on Earth. When I wrote about him in the chapter on resource depletion six months later, he was fifth. Today, he is first. In his case, wealth can be considered a measure of progress. C. Isidore 2021. Elon Musk, the world's richest man, is about to get a whole lot richer. Available at: https://edition.cnn.com/2021/02/11/investing/elon-musk-pay-wealth-tesla-stock-options/index.html (accessed 12.02.2021).
827 N.N. Taleb 2007, *op. cit.*
828 J.E. Lovelock 1972. Gaia as seen through the atmosphere. Atmospheric Environment, 6 (8): 579-580. DOI: 10.1016/0004-6981(72)90076-5.
829 J. Randers 2012. 2052. A Global Forecast for the Next Forty Years. White River Junction, Chelsea Green Publishing Co.
830 B. Lomborg 2001. The Skeptical Environmentalist: Measuring the Real State of the World. Cambridge University Press.
831 M. Heffernan 2020. Uncharted: How to navigate the future. Avid Reader Press/ Simon & Schuster.
832 Many more interesting examples of previously unimaginable and unpredictable events can be found in: N. Gowing, C. Langdon 2018 Thinking the Unthinkable: A new imperative for leadership in the digital age. John Catt Educational Ltd, Woodbridge.
833 VOA News 2021. Norway Says More Than 50% of New Cars Are Electric. Available at: https://www.voanews.com/europe/norway-says-more-50-new-cars-are-electric (accessed: 23.02.2021).
834 B.R. Forer 1949, *op. cit.*
835 Y.N. Harari 2018, *op. cit.*, p. 233.
836 J.B. Calhoun 1973. Death Squared. The Explosive Growth and Demise of a Mouse Population. Proceedings of the Royal Society of Medicine 66(1 Pt 2): 80-88.
837 R. F. Inglehart 2020. Giving up on God: The global decline of religion. Foreign Affairs. Available at: https://www.foreignaffairs.com/articles/world/2020-08-11/religion-giving-god (accessed: 28.02.2021).

Appendix

838 More important sources: R. Abanes 1998. End-time visions: the doomsday obsession. Broadman & Holman Publishers, Nashville, TN; E. Weber 1999. Apocalypses: prophecies, cults, and millennial beliefs through the ages. Harvard University Press, Cambridge; J. Boyett 2005. Pocket Guide to the Apocalypse: The Official Field Manual for the End of the World. Relevant Books, Orlando; J.W. Murphy 2014. A View from Above: Options for Understanding the Revelation of Jesus Christ. WestBow Press, Bloomington, IN.; W. Łaszewski 2016. Nadchodzi kres: Mistyczne wizje końca świata. Fronda, Warszawa; A Brief History of the Apocalypse 2011. Available at: http://www.abhota.info/end1.htm (accessed: 15.08.2020).